MORGENTALER

A DIFFICULT HERO

A Biography by

Catherine Dunphy

RANDOM HOUSE OF CANADA

Published in Canada in 1996 by
Random House of Canada Limited, Toronto.

Canadian Cataloguing in Publication Data

Dunphy, Catherine, 1946-
Morgentaler: a difficult hero

Includes index.
ISBN 0-394-22391-8

1. Morgentaler, Henry, 1923– . 2. Abortion - Canada - History.
3. Abortion services - Canada. 4. Pro-choice movement.
5. Physicians - Quebec (Province) - Biography. I. Title.

R464.M67D85 1996   610'.92   c96-930769-1

Cover photograph: © John Felstead, courtesy of CanaPress.
Cover design: Gary Stüber, Orbit

Printed and bound in the United States.

10 9 8 7 6 5 4 3 2 1

For Nell, my daughter

TABLE OF CONTENTS

CHAPTER I

THE ABORTIONIST'S PARTY

THE BRIGHT ORANGE-RED SOCKS on twelve-year-old Yann Morgentaler's twitchy feet were like sparks of neon in the darkened theatre. Yann had shrugged off his shoes and plopped his stocking feet on the railing of the deluxe box where he lounged with his father and family. Dr. Henry Morgentaler sat characteristically straight and alert, bantam chest outthrust, his smooth, sloping forehead caught in the glow of the stage lights. To his right, the slim hands of his companion, Arlene Leibovitch, fluttered as she translated for her deaf parents, Abraham and Ruth. Henry Morgentaler's eldest son, Bamie, a doctor, had flown in with his wife, Susan, from Boston that afternoon, and would fly back that night to be at home when their young daughters, Henry's only grandchildren, awoke the next morning. Henry's youngest son, Benny, born to Arlene three weeks before the Supreme Court of Canada ruled that the country's abortion law was unconstitutional, squirmed in his seat. This would be a long night for the five-year-old.

"The security for this evening, which you cannot fail to have noticed — I hope you love a man in uniform — we have twelve uniformed officers in the theatre and they will remain until the last person has left," the evening's host, actress Fiona Reid, was saying. "At five o'clock today there was a thorough, electronic search in the theatre. We also have twelve plainclothes security people scattered about.... As a further precaution we have conducted random searches of handbags and briefcases.... It is significant that the only other time this theatre has seen such elaborate security precautions was when Salman Rushdie was the surprise guest at a benefit for the Canadian centre for PEN. Like Salman Rushdie, Henry Morgentaler has cause to fear for his life at the hands of fanatics."

Outside Toronto's latest showplace on the overcast evening of May 17, 1993, members of the police riot squad, including its mounted division, flicked impassive eyes over the women clutching $82, $55 or $34 tickets as they streamed past the ornate ticket office into the refuge of the Winter Garden Theatre for a seventieth-birthday tribute to the unlikeliest of heroes.

As usual, Henry Morgentaler had refused to wear his bulletproof vest. The only threat police had received was hapless as such things go — from an unknown entity calling itself "The Sword of Gideon." They had announced their strange-but-true intention to pelt Morgentaler and fans with chicken livers, representing aborted fetuses. They never showed up.

But so many others did, people of prestige and influence if not actual power, respected activists like June Callwood and lawyer Clayton Ruby and Toronto politicos Jack Layton and Olivia Chow, all of them saying wonderful, flattering, grateful things about him. "Every struggle needs its elders, the old people with long memories to remind us of how it used to be — the back streets and kitchen tables, the infections, the shame, the deaths," said icon Rosemary Brown, former British Columbia politician, now chief of the Ontario Human Rights Commission. "We have to think of Henry Morgentaler because...he was the best one, the greatest one, because he was the one with courage."

Henry's "great and good friend," as wealthy Forest Hill socialite Selma Edelstone was introduced that evening, had organized the event — the performers, speeches and, at the reception, the jazz trio, birthday cake and the balloon clown, who dogged Henry's every move — because nobody else was honouring him. Henry Morgentaler had made history, gone to jail to change the law, altered society, endured bombings, death threats and an armed attack and monopolized the front pages of the country's newspapers for the past quarter century, but he was still the upstart and outsider. He had been recognized by the Canadian establishment just once, and that had been only a few weeks earlier when his alma mater, the Université de Montréal, had presented him with its merit medal on the fortieth anniversary of his graduation. But there was no Order of Canada (although Edelstone had tried), no honorary doctorate, not even an invitation to lecture medical students.

In championing women's rights to reproductive freedom, he had waded into the still and dangerous centre of the most divisive, primal and painful issue ever faced by the whole of Canadian society. His courage was never questioned by anyone but him. If anything was suspect it was that he was always so certain, so unwavering, that he'd never had any second thoughts about what he was doing and why.

———

Along with thousands of Canadians, I had sent off cheques whenever an ad for the Henry Morgentaler Defence Fund ran in the weekend newspaper. I was grateful women had the right to choose; I was even more grateful I had never had to make the choice for myself. I was — am — a feminist, with the strongly held belief that a woman's right to have an abortion is central to women's equality and emancipation, and if a Dr. Henry Morgentaler was the one leading the fight to ensure that all women have that right, then he would have my wholehearted support — as well as my sporadic donations of $25 or $30. Then my daughter was born in 1981. Sometimes late at night as my child and I rocked on the ladderback chair, I would think about abortion. I would think, "What if I had?" and shudder. That was not the point, of course; it was never the point of the struggle for choice. The issue was always one of having a *wanted* child. Now that our daughter has entered her teens, what I want for my wanted child is for her to have that choice, too.

I like to think that is why I purchased one of the few remaining $55 tickets for the Morgentaler Tribute, but I can never be certain. By then I had met Henry Morgentaler twice — on both occasions to discuss writing this book. For our second meeting, he had invited me to lunch in a cramped and crowded Thai restaurant down the street from his stunning Toronto clinic. Every single person there that lunch hour knew who he was. Henry was aware of this but didn't acknowledge it. Our meal was a jagged dance of conviviality and confrontation. We began on a first-name basis. He was casual and so was I, but he was always the one in control. I had envisaged this lunch as my chance to convince him of my honourable intentions (the Tribute ticket was in my wallet, ready for brandishing) and the necessity of recording his life, but I quickly realized I would not be given the opportunity to do either. He never asked me my stance on the issue, relying, I supposed then, on the truth of many Gallup Polls, which showed that an increasing majority favour a woman's right to choose, and on the odds that I would be part of that majority. As for my sales pitch, no one convinces Henry Morgentaler of anything he doesn't want to believe in.

And he was not at all sure he wanted a biography written about him. Accuracy was a concern, of course, but he just might write his own book. He enjoyed writing and was a good writer, he said, with a quick, sidelong glance, awaiting my reaction. But to what? The news of a rival book or of his writing talent? I replied that I thought the market could sustain two books, which might, in the best of all possible worlds, eventually be seen as companion texts. Now I think I was wrong not to understand I was to comment on his writing ability. Henry is an affable man, but my words were a nuisance, and he brushed them away like hovering flies. Even now, after hours of interviews, he is not convinced he should be co-operating, at least not all of the time, and says he may soon hire a writer to help him create a fictionalized novel about his life, a form of autobiography he feels safest presenting to the public. He says he'll do it, but he has so many other schemes and ideas, he knows he may never get to it. As aware as he is of all those who consider him a great man, he has never grasped that those same thousands never expected him to be a selfless, fearless paragon of all virtue and little vice. At times he thinks that what he is — a sensitive doctor, scientist, champion — is not enough, and would prefer to also be known as a childlike spinner of whimsy and a creator of beauty. But when the arena is biography, the sides clash and he becomes a very difficult hero and a very discomforted man.

When a young woman approached our table, I was grateful for the interruption. She was part of a party of four — two handsome couples, perhaps midtwenties, well dressed, full of promise. "I just want to thank you for the work you've done," she said, sliding a folded cheque across the table to Henry as her companions waited at the door. He was gracious, but neither surprised nor embarrassed. He was a wealthy man, his government-funded Toronto clinic operating at full and very profitable capacity. Nor did he appear aware of the incongruity of pocketing one cheque while paying for our restaurant bill. But he was aware of the time: he had a full slate of patients that afternoon. He asked if I wanted to witness a procedure. "It's very interesting," he murmured.

Back in his clinic, Henry introduced me to the staff in the lunchroom as "the woman writing his biography." The nurses whispered among themselves — not about what I should see, but about whom. I assumed they would select the patient deemed "best" in public relations terms — perhaps a harried mother of five, for instance, or someone whose health would be endangered if she was to give birth — but their decision rested only on who would be willing to have a notebook-toting stranger hovering throughout the time (ninety minutes) it took from the counselling interview through the procedure and recovery period. I almost hoped no one would be willing to have me along for her experience. Had I been honest, I might have blurted to Henry right there that the only reason I had agreed to watch an abortion was that I had assumed his invitation was testing my politics, my intentions, my mettle and I wanted to prove myself. It never occurred to me that Henry had not issued the invitation for its shock value. He had issued it because he was proud of his sleek, beautiful clinic, and he intended that I see for myself how safe and pain-free the procedure had become, thanks in great part to innovations he himself had instigated.

So I was introduced to Dominique, twenty-five, a quarter of an inch above five feet, 118 pounds, dull brown hair straight and long, lower eyelids lined aggressively in black. She said she lived in Oshawa and worked there in the "entertainment industry." Her French accent was slight, but Sheri Krieger, the counsellor, seized on it and wanted to do the interview in that language. Dominique balked. Yes, she was born in Montreal, but she had lived in Oshawa for six or seven years and had forgotten French, she said. She was English now. So was the man who had impregnated her. He was a good man, but he was not her real boyfriend, the guy she really loved, who was spending the next eight to twelve years in prison. Sheri didn't flinch, her smile was still wide and warm, but Dominique was defensive.

"A girl's going to have her urges," she said.

"Absolutely," agreed Sheri with a grin, glancing at Dominique's chart.

What concerned Sheri were the migraines Dominique said she was getting from using the birth control pill. Sheri wanted her to consider having an IUD (Intrauterine Device) put in that day. Again Dominique balked. Sheri slapped a yellow Post-it® note on her file. "Dr. Morgentaler can talk to you about it," she said. Later, as Dominique sat in a semi-circle of silent women in paper dresses and their own socks, wrapped in identical white blankets, she agreed that Sheri was "cool," then joked about wanting a television to watch "her" soap, "The Bold and the Beautiful." No one in the room smiled. The composed Asian woman; the tall teenager in thick, studious glasses, her shoulders already rounded from stooping; the very young girl whose face had not yet shed its baby fat; the married woman who had just bought a house — they were all there for the same thing but for very different reasons, and those, at least, would remain private.

The sound of gypsy violins, passionate and mournful, flooded the waiting area. "Dreadful, isn't it?" said Cathy, who was on diagnostic ultrasound duty. "Henry loves it. We always know when he's working in the operating room." The radio in her office was tuned to a station playing golden oldies. "A lot of the girls tell me they like it." She asked Dominique if she wanted to see the fetus. Dominique didn't, but if it was twins she wanted to know.

"Are there twins in your family?" Cathy inquired.

"I don't know who my family is. I just wanted to tell the father if it is twins."

Cathy paused. "Would that change your decision? If you can't keep one, you can't look after two. I know — I have twins."

Dominique didn't have twins, but was close to eleven weeks pregnant. She didn't seem disappointed when she returned to the room to await her turn for the procedure. Nor did she react visibly when she entered the operating area and saw a very cheerful Henry Morgentaler waiting for her.

A scrub nurse was setting out the equipment as Karen, the nurse doing what clinic staff call the "handholding" that afternoon, made sure that Dominique's feet were in the stirrups and that she was comfortable on the padded table and prepared for the curettage, or cleaning of the uterus. Vivacious and inquisitive, Karen persisted with her friendly questioning until finally Dominique confessed she was a stripper. Karen beamed; Henry beamed. "We get a lot of dancers," he said. Dominique grimaced and tensed as Henry injected her cervix with an anesthetic before inserting the tenaculum, a kind of clamp to anchor the cervical area without pinching the patient. "Am I causing you any pain?" Henry asked, surprised. He often tells patients this is just like dentists freezing the area around the tooth they'll be drilling. Henry believes the procedure to be pain-free, but some of his nurses say it most definitely is not. The women have an aspirator in their womb; some experience what feels like a menstrual cramp that has gone off the pain scale.

Glaring at Karen, who was smiling and stroking her tight shoulder, Dominique wouldn't admit her fear. But she gripped Karen's right hand with her left one and pressed shut her eyes as Henry inserted a Dalsace Sound, a French-manufactured flexible rubber rod, to measure the angle of the uterus and length of cervix and then guided two more injections along both sides of the cervical canal. Pain-sensitive patients like Dominique are often given a short-acting narcotic, Sublimaze (fentanyl). Sitting at the end of the table, Henry worked quietly and very quickly, dilating the cervix by inserting increasingly larger tapers smoothly in and out of the uterine cavity. "You see there is no resistance," he noted, his hand reaching for the cannula, the clear hollow plastic tube attached to the aspirator. He inserted this through the cervix into the uterus and Dominique strained to listen to Karen's comforting inanities as blood-covered tissue and liquid were evacuated from her body through the tube into a metal tray. The aspirator made a low gurgling sound; Dominique would have felt some cramping as her uterus contracted when the fetal material was evacuated. Then Henry announced: "I'm happy to tell you you are no longer pregnant."

Dominique was one of about 8,000 women served by the clinic that year, but Henry smiled at her as if she was his only patient. Dominique's posture softened. It was over. The actual procedure had taken less than five minutes. She looked very young, very relieved, very vulnerable. "I just need to rest," she said. In the recovery room she curled up on a leather recliner under a yellow blanket and turned her face away.

———

It was Henry at his finest — and his most genuine. Not a crusader, just a caring doctor with the gentlest of touch. That may be why thousands of feminists allowed him, a man, to speak incessantly on their behalf, as if "the women of Canada" were some mute group shackled into silence and not vociferous colleagues matching Henry every step of the way, demanding and working hard for the right to freedom of choice. *Toronto Star* columnist Michele Landsberg, a leading feminist, said she truly understood and accepted Henry Morgentaler when she saw a film clip of him performing an abortion and watched him brush a stray lock of hair off the forehead of his patient as he talked to her.

But that was not the Henry Morgentaler who stood squarely on the stage at the Winter Garden at his tribute, and reached into his suit pocket for his speech, a thick sheaf of paper he stroked smooth on the plexiglass podium, eager to claim his moment. He loves making speeches. He stands motionless except for his right hand, which always creeps about the flap of his suit pocket. "Some of you may wonder — and I get asked this a lot — 'Where did you get the strength to endure such a long and arduous battle for over twenty-five years?'" he said. He didn't tell them that he needed his crusade. That the pro-choice cause was how he lived up to the legacy of his Jewish socialist martyr-father, Josef Morgentaler, and to the stern ideals of his remote, artistic mother, Golda. That it had given him meaning, rescued him from despair. It let him be brave. It provided the enemies he needed, the media attention he sought, the adulation he craved and a platform with which he, a survivor of Auschwitz and Dachau, could fight the state and win.

Performing abortions and crusading for reproductive rights had liberated Henry from obscurity, although it condemned him within the profession he loved. He would always be an abortionist, which is not regarded as a highly skilled specialty within medical circles. No one would accept him as anything else. Many haven't accepted him as that. A Polish-born Jew raised as an atheist, he has deliberately remained an outsider. Even from other Jews, who would sometimes say to him after a speech, "You're a Jew, an immigrant. Don't you think what you are doing will cause anti-Semitism?" In her tribute column to him Landsberg wrote: "He, like us, is aware that he is the very stereotype of classic anti-Semitic propoganda: small, wiry, with an East European accent, dark eyes, a prominent nose and a black beard. It has taken double daring for him to hurl himself against the establishment; many of us (Jews) are doubly proud of him, and it's past time that we said so. As one who has a beloved relative who was permanently maimed by an illegal abortion, I have long regarded Henry Morgentaler as a personal hero."[1]

That night in his speech, Henry in turn credited "my mother, from whom I inherited strength of character, steadfastness in adversity and artistic sensitivity, and my father, from whom I learned gentleness and compassion and idealism and a commitment to social justice." He was not a modest hero. He was never a modest man. But he was the only person that night who called himself an abortionist. The word carried no sting for him, but spoken aloud, it cut through the darkened space; even to his friends and supporters it sounded harsh, shocking. Henry has become oblivious to its effect, just as he has always been unconcerned about the internal skirmishes generated by politics and personalities. Judy Rebick, media personality, former national feminist leader and Henry's colleague on the abortion front lines for eight years, had to ask repeatedly to be a speaker at the tribute. And the woman who ran the Canadian Abortion Rights Action League (CARAL) for ten crucial years did not attend that evening. Norma Scarborough stayed away because of the high cost of the tickets and because proceeds were paying for the party, not going to the cause. That was not a concern to Henry, nor did she expect it to be. Throughout the years of trials and turmoil, when constitutional law expert Morris Manning took the charges against Henry Morgentaler and two colleagues up to the Supreme Court, Norma Scarborough, Judy Rebick and Henry were a united front, but Henry was the focal point. He did what he wanted. He didn't consult others, and rarely could anyone talk him out of one of his decisions. He used to ask CARAL for money, not advice. Although he never demanded they fall in line, he assumed they would and they did. They did because, ironically, they had almost no choice on this matter. Henry Morgentaler was their own action hero, impulsive and reckless, and almost always right.

Reproductive rights was the most urgent, volatile and important issue of the contemporary feminist movement, and it belonged to him. And he wasn't even a feminist but a humanist; he was a man who loved women and couldn't be monogamous. His first wife, his childhood sweetheart, with whom he survived five brutal and tense years in the Lodz ghetto during the war, refuses to speak about her former husband and has as little as possible to do with him. Just months before the tribute his second wife bolted from Montreal to Chile, taking their son, Yann, with her; Yann has said this was what he himself wanted. Henry's eldest child and only daughter, Goldie, cut off any communications between them many years before. She has said her surname, Morgentaler, is just a coincidence. Henry's younger brother saved his life in the concentration camps and stayed by his side throughout his first decade of trials. People used to say Mike would walk through flames for Henry, but he would not come from Montreal for the tribute. Henry told them Mike was ill, which was true. But Mike was also angry, and has said he would never again honour his brother.

So new friends, his latest family, his staff, his pro-choice colleagues and strangers had gathered to pay tribute to him. "People think Henry is the most admired and most reviled man in Canada," Rebick said that night. "But you know, that's not true. I've been with Henry in airports and restaurants and all I've ever seen is admiration and love." Henry is not immune to this and in many ways he has come to expect it. He throws a celebration of what he calls the "historic" Supreme Court decision every January 28, where he makes the longest speech of the night and retells the triumphant story. Usually he'll hold a birthday party for himself on or around his real birth date, March 19. In 1993 — the year of his seventieth birthday and this long-awaited tribute — he had friends to a private dinner, at which people stood to make speeches about him, and he basked in their content. But he has never been able to shake the notion that he has to work hard before he can party, that he has to deserve his big, fine Toronto house, his vacation home in Muskoka, the fine wines, the lavish restaurant meals, all those resort holidays — and every single accolade.

"Part of me wonders if I really deserve such a tribute," he admitted publicly that night. "Another part of me is jubilant and grateful that my long and arduous struggle for reproductive freedom, and the sacrifices necessary to sustain it and triumph in the law, has been recognized." His "unflagging energy" is intact, as is his sense of humour, he told the audience as the heavy stage curtain behind him rolled away to reveal a blazing three-tiered birthday cake the size of most banquet tables and a chorus of performers waiting for their cue to sing "Happy Birthday." Singer-satirist (and pro-choice advocate) Nancy White tried subtly to give him his cue to step aside from centre stage and let the others perform. But he wouldn't.

Henry Morgentaler loves a party and the spotlight, and here he had both. Those who knew him only as a crusader, a man of medicine and a stern and effective messenger for the reproductive rights of women gaped at what followed. Nancy White gamely held on to her hand mike as Henry whirled her in an impromptu waltz. He warbled a few improv bars with blues singer Salome Bey; then, taking the hand mike from her, he walked back to the centre of the stage and announced to the tittering audience that he would sing a song. "I didn't tell you before, but I am known as the singing abortionist. I used to sing in the operating room to my patients — with their permission, of course," he confided into the microphone, omitting that his nurses teasingly grouch that his repertoire ends at "Michael Row the Boat Ashore" and all his songs sound like Yiddish songs.

"Tonight I'll sing for you a French song," Henry declared. Many laughed at what they thought was a joke. But hand in pocket, crooner style, Henry sang, not stopping when he forgot the line that followed *"Parlez-moi d'amour"*; not even stopping when embarrassed laughter escaped from some parts of the theatre. Henry Morgentaler has a sense of joy, not humour; he is playful, not ironic. But many in the audience didn't know that.

And as the horns of the Flying Bulgar Klezmer Band finally swung into the Yiddish version of the birthday song, Henry closed his eyes and swayed to the music. The showman lifted up his arms high, hands slowly, sensually extending, shoulders shrugged loose, and he whirled, then whirled again, skipping childlike upstage on the balls of his feet. It was such a private moment and so public, as mysterious and disconcerting and contradictory as the man himself, whom almost all those in the audience then realized they did not know at all.

CHAPTER 2

THE LODZ LEGACY

T HE LODZ WHERE HENRY MORGENTALER was born March 19, 1923, was a soot-soaked chaotic centre of sweatshops and huge, clattering factories. Fuelled by German and Jewish capital, it prospered on the backs of its Polish and Jewish work force. At any time it would have been an unlikely locale for the brave new egalitarian world dreamed of between the two world wars by Jewish socialists like Henry's father, Josef. With time the idea became ludicrous: Lodz was never to be a Jewish socialist showpiece but instead was the last Polish ghetto, which avoided annihilation for five war years only because it was useful to the Nazis.[1]

Josef Morgentaler was a hero, and Henry worshipped his union-activist father, although he rarely saw him. Like many Jews in Lodz, Josef began as a weaver, enduring the strain and repetitious toil of operating stubborn and heavy looms. Lodz was the centre of Poland's thriving textile trade; more than a third of the city's 600,000 population were Jewish. A few were prosperous and prominent, a few more were middle-class professionals. But most worked in airless factories, producing the bolts of cloth destined for the manufacturing centres of Europe.

Josef's father, Heinoch, was probably one of those workers. Henry knows little about his paternal grandfather other than he was named after him. Heinoch Morgentaler smoked too much and spit too much and died a few years after his wife. That was when Josef, the middle of five children, was twelve. Acknowledged within the family as the bright one, Josef stayed in school. The others, including nine-year-old Leibish, immediately went out to work. The eldest Morgentaler boy,

Avrom, was a cheerful ne'er-do-well who eked out a living selling lot-
tery tickets. A dreamer and a good man, he would tell his customers
they were going to win. And he believed it, too. He was the only one in
the family who was religious. A sister — the only girl — soon married
and moved to Switzerland. Leibish became a weaver. Joshua, or Shia,
the youngest, left in 1918 for Russia, the promised land of social justice
for many of the young and idealistic. He was never heard from again.
Josef followed his father and brother into the textile business. It wasn't
as if he had a choice. Although Lodz was Poland's major manufacturing centre, many industries would not employ Jews.

Josef quickly rose to a supervisory position. He helped establish the
Textile Workers' Union and began agitating for an end to sixteen-hour
days and for improved working conditions and better pay. Word soon
spread that Morgentaler was a revolutionary, a troublemaker. Leibish
paid for his brother's zeal. Eventually none of the textile factories in
Lodz that paid fractionally more or offered minimally better working
conditions would hire him because they feared any brother of Josef
Morgentaler would automatically organize workers and cause trouble.
Leibish was forced to weave in others' homes, once even in his own one-
room apartment, in order to feed his family of six. But the brothers were
close, united by their socialist reforming instincts and by their affilia-
tion with the Bund.

Created in 1897, the Jewish Socialist Labour Bund was never just a
political party. It was central to the lives of thousands of secular Polish
Jewish families. Its dogma was their faith, its heroes their saints. Its
women's committees and youth groups, subcommittees and societies
provided music and poetry, schools for the children and, in summer,
camps in the country for entire families. Its parties were never just
get-togethers. They were exhilarating, noisy and joyful encounters, full
of laughter and talk about the glorious future. They were celebrations,
a secular society's stand-in for religious holidays and rituals. They are
what Henry likes to remember about his childhood, not the poverty,
the pervasive anti-Semitism and the sense of being an outsider twice
removed.

Although the 3.3 million Jews then living in Poland formed 10 per

cent of the country's population, they were not assimilated. According
to the 1931 census,[2] three-quarters of Poland's Jews lived in the city;
three-quarters of the Poles did not. That same census found that 79 per
cent of the Jews spoke Yiddish and only 12 per cent gave Polish as their
first language. The rest stated that Hebrew was their primary language.
The Jews were a people apart, a visible minority in custom and conduct,
marginalized since the fourteenth century, when Kazimierz the Great
had invited them to settle in the country.[3] By the 1930s, politics dominated Jewish life in Poland. There were almost as many political parties
as opinions on how to end poverty and battle anti-Semitism. A religious, non-Zionist party had sprung up, as well as a host of Zionist
political groups that ran the gamut from left-wing to right-wing. The
socialist movement was divided along ethnic lines. In Lodz there was a
German socialist party as well as a Polish socialist group. But Jewish
socialists flocked to the ultraleft-wing Bund, which before the war was
Poland's largest Jewish workers' organization. Henry's parents were
attracted because the Bund broke with the fatalistic Jewish religious
tradition of wait, hope and adapt as a way of overcoming problems.
"*Kiddush Hashem*" — in his blessed name — they would say, in what
amounted to a shrug. To the devout, this credo meant that those Jews
killed amid persecution were martyrs to God; to the idealistic socialists, it meant an abdication of individuality, plus a passive pessimism
because of its acceptance of a status quo they deemed inequitable and
often untenable. That was also why they rejected the Zionist goal of a
Jewish Palestine. They wanted to be accepted as equals, as full Yiddish-
speaking citizens within Poland; they believed it was possible.

The Bundist dream caught on. The party's popularity and clout
peaked in 1938, when, along with the Polish socialist party, it formed
the majority on city council. By that time, Josef Morgentaler was a city
council veteran, renowned for his activism and revered for his courage.
Elected half a dozen times, he had been jailed for his socialist opinions,
and sometimes would arrive home bandaged and bloodied from meetings of a council then dominated by Polish socialists. When he wasn't
negotiating for better wages and conditions for textile workers, he was
representing workers in the courts. He learned Polish to be able to do it.

Henry was thrilled to be known as "the son of Morgentaler," and would bask in his father's reflected glory on the rare Saturday mornings when they would walk together down to the baths. In the tightknit, impoverished world of the ghetto, Josef was someone who lived, and lived up to, his beliefs. And although he earned less than many of the textile workers, his political work and commitment to the socialist cause were seen and valued by the community. That was duly noted by his son, an alert boy sensitive to the double indemnity experienced by non-practising Jews within a devout Jewish community existing uneasily within a fervently Roman Catholic country. From birth Henry had known he was an outsider, with a place only in a minority within a minority, and that only Josef Morgentaler's adherence to his ideals gave the family their place, their prestige and their purpose.

Because of Josef's position, the Morgentaler family was among those lucky enough every summer to leave the dirt and congestion of Baluty, the inner-city ghetto of Lodz, where they and most of the Jewish people lived. They would pack the bedding, pots and pans — most of their meagre possessions — onto a horse-drawn cart and travel to a farmer's cottage fifty kilometres outside Lodz. There Henry would spend his days lying on his back in the grass, reading about Louis Pasteur and heroes of the American West. In the evenings, he would sit with the others around a campfire, warmed by the passion and beauty of the intense talk.

Those were not the only good times. In Baluty a dozen or more Bundist colleagues would often crowd around Josef Morgentaler's table to laugh, sing, talk about politics and the vision — never far behind — of the new society, in which the innate and common goodness of man and not a religion or a too-autocratic government would decree a fulfilled and comfortable life for all. One of Josef's friends used to say they would all bathe in milk come the revolution.

Sometimes Henry's mother would sing. Her voice was exquisite, and their friends would be spellbound. Then Henry could see how his mother looked when she was happy. A sensitive, creative woman, Golda Nitka Morgentaler was brought up in Lodz in a traditional and religious home where candles were lit on the Sabbath and Henry, his brother and his sister would visit weekly for the traditional Friday-night meal. Golda's parents were hardworking textile labourers, who had set up three looms in the home, on which two workers produced cloth from morning to night. A quiet, bearded veteran of the Russian army, Golda's father would start his long days with a morning shot of whisky. But it was his wife who ran things. Henry remembers her dealing with all the household and business matters, along with putting in her share of time at the loom.

Golda had little to do with textiles until her marriage. If Josef Morgentaler's idealism and activism kept him innocent and unworldly, they forced her to shoulder the formidable work of bringing up three children in poverty and amid anti-Semitism. She was often stern, tense and tired because of this responsibility, as well as from the sewing she did to make ends meet. She was a talented seamstress who created patterns for her clients with a few swift, sure lines of chalk on fabric. But Golda took no comfort from her abilities, and pushed aside her artistic impulses in order to maintain the home. She intimidated Henry, and he has always felt she didn't love him. His had been a painful breech birth; she had been ill for the first six weeks of his life and he was cared for by a wet nurse. More to the point, perhaps, he was pale and awkward, always underfoot, as well as sickly.

Like most Jewish families, the Morgentalers — Josef, Golda, Henry, his sister, Ghitel, and his brother, Mike — lived in one room, about three metres by five metres. It was where they ate and where they slept. Their apartment was on the second floor, and overlooked a central courtyard where the children played. The courtyard was also the location of the communal outdoor toilet facilities, literally holes in the ground. More apartments in Baluty had electric lighting than plumbing facilities.

When Henry was seven the family moved to Polesie, a Polish suburb of Lodz. Their city-built apartment was huge — four whole rooms — and there were parks, a lake, fields nearby. This was the Bund's way of acknowledging Josef's stature and prestige in the community. The fresh air helped Henry conquer the respiratory problems that had plagued him since his birth. And this is the part of Henry's life where his memories kick in — clear and suddenly detailed. He came out from behind his books; soon he was playing soccer with the local boys three or four hours a day, all day on weekends.

He learned Polish this way, and was usually among the first to be chosen when the soccer team was picked. That's how good he was. That's how good the times were. He still travelled the three or four kilometres by tram into the city to the socialist school every day. There wasn't enough money for return fare, so he usually walked home. One winter he walked both ways to save money for a pair of skates. He remembered gliding alone on the frozen lake in the cold, clean mornings. "It was a wonderful achievement," he said, especially because he had endured his own version of running the gauntlet to have his skates. Walking home, he would pass a Polish Roman Catholic school just as its students were getting out for the day. They poured from the building, blond kids, faces reddening as they screamed, "Jew! You killed Jesus Christ," at him in a tightening circle. He was beaten up. Soon Henry began to detour through the fields, giving a wide berth any time he saw a group of Polish boys, no matter how far away they were.

It was the prudent thing to do. It fit his family's — his *father's* — pacifist ideals. His father had been sent to jail more than once for holding firm to his beliefs; his father had been beaten for what he was; and Henry worshipped his father. But it still gnaws at him. "Walking around, walking away, avoiding those Polish boys gave me a feeling I was a coward. I had to battle against that feeling for a long time. And later on I had to prove to myself I wasn't."

But four years later in 1936, when Henry was thirteen, the Morgentalers moved back to the ghetto. Anti-Semitism was rampant; violence was increasing. It was no longer possible for a Jewish family, even a nonreligious Jewish family, to live in the Polish parts of the city. "[Polesie] was something like lost paradise," Henry admitted. The Bundist dream of living as equal citizens of the world had failed. There would be no more fresh air, frozen lakes and playing soccer in the fields.

———

In the beginning it was good to be back. Life was safer — and busy. Caught up in the youth branch of the Bund, Henry was proud to wear its blue shirt and red cravat. At school he excelled, just as he had on the soccer fields. His only rival for top honours was the daughter of Bundist colleagues of his parents. Chava Rosenfarb was a tall, sensitive and dreamy young woman who wrote poetry, something Henry wanted, and frequently tried, to do. They met in school when they were both nine. By the age of fourteen, they were a couple, always together, talking of the future and their futures. "I had vague ideas of some sort of intellectual career, of going to university, even though there were big obstacles. There was discrimination against Jews. We were a minority and we knew it."

Nevertheless, that year Henry was one of only five Jewish boys accepted into the prestigious Pilsudski gymnasium, a Polish high school, named after the country's national hero, Marshall Josef Pilsudski, with whom Henry shared a birthday. Like many Poles of the time, his first-year instructor, the arts-and-crafts teacher, was an anti-Semite who resented the Jewish boys in his class. "I was so frightened of him, his expression, his tone of voice. Nonverbally I could feel his attitude," Henry remembered. "I would freeze up when he came around. This is how I got the impression that I was very awkward, clumsy with my hands."

Clearly the brightest in the class, Henry was sure he would be awarded the medal for scholastic achievement at the end of the school year. But his instructor had other ideas and inflated the marks of a Polish student, who received not only the medal but also the official recognition. Everyone knew Henry deserved the honour; everyone understood why it was not his. But in those highly charged times, this was just one more minor indignity to be sloughed off. Anti-Semitism had become so pervasive it often showed its face in brutal offhand and impersonal petty humiliations.

The next year when Henry defeated boys two and three years older to win the school chess championship and it was reported on the last page of the student newspaper, he merely shrugged. He knew such news made the front page only when a Polish Catholic won. As a Jew, this is what he had come to expect and, reluctantly, accept. If he wanted to get the best education, if he hoped to fulfil the Bundist ideal of equality regardless of origin and live as an internationalist beyond the ghetto, then this is what he would have to endure.

.And he did. His family expected no less from him. He was to receive the best education they could manage for him. Like his father, Henry was deemed the intellectual child, the thinker, the visionary. He may have seemed somewhat awkward, but that was all right. Henry was bookish; Henry's thoughts were elsewhere. His brother, Mike, four years younger than Henry, was considered the one with the charm and the energy. A cousin who lived down the street from them remembered Mike as quicksilver, a small, good-natured boy full of mischief. "I used to catch butterflies with a blanket and put them between two panes of windows to look at them," said Sara Schwartz, a daughter of Leibish Morgentaler, Josef's brother. "Mike would open the windows and let them out. I remember I wanted to kill him. But I always laughed. That was Mike."

Henry believed Mike was his mother's favourite and that he and his sister, Ghitel, bore the brunt of their mother's exhaustion. But dark-haired and popular Ghitel, older than Henry by four and a half years, distinguished herself early. She followed her father's lead and became an active and essential member of the Bund's youth movement. Bright and articulate, at seventeen she gave a speech at city hall in 1936 and was hailed as a rising star, a credit to the Bundist movement and the standard to which her younger brother should aspire. She was a serious and intense young woman, whose sights never wavered from the world she was creating for herself away from home. She and Henry were never very close, yet that didn't mean there was no affection between them. Ghitel was always "nice" to him, he said.

But Henry's focus was always his father, whose time with his family was so limited Henry described it as "visits." Suddenly Josef would be with them. To his eldest son, it was as if the family were doused in brilliant sunshine when he appeared. The day-to-day drudgery gave way to exciting, energizing talk of politics and ideals. Josef often brought a stick of kielbassa for the family, but ever so much better, he might have enough time for a game of chess with his worshipful son.

Henry was often alone with his books. He hung around the edges whenever Ghitel brought her friends home. They were the leaders of the Bundist youth. Like Josef, Ghitel was attracted to the excitement of fighting for a better life and thrived on group dynamics. She was also attracted to one of the youth group's acknowledged leaders. Pav Schloimo was bright and charismatic, and he and Ghitel made a golden couple. She was only eighteen when they began living together, and twenty when they left for Warsaw. Schloimo worked with the Jewish underground resistance forces; he was to be a leader in the magnificent, but doomed, Warsaw ghetto uprising of April 19, 1943. Henry would never know for sure, but he believed that by then Ghitel had died in Treblinka. He knew she had been caring for children in the Medem Sanatorium health facility outside Warsaw, which the Nazis liquidated early on in the war.

Long before Hitler invaded Poland on September 1, 1939, the country had been gripped by fear and dread of what appeared impossible but inevitable. At the Morgentaler home there was no more spirited talk of the Spanish Civil war, ethics or politics, only a tightening anguish as the dangerous German war machine drew closer. From long and bitter experience, Baluty's Jews knew they would be targeted first. Before they could be arrested by the Nazis, Josef Morgentaler, along with many of the Jewish socialist leaders, fled Lodz. Some went into hiding and made their way to Russia, and from there eventually to Shanghai and onto the United States. Josef stayed closer to home.

By the time the Germans had officially taken over the city, a sixteen-year-old Henry was already on his way to Warsaw. There had been no time to say goodbye to Chava, or to do anything other than take the rucksack of food and a little money his worried and shaken mother gave him and leave. He found a terrible pandemonium on the road leaving Lodz. It was crowded with frantic people fleeing in carts, and already littered with the carcasses of horses struck down by wayward bullets. Henry fell in with some other schoolboys also on the run.

They told one another they were on a grand adventure, and that when they reached Warsaw or before, they would help Polish forces beat back the Germans. They slept in an abandoned farmhouse, and had covered more than thirty kilometres the next day before they saw a silent, menacing phalanx of German soldiers advancing up the middle of the highway, straight towards them. They were arrested, herded into a field, encircled by barbed wire and left there. Hours passed, broken only by hysteria and grief as the rumours that they were all going to be shot buzzed about them.

Once a soldier with a pail of water approached Henry.

"*Jude*?" he asked. Jew?

"*Ja*," Henry replied. Yes.

"*Nein*," the soldier said. The water was not for Jews.

Finally, the soldiers began checking for identification. The word quickly spread. Anyone under sixteen and not a soldier would be allowed to return to Lodz. Henry was sixteen and a half. He joined the line of youths, where he borrowed documents from a stranger. He was allowed to return with the others, but nearing the city, he was set upon by a group of Polish-German nationals looking for Jewish labour to dig some trenches. Henry's luck held. A Polish passerby told the Polish-German nationals Henry wasn't Jewish because the school hat he happened to be wearing came from a prestigious Polish school. "Let him go," ordered the Pole, and they did.

Back in Baluty, Henry tried to pick up his old life. He was in the gymnasium less than a week, when he and the rest of the Jewish students were told to go home and not to bother coming back. He was devastated. But suddenly his father was back. Then as now, Henry could not understood why Josef had returned from his hiding place in the country. He did not want to think his heroic father might have given up, but Josef Morgentaler was subdued and depressed, and looked very much a broken, disheartened man those last days he spent with his family. There was no laughter, no more fist-pounding politics or earnest confessions of simple dreams.

Henry's mother told him his father didn't have the money to run away. Others have said Josef was a leader who would never have left his people. He may have wanted to share his family's fate instead of carving out his own. Henry had not yet worked up the courage to ask his father himself, when the military police knocked on their apartment door the afternoon of September 21, 1939. They were very polite as they requested that Josef Morgentaler accompany them. He was taken to a detention camp in Radogoszcz, a suburb of Lodz, where he was interrogated and tortured. Golda managed to visit her husband and bring him some food once or twice before he disappeared, but Henry never saw his father again.

Golda Morgentaler and her sons moved to her parents' apartment in Baluty, where her sister and brother and his family were also staying. They remained for a year, until they found their own place within the ghetto. The Nazis had moved swiftly to install the barbed-wire fences that cut off Baluty from the rest of the city. Entry was gained only via three bridges built over the barbarous border by the German soldiers and paid for by the ghetto Jews; there was no exit. Soon the phrase "going to the wire" meant someone had committed suicide.[4]

The Gestapo-ghetto liaison was Mordechai Chaim Rumkowski, head of the Jewish Community Council and a Zionist. The former factory owner and orphanage director had a distinguished carriage, a head of thick, white hair and a penchant for finely tailored shirts and highly polished leather boots rising to the knee. He was referred to as the Eldest of the Jews and believed he was the ghetto's ruler. Rumkowski also believed the ghetto's salvation would result from its use as a compliant and efficient work centre for the Nazis. Initially, the Bundists were wary of him; eventually, they loathed him. They were behind some of the work stoppages and strike actions that took place in the ghetto's early days. They saw Rumkowski as a puppet of the Nazis, not as a saviour of the Jews. Through the Labour Assignment Office he offered daily to provide the Germans seven hundred, then one thousand — later, even greater numbers of — Jewish workers to end the Gestapo custom of grabbing people in bread lines off the streets. But Rumkowski could do nothing when the Germans decided that ghetto rations were to be limited to half that fed to German prisoners.

Early in 1940, on January 11, Baluty was declared an "area of epidemic danger." On February 8, the Lodz ghetto was officially established and the few remaining Poles and Germans in Baluty moved out. Twice the number of Jews were moved in. In the fall of 1941, another twenty thousand Jews from all over Europe were relocated to the enclave. The new arrivals came from Prague, Vienna and Berlin. They were devout, sophisticated Westerners, who had little in common with the Yiddish-speaking Jews of Lodz. By the time city authorities fled before the Germans invaded in September, most of Lodz's educated professionals had already gone. One unofficial tally put the number of doctors, masons and tailors remaining in Lodz when the Germans arrived at 128, 76 and 14,987 respectively.[5]

Rumkowski declared the Lodz Jews to be a work force of skilled machinists, steelworkers and mechanics, as well as tailors and textile workers, as he organized a manufacturing base that helped keep the German war effort in munitions and uniforms. They made the boots the German army wore on its march to Stalingrad; they built furniture for the comfort of the German moguls. Each task was seen as furthering the war effort. It was an orderly system, designed to appeal to Teutonic precision. Better still for Rumkowski and his plan to buy time for the Lodz Jews, it was profitable: twenty million Reichmarks were sent to Berlin from the Lodz ghetto between November 1940 and August 1942.

The ghetto survived until August 1944, more than two years after the adoption on January 20, 1942, of the policy euphemistically known as the Final Solution. Henry managed to maintain a semblance of his former life until 1942. He had been among those rounded up by the Germans while waiting in food lines at five in the morning, before being taken out of the city to work "like a slave." He was often picked up and directed into the fine homes being seized by the Germans and ordered to move around heavy furniture. Then, at age 19, Henry was asked to teach at his former school, the Medem school.

He loved teaching and the way the children's eyes lit up when he entered the room, in anticipation of the Yiddish stories he would read them to "take them away from the drudgery and danger of their daily lives." But he could not keep them safe. In 1942 the schools were closed and Henry was forced to work in a steel-making plant, then a paper-box factory where Mike was a mechanic operating the lathe. In 1943 the Germans rounded up all children under twelve, to take them away for extermination. It was a cruel way to ensure that Jews would become extinct. It was also another deal Rumkowski had negotiated with the

Germans. Whether the Elder believed it was a compromise hammered out to save the entire ghetto from being annihilated or that he kow-towed to the Nazi liquidation policy to maintain his regime is still a point of debate. At times, Rumkowski agreed the Germans could gather up the elderly and frail of the ghetto, ostensibly to move them to alter-native accommodations. The official line was they were being "reset-tled" in the East. Most knew otherwise.

"They left the ghetto and went, probably, to the extermination camps and certain death. By this time everybody knew this was the pol-icy, yet this guy Rumkowski was telling everybody to surrender," Henry recalled. Rumkowski urged mothers to give up their children to save others. Henry's class of eight- and nine-year-olds died in the gas cham-bers because of that system. And Henry remained alive because of that system, which was based on Jews maintaining a murderous status quo, capitulating to the Nazi liquidation policy. As repugnant as that was, Rumkowski stated repeatedly it was the only way to live another day, and the day after that, and it was the only way some of them were going to outlast the enemy.

Because they were useful to the German war effort, the Jews from Lodz were not rounded up and herded into airless railway cars with the rest of Europe's Jews, although in all, seventy thousand were sent away. They were, however, a slave labour force without dignity or self-respect, in a galling arrangement with an establishment that was destroying their people. Henry hated living like this, but he wanted to live. Rumkowski's arrangement meant the Jewish ghetto police didn't bother workers like him or fifteen-year-old Mike. But one day they did arrive at the apartment next to theirs. A fair-haired five-year-old lived there. Henry, who loved children and had often played with the little boy, watched as the boy's mother refused to release her son. She went with him, knowing she was going to her death but determined her child would not die alone. The father was left alone and grief-stricken. This was not an isolated case. All over the ghetto, soldiers plucked children right out from their families. Many mothers knowingly went with their children to their deaths. Others gave away their children, knowing they themselves did not have much longer to live. "Of course I was afraid I was going to die, but I had to suppress all my feelings of rage to try and survive," Henry said.

There were small mercies. In 1942, Golda Morgentaler was also loaded onto a truck to be taken away. She was saved by the intervention of a neighbour who was a Jewish ghetto policeman (a member of the squad Rumkowski had established to keep order and enforce the Germans' bidding in the ghetto). At one point Henry was told he was on a German hit list, and for two days and nights he hid out in the wood factory where his brother Mike worked, until informed his hunters had lost interest. Once Henry met the great Rumkowski himself when he went to his office to remind the elder he had known Josef Morgentaler and to ask for extra food. He was given a basket of salami, cheese and flour, a virtual lifesaver for the starving family. And always there was the Bund. For the first two years of the war, it was a mainstay of ghetto life. The new generation of leaders who took the place of those who had been murdered or who had fled was indefatigable. In essence, they assumed responsibility for maintaining individual dignity and collective humanity. Runners, for example, would check in daily with the ill and the heartsick.[6] The ghetto doctor was a Bundist who worked hard to obtain prescriptions for those suffering from the typhus and dysentery that tore through the ghetto during the first months. One of their number had a radio — he would have been put to death had the authorities ever discovered it — and even though the news was dismal those first years, at least a connection existed, albeit one way, with the outside world.

Golda Morgentaler was a leader of the Bundist's women's organization, the Yiddish Arbeter Froien. She founded a kindergarten and ran one of the two soup kitchens. These became the centre of ghetto life, where people could attend concerts by the symphony orchestra, poetry readings and theatrical productions. Chava Rosenfarb was prominent in die Zukunft, the illegal youth organization. She and her sister also helped run the library in their home.

And for a time, life was as good as they could make it. Chava was recognized as a nascent poet, and she thrived within a group of poets who believed they must record their lives for future generations. They met secretly but regularly to read their new works. Books in the library sustained Henry. So did the extra food his mother brought home from the kitchens for the family. But Henry spent little time at the Morgentaler home. Ghitel had left with Pav, and Golda was sad most of the time, even though she would not give up her work with the Bund and never faltered in her efforts to feed her own family. Henry spent his time at the Rosenfarb house with Chava, her younger sister, Henia, and their parents. This house was intact; no one was missing. Henry was happier there.

By August 1944, the Russians had arrived near Warsaw and the Germans had decided to evacuate Lodz, the last ghetto. But by then the Lodz socialist infrastructures and organizations were in tatters. The crisis point had come in the winter of 1942, when the Germans almost stopped sending in food. What did arrive was frozen — the potatoes, beets and turnips had been destroyed by the frost; bread rations were meagre. People gave up; to exist seemed futile. Clinging to a socialist culture and its ideals required more energy than anyone had. There was no point in the Bund maintaining a library or organizing poetry readings. Its political activities ceased. The Bund continued to oppose Rumkowski, but within limits. After he sent the children to their deaths, the Bund leadership discussed assassinating Rumkowski, but eventually dropped the idea because the act would have been a futile one: the Jewish elder had four or five lieutenants who would continue his work.

Throughout 1942 and 1943, the Germans continually demanded more and more Jews for one more transport. Many Bundists thought Rumkowski was too eager to satisfy the Germans' every request. He released thousands of Jews to the transports and they knew all too well what that meant. But, to verify the fate of those sent out of the ghetto, one of their members, a woman, volunteered to go. She was to report back what she found when she reached her destination. They never heard from her, which was enough documentation for them.

They knew they were helpless, and that Rumkowski was very determined to eliminate all those opposed to his ways. During what amounted to a state visit to the Warsaw ghetto in 1942, he said in a speech, "For a price of 50 marks, I got reports on all the workers' top secret meetings. In the meantime I set up a detention camp and slowly, one by one, I put the leaders inside."[7] Rumkowski never succeeded in breaking the Bund, but during the waning months of the Lodz ghetto, it was too concerned with keeping its followers alive, and keeping some hope alive in its followers, to be much of a thorn in his side.

The Bund leaders were exhausted by their private agonies. Two members of the leadership were women. One perished when she decided to go with her children; the other tried, unsuccessfully, to hide hers. In August 1944, nobody was surprised when the Nazis overran the ghetto and rounded up everybody into waiting cattle cars. Henry, Mike and Golda Morgentaler fled to the Rosenfarb house. They were not going to wait around for another knock on their door. The Rosenfarbs had a secret room, where the two families hid. Its doorway was obscured by a weighty commode and the Gestapo and Jewish police made several passes by the house without incident.

For ten days they were safe. Then a steady but muffled sound was heard on the outside wall. It was an official tapping on the walls of the building; the discrepancy between the outside and interior building measurement had been detected. The next sound was that of the commode being shoved aside. Then a Nazi officer and Jewish police burst into the small room and herded the ten cowering people living there onto wagons to transport them to the collection square.

It was over. Henry and his family joined the thousands of other Jews huddled on the square, clutching a bag of food, a keepsake, each other. Zionist or Bundist, it didn't matter now. Still, amid all the despair and grief, Henry noted it was Jewish police who prodded them into the wretched, filthy cattle cars, jamming in more and more people until it seemed there was no air left to breathe, and not one inch in which to move.

The doors thudded shut, shrouding everyone in the thick darkness. Hours later when they opened up, it was to a line of guards, their screaming faces pale against the backdrop of the black smoke of Auschwitz.

CHAPTER 3

"SCHNELL, SCHNELL..."

THEY STUMBLED FROM THE CARS. For fifteen hours they had been drenched in their own and each other's fear and ignorance. It was more than Henry could stand. He needed his bearings, which meant he needed to know.

"Where are we going?" he asked one officer. By now Henry could speak German, as well as Polish, Yiddish and a little English.

"*Himmel*," said the officer. Heaven.

Golda Morgentaler drew Mike aside and begged him to go back to the train. She had left behind a basket. Mike sped away and leaped onto the cattle car they had just left. But he was seen. Officers converged on him, beating, slapping him, before he staggered back empty-handed to the section of the platform where his mother had been standing. She was nowhere to be seen. The women had been separated from the men. And the men were being marched past an officer who was dividing them into two lines, one to the right, one to the left. The officer was Josef Mengele, who was in command of Auschwitz-Birkenau — that was what Mike Morgentaler remembered. Henry recalls only that their mother had forgotten her winter coat. Other than that he does not remember where or when she vanished from their sight and their lives. Soldiers were screaming "*Schnell, schnell*" — fast, fast — at them as they stumbled off the squalid cattle car. Although only fifty, Golda Morgentaler had probably been ordered into the line of the ill, the elderly, those too young or not fit for work and sent to the gas chamber. They had heard of the ovens; everyone had been told the stories of showers that emitted no water, only a deadly gas. Chava, her sister and their mother had also vanished, and the brothers feared the worst.

Henry told Mike to pinch his cheeks for colour to look strong enough to work, and to tell the officer he was nineteen, not seventeen. The officer jerked his thumb to the left, as he had for Henry. They joined at least five hundred others in a huge room. A uniformed German stood on a stage at the front of the room and declared, "Your life is worthless spit. If you don't obey orders it will be shorter than that." They were stripped, searched and sent away to shower. Henry knew what that might mean. A collective sigh of relief sounded when water came out. "There was still some hope then." They were shaven from head to foot, given pajamalike striped tops and bottoms and crammed into an A-frame wooden structure built into the bare earth and designed to hold two hundred. Now more than five hundred men crushed into the space. With no room to lie down, Henry spent the whole night crouching.

In the morning they were led to a field. Henry remembered how they chose one obese man — he had been a leader in the ghetto government and privy to a generous source of food supply — to humiliate, beat and intimidate. No one attempted to stop it or help him. They were fast learning how to survive from hour to hour. Henry was now prisoner 95077; Mike was 95095. They had deliberately stayed apart in the line because they hadn't wanted anybody to recognize them as Josef Morgentaler's sons and send them off to a swift death. They left the camp after four days, before the Nazis could burn their new identities into their forearms, as they had done with those imprisoned earlier in the war. It was a small indicator the enemy war machine might be wearing down. Someone had told the brothers they should try to be transferred from Auschwitz and its terrible smoking ovens, so they told the authorities they were skilled workers because Mike had worked in a furniture factory in Lodz.

As a result they were herded onto another train, this time for a ride of seventeen hours without food or water. When it ended, they were in Bavaria at Dachau's Lager Vier (Camp Four), where they would work to build an airplane hangar. They were no more than beasts of burden, ordered around by supervising Kapos, in this case Polish Jews, to carry cement bags and metal parts. They were barely fed, but at least there were no working ovens at Dachau.

The days took on a gruesome pattern. They would be awoken when it was still dark, about 5 a.m., and sent down to a central square, where they were kept for about two hours as officers counted them many times. Then they were marched to the factory to work. "The sacks were really heavy. I wasn't sure I was going to survive it," Henry said. They got their meal of the day about 7 p.m., a watery soup and a piece of bread weighing between 115 and 170 grams, to be shared between two. The prisoners had no knife to cut the bread and soon fights erupted over who had the larger piece. Henry devised the plan that ended the battles: one day A would divide the bread and B would choose which piece; the next day B divided and A chose.

Henry and Mike were a team. At seventeen, Mike was the youngest in the camp, a favourite who could wheedle potato peelings, if not the potato itself, from otherwise hard-eyed camp staff to share with his brother. Mike figured out that by going to the front of the soup line he could get in line again for seconds. It worked for him, but when Henry tried he was caught and beaten. "Mike got away with it because he was the baby," Henry claimed, but Mike got away with it because he worked the system like a Tom Sawyer. He had the savvy to hang around the kitchen, then the charm to parlay himself into a regular job there. After a while he never had to leave the camp to go out to work. But Henry did. Like the others, he faced twelve hours of excruciating labour every day. He was just twenty-one, but he had been hungry for five years. Mike was strong and wiry, reverberating with energy. It was harder for Henry, who sustained himself through force of will. He drew on poetry, remembered fragments of books, anything he could conjure that was beautiful or noble. But he watched the shameful failure of poetry to sustain the life of a promising young poet, a colleague of Chava. The poet had been vital and passionate about the beautiful mystery of words, but in the camps he became just one more starving, bloated *Musselman*. (In the ghetto and in the camps, the people who gave up were called *Musselmen*. In German and Yiddish that meant Muslims — in this sense, those resigned to the fate meted out to them by the will of God or Allah.)

Other prisoners faltered under the oppressive work regime. Exhausted, they either asked for a transfer or volunteered to go back to Auschwitz. "No one came back from there. It was a one-way ride," Henry said. He could see that as clearly as he noted the self-delusion and how strong people's need was to deny reality. Along with Mike, he was determined to beat reality, not ignore it. A small group of prisoners, including Chava's father, looked out for one another, sharing what little information they could find out about the war. When winter came they needed one another more than ever. They were filthy from sleeping and working in their striped suits. Fifty slept in each dugout under an A-frame roof. A central corridor ran between and below planks on each side. The men slept on the planks, no more than five or six hours a night. A few marked their spot with small possessions — a comb, perhaps a mirror. They were given no extra clothing for winter, so they took the paper from the sacks holding 22 to 27 kilos of cement that they were forced to carry, and wore it as an extra layer against the chill and the wind. "If you got caught you got a severe beating. If you didn't you died of pneumonia."

By midwinter, between ten and fifteen men were dying daily, among them Chava's father. Some had bartered away the food that might have sustained them longer for cigarettes. That repelled Henry. They had given away their only chance of survival for a smoke. Henry and Mike and anyone else still alive were transferred to Lager Eins (Camp One), where conditions were as brutal but the supervising Kapos were Lithuanian Jews. Traditionally, Lithuanians and Poles didn't get along, but Henry had heard them speaking in a dialect close to Yiddish, so he approached one of them and explained in literary Yiddish that he wanted to be a foreman. "You tried whatever you could to survive." Mike had once again arranged it so he worked in the kitchen and never had to go on a work crew with Henry. Then a few days later a foreman went missing — whether he tried to escape or he died from ill health was never made known to Henry, nor did he ever

ask — and the Kapo Henry had spoken to appointed him the new foreman. He was responsible for a crew of fifteen who worked the twelve-
hour night shift, digging railway beds. He was not in charge; a German
civilian with a vicious temper was. Henry says the German once hit him
on the head with a stick so hard he passed out. He remembers scrambling to his feet as he regained consciousness and feigning that nothing
had happened.

But early one morning as Henry was on his way to the latrine after
working another shift through the black, bitterly cold night, he was
picked up by a Kapo needing another person on his crew and ordered
to fall into line for work. He had no choice, even though it meant he
would be working twenty-four hours straight. He was staggering from
exhaustion when he came back to the camp, but Mike was manic with
energy. He was burning with fever from typhus, and would be going to
another camp. He wanted Henry to go with him.

"I can't possibly go. I'm beat. I've worked twenty-four hours."
Henry pleaded with his younger brother to stay.

But Mike had made up his mind. He had been sick with diarrhea.
He kept saying, "I've got to go. I've got to go." He wanted out with or
without Henry. Henry fell back onto his pallet on the rough, wooden
boards. All he could think to do was sleep. When he awoke hours later,
Mike had gone. For the first time, Henry was alone in that terrible place
filled with dying, defeated, starved and exhausted men. There was no
one lying beside him.

He was grief-stricken, although he had chosen to stay. Because he
was a foreman, he received extra food rations and wasn't expected to do
as much hard labour. He was given a pair of clogs to replace the deteri-
orating leather shoes he had left Lodz in. But a few days later someone
stole them from the head of his bed, where he always left them. That
morning he walked the two kilometres to work barefoot. The next day
he, too, was felled by a fever. He sought help from the Jewish doctor
in the infirmary. Usually, sick prisoners were sent back to Auschwitz,
but by then some men received treatment without incident. It was
February 1, 1945. It seemed a safer time to be sick. The infirmary had a
mirror. Gazing into it, Henry saw a gaunt, bearded man with haunted

eyes. He resembled all the others in the camp. "I looked like death." He started to cry; he thought it was over.

But he was diagnosed with bronchitis and treated with whatever medicine was available. He got rest, bread and soup. And for two weeks he was left alone by the camp personnel, who assumed anyone in the infirmary would soon die.

Then, on February 15, he and about a dozen others were suddenly shipped out to Lager Vier. Somehow they learned Auschwitz had been taken by the Russians — the reason the Germans had stopped transporting prisoners there. Now Lager Vier was the place where prisoners like Henry were being sent to die. They didn't have to work there, but neither did they get much food. They remained in the camp, virtually abandoned, as spring approached. Henry could see a German soldier walk with a girl on the grass outside the camp, but where he lay there was nothing — no hope, not even a blade of grass. He still wanted to live, but his strength was ebbing away. He thought, "Maybe I should believe in God." But how could a God let such a thing happen to his people? To people who believed in him? All around were the faithful praying to their God, then dying wretchedly the next day. How could millions of people be so sinful that they would be punished by this horrible death by degradation? So he picked a star in the sky, an active one that zigged, then zagged with brio. That's what he would believe in.

And then, suddenly, Mike was back, laughing and healthy. A doctor at the sick camp had promised him double rations if he pulled through, and had kept his word, obtaining the extra food by not reporting some of the deaths. When Mike had been forced to labour outdoors, the winter air had cooled his raging fever, and with the help of this doctor, a former neighbour from Lodz, he had recovered. This man may have been half German; in the skewed reality of the death camps this could have accounted for the influence he held there. What mattered is that Mike was a favourite of his and therefore Mike received enough food to regain his health.

When he had heard Henry had been sent back to Lager Vier, Mike had known what that meant: his brother was expected to die. Mike had acted fast, wrangling a transfer to be near Henry and another job in the kitchen to get the scraps to feed his brother. Before the family was sent away from Lodz, Golda Morgentaler had asked Mike to look out for Henry. She'd known her sons well. Henry may have been the elder by four years, but he was the dreamer, disconnected from everyday life. Mike had the street smarts. He was quick and strong, able to think fast and think on his feet. He adored his mother, worshipped her strength and steadfastness as much as Henry idolized his father's idealism. Mike was fiercely proud of his mother; he would do anything she asked of him, especially take care of Henry.[1]

———

As the Germans plunged into a deeper and darker gloom and those prisoners still alive began to worry about whether they would be killed before they could be rescued and bear witness against their captors, Mike grew more irrepressible. Henry's health improved. Mike, Henry and a third man, a Czech, caught, killed and cooked the chef's cat. "One of the most delicious meals of my life," Henry said.

They could see the Allied planes circling overhead, but this was no cause for celebration. What would the Germans do with them now? Shoot them all? In mid-April the call came to gather at the meeting grounds where they had stood subserviently in rows so many mornings before to be counted. Believing they were about to be shot, Henry and Mike hid, instead, in the bunkhouses. Until three that morning they scurried from one bunkhouse to another, attempting to elude the Germans. At the same time, a couple of SS officers, doctors, prowled the infirmary Henry had just left, shooting in the head anyone they found, anyone who couldn't move. Then they set the hospital tent on fire, before killing themselves.

"They didn't have to do that, but these were their orders. They knew those people in there couldn't defend themselves," Henry recalled.

When Henry and Mike were found, the first group of prisoners had already been herded out of the camp, for what would be a ten-day march to another camp. Anyone who faltered or dropped out was shot. They joined another group, which was rounded onto a train heading south. Armed American planes swooped overhead. In a desperate bid to avoid being targeted, the Germans forced the pyjama-clad prisoners to stand on the open cattle cars. The low-flying American pilots could see the telltale stripes of the concentration camp uniforms. But they didn't turn away. They circled once, then once again, over the trains to warn the prisoners to jump and flee before the trains and Germans were machine-gunned.

Henry said the man he was standing beside was hit by shrapnel. The train may have stopped, but he isn't sure. There may have been two German guards and about 150 prisoners too emaciated, too numbed to cheer. The truth is Henry cannot remember. The moment of liberation remains a shadowy, elusive memory, and was anything but triumphant. Mike claimed he remembered everything. One American plane, then another and another came screaming down. Mike jumped off the train after the first plane, expecting Henry to be behind him. He wasn't. Mike zigzagged through the shrapnel and the gunfire back to the stopped train, where, he said, Henry was standing, oblivious, arguing politics with someone.

"Jump, Henry, jump," he screamed.

Dodging bullets, they ran through the fields, past the bodies of fallen Jews, to the relative safety of the nearby woods. Then they headed away from the train towards a road. It was wide-open; they were as exposed to random violence as they had ever been in the camp. But they had exhausted their hiding places, and the war was so very nearly over; they could not and would not hide and cower one more time.

When the inevitable happened — when the line on the horizon turned grey with the uniforms of the retreating Germans — they neither stopped nor sought cover. They would meet face to face. But the Germans, intent on saving themselves, knowing all was lost, ignored the two small, frail figures trudging past.

Henry was so tired he begged Mike to stop and rest awhile. But Mike insisted that they keep going. Five kilometres down the road they came upon a village. A German peasant family grudgingly gave them shelter — a chicken coop — for the night and thin soup as supper. A third man, also an escaped prisoner, joined them. Everything changed the next morning when the American soldiers came over the hill.

Henry hailed them. "Hi, I speak English," he shouted. Whatever English he knew he had learned from reading *Little Lord Fauntleroy*.

The Americans were looking for Germans. Henry told them the direction to take to find them. Mike remembered a red-haired soldier tossing out a weapon, saying in Yiddish, "Here's a gun. Go shoot them." Mike didn't take the gun. After the Americans arrived the peasant family were markedly more hospitable. That night, Henry and Mike slept on a bed in the house. That evening, they sat at the dinner table with the family and were fed meat, even some vegetables. And they had a glass of wine. The family claimed they had saved the Morgentaler brothers. They had not told some passing German soldiers of their whereabouts, they said. They were no longer supporters of the Reich, perhaps never had been, although they may have been among the area farmers who had used the free Jewish labour to work their fields.

Henry didn't bother to argue with them. "It was not our nature to take revenge. That was not how we had been brought up."

He weighed about seventy pounds, but "I could move and I could speak. When I told that American I could speak English, I knew I had survived. That was my moment of liberation." Two days later, however, Henry fell ill. Feverish and giddy, he knew he had to get himself to a hospital. With Mike, he dragged himself the twelve kilometres to a former Roman Catholic monastery that the Americans were using as a hospital, then fell onto a stretcher. He lay there for hours, unable to move or even turn over. He had no strength left in him, just despair that this was how it was going to end for him, after only two days of freedom. He sank into a frantic sleep. When he awoke the next morning an American and a German doctor were tending to him. He had typhoid fever, probably contracted from lice infesting the man who had shared the chicken coop with Mike and him that first night.

With Mike still at the farmhouse, Henry spent two weeks convalescing, before being transferred to facilities at St-Ottilien for recuperating patients. He could stroll the hospital grounds; finally, he was walking on grass. The freshness in the air was overpowering; he had also forgotten how intense the colours of nature could be. His shoulders straightened; his step quickened; he was reborn. He wasn't savouring life — he was reaching out and shaking it. He decided to become a doc-tor, a healer, a saviour, a man like Louis Pasteur. He would never be afraid again. He would never play by anyone else's rules. That was for his father. The Nazis had not beaten Henry Morgentaler. Anything was possible again.

By the time Henry left St-Ottilien, some lists of survivors were being posted in former concentration camps where Jewish survivors were gathering and pieces of his past started to emerge. Henry and Mike journeyed to Feldafing, a refugee camp near Munich, where they searched the lists. People knew Chava, her mother and sister to be alive in Bergen-Belsen; there was no trace of Ghitel or either of Henry's parents. For five days, Henry and Mike hitched rides on American transport trucks, tanks and railroad cars to northern Germany. Once while waiting for a train at a small town by the side of a river, the broth-ers watched people swimming across to the other side. Neither man could swim, but Henry was too euphoric to concede anything was beyond his grasp. If he could live, he could swim, and by imitating the other swimmers' movements he did, although he almost was lost in the midriver currents. But he blithely thrashed on to the other side, where he basked until he had to swim back to catch the train.

Bergen-Belsen had become a displaced persons camp, where Chava and her family had been staying for a month. But Henry's reunion with her was delayed a day or two, because Chava had left to look for him. Once together, Chava, Henry, Mike and Chava's sister and mother relo-cated to Feldafing, where the United Nations Relief and Rehabilitation Agency was offering scholarships to German universities to the few of the nearly 200,000 Jewish survivors not fleeing Europe at their first opportunity. On a now-yellowing piece of paper notarized at Feldafing, Henry declared his intention to study medicine and that he had the equivalent of a high-school diploma. From that moment, he never looked back to Lodz. Nor did he ever go back.

But a reckless, eager Mike rode the top of a box car home, carrying letters to people in the ghetto. Always adventuresome, even bolder and more fearless after surviving the camps, Mike felt compelled to return home. He went back to the family's apartment, now occupied by a

Polish family. He was hoping to find some family photographs, any memento of his childhood home and family, which some Jews were fortunate enough to have, but the new occupants had saved nothing. He was restless and kinetic. A friend of the time remembered how his eyes seemed to dart in all directions. He hitchhiked back to the refugee camp. There Henry was studying and Chava had organized a literary group where her poems and the works of others were read. There the circle was unbroken. They might even have been forgiven for believing it was charmed.

The Bund had sprung back to life. They were soon running covert convoys to Brussels, smuggling Jewish socialists to new lives in what they believed to be a more benign, less ravaged part of Europe. But on the day Henry, along with Chava, her family and many of their friends, was scheduled for the Brussels convoy, he fell ill again. This time it was jaundice due to viral hepatitis. He was in the hospital when word came he had been accepted into first-year medical school. However, the school was in Germany. Chava was adamant. She would never go back to that country. She had left for Brussels with her family believing Henry would soon be joining her. Henry was equally adamant. He was going to become a doctor, and if the Germans inadvertently were aiding him in that goal, so be it. The irony of his situation was not lost on him. He was in the position of privilege; they were the conquered people. He was free and studying to join one of the noblest and most prestigious professions; they were under the rule of the Americans.

Nevertheless, Chava and Mike were appalled at Henry's decision. Henry hid behind pragmatism. "There's not much I could do. I had to go where the education was available to me." Still, he loved his year at Marburg-Lahn University. He was one of a dozen Jewish students, all of them on scholarship, and every one of them a living reminder to the townspeople that the Final Solution was a failure.

Henry boarded with the Launs, a tight-lipped, wintry couple forced by authorities to take in a Jewish scholarship student because they were childless and had room in their modest home. In the entire year he lived in the small room behind the glass doors off their parlour, Henry never exchanged more than a *"Guten Tag"* or *"Guten Abend"* with them. Even after he had lived there several months, they would start whenever he entered, as if they had forgotten he existed. Henry maintained the charade of civility; he would neither acknowledge his status of interloper nor indicate he was affected by their deliberately slighting correctness.

He was rarely there anyway. The other Jewish students were housed in a large, old home near the university. It had a study room, a dining room and, on the third floor, a common room with a Ping-Pong table, where Henry could always be found. At first he hung around because he didn't want to go back to his own lodgings, but later he was always there because he had discovered his sport. He was obsessed with, and soon unbeatable at, Ping-Pong. He was willingly distracted from his studies; the lectures bored him, he said. He attended few, although his marks were excellent, buoyed by a fluency in German, a memory close to photographic — he said he could remember whether a fact was on the third line from the bottom of the page — and his habit of last-minute, all-night study sessions. What really engaged him was the thrust and parry of competition. He revelled in his agility with a Ping-Pong paddle, but coming up with a winning analysis of an opponent's style and strategy pleased him more. "I can adapt to the style of my opponent. I can analyze the weaknesses and capitalize."

The university was located in a pretty mountain town so unscathed by the war that it seemed, Brigadoon-like, to have vanished during the war years, only to be discovered by occupying American troops and their tanks. The all-pervasive anti-Semitism had evaporated with the troops. German townspeople would tell anyone who cared to listen they had not known of the atrocities; they had not been Nazis. Henry paid them scant attention. Of the 120 medical students at the university, all but the twelve Jews were German. Henry ignored the Germans because — finally — he could. It was safe to. Only one German student — formerly a pilot in the air force — was friendly. "Too friendly. He probably felt guilty," Henry said. He rebuffed him and all Germans. "These were a conquered people, unsure of their future."

How the tables had turned. Henry and his friends believed they were living in a state of grace. They were Russian, Ukrainian; some of the women were Latvian and Lithuanian; another was a Pole who was already married; they were all survivors who were going to help mankind. They had their dreams well within reach and they had one another. They were all going to stay until they got their medical degrees, everyone except Henry. Although he had become close with one of the women, he decided to take his first-year diploma, return to Chava and finish the remainder of his studies in Brussels. Mike had long before eagerly left Germany and Poland for America, the land of their liberators, the country that symbolized everything to them, including winning. Henry probably would have gone to the United States had he had the opportunity, but he was too old for this particular study program for young Jewish orphans who had not completed high school. Not yet eighteen, Mike lived with a Jewish foster family, but soon ran off to join the merchant navy.

After living as one, saving each other's lives, the brothers lost touch with each other. Mike never was much of a writer, and Henry, disgusted that Mike would forfeit his whole future, didn't overtax himself keeping track of his adventuring brother's whereabouts. He had other things on his mind. The only way to get to Brussels was still via the Bund's underground convoy. Henry had heard of what had happened to friends of theirs just a few months earlier. They had been let off too close to the German-Belgian border by the people paid to escort them into Belgium and were found by border guards, who turned them over to the authorities after being told they were displaced people with no documents allowing them entry into the country.

They spent months in a German prison before the Bund managed to negotiate their release. By the time Henry was ready to leave, the Bund was using a safer route via the French border. With five strangers, he crouched on a bench under a tarpaulin in the back of a pickup, in silence and darkness for hours. They were stopped at the border — Henry was never told why or what was said — but after what seemed an eternity, yet was actually no more than five minutes at Customs, the truck was on its way again.

They arrived in Paris at about three in the morning. The refugees were put up in a hotel and given strict orders not to leave their rooms, because they had no papers. They would get those first thing in the morning, but until then they were illegal aliens. It was a benchmark moment. Henry had made it into the premier city of his imagination, Pasteur's birthplace, Western Europe's City of Light. With so many Jews heading for Israel to start new lives, Henry had stayed true to his father's Bundist beliefs. He'd remained an internationalist, a modernist. The idea of Jews living on their own even outside a Polish town or city had seemed "obsolete, entrophic, something from the Middle Ages. With Israel, Zionists were saying Jews had suffered enough — we will create our own world." But Henry believed that this was just putting more walls around Jews, creating another ghetto. "The fact that you are Jewish doesn't mean you have to put a ghetto around you, a wall around you." Besides, Bundists were still at loggerheads with Zionists. The cruel reality was that few countries were offering open-armed hospitality to Europe's Jews. "But I wanted to be part of modern humanity, where all people were not Jewish." He dared to think of going to the United States, or to Canada, but first he had to become a doctor.

And before that, he would have to make it past the bureaucratic red tape. He knew it would take all day, if it happened at all. There was nothing more he could do except get some sleep.

———

Chava loved Brussels. She, her sister Henia and Sima, their mother, were surrounded by old Bundist friends; every day it seemed that another reunion took place. Or a departure. Many friends were leaving for Australia. She and Henry moved into an apartment above a store on rue Aerschot. It was the red-light district, but they believed they were living in luxury. Chava had work once a week teaching in a Yiddish school in Antwerp, just as she had taught in the illegal schools set up in Baluty for the children who had not been deported.[2] When the ghetto had been liquidated in August 1944, she had packed up everything she had written and taken it with her. It was confiscated in Auschwitz. Now she was reclaiming all the stories the Nazis has wrested from her. She wrote poetry; she wrote plays; she wrote with a passion, sensitivity and urgency, and was soon acclaimed an extraordinary new talent.

She was a rising star, centred within the small and loyal Bundist circles who met at the community centre. The Bund had risen from the ashes and was recreating itself. To Chava, it was reassuring that the old ways were continuing; to Henry, when he arrived, it was claustrophobic. He was in a hurry; the world beyond the Bund was waiting. Bundist friends told him of Madame Allard, a wealthy widow whose sister had married Victor Alter, a Bundist hero shot under Stalin's orders. She had some scholarship money for worthy young Bundists. Henry met with her in her sumptuous apartment. She knew of Josef Morgentaler. Henry was given two thousand Belgian francs (about $40) a month. As Chava's stature grew and she was invited to London, England, for a reading organized by a gentleman taken by her talent, Henry studied, completing second and third years of medical school in one year. He was on his own, with no mentors and little connection with the Université de Bruxelles medical school. He was living with Chava and her mother in a three-room apartment near the railway tracks, which they had moved to from their tiny one-room place in the red-light district. He got along well with Chava's mother. Sima Rosenfarb was a warm, loving woman, who was a mother figure to many of their young friends. They called her Mameshi.

But that was Chava's world. Henry's was the inhospitable, day-to-day competitive medical school. Chess was a distraction. He began playing the masters and won some important tourneys while in Belgium. But he soon realized his downfall, his "strategic flaw." He was not analyzing and anticipating his opponents' moves. Instead of the two-dimensional game chess masters all play, he was playing one level only.

Within the Faculty of Medicine, he was only eligible to sign up for scientific studies, but Belgian medical students were enrolled in legal studies. Both streams took the same classes, same exams, even had the same teachers, but those in legal studies would be qualified to start up a medical practice in Belgium when they got their degree and Henry and the others in his course would not. Henry's identity card said he had to immigrate, and the card had to be renewed every six months. The only place where the diploma he was working towards would allow him to practise was the Belgian Congo. He redoubled his efforts to go to Canada to continue his studies and start anew one more time. A wealthy middle-aged cousin, a son of Josef Morgentaler's sister, who had left Lodz for Switzerland in 1903, was a prosperous furniture factory owner in Brussels. He agreed to advance Henry the money to pay for the passage for him and Chava. The two decided on Montreal. Henry's cousin Sara was already living there with her family and had agreed to sponsor them. Chava, who had just published her first volume of poetry, had an admirer there. He was Harry Hershman, a Montreal-based distributor of *Forward*, a Jewish newspaper published in New York City; he became her patron. Besides, the American medical schools were full.

They got married at city hall and began packing for Canada almost immediately. It didn't take long, since they had so little.

In February 1950, only a few friends were at the Brussels train station to see them off. Most people they knew had already left for Australia. They left from Le Havre for Canada. The *Samaria* was an old ship, and far from luxurious. The crossing was rough. Henry was one of the few passengers who wasn't seasick. Three months pregnant, Chava remained below deck in the cabin for almost the entire trip. Henry made a point of staying up on deck, sometimes the only person there, face in the wind as he looked across the sea as if to the new land. Down in the hold he had three cartons of psychology books — "it seemed a sacrilege to throw or give them away" — and in his pocket $20 (U.S.).

The day they docked in Montreal a blizzard was raging.

CHAPTER 4

A FOREIGNER AND A JEW

Years later, when millions beat an eager path to Montreal for Expo 67 to confirm the city's place on the world stage, Henry Morgentaler knew this was where he belonged. He knew he'd achieved everything he had dreamed of all those hours he'd stood in the wind on the deck of the *Samaria*. He had become a medical doctor, a general practitioner with a thriving practice. Although his lifestyle was not ostentatious, a swimming pool sat behind his low, rambling home in the Town of Mount Royal, an upper-middle-class enclave of Montreal.

This life was calm and good, but he was still uneasy in comfort. Henry was a successful physician, but tormented by a need to do more for society than tend to grateful patients' ailments. He often sat at his desk brooding late into the night, racked by the guilt of not equalling his father's dedication to an ideal and filled with remorse that he still didn't know why Josef Morgentaler had come back to Baluty from his hiding place — to his family, but also to certain death. Had he given up, like all those *Musselmen* in the camps? That Henry survived five precarious years in the ghetto and the last nine months of the war at Auschwitz and Dachau should be viewed as a triumph. But it was not that clear cut for Henry. For many concentration camp survivors, simply being able to lead an ordinary life after witnessing or experiencing the extraordinary inhumanity meted out to Jews was heroic.[1] But Henry was not convinced that living an ordinary life was enough. Nor could he shake off the anxious undercurrent of thought running through him that his present comfortable life was unearned until he had lived a courageous life as his father had done.

He was having a succession of affairs. His midlife crisis was a cliché: there was nothing he would not try. A patient had given him one tab of a hallucinatory drug. It promised more than the day-to-day human experience — something Henry craved. He put on a favourite cello concerto, lay down by the pool and dropped acid on a summer Sunday in Montreal when the air was so warm it clung to bare, tanned skin and the only thing bluer than the sky was the sparkle of the pool. The music roared inside him; never had he experienced anything like the emotion he was feeling. He wept as he watched the sunset because finally he knew he was living fully, that every fibre of his being was shuddering with startling clarity.

Then his hands began shaking, his vision blurring, the objects around him doubling. He cried out to his son to help him get inside the house and into his bed. It was another good trip gone bad, commonplace in this hippie era. Afterward Henry referred to this incident as an "interesting experience" of being in an altered state, but it was something more than that. It was indicative of the emptiness he knew was inside himself and the panic with which he faced his inner void. He didn't know what he wanted anymore.

And he had always known what he wanted. From the moment he'd walked off the boat into Montreal's chilled February air, he'd been in charge of his life. Most everything in the years that followed had gone according to plan, *his* plan and *his* goal, the one he had decreed for himself in the camps. He would become a medical doctor, a medical researcher. He'd approached McGill University almost immediately, having the savvy to first arrange a meeting with Dr. Wilder Penfield, neurosurgeon of international reputation. Henry held a letter of recommendation from one of his Belgian professors. Because his English was still weak and because he wanted to ensure his plea for help was communicated, he'd gotten the prominent Yiddish writer Ida Masse to accompany him and translate. But Penfield would only say he would see what he could do. It was probably a brushoff, but the reality of Montreal in the 1950s was that even someone as important as Penfield had little influence in some matters. The number of Jewish students McGill would accept was limited. Henry said he realized that any who were admitted needed a 75 per cent average, although non-Jews were accepted with only a 65 per cent grade.[2]

Another letter of recommendation from a Belgian professor to a colleague at Université Laval in Quebec City may have motivated the authorities at Université de Montréal, who didn't refuse him outright. Henry would be admitted if, and only if, he took his premed first- and second-year examinations again. "They didn't feel they owed me anything." No special favours were accorded this young and ambitious Jewish concentration camp survivor.

By then he was a father. Goldie Morgentaler had been born August 8, 1950, and named after the mother Henry was never sure loved him. He was smitten with his baby, but he moved away from Chava and Goldie into a friend's place for several weeks to study. His examinations were set for September and they were crucial; everything depended on him doing well. There was much he had forgotten, plus an entire first year of material he had studied in German that he had to translate into French.

He passed, and started classes three weeks later than everybody else. The secretary to the dean of the medical school caught up with him one day in the halls and told him in confidence that nobody there had believed he would pass the exams. Some friends — practical people — had urged him to work for a year and make some money before going back to school. But Henry was as impatient as he was determined to finish his medical studies and become a doctor. "I knew if I went into other work I would never get back, or at least the possibility was there I would never be accepted, and I had to finish my medical studies, no matter where."

Other than their first three weeks in Canada, when they had stayed in the luxurious apartment of Chava's publisher mentor-patron, Chava and Henry had been living hand to mouth. Henry had landed in Montreal without even owning a winter coat. His cousin Sara and her husband, Bernard, who had immigrated to Canada in 1948, took him out immediately and bought him one. A tailor, Bernard had then got Henry a job as an assistant bookkeeper at the textile firm where he worked. Henry had chafed at the $18-a-week salary. But Sara recalled that "it wasn't bad pay. My husband was a tailor and he didn't get more than $18 a week."

"It was menial and boring [work]," Henry said. "I stayed for maybe a week." His next job, also as a bookkeeper, was with a company that sold Venetian blinds. Henry told them he was experienced (glad they never asked how much experience he actually had) and landed a job paying $30 a week. He had never intended to stay at either place; they were stopgaps until he was accepted into medical school. If he had to return to Brussels to gain that acceptance, he would. Meanwhile, he told the faculty at the Université de Montréal that he had been working as a peddler going door to door, so they wouldn't check up on him and alert his employer of his intention to abandon his job to return to school. That was not a total fabrication. Henry had flogged encyclopedias door to door, and had sold sets to two friends too embarrassed not to buy from him, before he quit out of self-disgust. "They didn't really want to buy them," he acknowledged.

But he never told his employers at the Venetian blind company he had other career goals, and continued working there for three weeks after he had been admitted and should have been attending classes. (Henry had ascertained he had already studied what was being taught during that time.) Then he went to his employers and asked for a $5 raise. They refused, as he knew they would; he resigned and went to school with an unblemished work record.

Already he was beginning to move beyond the small and intensely loyal group of Bundists in Montreal to which Sara and her husband belonged and where Chava thrived. He was still the life of their parties; Sara remembers him singing heartily with them all, but even then he was not one of them. "We were all tailors, carpenters, barbers," said Bernard about the group of friends from Lodz who all lived in the Park district of the city and made up Montreal's Arbeiter Ring (Workmen's Circle). "He was not like those people. He went to the university. He was higher." Sara didn't care. He was family; it was enough: "Of course I helped them as much as I could." Her cousin Henry was like his father. And her father had loved Josef Morgentaler. He had begged him to hide in their home when the Germans first came to Lodz in 1939.

Josef refused. "He was stubborn. All Morgentalers are stubborn," Sara said. When the two families lived on the same street in Baluty, her father would say, "Josef, why don't you come to see us?" And Josef would reply, "I have no time." That was Henry, too.

Sara's father, Leibish, died in the gas chamber. So did her sister. Her mother had refused to go to Russia with the rest of the family. She said she didn't have the strength to run, and she died in 1940. Like many young people whose families begged them to escape, Sara and Bernard made it to Russia, where they were detained at the border for three nights. It was December, and Sara's feet turned black from the cold. The soldiers took everything they had in their knapsacks; they were left with nothing but the clothes on their backs and their lives. Both Sara's brothers were living in Montreal at the time, but she was eager to sponsor Henry and Chava to Canada and thrilled when their arrival in Montreal added to the extended family of survivors from Lodz. Goldie was close in age to her own daughter, and the two families shared a rented cottage part of one summer in Shawbridge in the Laurentians, a vacation and resort area north of Montreal. But they saw less and less of one another as Henry worked towards his dream. Sara, her family and their leftist colleagues were, he said, "our natural constituency," but they were living in the past. Henry was living for the future. He worked four hours every night and more on weekends, holding down two jobs. He taught French to newcomers at the Young Men's Hebrew Association and he also answered their phones for sixty, then later sixty-five, cents an hour.

The cousin in Belgium who had helped pay for Henry's and Chava's passage refused Henry's request for a monthly allowance to help the family while Henry attended medical school. He wrote Henry a stinging letter, chiding him for even asking such a thing. Why hadn't Henry thought about this before he'd left Belgium? Why had he not arranged things there in Canada so he could adequately support his family? For years after he had paid back every cent the cousin had ever given him for the voyage to Canada from among his first earnings as a doctor, Henry still resented the man for labelling him rash and irresponsible rather than bold and brave. "I could have stayed in Belgium and got my certificate, but I thought the risk was worth it, and I was right," he said. (Perhaps significantly, he bought the elegant rosewood desk in his home basement office from this cousin years later. "I forgave him," Henry said. "I can't carry a grudge forever." He did, however, ask for a 25 per cent discount; his relative offered 10 per cent. Henry laughed. "I said okay. He [my cousin] was seventy-eight. It was habit.")

The financial situation eased somewhat when Sima and Henia Rosenfarb arrived early in 1951 and came to live with them. Chava's mother was eager to look after her first grandchild while Chava worked part-time in a Jewish school. Chava found an extraordinary apartment for them all — four rooms and a bath for $150 a month — unprecedented luxury on the third floor of a fine building housing a bank at the corner of Bernard Street and Park Avenue. Until then Chava had been restless, and had moved them from one apartment to another, although staying within the Jewish area of town, known as the Main. Someone at the university told Henry he wasn't making much of an impression changing addresses so often, but he was as oblivious to the criticism as he was to where they lived. They had shelter; they were not going hungry. What more could they need? But he did concur when Chava decided they could not stay in one particular rented room because their landlords were religious Jews.

Yet Henry had chosen to live in a very Roman Catholic locale at a time when religion dominated most facets of Quebec life. It would be another decade and more before the Quiet Revolution would release Quebec from the shackles of church domination. In the fifties, the church completely controlled the lives of the people and, many say, the institutions of the state. The cavernous grey cathedrals looming over the centre square of every small town in the province reminded the inhabitants in the modest but gaily painted homes literally under their shadow just who was in charge. Montreal was urbane and cosmopolitan, but not immune from the influence of religion. Henry thought of his chosen city as a series of mutually suspicious, ethnically (therefore religiously) based small ghettos, none of them — be they Jewish, Anglo, Italian or black — having much to do with the other, but with French Canadians being the most mistrustful of all towards others. As the Université de

Montréal was a French-speaking institution governed by the Roman Catholic church, it graduated medical doctors who would naturally float to the top of the social strata and become society's elite, its opinion makers and influence builders. Some of the medical professionals who walked out in protest from Notre Dame Hospital when it took on a Jewish intern in 1939 graduated from that university.

To Henry, the university was "just another place dominated by the church and small minds." As a Jew and as a foreigner, he was distrusted and shunned. But so what? He had also been shunned in Poland. He had known anti-Semitism all his life and had experienced much more virulent forms of it in Germany. "It is part of the design of the world and there was not much I could do about it." So he tried to ignore it, rejecting the larger society of his newly adopted country, choosing carefully from his classmates just who would be his friends. "The French-Canadian students were polite, but most wanted nothing to do with me. I reacted in consequence." He was never invited to a French-Canadian classmate's home. He was aware of this "social discrimination" and quickly had it confirmed when one student, who became a prominent medical specialist, told another student, "Why are you inviting a Jew to your house? We don't do that in Quebec."

The student who had issued Henry the invitation was another outsider. Vincent Mauriello was the son of an Italian from New York and a Creole from Martinique. Henry thought Mauriello was Jewish, which is why he first approached him. He wasn't, but Mauriello and Henry formed a close friendship that continues to this day. Henry approached another classmate he also thought was Jewish. "Sssh, I'll explain later," Art Danzig whispered back. Danzig was a former American GI who had experienced so much trouble getting into a medical school that he stated he was Roman Catholic on his application to the Université de Montréal. "When he first arrived in Montreal, he pretended to be a Catholic. He would cross himself and things like that," Henry remembered. "After a while he went to the dean and said he was Jewish, but by then the dean couldn't do much."

The three became inseparable, although Morgentaler and Mauriello would often smirk about how long it took Danzig to grasp an idea.

Henry says Mauriello's IQ is 152, his own another twenty points beyond that, but Danzig was a hard worker and Henry definitely wasn't. He was never in class before 11 a.m. because mornings were for playing with Goldie. He had studied the information all before in Brussels, and became accustomed to marks of 95 and 96. He stood fifth in the class of 105.

———

By 1953, when Henry received his medical degree from Cardinal Léger, he was confidently anticipating the additional year it would take him to become a researcher and achieve Louis Pasteur-like fame. Passing the examinations administered by the Association of Medical Councils of Canada allowed Henry to practise anywhere in Canada except in Quebec, where Canadian citizenship was a prerequisite for a medical licence. But he chose to stay and wait it out in Montreal, where his friends and family were.

He spent his research year at McGill, peering into a microscope and counting cells, so bored he wrote an audacious satirical poem about a man driven to count everything in his life. He says he read it aloud to his colleagues at a Christmas gathering; his supervisors were not amused. Nor did they recognize it as a plea for action and involvement from a man whose years in the ghetto and concentration camps had trained him to present to the world an impenetrable, impassive face. His only pleasure was the lunch hours he spent playing very competitive, high-level chess with a fellow instructor, Mircea Enesco. Enesco was brilliant. Not only was he a physician, but he also held a doctorate in anatomy. Henry considered him one of the most accomplished people he had ever met, and believed Enesco would have inevitably ascended to the top echelons of one of his many areas of competence had he not been Romanian. Henry had already noted that both Anglo and French-Canadian Montreal promoted from within their own ranks.

Henry was remembered as a pleasant, very studious lab instructor. Bernie Trossman, now a Hamilton, Ontario, psychiatrist, was a first-year medical student at McGill in 1953. "I would have never predicted that man would have made the front pages of the newspapers. He seemed passive to me, not the type who was a doer." To have his microscope insured, Trossman had to get a signed statement from a medical authority that the equipment was worth at least $250. It was a run-of-the-mill procedure, but Henry was reluctant to sign the form. Trossman could see he didn't want to get involved or accept any responsibility, no matter how nominal. "I had to really push him. I had to tell him he had to do it."

Henry had re-evaluated his ambitions. If he continued along his career path, it would be years before he could achieve the recognition he knew he wanted. He decided to put away boyhood dreams and return to the ward, where patients appreciated his eagerness to care for them. When he applied for, and was accepted for, residency at Queen Mary's Veterans Hospital, he turned his back on conventional career paths forever. He did not join the other ambitious and talented Jewish physicians at the Jewish General Hospital and he chose not to specialize. He would become a low-status general practitioner, a doctor near the bottom of a professional pecking order headed by specialists running hospitals and a medical elite whose pronouncements and research profoundly affected lives and even society itself.

But he thrived at Queen Mary's, discovering he had a gift for diagnosis. He loved the direct contact with patients, and how they responded to him as well as to his ministrations. Soon he was experimenting with another form of personal power — hypnosis. He remembers one soldier, discharged under mysterious but unhappy circumstances, who had not moved his left arm for a month, without apparent physiological reason for this. Had the arm stayed immobile, it would have atrophied with time. With permission from the chief of psychiatry, Henry hypnotized the man, who confessed he was afraid of returning to the army because he knew he had an uncontrollable impulse to hit, even kill, his supervisor (who may have made sexual overtures to him). Then he awakened the man at a moment when his arm was up in the air, explained the latent meaning in the gesture and reassured the man he would not have to return to the army.

Henry now had a giddiness about him. Released from the dream of achieving world fame for his research work, confident that he was a trailblazing maverick because he had turned his back on the competitive medical circles within Montreal's intense, powerful and 120,000-strong Jewish community, he worked summers as a doctor at Camp Massad, a Hebrew-speaking camp, and waited until August 11, 1955, the day he received his Canadian citizenship, to obtain his licence to practice in Quebec. Henry also liked to think that was the day he and Chava conceived their son Bamie, or Abraham, who is named after Chava's father and is now a successful doctor in Boston.

Henry moved swiftly, gaining medical privileges at Jean-Talon Hospital, a private institution, and deliberately renting, then buying, a retiring doctor's practice in Champlain Village, far from the Jewish enclave. This was east-end, French-speaking, working-class Montreal, "where Jewish people didn't venture." He bought second-hand equipment, including a $40 examining table, which he, Chava, who was now known as Eva, and Henia painted white. He had been moonlighting the previous year at Queen Mary's, taking some of the other doctors' night calls. As a resident, he wasn't supposed to, but he needed the money. He started his practice $10,000 in debt, having borrowed some from the bank and $1,100 from Harry Hershman, Chava's literary patron.

The retiring doctor had not made a success of his practice, according to a local pharmacist, but Henry sent out three thousand announcements and began making house calls, and soon his business was thriving. It was a varied caseload. Henry cheerfully delivered between three hundred and four hundred babies until the hours took their toll. He was free to do whatever he liked in a general practice. His interest in psychotherapies, particularly hypnosis, continued; he chaired a group of doctors and dentists who used the technique in their practices. Henry had employed it effectively once or twice to relieve pain for women in the throes of childbirth, but Trossman, then a psychiatrist with a practice less than two weeks old, vividly remembered getting a phone call from Henry one evening after office hours. Trossman thought Henry was calling because Trossman had just sent him a card announcing his new practice. Whatever the reason, Henry needed help. "He said, 'Look, I'm doing hypnosis. I have this patient and she's in a hypnotic trance and she won't leave my office and I can't get her out of it.'" Henry asked him to drive to his office and somehow or other get this woman out of her trance. Trossman knew little about hypnosis and said he couldn't help. He did call an ambulance and got the woman into emergency and then the hospital for a couple of days. She recovered completely.

Although it was Henry's hypnotic session that had created this minicrisis, Trossman still felt guilty he didn't drive the fifteen miles across town to help out his former lab instructor. "Henry may have thought I wasn't gutsy, because he never did send any other patients over my way. I may have disappointed him, but truthfully, I wouldn't have known what the hell to do." Trossman wasn't sure whether to admire Henry for being courageous or criticize him for being reckless, but he was certain Henry had changed from a meek lab instructor who had been too afraid to sign an insurance form into a confident and daring GP.

From Bernard Street, he and Eva (even Henry now called his wife by her anglicized name, although she continued to write as Chava Rosenfarb) had moved to the top floor of a triplex in Outremount. Henry was comfortable in all of Montreal's three dominant cultures — the Anglo, the Jewish and the French Canadian. English had become his main language. He read in it, and along with most Jewish children, Goldie had started kindergarten in a Jewish parochial school. With patients and friends like Mauriello, then away studying psychiatry in France, Henry switched to speaking in French. Henry was a gifted linguist who could grasp the nuances and cultural subtleties of a language as swiftly as he could its syntax, but his European accent may have precluded whole-hearted acceptance into either the French or the Anglo community.

That suited him. He wanted casual acceptance, not group membership. Any religious-based social structure rankled, and he was becoming equally exasperated with the socialist Bund crowd, particularly with the writers with whom Eva associated. "They were just people like everybody else. They had kind of a Messianic overexaggerated fervour that Jewish and Yiddish literature was the tip of everything and that Jews were the moral guardians and moral guides to the world. They exaggerated their mission, that they were the chosen people. To me, it was a lot of exaggerated foolishness. I didn't buy it." That it was emanating from secular Jews offended him even more. "This was a secular version of religious superiority. They, too, were very conservative people." He speculated they may have resorted to self-belief because they had been disappointed by the Germans, the Russians, the Poles, even by the Canadians and their passivity about letting more Jews into the country. All and any religion was toxic to him. It had poisoned the Poles and the Germans, and had affected even his French-speaking fellow Montrealers. The only faith Henry clung to was his father's belief in a secular-based world where cultural Jews would live freely and equally.

Henry never spoke up about what he thought because Eva was so deeply committed to Yiddish culture, its nobility and dignity. In fact, it was central to her art. She had begun work on her massive, profoundly moving and unutterably sad trilogy, *The Tree of Life*. Grieving for her father and all the other victims infused her life and creative source; it became her life's work. As she wrote about the Lodz ghetto, she re-experienced its horror. Her despair and depression often hung heavy throughout their home, by this time a spacious, modern house on Barton Street in the Town of Mount Royal. Henry refused to go back with her to the memories, where he knew feelings of hopelessness and helplessness awaited him; many times he could not bring himself even to read her work. He has never read her much-praised trilogy.

Even staying firmly focused on the here and now, so many mornings he would awaken drenched in sweat from his latest dream, where he was surrounded, engulfed, suffocated by huge, vicious German soldiers, where he would feel furious and helpless, passive, pitiful again. In Montreal, the flashing blue lights and siren of the snow removal equipment, which were exactly like the siren and flashing lights of the Gestapo, triggered nightmarish memories in many survivors. Psychiatric journals acknowledge the existence of a survivor syndrome, albeit one with much variation. There are psychiatrists who think it impossible ever to recover from the Holocaust, even for a survivor like Henry, who believes it was luck, not any divine guidance, that let him live.

"You can get over a car accident, but to be beaten and humiliated and starved for four years and never know when you are the one going to be hauled away — I don't think you ever get over that," said Trossman, who has worked with many survivors in his psychiatry practice. Research (and the passage of time) has indicated that many survivors of the Holocaust showed no obvious effects of their experiences until years and years after the war, when they finally let go of the faint hope that a loved one might still be alive and, paradoxically, when many more finally understood they were financially and physically settled and safe, that they could breathe out deep and slow, that it was all right now. The blue lights of Montreal's snow machine didn't bother Henry; however, the sound of certain trucks could freeze his soul.

He wryly once said to a journalist that he had "the wife, the mistress, the son and daughter and house," everything he always thought he wanted to be happy, but he wasn't happy. Of course he understood the source of the nightmares. Nevertheless, he went into therapy for four years from 1960 to 1964. He used his thrice-weekly sessions to explore their cause and effect. "Surprisingly, I was not afraid [to go back in the past]. I was patting myself on the back."

André Lussier was a Freudian lay analyst recommended by his friend Mauriello. Five years later, when Henry was forty-two, he tried to become a Freudian psychoanalyst, submitting himself to an intensive interview by three analysts who belonged to the Freudian psychoanalytical society. Had they approved of his application, he would have been allowed to train with them to become an analyst, but they didn't. He was two years over their age limit of forty and his interview had gone badly. When one of them asked him how he visualized himself as a practising analyst, Henry suddenly saw himself sitting on a chair, listening to nine patients for nine hours a day. At that moment, he knew he didn't want to do it, but he was furious that the society didn't have to give any reasons for rejecting him. He sent off an angry letter before he let the matter drop, finally acknowledging he hadn't wanted to be a psychoanalyst as much as he had craved to learn what lay within his own soul.

He finally left psychoanalysis, declaring himself cured and knowing he was too impatient to practise that kind of wordy, sluggishly paced

intellectually based analysis — but nevertheless eager to change the
world. Therapy had given him an understanding: the Holocaust had
made him afraid to compete; he was not necessarily genetically predes-
tined to be anxious or passive. And this was galvanizing. "It opened up
a lot of energy." At that point he had already found humanism and
founded the Committee for Neutral Schools.

By chance, in 1963 Henry read a small newspaper announcement
of a Montreal talk by a member of the Ethical Cultural Society from
New York City. It was sponsored by the Humanist Fellowship of Montreal, an organization Henry had never heard of, but when he showed
up at the community hall at the corner of St-Antoine and DeCarrie
Boulevard that night, he knew he had come home. Everything Jerome
Nathanson said was everything Henry believed in. It was thrilling. Suddenly his ideas and experiences were being presented as an organized,
thoughtful entity. Henry joined the Humanists that night. Soon he was
appearing on radio and television shows and accepting every invitation
to be on panels to promote the group's ideas. With humanism, Henry
finally had met his match. A philosophy and lifestyle that is not only
nonreligious but antireligious, it advocates bettering society through
reason, scientific inquiry and humanitarian compassion.

Here Henry found everything Josef Morgentaler believed in —
social justice, brotherhood and the belief that people are inherently
good and society's institutions are what cause the evil men do. In Montreal's Humanist Fellowship, Henry believed he had found a place
where Jews were equal partners in social activism with Unitarians,
atheists, intellectuals and other humanitarians from far-flung and varied ethnic origins. This would be where Henry would keep his father's
faith — and rejuvenate his own, which had been battered by the brutality he encountered from the Third Reich and the indifference of
this new country. In 1964, Henry became president of the Montreal
Humanist Fellowship. He went out looking for a cause for the Fellowship — and he found it very close to his own home. The two Quebec
school boards were divided according to religion — Roman Catholic-
ism and Protestantism. The only nonreligious schools were private, and
Goldie and Bamie Morgentaler were enrolled in one of them. St. George's

was a progressive and expensive school for the very bright offspring of the well-off. A francophone group, Mouvement Laique de Langue Française, was already working towards the goal of a public secular school system, but Henry plunged right in and started the Committee for Neutral Schools. He kick-started the English side of the movement, writing furious, pungent letters to the editor of the two English-language newspapers, re-invigorating the issue. He didn't want any religion taught in schools and he didn't want schools divided according to religion. "This was a democratic country and if people weren't Catholic or Protestant, they shouldn't have religion that is not theirs imposed on them. It separates people according to creed and we want people to live together in peace."

In another, less opulent part of Montreal, Gertrude Katz had been quietly researching the same issue. One of her daughters had come home from her grade two class parroting her teacher: children who believe in Jesus are good children; the people believing in Jesus are the good people of the world. A published feminist poet, social activist who had helped found Montreal's first English women's centre, night-school philosophy student and daughter of Russian Jews, Gertie Katz was enraged enough to do some independent research into the local educational system.

"I was wondering what to do with my research, when someone told me about this committee that I should join and that a Dr. Henry Morgentaler was its president." She phoned Henry that very evening. He told her to come to the next meeting and that she would now be the committee's research chair. She remembered a small, friendly, very animated man escorting her to the den and introducing her to a Unitarian minister, a pair of chemistry professors and civil libertarian lawyer Claude-Armand Sheppard. "Henry was very emotional about the issue. He was talking about an idea he had to withhold his taxes as protest. He wanted to put himself forward as a test case." She knew a little bit about this and told him the government would confiscate his house. Sheppard also told him it was a dumb idea.

"He seemed to have such a great compulsion to do something right now for change." Katz recognized someone with a passion equal to her own. Henry did the open-line radio talk shows; she wrote the letters. Henry gave interviews to the print media and the major speeches; she went to home-and-school meetings on the island. He was high profile; she was grassroots. Each was happy with his or her part, and together they were indefatigable and efficient. They would meet evenings, after their respective working days were over and the kids were in bed, to write letters to the editor. Many times, Katz drove to the *Montreal Star*'s offices at 1 a.m. to hand them in. "We would make decisions on the telephone — bup, bup, bup, done. We didn't spend hours discussing these things. We were both highly motivated. We just did it. For me it was a pleasure. At home-and-school meetings they would talk, talk, talk. It was so wonderful to say ten words and we're moving mountains. It was a high working with Henry." They moved as one, Henry though, definitely in the forefront, where he wanted to be. He was becoming a well-known local personality because of his activism. His children were accustomed to seeing him on the supper-hour news telecasts. When Bamie's teacher asked her young class for their heroes, Bamie named his father. Henry laughed about it — "Me! Not a cowboy or an athlete or a fireman like the other boys." Henry never forgot that feeling of joy inside him knowing he was following his own father's lead.

The shadow of the Holocaust still hung low over him. He dreamed about an irate phone call from an education minister. "Who are you to interfere with our educational system? How dare you?" the man shouted at him. What Henry heard was the voice of his own experience: people who don't like you or what you are doing could kill you, hurt you. Those years of being a victim had trained Henry not to get himself into any situation in which he would be exposed. The Nazis tended to pick their victims from the edges of a group. He and Mike had always squeezed their way into the middle of a group in the concentration camps. The tactic had become so ingrained as to become an instinct for survival.

"We both had no time," Katz remembered. "Life was too short for all the injustices to correct. Henry used to keep a file on all the other issues and he would mention to me *en passant* that when this matter was corrected he wanted to go on to this, then to that. I would say, 'Okay,

Henry, one thing at a time.'" The schools issue proved stubborn. They never did get it "corrected."[3] The Catholic and Protestant education systems were entrenched in the British North America Act of 1867, then the Canadian Constitution. Both the English minority and the French majority clung to those documents as safeguards of their language rights. When the committee ran into that roadblock, all the public education meetings and all those letters and interviews and talk shows came to naught. The cause had just about run out of steam, when the Montreal Humanists decided to present a paper to a special government standing committee of health and welfare looking into abortion law reform, which would be meeting that fall.

Naturally, Henry turned to Gertie for help. Gertie Katz was a trim and confident woman, with a warm intelligence and a rich laugh. They were instant friends. Comrades in a cause, yes, but Gertie intuitively understood and accepted Henry without the usual uncomfortable confessionals. She knew him without pressing him for details. And for once, he was at ease with that intimacy. Henry trusted mankind in general and in theory — it was people he was wary of. With Gertie he knew he was safe. She knew him like family. And with Mike settled in Cleveland, where he worked as a machinist, that was what she was to him. With Gertie, Henry could take on a cause, right some wrongs, go beyond merely surviving. That is what he had needed Mike for.

When Henry turned to Gertie in 1967 for help in writing the humanist brief on abortion to be presented to a House of Commons standing committee, abortion law reform was just one of many issues rocking Canadian society. Henry didn't know it would become his life's work; he was doing the brief because he understood something of the issue as a doctor and because he hoped it would promote humanism. Gertie, however, had her reservations. She said she would help only with the speech and that was all. She wasn't at all interested in the cause of abortion rights. Besides, she was working in a penitentiary as a literary instructor. (Eventually, she would edit a collection of the prisoners' writings. In the introduction to the book, the noted author and board chair of the literacy project, Hugh MacLennan, wrote that Gertie was one of those people "who have always existed and always will, who are prompted by something deep within them to pick up the pieces after a disaster.") She had also suffered several miscarriages. To give birth to her two daughters, she had resorted to bed rest for the duration of her pregnancies. "[You can see why] I wasn't motivated," she said.

Henry was.

Here was an issue he knew something about, a medical matter that spilled over into society and into real people's lives. It provided an un-precedented chance to mesh his work with his philosophical and value systems, and gave Humanists the opportunity to rally around an idea central to their beliefs. It was also an issue on which all the Fellowships could agree. (The brief was endorsed by Humanists in Victoria, British Columbia, and Toronto, and Henry believed it served to instigate the formation the following year of the Humanist Association of Canada. Henry was its first president.) But first he had to convince his fellow Humanists to take a more radical position from the one they preferred, which mirrored the Canadian Medical Association's middle-of-the-road stance that abortions be granted when a committee of three doctors decreed a woman's life or health was in danger.

Many of the lawyers in the group, including Fellowship president Richard Gottlieb, wanted to adopt the moderate position of the Canadian Bar Association, the CMA, even the Association for the Modernization of Canadian Abortion Laws — in fact, the position of every other organization that would appear before the standing committee. But a year earlier, in 1966, Henry had convinced the Montreal chapter of the Civil Liberties Union to endorse his resolution that women should have abortion on demand within their first trimester of pregnancy. He'd hailed it as "a great moral victory," but that is all it was, because the group never acted on it. However, it probably strengthened Henry's persuasive powers with the Humanists, since most Montrealers knew that then justice minister Pierre Elliott Trudeau had been an enthusiastic civil libertarian, and had only vacated his seat on the board of the Montreal Humanist chapter when he left for Ottawa. Henry had been elected to fill Trudeau's spot. Henry did convince Gottlieb and the other Humanists they had to be more progressive and recognize a woman's right to an abortion if she wished to have one. Gottlieb was slated to accompany Henry to Ottawa to present the brief, but he called Henry the night before and said he couldn't make it. "He never gave a good reason why he wasn't going," Henry recalled.

The next morning, October 19, 1967, Henry drove the stretch of the Macdonald-Cartier Freeway between Montreal and Ottawa alone. A bright sun lit the crisp autumn day, transforming the flat, featureless terrain he was driving by into a land brimming with possibility. He was in a state of heightened anticipation, happier than he had felt in years. In recommending that women have abortion on demand, he knew he was going to make Canadian history.

It was the second session of the twenty-seventh Canadian Parliament. Chaired by Dr. Harry Harley (Liberal, Halton), health and welfare's standing committee met at 11:10 a.m. The idea was to hear and question a Dr. Henry Morgentaler, who represented the Humanist Fellowship of Montreal, before breaking for lunch. So intense was the questioning that at about 1 p.m. committee member Stanley Knowles complained, "If we don't eat soon we will all have less than life." But the barrage of questions to Henry, most of them pointed, many antagonistic, continued for another half hour.

Knowles was supportive, as was fellow New Democratic MP Grace MacInnis, but Henry was grilled by the others about everything from the Humanists' income-tax status, to his own definition of a religion, to the reasons behind the fall of the Roman Empire, to abortion statistics in Japan and Sweden, to whether he believed in a master race. Henry rose to the occasion. He had honed his skill at the verbal thrust and parry of debate the way a top pitcher practises the fastball or a hockey forward perfects a slapshot that can win championships. He was eloquent and unflappable, and only Liberal MP Warren Allmand, appearing before the committee by special request, provided any real challenge when he asked why a fetal age of five months should be a cutoff point for allowing abortions (as recommended by the Humanists), when science should be able to keep a child alive outside the womb after three months.

"I think that is a very interesting question," Henry replied. "I also think I will have trouble answering it. ... "

The official transcript of the meeting indicates that most of the committee members were having trouble comprehending the enormity of what Henry was so calmly and reasonably putting forth:

MR. [JAMES] BROWN [LIBERAL, BRANTFORD, ONTARIO]: The Humanist Fellowship desires the law to be changed so that an abortion will be granted during the first three months of any pregnancy simply upon request of the mother.

DR. MORGENTALER: Right.

MR. BROWN: Without giving any reasons. That pretty well summarizes it. Without giving a reason?

DR. MORGENTALER: Yes.

Some of them found it offensive:

MR. [JOSEPH] O'KEEFE [LIBERAL, ST. JOHN'S EAST]: Have you no serious qualms, Doctor, about ending the life of a Steinmetz because he is so crippled? I could give you many thousands of examples. The classic one is of a syphilitic father and a tubercular mother who produced Beethoven. Forgetting all about religion, have you no qualms about that?

DR. MORGENTALER: I do not consider that a fair question, Mr. O'Keefe.

O'KEEFE: It is a question. I am asking him if he has any qualms. He has none?

DR. MORGENTALER: Qualms about what?

MR. O'KEEFE: About aborting a baby born of a syphilitic father and a tubercular mother? I am very confident that the majority of doctors who did not have a Catholic conscience would abort the foetus. Would you agree?

DR. MORGENTALER: I would agree definitely.

MR. O'KEEFE: Then we would have lost Beethoven....

DR. MORGENTALER: Oh, that is a good argument, but it is one...

MR. O'KEEFE: Or Helen Keller, or a Steinmetz...

THE CHAIRMAN: Mr. O'Keefe, please let the witness answer the question.

DR. MORGENTALER: This argument is completely nullified by the fact

that if you had had legal abortions you perhaps would not have
also had Hitler, or Mussolini, or Stalin, or many other…

MR. O'KEEFE: I think they have the right to life.

DR. MORGENTALER: Therefore it evens itself out.[4]

Henry didn't get the last word, though. As Harley was wrapping up
the meeting, Dr. Lewis Brand (Progressive Conservative, Saskatoon)
interjected, "I have one further comment in view of your brief, Doctor.
If this law of abortion is proclaimed, would you in the first week like to
have it called 'Accident Prevention Week'?" That comment prompted
Stanley Knowles to suggest the committee extend "special thanks" to
Henry.

Harley did. "Many thanks, Dr. Morgentaler," he said, "for having
braved our committee this morning."

That night at home, Henry turned on the television to watch the
national news and saw himself. The next morning major newspaper
articles about the brief appeared in both Montreal papers and in the
Toronto *Globe and Mail*. Henry had described the proposal as revolutionary. The media seemed to agree. They had also noted, and respectfully reported, Henry's comments about the proposal ending the illegal
and dangerous backroom abortion racket.

Henry went back to being a family doctor that morning, but the
phones in the modest bungalow on rue Honoré-Beaugrand never
stopped ringing. It seemed as if everybody in the fifth estate wanted a
quote from him, and he was happy to oblige. But the other phone calls
unsettled him. They were from women begging him for an abortion.
He tried to explain it to them: he was a general practitioner; he did not
do abortions; he would not break the law. He was speaking theoretically; he had been talking policy only. No, he was sorry. But they kept
calling from all over Canada, women who thought they had finally
found someone who would perform abortions on demand. Joanne
Cornax, Henry's head nurse, stopped putting the calls through to him.
That didn't help. He could hear the phones ringing and he knew why.
Some women came right up to the door of the clinic, begging him to
help their daughters, nieces, themselves.

Over at Gertie's, he sank into one of her kitchen chairs and held his head in his hands.

"Oh, God, what did I do? What did I do?" he moaned.

CHAPTER 5

THE CAUSE CÉLÈBRE

H E HAD BEEN PLAYING WITH FIRE, but he wouldn't know that until after he had been singed. Henry had approached this issue as a good humanist: he had applied pragmatic, rational, scientific-based thinking to an abstract.

It was, after all, a medical matter, and he was a medical man. He was also a thinking man, a self-styled scholar. Henry delighted in turning a complex issue this way and that, savouring its many sides. He well knew abortion was no modern conundrum but a challenge of the highest intellectual order, a majestic puzzlement that had intrigued and entranced not just his mind, but the greatest minds of all time.

Aristotle had believed the fetus acquired a soul, or was animated, forty days after conception if it was a boy, eighty days if a girl. Many Christian theologians concurred, including the medieval philosopher Thomas Aquinas. In fourteenth-century England, abortion was allowed up until the point of "quickening," or the moment that the woman could feel the fetus move. In 1803, British Parliament passed Lord Ellenborough's Act, which made it illegal to administer anything to cause a miscarriage if the woman was "quick with child." The motivation was to protect a woman's life. Subsequent British legislation in 1828, 1837 and 1861 banned abortion.

In New York in 1823, government decreed that unless a woman's life was in jeopardy, it was illegal for her to have an abortion. In 1869, Canada's Parliament said abortion was illegal and anyone performing abortions was subject to life imprisonment. That same year, Pope Pius IX ended once and for all any church compliance with Aristotelian thought. The birth-control rate, in France particularly, was in decline and the pope was adamant: henceforth the church would no longer entertain a distinction between an animated and a nonanimated fetus. Animation existed from the point of conception. The fetus had a soul; it was a human. In 1892, Section 179C of the Canadian Criminal Code deemed it an indictable offence to "offer to sell, advertise, publish an advertisement of or have for sale or disposal any medicine, drug or article intended or represented as a means of preventing conception or causing an abortion."

In Britain, the restrictions on abortion appeared to ease in 1938, when Dr. Alec Bourne turned himself over to authorities as a test case for the law. He had performed an abortion for a fourteen-year-old girl raped by four soldiers. But he won an acquittal, because, as Justice McNaughten told the jury, the doctor believed that if the child's pregnancy continued it "would make the woman a physical or mental wreck." Deemed a pivotal, legal precedent, the Bourne decision, with its legal loophole (abortion was allowable in some cases where a woman's health was endangered by a pregnancy), was adopted as jurisprudence by Canada along with other Commonwealth nations. But the thalidomide scandal of the early 1960s (in which about a thousand British woman who had taken the drug during their pregnancies gave birth to cruelly deformed children missing whole limbs, after many of them had been refused an abortion) finally forced the House of Commons in Britain in 1967 to pass an act allowing abortion if two doctors agreed there was a high risk of a deformity, or if being pregnant would be more dangerous to a woman's physical or mental health or that of her children than if she were not pregnant.[1]

Canada appeared to want to follow Britain's lead. In 1967, Justice Minister Pierre Trudeau tabled an omnibus bill reforming the Criminal Code. (It became law in 1969 when he was prime minister.) Homosexuality was decriminalized; so was the dissemination of contraceptives or contraceptive information, after a long campaign spearheaded by Planned Parenthood founders Barbara and George Cadbury. Even divorce became more accessible. But abortion, always the thorn, even in as prickly a bouquet as this bill, was the issue the legislators couldn't seem to handle. In spite of Henry's spirited debate with the standing committee, they handed it all over to the medical establishment, saying in as many words, "You be the judge."

What Trudeau actually said, ringingly, was "The state has no business being in the bedrooms of the nation." But politicians and medical professionals had no intention of listening to him or accepting Henry's advice and leaving the issue of abortion to women, who had been taking this matter into their own hands for some time anyway. Many women were coming to the realization that this was a matter of life or death — their own. In the first of the five parts of the 1986 documentary film *The Struggle for Choice* Arlene Mantle, the narrator, set it out: "Prior to legal reform in 1969, abortion was the leading cause of death to women in their maternal years. Despite social condemnation, legal barriers and dangerous conditions, many women sought out abortions."

Angus McLaren and Arlene Tigar McLaren, the authors of *The Bedroom and the State*, noted that Canada's long-term fertility decline began about 1851. Family size fell from 4.1 children born to parents in 1871 to 2.9 children for parents born in 1911. "Contraception and abortion were both being employed early in the nineteenth century," they wrote. "A woman would 'put herself right' by drinking an infusion of one of the traditional abortifacients such as tansy, quinine, pennyroyal, rue, black hellebore, ergot of rye, savin or cotton root."[2] It was strictly a private, not state, matter; women would attempt to look after themselves. "If these [methods] failed, women often tried anything from leaping off tables to imbibing gin, followed if necessary by dilating the cervix with slippery elm.... If it were not beyond the sixteenth week ... the woman would turn to the abortionist. How would one find the help required? It was only necessary to glance at the advertisements in the personal and medical columns of the local paper."[3]

Only in 1937, when an Ontario public health nurse named Dorothy Parker was acquitted of disseminating birth control information due to the little-known loophole that held up public good as reason enough for her actions, was it accordingly acknowledged that disseminating information and birth control might be a good thing for the public. Parker worked for birth control advocate, many would say zealot, A.R. Kaufman, the owner of a factory in Kitchener, Ontario, who wanted the poor to stop overreproducing themselves. Alvin Ratz Kaufman (1885–1983) was driven by compassion (it was better for all if the poor had fewer mouths to feed) and an acute class sense (it was better for all that there not be as many poor). He regarded the fertility rate of the lower class as a threat and the falling fertility rate of the tax-paying middle class as a worry.

Then, in 1959, *Chatelaine* magazine published a cautious article by Joan Finnigan entitled "Should Canada Change Its Abortion Law?" As is the case with all articles that take their cues from a question, it decided that the country should, perhaps, consider allowing abortion in cases where the mother's physical or mental health was at stake. With the invention of the birth control pill and its use burgeoning in the sixties, the issue became, suddenly, respectable, a tool to be used for the greater cause of world-wide population control in the advent of the intellectuals' newest worry: the population explosion. North America's sexual revolution was being played out on the homefront and in the lifestyle pages of the nation's print media. For a time abortion was discussed as something personal, not political; politicians collectively let out a huge sigh of relief. Birth control would now be known as family planning — such a pleasant euphemism. It was everywhere and, yes, it was illegal, but everyone would turn a blind eye.

But the law would not, could not, be denied. In 1960, a Toronto pharmacist was jailed for selling condoms. And both medical and legal circles were alarmed at the proliferation of backstreet abortionists. A police chief complained long and bitterly in a Toronto *Telegram* article about the many women going to Cuba for abortions and those using the dubious talents of local abortionists. "Most abortionists are unskilled persons who do their work in the client's home or in their own home with no regard for sanitation," noted reporter Helen Allen. The motive was age-old and it wasn't noble. "It's the money that gets people into this business," said Detective Sergeant William Quennell, whom Allen described as head of Metro Toronto police's abortion squad. "Just like it's money that attracts people into any kind of crime. They probably don't like actually committing the crime, but they do like the financial returns." Which were, he estimated, between $300 and $1,000 a

procedure. In 1960, police won convictions against thirty abortionists —
every person they charged.

In the United States, feminists took matters into their own hands.
From the late sixties until 1973 and the *Roe* v. *Wade* decision making
abortions legal, the Jane Collective, an underground abortion facility
in Chicago, arranged and then later performed more than eleven thousand abortions, an action hailed as heroic by journalist Lindsy Van
Gelder in the September/October 1991 edition of *Ms.* magazine. But
Canada was slower than the States to rearrange its thinking to encompass the women's perspective. In her book *Abortion, The Big Evasion*,
author Anne Collins noted the United Church was the first professional
body to publicly advocate abortion for women whose health or life was
in jeopardy because of the pregnancy (in a 1960 meeting of the church
Council). But it was only when medical professional bodies joined the
fray that legislators were convinced it was time to come out of hiding on
this issue.

In 1961, the British Columbia branch of the Canadian Medical
Association called for abortion law reform. In 1962, an American
mother of four, Sherri Finkbine, decided to abort her fifth pregnancy
because she had taken thalidomide. When news of her impending abortion was reported in the media, her appointment was cancelled. She had
to fly to Sweden to qualify under the law for an abortion. From 1963,
the national body of the Canadian Medical Association, bolstered by the
Canadian Bar Association, lobbied the government long and hard to
change the law. This was neither radical nor rash, just prudent. By then
plenty of doctors were doing abortions; in hospitals, not in back alleys.
These were respectable, often courageous physicians. In *The Politics of
Abortion*, professors Janine Brodie, Shelley Gavigan and Jane Jenson
estimated that thirty-three thousand abortions were performed in
Canada in 1959 alone, and the possible number of illegal abortions performed in Canada between 1955 and 1969 was estimated by others,
including McLaren and Tigar McLaren, to be as high as 120,000. Doctors often set up informal therapeutic abortion committees in the hospitals for protection. Three to five doctors would convene to judge in
private which applicants would get abortions.[4]

But no hospital wanted to be known as being soft on abortion. In *The Politics of Abortion: Trends in Canadian Fertility Policy*, St. Francis Xavier University professor Larry Collins's study, published posthumously in the Spring 1982 edition of *Atlantis,* stated: "The abortion committees served to diffuse responsibility for decisions made by the individual doctor. Such decisions reflected the physicians' personal moral standards and class biases, while relieving them of them of personal responsibility.... This helped to rationalize on personal and compassionate grounds those abortions actually performed as favours to friends and community elites."

Because, increasingly, middle-class, married women were the ones who wanted abortions, the destigmatization of the procedure had begun. Fewer considered an unplanned pregnancy the price of wanton "sinning" by the young and lustful anymore, but that was never the doctors' area of concern.

Anne Collins remarked on it succinctly in her book: "Some doctors had always done abortions for socio-economic reasons.... Other physicians had rarely seen the necessity for abortion and had condoned it only in literally life-threatening cases. But by the 1960s, medical advances in the care of pregnant women had made it impossible for the two attitudes to continue to co-exist. When it became possible even for pregnant women with diabetes or severe heart disease to bear children safely, doctors who had been using vague 'medical' grounds to justify abortions suddenly had no protection from doctors who knew that few purely medical grounds existed." They wanted the law changed so they wouldn't ever be prosecuted for breaking it.

Other organizations were equally cautious, and in retrospect perhaps self-serving. In 1964, the National Council of Women of Canada said the abortion law was, among other things, "confused" and "conflicting."[5] But its complaints were based on the inequity of access to abortion for women, not on their right to choose. As Jane Jenson wrote in *The Politics of Abortion*:

The National Council of Women was the largest and most accepted representative of Canadian women at that time. Founded in 1893, it had committed itself to serving "the highest good of the family and the State and application of the Golden Rule." Within these terms of reference, any advocacy of women's rights to control their own bodies or expression of the anger and anguish of women who had been forced to seek backstreet abortions was difficult. Either would have gone against the traditionally restrained behaviour of the Council and its fear of rocking the very delicate political boat in which it found itself. The most it could do was argue the current practices were unjust and inequitable and demand reform in the direction of greater social justice.

The 1967 Royal Commission on the Status of Women released its final report in 1970. It recommended that "the Criminal Code be amended to permit abortion by a qualified medical practitioner on the sole request of any woman who has been pregnant for twelve weeks or less," and after twelve weeks if a qualified practitioner determined the woman's physical or mental health was endangered. The commission put forward 167 recommendations, but those two, numbers 126 and 127, stirred the most dissension. Commissioner Elsie Gregory McGill wanted the recommendations to go further, while two of her colleagues — Jacques Henripin and Doris Ogilvie — thought the commission had already gone much too far.

Later, abortion would become the most divisive issue of a decade. It would ignite a movement, incite violence and grow so corrosive it would very nearly divide and conquer a people. And it would soon be wrested from its birth control context of family size and women's health and relocated in a more contemporary, confusing and perilous territory. It was the object of a power grab.

When the doctors came before the Canadian parliamentarians in 1967, suggesting there be a changing of the moral guard, it was all so simple and sensible. Certainly more sensible than that headline-grabbing notion being touted by a Dr. Morgentaler that there should be no value judgments, just abortions for whoever asked for one. Even Montreal's police director had recommended abortion be removed from the field of the criminal and handled by medical and hospital authorities. "Hardly a day goes by without a woman coming or being brought to the hospital after an attempted abortion," Jean-Paul Gilbert wrote in a submission to the standing committee, quoted in the *Globe and Mail* on January 26, 1968. "If this is the case, and we are convinced that it is, it is our opinion that abortion is one of those offenses which should be removed from the penal or criminal field so that it can be handled by the medical and hospital authorities rather than by the police and the judiciary." On August 28, 1969, parliamentarians voted 149 to 55 to give the doctors just what they had ordered. Justice Minister John Turner quickly tried to make clear that this new Section 251 of the Criminal Code "does not authorize the taking of a fetal life; it does not promote abortion."

Section 251 was all spelled out in the Revised Statutes of Canada, 1970 Criminal Code, from the bottom of page 1,627 through to midway through page 1,629, where the law on Venereal Diseases began. Subsection 1 stated: "Every one who, with intent to procure the miscarriage of a female person, whether or not she is pregnant, uses any means for the purpose of carrying out his intention is guilty of an indictable offence and is liable for imprisonment for life."

And Subsection 2 said: "Every female person who, being pregnant, with intent to procure her own miscarriage, uses any means or permits any means to be used for the purpose of carrying out her intention is guilty of an indictable offence and is liable to imprisonment for two years."

Abortions were legal only if a hospital therapeutic abortion committee said in writing that the pregnancy would endanger a woman's health or life. No hospital was obligated to have a therapeutic abortion committee, but every committee was obligated to hand over the names of all patients having abortions to the provincial ministry of health if so requested. Only accredited medical practitioners could do abortions, but they also were obligated to turn over the names of all their patients having had the procedure, if told to. And finally, abortions could only be done in an accredited hospital that also provided medical, surgical and obstetrical treatment.

However, no abortionist was allowed to serve on a hospital therapeutic abortion committee, nothing prevented a province from smothering a therapeutic abortion committee in governing regulations and nothing could stop hospital boards and medical professionals from applying "diverse interpretations of the indications for the procedure," wrote Hamilton psychiatrist and pro-choice advocate Dr. May Cohen in an article entitled "Therapeutic Abortion and the Law." She concluded that "the abortion law as it exists today ensures that equality of health care in this area can never be available to Canadian women."

It was true. This was checkmate. The new statutes changed very little other than to state that only doctors, in the guise of therapeutic abortion committees, could decide who would have an abortion and who would not. By not defining "health" in this crucial context, the law gave the country's medical professionals free rein, and the power to define the country's morals. Government may have been trying to contain the tide; it may even have been trying to convince itself that abortion really was simply a health matter with no legitimate bearing on the incipient social revolution that threatened to blow the lid off most things. But it was 1969. Society was in extreme flux, and the boundaries between medicine and mores were blurred and shaken.

And in east-end Montreal, Henry had decided to fold up his family practice and specialize in abortion.

CHAPTER 6

DANGEROUS PRACTICES

Abortionist! What a terrible word!
— Anonymous, *The Humanist*

"I STILL CANNOT BELIEVE THAT I, who have always been a law-abiding citizen, could bring myself to defy the law of the land and the state and to risk imprisonment, loss of licence to practise medicine, the contempt of my colleagues, the ruin of my family, and the opprobrium that goes with that terrible word: *abortionist.*"

Henry wrote this in one sitting, dashed it off without hesitation with not one rewrite or crumpled scrap of paper. It was a perfect first try; he was elated. That's the way Henry preferred to remember the time he went public — or as public as his anonymous byline in the January/February 1970 edition of the *Humanist* allowed. This wasn't a point of view taken; it was a stand. "... I intend to go all the way to the Supreme Court before I give up this fight," he wrote.

"I consider my attitude one of civil disobedience to a cruel and immoral law. I do not believe we should disobey all laws. I am sure there is an element of danger in every citizen's deciding for himself which law is good or bad and which one he will obey or disobey."

By the essay's halfway point the bravado and the posturing were offset by a sweet naïvete: "I have come to believe that women with unwanted pregnancies are the most discriminated against segment of our society." Except for his genuine, quiet resolve and courage, he could have been auditioning for leadership of a cause. "I claim that every woman on whom I have performed an abortion with good results was in danger of life at the hands of an incompetent abortionist. This is the line I intend to take if ever I am prosecuted for performing abortions."

And: "I have not publicly declared that I am an abortionist and am breaking the abortion laws, as is supposed to be done in the classical cases of civil disobedience, although I have toyed with the idea and might still do so if I think it would be useful. The reason is simply that I prefer to live for a cause rather than be martyred for it."

Later, an informal poll concluded only Prime Minister Pierre Elliott Trudeau was more recognizable than he. Henry had given a thousand interviews, each more masterful than the one before. He alone understood how well the uneasy blend of statesman and Everyman played in the media. No one thought to wonder why he was always speaking for "the women of Canada," instead of letting the women speak for themselves. When his courage had been proven over and over, to the point where he had almost convinced himself, he began to gloss over his personal commitment to the cause — perhaps because he had become the cause.

Only once did he tell a journalist that Eva had had an abortion. In the mideighties, Ian Brown, then a feature writer for the *Globe and Mail*, reported that "Eva has endured a 'very illegal' and very painful abortion in the early 1950s — no anaesthetic was used." Henry admitted he felt helpless and demeaned. They had been ordered to use the servants' back entrance into the imposing stone Westmount mansion of the abortionist. The nurse there was brusque and disdainful; Eva had been ill and shaken; Henry had been of no comfort or use to her.

Henry much preferred to champion the cause of abortion from an intellectual tack. His allegiance had always been to the humanist overlay — that of the sheer unreasonedness of an inequitable law. He was mindful of the plight of others — it genuinely motivated him. But he saw his approach as rational, not political or ideological, and never personal. In his ground-breaking article in the *Humanist*, he wrote that when he was a resident in pathology he saw the bodies of two young girls killed by botched abortions. They were "silent reproaches," he said, painful reminders of a patient of his who had needed an abortion and who committed suicide when he didn't help her. Since then he has

admitted that the reference to the suicidal patient was not entirely accurate. "I wanted to make my point. I don't think I ever had a patient who
committed suicide, although I had lots of women who threatened to
commit suicide if they didn't get help."

In the same piece in the *Humanist* he described a patient he finally
did help as

> the daughter of a colleague who was forever telling medical stu-
> dents of the viciousness and immorality of abortion came to seek
> my help. I did not refuse her. I inserted a catheter, which is a soft
> rubber tube, inside the uterus and this brought on a miscarriage,
> which was complete and did not require a curettage. The girl
> was ecstatic with joy; her father, whom she feared would disown
> her, never found out. . . . [t]hat was five years ago and I have
> never refused a serious request for an abortion since, provided it
> is within the 11 week time limit within which a dilatation and
> curettage is possible without complications.

And that description, too, was not the whole truth. It was based on
his experience with a Scottish woman whose father was a physician and
a leading anti-abortionist in Britain. Through the years, Henry's stories
became less mawkish and avenging. But at that time, he was determined, at all costs, to make his point. When women kept asking for his
help, he did some investigating and found the situation appalling. He
knew from his days as an intern and resident that hospitals, including Montreal's revered Royal Victoria, routinely had entire wards of
women — some dying, some with pelvic inflammatory disease, others
having hysterectomies — there because of botched abortions.

In the late sixties, Montreal pharmacies stocked slippery elm, which
women inserted in the cervix. "It would open the cervix," Henry explained. "It acted like a piece of wood, and when inserted with the
secretions and warmth it would expand and open the cervix and occasionally bring on a miscarriage. But not always."

Some women injected water into the uterus, which would get
behind the placenta, detach it from the uterus and, sometimes, after

twenty-four hours induce a miscarriage. But this method ran the huge risk of causing a fatal air embolism. Women were also known to douche with Lysol — permanganate potassium — to induce an abortion. "This is a caustic substance that produces a hole on contact. I've seen this myself. A woman would insert the actual round tablet of the substance into her vagina. It is very toxic and can cause vaginal ulcerations. When the bleeding started, the women thought it was okay, that they had induced a miscarriage." These were desperate measures, because the alternatives were often despicable. Henry had heard the stories about the mountebanks. One demanded sexual favours before proceeding and masturbated the women, ostensibly to ascertain if they were orgasmic. (His rationale that he was doing professional research — he professed to believe orgasmic women recovered more easily from abortions — certainly gave a new fillip to perversion.) To complete the humiliation, he made the women lie on the old newspapers he had covering his examining table.

Henry knew of another — a nonlicensed — doctor, trained in then Yugoslavia, who refused to insert a tenaculum to hold the cervix in place. Henry believed a tenaculum — the instrument that holds the cervix steady and is essential for the completion of an abortion — should always be used because the doctor has delicate, manipulative work to do inside the uterus. But this doctor told Henry he was afraid the tenaculum would leave a mark that police could use to prove an abortion had taken place. Henry was nonplussed at such an attitude: "You can't do an abortion without a tenaculum. You are very likely to fail and cause damage. If you do pull it off you have to be very, very skilful." He ended up performing more than one rescue mission on this doctor's patients.

Of the three doctors doing abortions in Montreal in the sixties whom Henry considered reputable and trustworthy, one died in a boating accident, another left the country because he knew the police were closing in and the third, Henry later discovered, wasn't a doctor at all. Henry was on the spot. By 1968, there was no one he felt he could recommend to his patients. Many doctors were so afraid they could be charged as an accessory they would not even refer patients for an abortion. And in the taut medical circles of Montreal, even being fingered as a doctor who could refer patients to the abortion netherworld was perilous — medical reputations had been felled by lesser deeds.

Then a close friend, a woman from the Unitarian community, came to Henry with a problem. Henry had often been a featured speaker at her church, and the congregation agreed with him that women should have access to safe, legal abortions on demand. This kind of approval was rare before the formation of many of the pro-choice groups. In fact, Henry was impressed by the Unitarian stance on many issues: "There wasn't much separating Unitarians and Humanists. They were just attached to a vocabulary we didn't like, like 'worship' and 'church' — words we didn't like." Henry had long admired his friend for her quiet commitment and hard work on many matters of concern shared by humanitarians and Unitarians and now she needed his help. Her eighteen-year-old daughter, a lovely nursing student Henry knew by sight and reputation, was pregnant. Would he do the abortion?

He had turned away so many people. And every time he'd said no, he'd felt a wave of disgust pass through him. He was a coward, a hypocrite for saying what he was saying all over the Montreal and national media and doing nothing. The son of Josef Morgentaler was so brave at demanding that women have their rights and so good at hiding himself behind the law.

He did the abortion. It was January 9, 1968. He never tried to fool himself; he knew this was a turning point. He was not a doctor doing a one-time favour for a friend; he was now a practising abortionist. Later, he'd intuitively understand that the pro-choice movement had to have a declared abortionist leading it if it were to topple politicians from their fence-sitting comfort. He would become the only abortionist in the entire country not afraid to say loudly and often what he did for a living, and he would be vital to a movement that might otherwise have been stymied by the tepid legislation. But for now he was discreet. "Here I was for the first time in my life doing my most daring thing in my life, really, defying the law of the new country that had adopted me, basically, and playing for very high stakes, risking prison, possibly my medical licence, the security of my family."

He felt uplifted, mythic; finally he had reached for and embraced his destiny. Now that his cause had his total commitment, now that he was an action hero, it was more than a cause — it was a crusade. The romantic boy who had daydreamed adventures in the farmer's field outside Lodz had metamorphosed into a man as brave as any from the pages of those books. He knew he had to be brave or all the therapy in the world would not allow him to live with himself. Yes, the cause was genuine, but so was his own need.

He read everything he could on abortion. He had used a catheter on his friend's daughter to precipitate the miscarriage, a method used in France. In this method, the uterus senses a foreign body and contracts enough to expel the pregnancy. Henry insisted the girl come back for an examination forty-eight hours later. She did and everything seemed well. He followed her recovery for a few days more until he was satisfied there were no after-effects. But this method did not impress him. "It seemed like a hit or miss and there was always the possibility of a hemorrhage or infection."

Henry prided himself on his medical standards; his clinic was immaculate, his doctoring above reproach. This is how it would have to be for the abortions as well. He was sure some better way existed. He found it when a member of the Ottawa ARCAL (Association for the Repeal of the Canadian Abortion Law, a group that had formed in 1967 to make a presentation before the Royal Commission on the Status of Women) gave him a pamphlet by a British doctor, Dorothy Kerslake. She had witnessed abortions in the then Soviet Union and in China that used a suction method invented in 1958. She had kept scrupulous records, and reported less bleeding and fewer instances of after-procedure hemorrhaging.

Henry sent to England for the $3,000 vacuum aspirator, and when it arrived on January 26, 1968, his nurse, Joanne Cornax, went to collect it at customs. Henry loved to recall how the very proper, middle-aged mother-of-two brazenly told a customs agent she was picking up some run-of-the-mill medical equipment, but that she would go to the trouble of opening the box for his inspection if he really wanted her to. He didn't, which was just as well, because instructions for using the equipment accompanied it. Henry visited British and American clinics to learn how the aspirator worked, and soon he understood enough to modify and improve the equipment and method.

"I was the first one who used this procedure in Canada, possibly even in North America," Henry told fellow pro-choice activist Eleanor Wright Pelrine a few years later when she wrote *Morgentaler: The Doctor Who Wouldn't Turn Away*. "Along the way, I improved upon the technique, which was relatively new and not yet completely standardized.

"I made a habit, after using the vacuum suction with a straight cannula, to pass a metal curette around to gently scrape the insides of the uterus, just to make sure that nothing of the placenta remains attached to the uterine wall. Then I again use, for a few seconds, vacuum suction with a bent cannula, to ensure the procedure is complete and that there is absolutely nothing remaining in the uterus that could cause bleeding or infection."

He sent out notices to his patients saying he was limiting his practice to family planning and reopened for business. He set his fee at $300, the same amount charged by Dr. Robert McCallum, a British Columbian doctor who had been doing abortions quietly since 1948.[1] McCallum was given a suspended sentence and stripped of his physician's licence in January 1968. He had insisted on pleading guilty and never went back to active medicine, even after his licence was restored. Henry seemed oblivious to his colleague's fate. "He charged $300, which seemed like a nice number. Then I decided that nobody would ever be denied treatment because they couldn't pay. The maximum was there, but people could pay what they could."

Cornax, a Roman Catholic, wasn't happy with the change in her job description. But she had been Henry's only nurse, manager, assistant and right hand for ten years, and by then she was a friend as well as a loyal employee. From the beginning she had impressed Henry as a quick study. She'd learned to operate the x-ray machine and routinely did blood tests and the urine tests, services Henry provided in his office so he could give his patients a complete checkup without their having to go to a hospital. But Cornax was the one on the front lines of the abortion issue. She fielded all the calls from frightened, weeping women pleading for abortions. She knew the need and she chose to stay.

He never asked her what she thought of his decision to perform abortions. He spoke with no one about it, not even his family. "Why didn't I discuss it with Eva? I don't know. At the time we were pretty much apart in our lifestyles." Nor can he remember when or how or even if he did tell her. In his mind there is no pared-down still and sad scene of two figures sitting at a kitchen table, traversing their great divide for one of the last times, although they were once so close one would breathe in the other's exhaled air. Instead, he offered conjecture: "I'm sure Eva was worried about the safety of the family and the stress on me, but her reaction was that this was a great thing. It's courageous but also dangerous."

He knows he didn't tell his children until more than a year later. Goldie was away in Vermont at Bennington College, and Bamie, bright and popular, an athlete and president of the student council, was attending St. George's. Henry wanted to preserve their status quo. Within the first month, though, he had taken aside Claude-Armand Sheppard, lawyer and fellow rebel for a just cause, and asked how he could minimize the risks of being an abortionist. Sheppard told him the risks were enormous — he could lose everything — and that one preventative measure might be to allow only the woman having the abortion inside his clinic. But Henry wanted women to feel comfortable when they came to his clinic, and that meant permitting husbands, friends or family to accompany them. "The women were afraid of dying, hemorrhaging, all those things. I couldn't deprive them of someone who would give them emotional support and comfort. If I was going to do this, it would be in the best possible conditions."

He had already decided he would not deny he was doing abortions if he was ever caught. He was going to say, "Yes, I did it for these and these and these reasons and I believe in what I am doing and I believe the law is wrong." Those people he eventually told were not his confidants but his ideological associates, the people with whom he debated. The reaction of one Unitarian minister when he revealed he was doing abortions was gratifying: "He was very understanding. He said, 'Henry, you are putting your head on the block.' I said, 'Well, I'm not going to stop doing them.' He said, 'I think you are doing a noble thing and I wish you well.'"

That's also what Henry wanted to hear from the Humanists. Instead, a respected neurologist, Irving Heller, then president of the Montreal chapter, invited Henry over to his home one evening for a fireside chat. He had heard Henry was doing abortions illegally; was that true? Henry confirmed the rumours. "If you get arrested and convicted it will reflect on the Humanist Fellowship of Montreal," Henry said Heller told him. "Either you should stop doing abortions or resign as president of the Humanist Association of Canada." When Henry refused to consider either option, Heller declared he would talk to the executive. If they did not agree with him, he would quit. Heller was outvoted and he did resign. "I felt partly vindicated," Henry said. (Two decades later, Heller's niece would work for Henry as executive manager of his Toronto clinic.) But the sting never subsided. Henry never forgot it was the front-ranking Humanists who had voted against him. He viewed it as betrayal. "You expect your enemies to throw mud at you and vilify you, but to be slandered by your own friends, the people who should know, the people who should understand — I vowed to myself I would be vindicated, that they would be proud of me one day." (In 1974, Henry was voted Canadian Humanist of the Year. He had always had the majority on his side, but Henry wanted the approval of everyone, particularly those at the top. For a time he was careful to avoid the meetings at which he was the subject of often acrimonious and heated debate, but he found out who stood by him and who did not just the same. He said McGill psychology professor Ernest Poser was one who agreed with Heller. "Lots were on my side, but Poser and Heller had positions of prestige," both inside the Humanist organization and within the medical establishment. No wonder it was so important to Henry he win them over.)

Stung, he began to use his new role as a sort of litmus test with his friends. He waited for six months before telling Mauriello. "I knew what he was going to say. 'Don't do it. It's dangerous. What do you need this for?' And when I did tell him sometime later, we discussed it and he said he would rather be a live coward than a dead hero." He and Gertie were out for a stroll when he told her what he had done. He blurted it out, with little preamble. "I didn't ask him any questions. I didn't want to hear about it," Gertie recalled. "I was into my own brain. I told him, 'Don't do it again. You were lucky this time. Forget it.'"

But he had too many people counting on him now. The Point St. Charles clinic had begun referring many of their clients who were on welfare and/or single mothers when they found out he would only charge those women $25 or $50. Other agencies were ecstatic that Montreal finally had a doctor willing to do abortions who was not only aboveboard but a thorough professional and extremely competent. As he carried out the routine examinations on his regular patients, Henry's mind would be on the women sitting in his reception room waiting for abortions. They were risking so much by coming to see him. He marvelled at their courage as he became more aware of the depth of their desperation. "Here all these cases of general practice, headaches and stomachaches and colds and everything else, and their value seemed pale next to a woman needing an abortion, and I was the only one who could help her. It was hard to keep these people waiting."

In March 1969 when he'd written the letter to all his patients saying he was changing his practice to specialize in family planning, he'd known he could not turn back. "It was a hard decision. I liked my general practice. I had a lot of loyal patients." Ostensibly, he would now be prescribing birth control pills, inserting IUDs, even performing a few vasectomies. He did all that, but he did even more abortions. He told himself he was undoing "centuries of oppression"; he told himself he was being courageous in defying a law, religious traditions, a way of life. "It was a big step, and I was proud I was able to [take] it. I was getting a lot of gratitude from my patients."

But Henry wasn't sleeping — the nightmares were back. He was exhausted and frightened about everything, including the fact he might be too tired to do the procedure properly. What if something went wrong? What if he lost a patient? What if he got caught? "There was constant anxiety in the background." Yet somehow his hands stayed steady. He swooped between jubilation — "Finally I am doing something I believe in, in spite of the law, in spite of everything" — and sharp jabs of despair — "I'm an outlaw, a potential outlaw. Anyone can denounce me. The police can arrest me."

He tried to laugh about it. So what if he was arrested? That would only make him a criminal. Much worse was being an incompetent criminal, which is what he would be labelled if anything ever went wrong while he was doing an abortion. All this talk of ideals and rights and women's choice would be for nothing if he became known as the man who caused the death of a woman. At home Eva noticed his stress. "Maybe you have done enough," she would say. One afternoon, at the end of a day full of complicated cases, he sat down at his desk, put his head down and wept. His receptionist came in, saw him and left without a word. He told himself he deserved to cry. It was only emotion, an overload. He wasn't going to stop now.

Then on June 1, 1970, there was a knock on the door.

CHAPTER 7

COURTS AND CARAVANS

THAT DAY, as it was getting close to lunchtime, Henry was having a break in his office. In the former recreation room Henry had converted to a comfortable recovery area was a young woman from Minnesota, one of many women referred to Henry by an organization operating out of Boston, New York and Minneapolis called Clergymen Counseling On Abortion. It was run by Bob McCoy, a fellow Humanist, who was becoming his good friend.

Randy was seventeen, and seven weeks pregnant. What she didn't know was the man who had accompanied her, not apparently responsible for the pregnancy, had tipped off American police about what she was going to do in Canada. He told the Federal Bureau of Investigation he could expose an abortion ring. The FBI alerted Canadian authorities and gave the young man marked bills to pay for the procedure.

When Joanne Cornax told Henry three men were outside his office waiting to see him, he was less startled by the search warrant the three police officers flashed than by the fact that almost immediately they began a search of his left-hand trouser pocket for his wallet. They took out all the money. Then they searched his right-hand pocket, and found more money. Henry had always been casual about cash, usually shoving it into one pocket or drawer or another, when he wasn't blithely accepting cheques (many of which bounced). In the beginning, when he was doing only three or four abortion procedures a day, the system — or lack thereof — had worked. Now about a dozen procedures a day were the norm and Henry's staff had begun making bank runs at the end of office hours. At the time Henry had set his top rate at $350 (later $300), dropping it to $200 for students, but he was always willing to make a deal and do an abortion for whatever amount the woman said she could afford. Nevertheless his clinic was cash rich; in fact, word may have slipped out, because once Henry was robbed in the clinic at gunpoint. But this time it was the police who were removing all the money, examining it and looking as if they were even counting it. Henry was puzzled by their behaviour and said so. They were searching for the marked money, said one of the officers; then he moved on to rifle through Henry's untidy desk. He packed any and all papers suspected to be of importance, and confiscated much of Henry's equipment, but not the vacuum aspirator. Henry was ordered into an adjacent examination room; Cornax and the other nurses were ushered into another room. The patients were also taken into custody.

Henry headed to the refrigerator for the sandwich he had put there that morning. The action was a reflex from the Holocaust, when accompanying authorities meant no food for days. He was permitted one phone call before being taken away for questioning. Eva Morgentaler assured him she would phone Claude-Armand Sheppard. At the police station Henry stalled for more than an hour, until police realized he was not going to make a statement without the presence of legal counsel. Police finally stopped giving the runaround to the lawyer Sheppard had dispatched to the station and allowed him to see his client.

Henry made his statement to Daniel David, "a jovial, overweight detective." The junior lawyer sent by Sheppard cautioned him about saying anything. But Henry had waited a long time to make this statement; nothing could have stopped him. Yes, he had indeed been doing abortions, and for the following reasons. As the police typed up the statement, the lawyer left. "Maybe he went to dinner," Henry said laconically. When it was completed Henry helpfully pointed out all its grammatical and typographical errors, then refused to sign it without his lawyer present. Meanwhile Joanne Cornax, who had also been detained, was shown a small part of the statement and led to believe Henry had signed it. She signed a statement of corroboration, not knowing she had just guaranteed she would be subpoenaed as a witness for the prosecution at some future date. Oddly, everyone was finally released and nobody was charged. The next day they all returned to Henry's clinic, where it was business as usual, except that the staff were understandably nervous and the operating room nurses jittery whenever they heard a knock on the door. Henry also wondered when the inevitable second raid would occur. He had been peppering the police station with calls, asking police to return the confiscated equipment. On June 5, three detectives visited the clinic again. This time they phoned ahead. And this time they had a warrant for Henry's arrest, as well as a search warrant.

Henry suddenly realized this was more than an academic exercise in freedom of speech and the opportunity to be seen as a hero. He could be slapped with a sentence of life imprisonment, ultimately. He had a taste of what prison might be like when he spent that night in a small, spare cell. The only interruption was the 2 a.m. session to take fingerprints and mug shots. His companions consisted of a few drunks and one Greek man in the cell across the hallway, to whom Henry tried to talk:

"Do you know Cavafy, the Greek poet?" he asked. As a conversational gambit, this was the best Henry could do. Small talk had never been his forte.

"Baa, Cavafy," the man spat back. "Cavafy no good. He a homo."

Henry spent the rest of the long night lying quietly, comparing himself with "all the people who [had] fought for principles and spent time in jail, like Ghandi and others." He attended the following day's bail hearing rumpled and unshaven.

During this raid the police had confiscated the aspirator — it was exhibit 1A — and had searched the pockets and purses of all the patients at the clinic. They came to court prepared. The junior lawyer from Sheppard's firm was also there. Henry wanted him to ask the court to give back the clinic's equipment; the junior was shocked at such a suggestion. This was a bail hearing, routine procedure, neither the time nor place for ideological grandstanding. But Henry wanted the aspirator so he could keep the clinic open — out of professional pride, as well as for all the women who would be needing abortions. He tried to make the request himself. The judge cut him off. "You have a lawyer for that," he told him. (It was six years before he got back that particular aspirator.)

The police had found a witness — a woman arriving for an abortion, and therefore in a particularly vulnerable situation. She was an unmarried secretary with a two-year-old. She knew she could be facing a two-year prison sentence and the possibility that her child would be taken from her. She agreed to make a statement. Henry was accused of performing an abortion on her; he pleaded not guilty. Bail was set at $2,000 and he was released. Henry immediately set about ordering another $3,000 vacuum aspirator and keeping the clinic open for referrals until the device arrived. He was eager to get back to work. He didn't want a long, drawn-out court battle; he wanted a quick victory. He expected Sheppard to deliver it.

The two men were an improbable pairing, physically. Both were very small, balding and middle-aged, but Sheppard was a rounded, miniaturized Churchillian figure, whereas Henry was hawkish and wiry, with bearded chin outthrust and bristling. Yet both were intellectuals; both were arrogant; each was accustomed to being listened to, deferred to and to being right. Henry admitted that Sheppard "probably thought I was a pain in the ass. I wasn't easy. I had to be convinced all the time." Sheppard was canny, as rebellious as Henry, but more inclined to view the case as a long-term skilful and polished manoeuvre rather than as one quick-hit, win-or-lose courtroom skirmish. One of the defenders of a group of twenty-one FLQ (Front de Libération du Québec) terrorists whose mail bombs had killed several innocent bystanders, Sheppard operated under the credo that a criminal lawyer had to defend anyone who asked for his services. And Henry had. Although they knew each other superficially from their days with the Montreal Civil Liberties Union, Sheppard had never been caught up in the abortion rights issue. But like his client, Sheppard coveted winning, loved being the long shot. Personally he believed this was one of those times the law was an ass, but that didn't mean an automatic or easy victory for Henry. Sheppard said at the time:

> I never hesitated to take advantage of whatever was favourable, in
> doing my best to change public opinion whenever I could. To do
> my best to change the judicial atmosphere, to use legal proceedings

to change the society in which I live. I'm impressed by the American use of the legal system to bring about social change. Our courts may be too reactionary to contemplate a move in that direction. The whole tradition in Canada is the British tradition, a totally technical, dehumanized, anti-social tradition to resolve technical problems in a technical way.

Typically we're perpetually told by the courts that the law is not just, that a situation they're called to deal with is a scandal, that the decision is not going to be fair, but that that's not their function, that it's up to the legislator. In other words they will look for any excuse to escape making a socially oriented decision.[1]

Henry was determined to be tried by jury, a jury of French-speaking Canadians, like the majority of his patients. Sheppard approved of this, and in fact he may even have come up with the jury configuration, although no one is sure now. Henry also wanted Sheppard to understand that his was "not an ordinary case, where he gets me off at any price." It took a while, Henry said, but Sheppard accepted his position, along with the knowledge that Henry was never going to deny peforming abortions, he would never plead guilty and he was going to be a full participant in all the tactics and strategies. "I wanted to understand everything that was going on. I was very insistent on that. I wanted to know and I wanted to have input. On an intellectual level we are equal and we could discuss things, then we would decide what we would do and how we would proceed."

They would play for time. New York State's newly liberalized law on abortion reform was coming into effect in a few weeks, on July 1, 1970. Society needed to see for itself the abortion law wasn't going to pave the way to Hell in the proverbial handbasket. When and only when public opinion on the abortion issue caught up with Henry would they stand a chance of winning in court.

————

Trudeau's compromise omnibus bill may have placated the doctors, but not the many women who knew all too well the difficulty they now faced having to convince a therapeutic abortion committee (should their hospital even have one) of their need for an abortion. When police arrested and charged the only doctor in Canada who had publicly stated the decision was up to the woman and only the woman, they were enraged.

Across the country, in the late sixties and early seventies, women's liberation groups were forming, particularly on campuses. *Ms.* magazine, a new and slick American feminist publication, urged women to take charge of their own lives and change society. The fact that Henry Morgentaler faced criminal charges for performing abortions underlined the fact that abortion on demand was the most pressing issue of the newly forming women's movement.

Many of these so-called women's libbers were middle class, newly radicalized by feminism, newly immune to the perks of their membership in the status quo. For hours they discussed who picked up the dirty socks in their homes and why. These discussions may have seemed mundane, but they fostered the liberation mind-set that made gender equality the pivotal component of any and all discussions. They knew Section 251 had created two laws. The law for married women with children, community standing and connections was entirely different from the law for disenfranchised women, poor and ignorant of any alternative help if their doctors frowned at the word *abortion*. Abortion-on-demand was not a luxury; it was feminism's bottom line. And during the heady days of the cross-country trek called the Abortion Caravan in the spring of 1970 — more than a month before police raided Henry's Montreal clinic — it rendered sisterhood more than a buzzword.

The Caravan came out of the Women's Caucus, a group of Vancouver feminists already operating an abortion referral service, who decided the situation called for lights and camera along with some action. In reaction to Section 251, abortion referral services in many major cities had been created, offering real help and advice to women wanting to terminate a pregnancy. The Vancouver service helped women get appointments in Seattle, coached them on how to deal with psychiatrists and warned them they might feel angry after enduring the process of convincing medical professionals something was dreadfully wrong with them just to get permission for a procedure they believed they had a right to. Other organizations providing the same kind of front-line services had sprung up in Montreal, Toronto and Calgary. But these organizations discovered there was always a tug-of-war between the need to provide direct help to women caught by Section 251 and the need to lobby and quash the law. In those days, lobbying was secondary. Even Henry was fighting the issue in the courts, not through lobbying.

But the Vancouver women wanted to bring everyone together, and they wanted everyone, together, to bring the issue right up to the front steps of the people who had plunged the women into this not-so-subtle legal entanglement. The Abortion Caravan planned to march on the Houses of Parliament in Ottawa on May 11, 1970 — the day after Mother's Day. The Vancouver women had already written to local and federal parliamentarians, and anyone else who had a point of view on the issue.[2] The Caravan even had a dress rehearsal when thirteen supporters camped in front of British Columbia Health Minister Ralph Loffmark's office for three days in March until he agreed to meet with them. The course of the meeting was predictable: the women asked the government to support abortion clinics, and Loffmark, according to one, patted them on their shoulders, called them all "dear" and promised nothing. The women had anticipated this reaction to their requests, and had a secondary plan all ready to go. On March 26, 1970, they went separately to the Victoria legislature and seated themselves throughout the gallery. When Marcy Cohen, one of the founders of the abortion referral service, tossed masses of red tape down over Loffmark's head, other women unfurled an eight-foot banner proclaiming Abortion Kills Women. "Mr. Speaker, there's a stranger in the House," Loffmark stated in parliamentese. With the exception of one woman who was lectured about decorum by House Speaker William Murray, the "strangers" were immediately but decorously ejected. Loffmark told the *Globe and Mail* he "doubted" he would ever establish abortion clinics "without the complete concurrence of the medical profession."

On April 27 of that year, about seventeen women left Vancouver in a covered pick-up truck, one large, gas-guzzling car and a Volkswagen van painted with slogans and bearing a coffin — a symbol of all the women who had died because of botched abortions. Slowly they proceeded across the country, stopping overnight in United church basements in Kamloops, Calgary, Edmonton, Regina, Saskatoon, Winnipeg, Thunder Bay, Sudbury, Toronto, on their way to Ottawa. The idea of the Caravan was to get the word out and get the people metaphorically on board — not a difficult task, since their cavalcade was a definite traffic stopper. The van was outfitted with a loudspeaker that blasted a prerecorded tape of liberation songs, including Judy Collins's "Marat /Sade," and explained who the women were and what their issue was. They had written to women's organizations across the country, asking for hospitality and support. They had also written to Prime Minister Trudeau, Justice Minister John Turner and Health and Welfare Minister John Munro, asking for meetings. (The politicians all had previous engagements.) Everywhere the Caravan went, women in cars would meet them on the outskirts of their town and create a joyful convoy of solidarity. During the trip they held meetings, after which local women would get up and recount their own experiences with illegal abortions, "appalling stories," said Caravaner Margo Dunn, one of the leaders.[3] The Caravaners were unconventional and theatrical — the women who did guerilla theatre would run into local malls, perform to astonished shoppers, then dash away — but they were authentic, and no matter where they went, many sensed and understood that underneath the spectacle of the hippie-decorated, coffin-carrying van was the real pain felt by real women. And so, as the Caravan neared Ottawa that Saturday, May 9, triumphant posters announced, "The women are coming."

They had left Vancouver a handful or two of "furious women" determined to "declare war on the government of Canada and accuse the government of Canada of being responsible for the murder by abortions of thousands of women who died from illegal abortions and of being responsible for the oppression and degradation of thousands of women who are forced into unwanted motherhood and who depend on inadequate medication over which they have no control," in the words of organizer Marcy Cohen.[4] They arrived in Ottawa the symbol of a new movement. Hundreds of women from Toronto who had rented buses to be there lined the streets. Even some women from the Province of Quebec came, although the Montreal Front de libération des femmes said that in spite of their support of the cause, they wouldn't be there to declare war on the government of Canada because they didn't believe in the government.

A public meeting was planned for the Railway Committee Room of the House of Commons. Speaking at it were the stars of the issue: Henry, as well as New Democratic MP Grace MacInnis, the lone female member of the House, who had put forth an independent bill in 1967 calling for the decriminalization of abortion. But it was a welfare mother and antipoverty activist, eight months pregnant, who electrified the crowd. The federal government couldn't seem to decide if a fetus was a human, yet "under Ontario's welfare legislation, a child does not exist until he or she is over three months old," said Doris Power of the Just Society. She believed the poor bore the brunt of this double standard. "One of the most painful results of that double standard is the isolation women feel in the face of what is called an illegitimate pregnancy... women alone are blamed for their pregnancies but men control the circumstances under which they can be terminated."[5]

Power had applied for an abortion to terminate her pregnancy at a Toronto hospital, where two psychiatrists and another doctor asked her how she had become pregnant. "My method was terribly unoriginal," she replied. "It's thousands of years old." When she was turned down, the doctor asked her if she would be getting an illegal abortion. "Many women have," she said. He told her, "Well, take your rosary and get the hell out of here." Many low-income women, when they applied for a legal abortion, suffered the additional indignity of being asked if they would agree to sterilization. "Let me make myself clear," Power told the crowd. "Had I agreed to sterilization I may have been granted an abortion."

It was Saturday, and the Abortion Caravaners had given the government of the country until Monday (May 11, 1970) to change the law.

By rights, they couldn't deviate from the clearly stated game plan. These were still law-abiding *Canadian* women, after all, who always played fair. Someone suggested they march to Trudeau's house. That Trudeau was somewhere in the Pacific Rim at the time was irrelevant.

Some women from Vancouver retrieved the coffin from the Volkswagen bus and dragged it over to 24 Sussex Drive, where only three Mounties were on guard. The women linked arms and easily made it by the officers to the stone steps of the residence. As the Mounties called for reinforcements, many women dropped down on the thick, lush lawn and declared that they would stay until the law was changed. But then it started to rain. An aide came to the door and stressed that Trudeau was not at home. Nobody had planned for this spontaneous demonstration, and fewer had any idea what to do next. They decided to carry the coffin to the doorstep and leave it there. Going by the name Elsa, Dunn presented the aide, Gordon Gibson, with a few items she had been transporting across the country — a coat hanger, vacuum cleaner hose, empty can of household cleaner, along with a speech she had prepared: "This is a vacuum cleaner hose. Women use it for the suction to withdraw the fetus from their bodies. It often removes the entire uterus. This is a can of Draino. Women inject it into their uteruses to attempt an abortion. It turns their insides into soup."[6] That evening and the next afternoon at the old high school where they were bunking, the women debated whether to call it quits or go ahead with their planned demonstration on the Hill. They decided thirty-five of them would go into the House (they had tickets to the four different galleries) and tie themselves with bicycle chains to their seats. Each of them memorized a short speech stating abortion should be removed from the Criminal Code because it caused the deaths of women and because women ought to have control over their own bodies. As the guards closed in on one woman, another woman in a different part of another gallery would stand and recite the speech again. The demonstration was scheduled for 3:30 p.m., about a half hour into Question Period, when the microphones hang low and the women could be heard throughout the House. And it all went according to plan.

In the meantime, hundreds in black kerchiefs gathered at 3 p.m. by the Eternal Flame, chanting, "Women are dying. Abortion laws kill." They marched two by two, round and round for half an hour. Then, as a declaration of war, they ripped off their black headgear to reveal red kerchiefs, a homage to the women of the French Revolution. Inside, the women stood and spoke and Parliament was halted for more than a half hour. A first in Canadian parliamentary history. Some women were reprimanded for their behaviour, but no one was arrested. John Turner was not amused, and expressed in the *Globe and Mail* his "surprise and dismay that these young women understand the democratic process so little." Acting prime minister Mitchell Sharp was amused: he told the *Globe and Mail* that the women's demonstration was not fair to him on his first day on the job.

As much as the politicians tried to downplay the event and blame the action on a few shrill women, the Abortion Caravan, chains and all, was "the first national expression of a movement which has been active and growing for some time. It was not, as the media pretended, simply five hundred women taking part in an event with no history and little social context....

"The demonstrations, meetings and speeches from the gallery of the House of Commons marked the end of one phase of the battle and the beginning of another. The women had mapped out strategies for confronting doctors, hospital administrators, and abortion committees in their own communities," noted Krista Maeots in the *Canadian Forum*.[7] Later, Vancouver women challenged Trudeau in a demonstration; in Toronto, Health Minister Munro was confronted about the issue at the Canadian Conference on Social Welfare; and in Winnipeg, women demonstrated at a luncheon meeting of the Canadian Medical Association and later held an open meeting to present their demands to the association's board of directors. When the Humanist Association of Canada presented abortion reform recommendations to Justice Minister Turner a large group of women were present to make known their approval. Similarly, when members of the Canadian Psychiatric Association voted to recommend that the federal government remove abortion from the Criminal Code and make it a medical decision between physician and patient, women were there to applaud and encourage.

Women across the country were now politicized, activated: when Henry was charged with procuring an illegal abortion that summer, a telegraph campaign sprang up to support him. Women made a show of support to any individual or organization that was bucking the system and siding with them on the abortion issue. Later Henry was alone at the forefront of the movement because he was the one who pushed it further and never let it go. But at that time, he was a courageous Montreal doctor, frequently invited to speak at rallies such as the one for the Caravan, but not yet seen as the linchpin of the issue. He always referred to humanism as the source of his stance, not feminism. And in the post-Caravan surge of actions and organizing, a funny thing was happening to many of the feminist organizations. They were being wrenched apart internally about whether abortion should be the sole issue on which women should mobilize or whether abortion on demand should be one plank in a larger social issue platform. It helped explain why another major action was not undertaken by women for years after the Abortion Caravan. The momentum was there, but the unity wasn't. In Toronto, the regular Wednesday-night meetings of the Women's Caucus above a downtown pub were noisy affairs. "I remember all these discussions about social tactics and were you using abortion as the single issue that would then rally people. That's what the Trotskyites and Marxist-Leninists wanted," said Ruth Miller, a public health worker who belonged to ARCAL and several other advocacy groups that later folded into the Canadian Alliance for the Repeal of the Abortion Laws (CARAL). The revolutionary rhetoric and obvious ulterior motives scared off many small-l liberal middle-class women from the movement. "So many meetings just fell apart," Miller said, sighing.

As Jane Jenson observed in *The Politics of Abortion*, "the Canadian women's movement is not only divided but also heavily weighted towards liberal feminism. Equal opportunities and individual rights claims have dominated the agenda of this wing of the movement since the middle 60s, affecting the representation of abortion by this wing of the movement."[8]

But as Bobbie Spark, one of women on the Abortion Caravan, told the *Socialist Worker* magazine years later:

You have to understand that patriarchy is a system of control, that those who control my body and my womb and those who control the courts are all linked. When you start to understand that, it fuels you with such pure rage, just like at the time of a crisis you might be able to lift a car to release someone who has been trapped, so in the fight for your rights that rage can be a source of energy. It's absolutely total, a complete sense of rage.

I think it's important to understand that when you take on what appears to be, in the public eye, a single issue, in fact if you really follow it through you find that they all interlock and dovetail. It puts you up against capitalism, against the church and against the state, and against all the structures that support these institutions, and they all have a vested interest in opposing women's rights to abortion.[9]

Back in 1971, this was the stage against which Henry's battle was set. He made an impassioned speech on Parliament Hill to thousands of women gathered to protest the abortion laws. He was a symbol, a recognizable figure affixed to a growing viable and visible movement. In Montreal he seemed to be all over at once, stirring up controversy in frequent letters to the editors, speaking on any open line and talk show that invited him. He loved the media spotlight because he liked thinking on his feet, feeling nimble, scoring points. The cerebral thrill he got from the debates was addictive, but some of the wounds received in those verbal set-tos stayed. Pro-life groups were popping up everywhere he went, like grass springing back upright after being trod on. One couple in Montreal were particularly adept at getting media air time. Dr. Heather Morris, who headed a Canadian-wide organization, Alliance for Life, became a bitter foe. "Heather Morris was the worst. She was very religious. Once I debated her in front of a labour movement group and she took out a recording of a fetal heart. It filled the room. Boom, boom. Boom, boom. On 'Canadian AM' [sic] I asked her if she would allow a fourteen-year-old who had been raped to have an abortion and I took by her silence that she would not even allow an abortion in this type of case. Afterwards, as we were leaving the studio, she said, 'I

know you are a good doctor, a good technician. Hitler also was technically proficient, you know.' I was so shocked I almost slapped her face.
She just left. To this day I hate her for that."

Henry had trained four doctors in his method, including the older
brother of his old friend Vincent Mauriello. His own practice was becoming so busy he had to turn away women, referring them, instead,
to one of the other doctors who were making Montreal known as a
mecca for safe abortions. Interspersed with his medical duties were
court appearances, preliminary inquiries into which Sheppard always
managed to toss one more delaying tactic. "Sheppard was very good at
standing his ground in front of judges. I realized that when you pay for
a good lawyer, it's not just for his knowledge of the law but for the ability to withstand the wrath, the bad tempers of the judges. He knew how
to stand his ground, insist on his rights as a lawyer. Many lawyers shake
in their boots." Henry was to learn that first-hand. One judge forbade
him to sit on the bench provided in the dock on his first appearance
before him. Another ordered him to take his hands out of his pockets.
Meanwhile, in the preliminaries Sheppard was making mockery of the
police's paper trail on Henry. If the police had taken all the papers from
Henry's desk in the two-part raid, then there must be good reason.
Piece by piece, he went through all of them.

"Is this the paper you found in Dr. Morgentaler's office?" he'd ask
the police officer on the witness stand.

"Yes," the officer would reply.

"The paper is blank," Sheppard would counter, waving it around in
the courtroom.

Or he would insist the court record each piece of paper as a separate item. The legal antics often veered towards the farcical, but whatever comic release they provided could only momentarily puncture the
underlying tension, as the lengths to which the police would go to convict Henry Morgentaler became increasingly evident. Henry had been
summoned to court again in 1970 when police laid a third charge of
performing an abortion against him. The woman was from Quebec
City. That she was a reluctant witness was an understatement. She had
been given a problem-free abortion two years earlier, but six months

afterwards a former boyfriend had turned her in to police. When she was asked to identify the man who had administered her abortion, she said "I don't see him here." Henry had just returned from a month's vacation in Greece, during which he had grown a beard. Before, he had been clean-shaven. Crown Attorney Louis-Guy Robichaud, a dogged prosecutor with a personal commitment to the anti-abortion cause, Henry always believed, wanted the court to require Henry to shave. Sheppard sprang to his feet, but the judge laughed. "Suppose I order it and she doesn't recognize him. Can we put the beard back on?" he asked.

That preliminary hearing for the third charge against Henry resumed some time later, after police had combed the prescription files of every druggist in Quebec City. They read as many as ten thousand pieces of paper, Henry was told, before they found a prescription for birth control pills which Henry had written out for the woman after her abortion — tangible proof she was at his abortion clinic.

The stress of being Henry Morgentaler steadfast rebel, Henry Morgentaler media pundit, as well as Henry Morgentaler compassionate doctor with calm gaze and steady hands, was exacting its toll. He began taking vacations every six weeks — one of many reasons that Gertie Katz was becoming very worried about her friend.

Gertie and Henry had grown even closer over the years, and when Henry's brother, Mike, moved to Montreal, she became like a sister to them both. Like Henry and Mike's sister, her name in Yiddish was Ghitel. Gertie had two brothers she had never met from her father's first family in Russia. It was from Mike that Gertie found out more about Henry, his family in Poland and what he had been through. Unlike his brother, Mike would talk for hours about the past and the people from it. He worshipped his mother, and scoffed at any indication that she didn't adore Henry. "She liked him very much. She was a very good mother. Whatever he has made of himself, he owes to our mother," he said. Mike had returned to Poland several times. In 1978, he took Gertie and Carl to Lodz. They hunted down the subcamp sites of Dachau where Henry and Mike had been. In Lodz they stayed at the Grand Hotel, and only after they registered did Mike tell them that the hotel used to be Nazi headquarters. "I was ready to run. How can you stay here now?" Gertie asked Mike, who laughed. "Where are you going, Ghitel? It's not the Nazi headquarters now." Later he told her he was going for a walk. It was dark and raining. Gertie got an umbrella and insisted she accompany him. He didn't tell her where they were going until he stopped and pointed to a courtyard: "That's where I lived."

"The kitchen was minute. No bathroom. The toilet was off in the courtyard, just a hole with an impression for your feet. Mike was showing it, laughing his head off," Gertie remembered. In Lodz they met the Warsaw ghetto resistance hero Marek Edelman. He'd known Ghitel Morgentaler; they had worked in the same factory unit before she was transported to the gas chambers at Treblinka. "We saw her go," Marek told Mike with conviction, understanding that there was more comfort in knowing a sister's fate than in not knowing. In Warsaw Mike bought flowers. They drove to Treblinka the next day to lay them there in tribute. Subsequently, Mike also returned to Auschwitz; to honour his mother, he said, who was the reason he'd come to Canada. "I did my share," he said. "My mother told me to look after [Henry] and I did. He asked for help."

Henry said Mike had come to Canada to get away from marital difficulties. He'd finally settled in Cleveland after years of army living in places such as Fort Bliss, El Paso. He'd picked up some training as an X-ray technician, even a little optometry. Mike said he was an inventor and that he still held some patents for machine tools. In Cleveland, he worked for years for National Acme, then went into a partnership with a buddy in a machine shop. Business was fine, he said, then his marriage fell apart. Mike took custody of the two older children, both girls, and the two boys remained with his ex-wife. Henry recalled that whenever Mike was late with the alimony his wife would send the police to the machine shop to arrest him. In 1969, Mike came to Montreal, where he found work at Canadair, but at a fraction of what he had been earning. He returned to Cleveland for a few months, then in 1970 came back to Canada for good. Henry gave him a job managing a couple of apartment buildings he had bought. With Mike's advice, he eventually bought five more buildings, all of them with small down payments, most of them before 1972, when income tax laws allowed depreciation on apartment buildings to be deducted against professional income. Henry was not the only professional on suddenly shaky financial ground when the law changed in 1972. Mike lived in one of the apartments before moving to a lower duplex in Montreal's pleasant but modest Notre-Dame-de-Grâce area. In 1970, he was again a newlywed when he married Nancy, a woman with one young son, Joey, whom Mike adopted. They'd met when she answered his newspaper ad for a housekeeper. Together they had a daughter, Donna. They divorced in 1974. Mike met Gertie's husband, Carl Katz, when Henry asked Carl, who knew something about real estate, to show Mike the ropes.

Soon Mike was calling Carl daily, then dropping by for games of chess with him. Perhaps because Mike treated Gertie and Carl like family, Henry began to talk to Gertie a little more often about his past. Not much, though. "It's almost like he opened the doors, looked in, shared something with me — sometimes a funny incident — then closed the doors, never to be referred to again."

By now Gertie understood her friend well. She knew why he was throwing himself into this cause, but she also knew Henry had never considered the consequences of losing. Because Gertie was working in prisons, teaching creative writing, she was convinced it would kill Henry if he ever ended up in one. "Having worked in a penitentiary, being Jewish, knowing what he went through in the concentration camps, I just felt that he was putting himself on the line, standing with his heels on one side of the cliff and his toes on the other. And he had put himself there. This wasn't something anyone was forcing him into. It wasn't the Nazis. He was doing this to himself. I just wanted to shake him, to say, 'You're safe. Don't go back into the lion's den.'"

One evening she tried to convince him to close up the clinic. They were at a Laurentian resort having dinner. He was not with Eva — although both still lived at the house on Barton Street, they had long been living separate lives. Gertie had never thought the couple would actually split, even though she could see how Henry was changing. Gertie cannot remember the name of Henry's companion that evening — a succession of women passed through his life then — but Carl stayed back with her while Gertie and Henry went out for a walk. "I have this vivid image of night and the two of us walking and me shouting at him and him shouting at me. He said he had to do it. He would do it alone if I wouldn't help. He didn't need me."

But he did and she stayed. She wrote to every member of Parliament. She personally lobbied Warren Allmand, who told her he had been very moved when anti-abortionists had shown pickled fetuses to the 1967 health and welfare standing committee. In 1972, when Henry decided to run for Parliament she managed his campaign office. He was running because it was another platform for his message. But he was also bored. His case was stalled somewhere in the legal system, and this was something to do. When he originally approached the New Democratic Party about his candidacy, he was told his identification with the abortion issue might alienate voters. About a month before the election, someone suggested to him he run as an independent NDP in the riding of St-Denis, a Liberal stronghold of about 60 per cent French-speaking voters. He spent $6,000 of his own money, rented a campaign office and put together a pamphlet, red ink on thick yellow paper, French on one side, English on the other, asking:

- Do you believe that all people should have a decent standard of living?
- Do you believe in respect for individual rights and freedoms?
- Do you believe that people should have access to family planning services and day care centres for children?
- Do you believe that women who need and want abortions should be able to have them safely and legally?

He made some radio ads, spoke at a few meetings, had a wonderful time and lost his deposit.

Early in 1973, after the U.S. Supreme Court legalized abortion with the *Roe* v. *Wade* decision of January 22, Henry decided he had waited long enough. The American decision was a signal that times had changed. In Toronto at the nation-wide conference of the Canadian Women's Coalition to Repeal the Abortion Law, he made a public statement: he had performed more than five thousand abortions, all of them safe, all of them illegal. The announcement didn't create the splash Henry wanted. In fact, it barely produced a media ripple. Wright Pelrine, an abortion rights activist and author of *Abortion in Canada* before she wrote *Morgentaler: The Doctor Who Wouldn't Turn Away*, was at the event:

> The meeting erupted in pandemonium. Enthusiastic feminists and civil libertarians went wild. They gave Henry Morgentaler a standing ovation....
>
> But from the press, a deafening silence. A reporter from *The Globe and Mail* assigned to cover the meeting had left before Dr. Morgentaler's speech, probably to meet an early deadline. A brief report on a private radio station went virtually unheard. Back in Montreal, Henry Morgentaler held a press conference in English and in French, making the same declaration implicating himself. Another crusader for the repeal commented that what might have been the beginning of a massive campaign of civil disobedience had fizzled to nothing.[10]

The only reaction was that the police stopped trying to hide the fact they had the clinic under surveillance. On March 27, 1973, Henry wrote the province, asking for approval for his clinic as a "specialized abortion facility"; then he wrote a letter to Marc Lalonde, the federal Minister of Health and Welfare, telling him of his request (copying this letter to Prime Minister Trudeau, Otto Lang, Minister of Justice, and six others). It was Wright Pelrine who contacted a CTV producer for the public affairs program "W5" with the idea that Henry appear on television actually doing an abortion after CBC turned down the proposal. Henry liked the idea of showing an abortion. He thought it would "demystify" the procedure. They had found a woman willing to participate. Slim and attractive, Petra Hartt was married and the mother of a toddler. She and her husband wanted to have more children, but first they were building a house and expected to be in Mexico all winter. She wanted to be identified. CTV aired the segment on May 13, Mother's Day. Hartt was about five weeks pregnant; the abortion took about five minutes. It was obvious the procedure was safe and pain-free.

This time there was a reaction — outrage, anger, fear. Pro-life picketers descended on Henry's office at 2990 Beaugrand. Their placards varied from the anti-Semitic — "Remember Auschwitz" — to the insulting — "Beaugrand Abbatoir (Beaugrand Slaughterhouse)." On the other hand, strangers would yell, "Lachez pas" (Don't give up) to Henry on the street. That television appearance made him a household face as well as name. In the legislature, Quebec Justice Minister Jérôme Choquette was bombarded with questions.

Henry wrote a signed article, "Report on 5,641 outpatient abortions by vacuum suction curettage," and submitted it for publication to the *Journal of the Canadian Medical Association* before he left for a month's vacation in Europe. (The report was only published on December 15, after he was acquitted.) It was sober and thorough, and included a chart of the complication rates. Of the total number of women who had undergone the procedure none had a lacerated cervix, twenty had temperatures over 102 degrees Fahrenheit (39 degrees Celsius) and twenty-seven were hospitalized. He had arranged for his staff to work with Dr. Yvan Machabee, whom he had trained, in his private hospital during his absence. But the police raided Machabee on July 4, his first day of performing abortions, while he was in the midst of his second procedure. Machabee's sister, who was the hospital administrator, sounded the alarm for the police when she saw two men dragging away her brother, not understanding that the police in fact were the ones taking away her brother. Machabee was charged, as was Joanne Cornax when she infuriated the Crown attorney by refusing to identify Machabee. She told the court she couldn't identify the doctor because he was wearing a mask at the time. To retaliate, the Crown attorney resuscitated her testimony from one of Henry's hearings and charged her with being an accomplice. (She was immediately taken into custody, manacled and fingerprinted. The experience so horrified her she moved to Florida and worked as a nurse there.)

As for Machabee, a judge put off his trial indefinitely, saying there was no point in proceeding until the Morgentaler case was resolved.

Machabee, a French Canadian, never came to trial. "They were never really interested in Machabee but in Morgentaler," Henry said. (That held true for one other doctor trained by Henry. Mauriello's brother was never arrested.) "I was a thorn in the side of the establishment and they figured they could get away with prosecuting me or persecuting me because I was an immigrant, I was Jewish. I wasn't part of the traditional community. On top of that I was riling the Catholic hierarchy and what not."

Sheppard once told Henry that the whole bar, including all the judges, hated Henry Morgentaler. They considered him a troublemaker and a bad example. They thought he had to be curbed, and suddenly the opportunity to do so presented itself.

CHAPTER 8

THE BEGINNING OF THE BANDWAGON

NOT LONG AFTER 10 A.M. ON AUGUST 15, 1973, a long-haired woman dressed in the flowing hippie-type clothing of the day, accompanied by her fiancé, bearded but looking not quite as counter-culture as she, paid Henry for the abortion she was about to undertake. But as she headed into the examining room to undress, she said "I've changed my mind."

Henry never asked questions. He didn't ask women if they were sure they wanted an abortion, or if they wanted time to think it over. He assumed they had already done that. He was happy to explain the procedure and allay the fears so many of them had about what they thought they were about to endure. He assumed that was what he'd be doing with this couple. "That's fine," he said. "Why don't you get dressed and we will talk a bit more?" On his way back to his office, the fiancé stopped him, flashed a police badge and announced, "You're under arrest."

Mike Morgentaler is so naturally exuberant he can sometimes sound hysterical, but when he called Gertie Katz that morning he was calm. The clinic had been raided. Henry had been arrested. The whole staff had been arrested. Sheppard had been trying to find out which station they were taken to, but so far he'd come up short. Detectives were wandering all over the clinic. Gertie worked in the penitentiary. Could she somehow help?

"Pick me up in fifteen minutes," Gertie replied.

When she walked into the clinic, a detective stopped her. She asked him for his credentials — "just to show who was in charge here." She asked him what he was doing. She told him he would be personally responsible if anything were missing and that she expected an itemized list of everything removed from the property.

Then she and Mike went back to her house. All afternoon they waited, keeping in touch with Sheppard's staff, who still hadn't been told by police where Henry and the nurses were being held. By 3:50 p.m. Gertie had had enough. She got out her media list from the days of the Committee for Neutral Schools and began dialling. She gave them all the same story: Henry had been arrested, and after several hours police had still not informed his lawyer of his whereabouts. She assumed that was illegal. Wasn't it? Then she and Mike sat back and tuned in to the four o'clock newscasts. It had made practically every station. At 4:15 her phone rang. It was the detective Gertie had met at the clinic with the information she wanted: Henry was being detained at Beaumont, a station near Jean-Talon Market. The nurses, held at a different police station, had finally been allowed to contact their lawyer; Henry had always told them not to worry if they were arrested, just to call Sheppard, which they did. Gertie phoned Joanne's husband, Bill Cornax, who usually picked up his wife after work, and told him where to find her. All the nurses had refused to sign anything implicating Henry. (Later they laughed about it, because they knew Henry had already submitted his research paper to the CMA's *Journal*.) Gertie decided Henry had to have his toothbrush and a newspaper — "it normalized it all for me" — and hounded one of Sheppard's staff until that happened. The nurses were released, but Henry spent two nights in custody, mindful of the nights his father had been incarcerated, grateful to be able to experience something his father had and elated that at last the authorities had reacted.

Gertie had to have a second phone line installed in her house to handle the hundreds of media calls. "My life was never the same." Both pro- and anti-abortion camps were activated. On August 23, Alliance for Life president Heather Morris sent out a notice to every pro-life group across Canada, announcing Henry's arrest and his conditions of bail. He was to refrain from making any radio and television appearances, from discussing his trial with any witnesses, from leaving Montreal and from performing abortions. "Although Dr. Morgentaler has been prohibited from open involvement with the pro-abortion cause, his supporters have not been so restrained," she wrote. "As a result of this, the Quebec Minister of Justice and the Montreal Police have been under enormous strain to suspend charges against Dr. Morgentaler. In addition, the Montreal press, with a very minor exception, have been pro-abortion — editorials, commentaries and letters to the editor have all been in support of Dr. Morgentaler. It is believed the pro-abortionists are deliberately trying to manipulate public opinion so that Dr. Morgentaler will become a 'cause célèbre.'"

Dr. Morris asked each one of them to act immediately, to write as individuals ("to be effective"), not as a pro-life group, in English and French, "letting them know that the abortion law must be upheld and that Dr. Morgentaler must be held responsible for his illegal acts." She listed Choquette, Captain Detective Jean-Claude Rondou of Police Station No. 18 ("He is the police detective who carried out the investigation and arrest of Dr. Morgentaler," she explained) and ten newspapers they should write to to say "how much you appreciate their action and that they have your support."

The day after the raid, Gertie Katz was on the phone to a well-connected friend from the Women's Information and Referral Service, a feminist organization that had been bussing women to Plattsburg, New York, for abortions. Soon word about Henry was out at the women's groups at McGill and Concordia, immigrant women's groups, francophone organizations, wealthy women and Trotskyites throughout the city. Several Montreal doctors met at Henry's home to offer their professional support. When Yvan Machabee's preliminary trial was held August 21, picket lines of women chanted, "Morgentaler — Machabee. Stop the charges. Set them free," in rallies in Montreal as well as across the country.

Not long after, the Montreal groups merged to become the Committee for the Defence of Dr. Morgentaler. On October 3 they registered themselves as the Quebec Ad Hoc Committee for the Defence of Dr. Henry Morgentaler. Gertie was treasurer. When Henry was arrested again on August 30 and police laid six more charges from the August 15 raid, bringing the count to thirteen, word spread to women across the country: the time to rally round Henry Morgentaler was now; the time to raise money was now. The group published a pamphlet outlining the abortion struggle up to that point and sold it for twenty-five cents. Cheques began to arrive. Gertie remembered one from Maria Scott, wife of the late poet Frank Scott, and its accompanying note, which said, "Keep it up, but don't say where this comes from."

After several false starts, including a failed attempt by Sheppard to quash the indictment because it was unconstitutional, Henry's trial finally began on October 18, 1973, more than three years after he was first charged. By then women had formed a French-language committee to defend Henry (on September 11), an Ottawa defence committee (on September 13), a Toronto committee (on September 18), one in Edmonton (on September 24), Vancouver (on September 25) and Hamilton (on September 26). Public rallies took place between September 22 and 24 — Toronto's rally occurred on September 23, when fifty women and twenty men, including three doctors, marched down Yonge Street in the rain to Nathan Phillips Square, where writer and activist June Callwood stated people must support Henry, otherwise "we're letting down everyone in this country — men and women."[1] She and fellow author Pierre Berton sent this telegram to the justice ministers of Canada and Quebec:

> We believe that motherhood should be voluntary.
>
> We believe that Canadian women should have freedom of choice. Those who are not prepared to bear a child, despite whatever alternatives to abortion society can offer, should be able to get their pregnancies terminated safely and without delay.
>
> We believe that medical facilities where abortions can be performed in maximum safety should be available to all Canadian women, even if they live in areas without such facilities, even if they are poor, even if they are young. A law which provides access to abortion only to a few and only in some locations is unjust.
>
> We ask that police and courts immediately stop persecuting Dr. Henry Morgentaler and those other professionally qualified

doctors and nurses who have been performing abortions in order
to help women.

We ask support for Planned Parenthood programs.

We ask that abortion be removed from the Criminal Code.

In October a letter went out from the Toronto Committee to
Defend Dr. Morgentaler. The names on the letterhead were impressive:
Callwood, Berton, Grace Hartman of the Canadian Union of Public
Employees, Elsie Gregory McGill from the Royal Commission on the
Status of Women, poet Irving Layton, local councillors, Stephen Lewis
of the Ontario NDP and York University professor Esther Greenglass,
as well as singer Pauline Julien, then British Columbia MLA Rosemary
Brown and Michel Chartrand of the Confederation of National Trade
Unions. Organizations endorsing the campaign included Atkinson
College Student Union, Young Socialists, National Action Committee
on the Status of Women, CUPE Local 251, plus both the Canadian
Women's Coalition to Repeal the Abortion Laws and the Canadian
Association to Repeal the Abortion Law. By October 17, the day before
the trial began in Montreal's Palais de Justice, defence committee mem-
ber Eleanor Wright Pelrine announced that the Toronto committee had
raised more than $1,000.

Gertie and other members of the Montreal group, including Lise
Payette and Mireille Lafortune, a woman who would become Henry's
new lover, attended the trial. Gertie was there every day for the entire
six weeks. "I used to sit in the courtroom and just stare at the jury. I was
talking to them in my head. You can't convict. You can't. You can't."
Whenever there was a public demonstration, Gertie was one of the
women picking up the event posters and delivering them throughout
the city. At the end of the trial, the group published a fact sheet because
it thought the facts "have not been adequately reported." They really
meant that the facts had not been *accurately* reported. Henry, always
aware of the media world, knew that the reporter for *La Presse*, for
instance, usually covered trials. "That's why he emphasized all the neg-
atives." He considered *Le Journal* somewhat "sensationalist" generally,
and this was no exception.

The jury consisted of eleven men and one woman. The courtroom was presided over by Chief Justice James Hugessen, a senator's son, scion of a respected, long-established Quebec family and father of seven. The courtroom observers were evenly split between Henry's supporters and the anti-abortionists. They sat as far apart from each other as one courtroom would permit. Henry was charged with doing an abortion on a twenty-six-year-old student from Sierra Leone, whom police had picked up in the last raid. She was initially referred to as V in newspaper stories about the trial; then Verona Parkinson's identity was revealed in some of the French-language newspapers. One week into the proceedings, Sheppard revealed his trump card. Article 45 of the Criminal Code allowed surgical procedures to be done without criminal liability, as long as reasonable care and skill were taken and the operation benefited the patient. When Mr. Justice Hugessen ruled Article 45 admissible, Sheppard leaned over to Henry and whispered exuberantly, "You've just won your case."

He was proven right late in the afternoon of November 13. The jury had deliberated twenty-four hours. As they so often had during the trial, Henry and Mike had spent the down time playing chess on a board they had set up on the windowsill in the fourth-floor mezzanine outside the courtroom. Recently returned from a European trip, Eva Morgentaler, tall and elegant, "walked and talked, sometimes alone, sometimes with friends," Wright Pelrine wrote in an April 1974 article for *Chatelaine* magazine. Henry's wife now in name only, she had a lover in Australia. But if she didn't support her husband, she supported his cause. Goldie, twenty-three, studying journalism at Columbia, telephoned often from New York City. Eva and Henry had decided Bamie should go on his much-postponed pre-university trip to Europe. He had left the day before.

Everything Henry believed in was at stake, not only a woman's right to decide for herself whether to have an abortion, but also his much-tested faith in humanity. He always believed "No jury will ever convict me." He said it many times to supporters during the trial, and since then has repeated the words on hundreds, if not thousands, of more occasions. They've become worn, as much a cliché as the hundreds of photographs taken of Henry making the V-for-Victory sign with two fingers of his right hand. (Even back then, a close friend threatened to cut off his arm if he repeated "that corny gesture" again.[2]) But this was never just a sound bite or a good quote, brief and meaty. He did believe in juries, because juries were his fellows. "No jury will ever convict me" became his mantra; it was at the base of his obstinacy and courage. It was also his truth: no jury ever did convict him.

With the verdict came the pronouncements. "This verdict strips away the veil of hypocrisy surrounding our abortion law," Sheppard declared. "There will be an appeal," the prosecution declared. "You are all invited to come and celebrate with us tonight. This calls for champagne," Henry crowed. The next day photos of a joyful Henry lifting the puzzled, chubby infant of a supporter high into the air appeared in the newspapers. He told reporters he would invite the provincial and federal governments to use the facilities of his clinic. "This is a first in Canada. From now on, any doctor who has performed an abortion can invoke Article 45."[3]

But that same night a spokesman for Justice Minister Otto Lang, a known foe of Henry's, reserved any comment, noting Lang "might have something to say after all avenues of appeal have been explored."[4] A new anti-abortion group called Coalition for Life demanded Parliament amend the Criminal Code to protect the unborn child. Henry may have been a hero in the newspapers, but he was facing another twelve charges and he still had to obey bail conditions. He could travel, but he still wasn't allowed to hold press conferences or speak on radio or television about abortions. The conditions didn't say anything about participating in public meetings, so two weeks after the verdict and the night before his appeal to have bail lifted, Henry was in Toronto at the St. Lawrence Centre on a panel with MP Grace MacInnis and American feminist Flo Kennedy. That night the crowd overflowed onto the street and almost all the people were there for Henry. Outside a few women carried placards stating they were "Nurses Ashamed of Morgentaler," and at the entrance was a neon sign for a forthcoming event called, disconcertingly, Dance of Death. For a moment, Henry believed someone was out to kill him, and at the end of the night he did get a sealed envelope containing an unsettling note: "This is a curse. You will not live more than 24 hours." Billed as a panel discussion, the event was a celebration for the man who had made Canadian history in a most un-Canadian way. A member of the most respected profession in the land had used civil disobedience, not polite petitions or well-researched studies or earnest subcommittees or even officially sanctioned royal commissions, to overcome what Sheppard would call the "technical law." National media buzzed, wanting to know the who, but especially the why, of this man; not the issue, but the person. It was the beginning of the longest love affair Henry Morgentaler would ever have. That affair with the media lasts to this day.

By February 1974, Quebec authorities were ready to make their next move. This time the men at the door of the Champlain clinic were from the province's Department of Revenue, with a notice stating Henry owed more than $355,000 in back taxes. They froze all his assets and properties. It was a lethal move. Burdened by legal debt, prevented from doing abortions since January 29, when his bail hearing commenced, Henry feared he was at "the brink of financial ruin. But one of the conditions of bail was I couldn't do abortions. I was in limbo. I couldn't do anything. I didn't want to go to jail for a year just for disobeying a court injunction." All winter and into the spring, abortion repeal groups staged country-wide demonstrations. On January 26, they protested the upcoming appeal; on February 23, outraged people marched in Vancouver after Joanne Cornax was charged and police raided the office of Morgentaler-trained Dr. Robert Tanguay, charging him with eight counts of performing illegal abortions. And on March 9 in Ottawa, Henry himself led a noisy phalanx of his supporters from all over Canada to Parliament Hill during the Abortion Tribunal to Defend Dr. Morgentaler. Despite the public sound and fury, the motion to withdraw Henry's bail conditions was denied.

Then on April 26 came word from the Quebec Court of Appeal. The five Roman Catholic judges were unanimous. Henry Morgentaler was not innocent, as a jury had declared him to be, but guilty. He only heard the news when a radio reporter called him for his reaction. He was of course stunned. Like most observers, he had predicted the Court of Appeal would order another trial. The right to appeal a jury verdict of innocence existed in Canada but not in the U.S. or in Britain. Since 1930, Canada had also permitted a Court of Appeal to cancel a jury verdict and substitute its own. But this was the first time any Court of Appeal had ever done so. It was also the last time an Appeal Court would overrule a jury verdict of innocence — almost two years later a new federal justice minister, Ron Basford, would introduce a new law preventing a jury's decision to be overturned ever again, naming it the Morgentaler Amendment in Henry's honour — but that was neither relevant nor a consolation in 1974. Quebec's Court of Appeal also ordered that the case go back to Mr. Justice Hugessen for sentencing. Sheppard immediately launched an appeal to the Supreme Court of Canada, so Mr. Justice Hugessen refused to sentence Henry. The appeal court ordered Henry be detained until released on bail. According to Wright Pelrine, because Mr. Justice Hugessen had refused to sentence Henry, he also believed it was not his prerogative to grant him bail.

Thousands were outraged. On May 4, civil libertarians and ordinary citizens joined abortion rights activists in demonstrations, protests and press conferences in six cities organized by that area's Committee to Defend Dr. Morgentaler. On May 15, a protest took place outside the courthouse as Henry was ordered to jail. A shift in focus had occurred: the jury system, the bedrock of the British legal system, was under attack. Editorial writers, opinion makers, lawyers rose to defend that which they held dear in tones of stately sentiment. Sheppard stated Henry "single-handedly made us aware of the preciousness of how our jury system is. There's no more incredible or glorious page in the history of the jury system anywhere in the world."[5] Lost in the moment was the struggle for women's reproductive rights.

Henry spent ten days in Parthenais Detention Centre. "It was a dreadful place, a bit like Alcatraz. It was on the eleventh, twelfth and thirteenth floors of a big apartment building on Parthenais Street. You couldn't go outdoors — there were no walks. There were sixty cells in a few sections, all automatically controlled from outside. At certain moments they opened all the cells and it was time to have food or go back in before they suddenly closed it. If you didn't get in or out in time, it just remained closed. It was some invisible person pressing a button controlling you."

He blamed Quebec Crown Attorney Louis-Guy Robichaud for his detention, because Robichaud had made it clear he was personally committed to convicting abortionist Henry Morgentaler. (Henry took to calling him "Robichien.") Robichaud stalled the arrangement of court dates to work out a deal for bail. "At that time he hated me. He wanted me in jail badly. He was a mean sonuvabitch," Henry fumed. Once, later, Henry encountered Robichaud on the street. "He noticed, became red in the face and speeded up his walk. I walked behind him for a while, then I said, 'To hell with it.'"

On May 24, Henry was released and Hugessen had reconsidered his decision not to sentence Henry. It was almost a month later, on June 11 at a presentencing hearing, that Henry made, in part, this statement in court:

> I am about to be sentenced for having helped Verona P. to obtain a safe abortion in my clinic on August 15, 1973, after a jury of my peers declared on November 13, 1973, that it was no crime at all and declared me to be innocent.... Yet for this most natural and decent act, to help a person in distress, to offer help to a fellow human being when needed, I am now being threatened with life imprisonment. THERE IS SOMETHING AWFULLY WRONG HERE.

> Had I refused to help Verona P. in spite of my ability to do so, had I exposed her to the danger that she might commit suicide, to the dangers of self-induced abortion or those of back-alley butchery, to the mental stress and anguish of women grappling with the problems of unwanted pregnancies, then maybe I should have been reproached or even prosecuted. Certainly my conscience would bother me if nothing else. But I find it to be the height of injustice to be punished for an act of compassion, which is no crime at all, which I am proud of and which is the symbol and embodiment of everything that is decent, courageous and noble in me, where my mind, my heart and my guts were used in the service of fellow human beings.

In Toronto a full-page advertisement ran Thursday, June 13, in the *Globe and Mail* and the *Toronto Star*. Under the huge headline "Free Dr. Morgentaler" were the names of almost two hundred individuals and organizations and an announcement of a protest rally at the University of Toronto's Medical Sciences Auditorium two days later. Henry was there. "No one will ever make me believe this is a crime," he said, then marched alongside rally chair June Callwood south to Toronto's city hall. In two days he would be sentenced, yet that Saturday he was so starstruck, so thrilled to be marching alongside the well-known and respected journalist and activist Callwood, that he couldn't bring himself to say a word to her. They marched along in silence. On Monday, Mr. Justice Hugessen sentenced Henry to eighteen months in prison and an additional three years on probation, but released him on $25,000 bail, pending the Supreme Court decision. "I was so shocked about it, since I believed in Hugessen for so long, that during my vacation afterwards, I couldn't get it out of my mind. It was like a record playing all the time. I seemed to be arguing with Hugesson, trying to show him how he was wrong and injust," Henry told Eleanor Wright Pelrine.[6] He felt small, ineffectual and very much alone.

He didn't know help that would remain steadfast for decades would soon be coming to him from the most unlikely of sources. Ed Ratcliffe's fiefdom of home, horses and office could be seen from Highway 401 near Cambridge, Ontario. His company, Arriss Craft, made angel stone — the grey, glittery aggregate so many builders lined up under the picture windows of all the L-shaped bungalows and split-level ranch homes they built in suburbia in the fifties, sixties and seventies. Ratcliffe had made a lot of money, so much that he could spend it as he wished. In 1962, he offered Sherri Finkbine the money to go to Sweden to have her abortion. He was on just about every newscast, but it was no publicity stunt. It never had anything to do with ego. Opinionated, hard-headed, Ratcliffe was disgusted with the lawmakers. "I'll pay your transportation to a more enlightened jurisdiction," he said to the American Finkbine via the media. "I'm sorry our own province doesn't have the facilities." However, Finkbine declined his offer.

Ratcliffe had the same reaction when he read about Henry's acquittal being overturned by the appeal court in Quebec. "I said, 'You can't do this with a jury appeal,' and I got on a train." Ratcliffe, who belonged to Planned Parenthood, had first heard of Henry when Henry made his presentation to the health and welfare standing committee in 1967, but the two had never met. Henry took him to a Humanist meeting, then to dinner at Moishe's Steak House. Ed said he paid for the meal. "It was the only time I have seen him financially strapped." Then Ratcliffe wrote out a cheque for $10,000. Just like that. No fanfare, no strings. "I liked what he was doing and he was the only one doing it," he said. Then he went back to Cambridge and began phoning a few people he knew — Eleanor Wright Pelrine among them. "I wanted to see if we could get something going to back this guy up." There were plenty of committees already — ad hoc defence organizations that had sprung up before and during the trial — but despite their august nomenclatures, they were all pretty powerless and definitely penniless. Even the stellar Toronto Committee to Defend Dr. Morgentaler was having its troubles. On August 17, co-ordinating committee member Heidi Fischer sent out a letter appealing for funds. "The support for our past projects has been tremendous. Between June 1st and August 15 . . . we recieved [sic] more than $3100.00 Our expenses approximately equalled this," she wrote.

Everyone knew the campaign was at a critical juncture. The Supreme Court hearings, Henry's last chance, had been set for October, but, Fischer wrote in the same letter, "Justice Minister Otto Lang's recent attacks on abortion — referring to the right of women to control their own bodies as 'silly' — has made it clear that he doesn't care what the majority of Canadians think. Despite statements about his determination to 'protect fetuses' and his office's instructions to hospitals to cut back in the availability of abortion, he remains the Justice Minister in the new government."

Ratcliffe was impatient. Before he met Henry, he'd written a couple of cheques to the Morgentaler Defence Committee in Hamilton and Toronto — probably for $5,000 each, Ratcliffe wasn't sure — to sustain their work. He also had written to A.R. Kaufman, the birth control advocate from Kitchener, Ontario, asking for his support for Henry. Kaufman sent back a cheque for $1,000, commenting that Henry had taken referrals for vasectomies from an organization he'd set up in Quebec called Parents Information Bureau, but that he thought it "unfortunate for Dr. Morgentaler that he agreed to broadcast the abortion operation." Ratcliffe wrote Kaufman back July 23, thanking him for his contribution, adding, somewhat wryly, "I've only spent about $20,000 so far" in the fight to legalize abortion.

Already Ratcliffe was thinking bigger. Henry's supporters shouldn't have to be continually fund-raising. He was willing to keep writing the cheques if his money would float an organized group working flat out and full-time to lobby Parliament to legalize abortion on demand. About a year earlier, on June 20, Wright Pelrine and some friends, including Henry and Callwood, had met in Toronto — once — as the Canadian Association for the Repeal of the Abortion Law, with a stated purpose of informing the public and members of Parliament about the inequities of the abortion law. As Ratcliffe subsequently noted, "At [that] time you were talking about losing your respectability...to come out and talk about abortion." One night he met with a man "supposedly on the inside in Ottawa with Trudeau" at the home of York University professor and abortion rights activist Esther Greenglass. "Look, everybody's really behind you on this," Ratcliffe remembered the man saying, "but the Right to Life are organized all over the country and you people are acting like amateurs. Why don't you get an organization going and we'll have somebody to listen to and react to?"

They recycled the CARAL (Canadian Association for the Repeal of the Abortion Law) name early in the fall of 1974. Ratcliffe hired Wright Pelrine as the national secretary, rented a small office on Church Street in Toronto, where his daughter also worked. CARAL would be a national body, communicating with ARCAL, all the Morgentaler Defence Committees and other freedom-of-choice organizations. Ratcliffe wanted to hold an organizing national meeting in Ottawa before Christmas. Women were more than willing and ready. "I think the feeling of women's groups everywhere was we were willing to rally around anybody talking about the rights of women to have access to abortion in those days," said Ratcliffe's wife, Elinor, who lived in Newfoundland then and was active in the cause. She met Ratcliffe when she came to the CARAL meeting that fall. "We didn't have enough money in those days to pay the telephone bills, but there were plenty of women who were aware of Morgentaler and his fight for our rights."

On October 4 shortly after lunch, Henry's hearing at the Supreme Court of Canada began. He was banking everything on it; he was that sure the jury acquittal would be upheld and the law exposed as cruel and barbaric. He had already begun to think about what he would do next. In an article that had appeared December 31, 1973, he told *Toronto Star* reporter Judy Creighton that his wish for the new year (1974) would be to give up carrying out the operations because "I've been doing them so long." Now that he was well known, he had so many other causes he wanted to promote. Only the fight to obtain a woman's right to abortion interested him, not the actual mundane procedure itself.

But from the beginning, their case faltered. "Sheppard had been brilliant before the jury. Here, before the Supreme Court, he was a chastened little boy, determined to recite every last word of the oration he had memorized," wrote Wright Pelrine.[7] In retrospect, Henry agreed with the assessment. "I don't think he did a very good job, but I'm not sure it would have made any difference. I think the judges' positions were already made up." The presentations by the well-known and successful criminal lawyer Eddie Greenspan on behalf of the Canadian Civil Liberties Association, and by Clayton Ruby for a one-time-only group founded by Ratcliffe called the Foundation for Women in Crisis (Ruby went as far as to say Section 251 violated the rights of Canadian women and physicians.) appeared to have little positive affect on the judges. The hearing was over in one week and Henry could legally do nothing but wait. However, he could legally return to his work.

In November he toured the West, speaking to sold-out, overflowing university crowds in Calgary, Edmonton and Vancouver. Adrenaline pumping, he would be escorted past the anti-abortion picketers outside the hall where he was appearing. In Calgary picketers distributed leaflets that read "Abortion-on-demand laws give to one person (the mother) the legal right to kill another (the baby) in order to solve the first person's social problems." They showed photos of fetuses. They brandished placards: "Morgentaler, Murderer" and "You had a chance to live. Why shouldn't they?"

Henry was impervious; the signs, the protestors, actually calmed him. He was back in the fray. From a podium, on a stage, he could answer them, make his points, be reasonable, plead for the women of Canada — everything he had been unable to do in all those courtrooms.

At the University of Alberta on November 8, 1974, he received a standing ovation from more than a thousand people as he blasted Justice Minister Otto Lang, a Roman Catholic, for being "more of a theologian than a minister of justice."[8] The donations of money for his legal bills littered one corner of the stage. Back on June 13, he had successfully debated Alliance for Life president Dr. Heather Morris for Pierre Berton's popular television show "The Great Debate." That same evening (June 13) delegates from the law profession and the medical profession, and "clergymen" (as the meeting minutes described them), had gathered at Toronto's Westbury Hotel. The topic? How to support Henry Morgentaler. Clayton Ruby had wanted to ask candidates in the forthcoming election to endorse changing the law; others had wanted to form committees to work on the media; one — psychiatrist Gus Tolentino — was getting international support for Henry. Lawyer (now Judge) Rosalie Abella had wanted to approach a government women's organization to do a survey. Those at the meeting all had agreed to work on running a full-page newspaper ad supporting Henry.

Nevertheless, it wasn't enough for Henry. He needed constant action and he needed crowds. The cause had become his entire life, and with a few exceptions such as Mauriello, almost all of his friends were his supporters. When there were no marches, rallies or court dates, his life and those of his supporters rarely intersected, convincing Henry he was alone in his fight. "There was a deafening silence from most of my supporters and friends.... Some friends seemed to avoid me, as though they didn't know what to say to me," he told Wright Pelrine.[9] And having a friendship with Henry was awkward for some. Because the women's cause of free abortion on demand had come to rest with the fate of one man, many considered Henry a symbol or a figurehead. For them it was difficult to forge a friendship with a hero. As well, Henry never did comprehend that for many of them friendship wasn't only fighting shoulder to shoulder, but also sitting face to face. Some of his interpersonal blueprints needed redesigning, but he was too depressed. Now that the tour in the West was over the pace of life had slowed. He missed the crowds of well-wishers, the crush of photographers aiming their lenses on him, the reporters, notebooks in hand, wanting a word from him. Yet he still had many people around him, including Gertie and Mike and his children. Eva was often in Australia with her lover, but Henry also had a new romantic relationship. University psychology professor Mireille Lafortune had written Henry a short note after his acquittal. As an abortion rights activist, she was thrilled by his win. She was interested in what he had to say about humanism. Could they talk sometime? Lafortune was sensitive, intelligent and often pugnacious in her beliefs, with many friends in Montreal's progressive circles. Henry fell fast.

Still, he continued to fight depression. He tried to escape into books and movies, but leisure was something he has always believed he must first earn, and as much as he tried to convince himself otherwise, this enforced leisure was a numbing reminder that once again, others were in control of his fate. Henry had to arrange with Harvard, where Bamie was studying on a partial scholarship, to temporarily defer payment. He borrowed from Ed Ratcliffe and from Dr. Robert Makaroff, another Vancouver doctor also convicted of performing illegal abortions. Makaroff had pleaded guilty. He had told a Vancouver courtroom on September 19, 1970, that he had performed so many abortions for three years — in an attempt to meet the demand — he had driven himself close to exhaustion. Makaroff served a three-month prison term and paid a $15,000 fine. Henry acknowledged that Makaroff's experience was not inspiring, as he listlessly went through the motions, alternating between despair and faith and between Mike's apartment and Mireille's place, avoiding his Barton Street house. Mike was relatively immune to Henry's cash-flow crisis because his salary had always come from the real-estate revenues. The only person remaining on staff at the clinic was Trudy Martens, Henry's receptionist-secretary, who had become involved with Mike. Trudy kept telling Henry to go back into general practice, until finally he sent out about a thousand carefully worded notices. But there was no going back. Perhaps sensing Henry's heart wasn't in being a GP, few responded to the notices.

CARAL's upcoming national meeting on November 18, 1974, in Ottawa was the only bright spot on his horizon. "Henry was our symbol. It was all built around Henry," Ratcliffe recalled. But first they had to build the basics and change some of the semantics. "The organization which regards itself as pro-repeal and civil libertarian, not pro-abortion, last night reiterated its statement of purpose," Wright Pelrine wrote in the November 19 press release announcing CARAL's existence. This distinction was integral to their repositioning. Later they would come to be known as pro-choice, further broadening the semantic context of their position. "The purpose of CARAL is to ensure that no woman is denied access to safe, legal abortion in Canada. Our aim is the repeal of all sections of the Criminal Code dealing with abortion, and the establishment of comprehensive contraceptive and abortion services across the country. We regard the right to safe legal abortions as a fundamental human right."

Henry, Mireille and Gertie drove to Ottawa to be at the Monday-evening inaugural session of CARAL, held in the gym of the Académie de Lasalle, a Catholic high school. The place was packed — suspiciously so, Ratcliffe thought. He had anticipated (and paid the way for) about a hundred people from across the country, but about twice that number were there that night. Henry already knew many of the friendlier faces, such as that of psychiatrist Wendell Watters, a fellow Humanist and an enthusiastic proponent of abortion on demand. As clinical director of psychiatry at St. Joseph's Hospital in Hamilton, Watters had created a rotating system of psychiatrists available to write "those stupid damn letters" for women wanting abortions. Before the law changed and therapeutic abortion committees were created, women needed a letter from a psychiatrist. "While we all knew it was stupid, we had to do it for the woman to get her abortion. Women would come in to see us and ask for the abortion psychiatrist." Watters had been rethinking his profession:

> I was raised on psychiatry from a very traditional psychoanalytical viewpoint. Psychoanalysis doesn't go very deeply into social issues,

and for good reason, I think, because if you have somebody in psychoanalysis the goal is to help them become more and more
responsible for their lives, and not take refuge in blaming other
people. So you don't want to get involved on focusing on social
injustice. It's there, of course, but if you focus on that during the
treatment of the individual you're going to give the individual
too many outs. So it was difficult for me to realize that you
can be involved in social issues that affect people and still not
make the mistake of blaming society for your foibles and short-
comings. Once I could make the distinction between the two I
was like a kid in the candy shop in the early seventies. The
abortion issue was tailor-made. I did not like the role psychiatry was being forced into. We were supposed to decide which
unwanted children should be born and which shouldn't be born.
It sounded to me like a position nobody should be in, and I
rejected it outright.

Although abortions were not performed at his hospital, the psychiatrists
there, on principle, always wrote letters supporting the woman's position.
   But when another doctor in the audience that night stood up and
began to say, "Since we're all friends here I would like to tell you how
many abortions I've been doing," Watters interrupted him. "Let me
correct you, Doctor. I'm not sure we all are among friends here." Ratcliffe solved the problem by announcing the second half of the meeting
would start right after the break and would be for members only; that
is, those who had signed a membership form and paid their $10. After
the break, the room was about half as full. The remaining people discussed the next day's lobbying of all members of Parliament. The CARAL
meeting then moved to the Château Laurier. Elinor Ratcliffe, then Elinor
Neubauer, remembered being partnered with a trusting doctor: "He
introduced himself that day to all the politicians by saying, 'I'm Ken
Walker and I've done five thousand abortions.'" Ken Walker was then
an obstetrician-gynecologist in Niagara Falls, who performed abortions
every Wednesday afternoon. And every Wednesday afternoon, Right-
to-Lifers from St. Catharines and environs would come by bus to picket

him. Later he wrote a popular medical newspaper column under the pen name of Gifford-Jones. Under his own byline he now writes a bi-weekly column for *The Medical Post* called "Doctor to Doctor" in which he has often featured Henry.

Walker was one of a handful of members on the original steering committee of a fledgling group called DRAL, Doctors For Repeal of the Abortion Law. Watters was also on the committee, along with another psychiatrist, Dr. Stuart Smith, who would become the leader of the provincial Liberals in 1976. Another DRAL member was Dr. Linda Rapson, now an acupuncturist and pain specialist, who had signed the petition-telegram drafted by June Callwood and Pierre Berton. "I must have put M.D. after my name, because not long afterwards I got a letter from a Wendell Watters from Hamilton, asking me to be on this committee for doctors," she recalled. Rapson said she had been "complacent" for the first few years after the 1969 abortion laws because few women had any trouble getting abortions at the east-end Toronto hospital where she then worked. "I remember walking through the foyer with a pal of mine, the head of the TAC, kibbitzing. When I asked him where he was going, he said, 'Abortion committee meeting,' and pretending to reach into his pocket added, 'here's the rubber stamp.'"

But then one of Rapson's patients, who had three of her own children and the responsibility for the children of a sister who had died, had received bad contraceptive advice from a doctor and become pregnant. That doctor told her to make an appointment with Dr. Heather Morris. Thinking it was for an abortion, she did. "Dr. Morris will look after you," she was told. Rapson remembers the woman sitting in her office afterwards, almost shrieking in frustration, "Dr. Morris will look after me? Who will look after the baby?" Rapson got her the appointment for the abortion, but she realized, "There are a lot of Heather Morrises in this world, and this woman would not have been able to get an appointment if she had not had the persistence to try elsewhere. That hooked me into carrying the banner." With Kate, the elder of her two daughters, Rapson marched in the June rally, part of the crowd led by Callwood and Henry. Linda carried a sign saying "Morgentaler and Machabee. Set them free." Kate, who was just starting school, wondered who or what a Machabee was. "Twenty-five years later I'm still carry-ing the banner," Rapson said, laughing.

She decided to go to Ottawa for the first CARAL meeting, and tele-phoned the elder sister of one of her best childhood friends, telling her to come, too. "I was the suburban mother of five kids. I was terrified," recalled Norma Scarborough. The only other meeting like it she had ever attended was a conference on strategy for social change. She'd been so intimidated that she'd spent most of the conference in the hallway or just inside the doorway. Before she left for Ottawa, Scarborough phoned about ten teaching hospitals throughout Toronto, giving them all the same fictitious story: she was forty, a mother of five and pregnant. Could she have an abortion? "Each hospital had a different story. At one I had to have two psychiatrists. Another said my husband had to agree." At the CARAL meeting, she stood up and reported her home-spun survey. Scarborough was immediately elected to the executive, where she stayed for the next nineteen years.

Henry met both Scarborough and Rapson at that first CARAL meet-ing. What he didn't know then was that each woman, in her own way, would change his life. Scarborough was beside him through a decade of struggles and legal battles — for four years she wrote a letter to a mem-ber of Parliament or some sort of official every single lunch hour of her working day — and Rapson told her husband about the small, obsessed, relentless, courageous abortionist. Rapson was married to Morris Manning, the lawyer who would take Henry all the way to his second, and very different, appointment with the Supreme Court of Canada.

CHAPTER 9

PRISONER #118658

TELEVISION CAMERAS and Ed Ratcliffe greeted Henry at Toronto's airport midmorning on Wednesday, March 26, 1975.

"Hi, Ed!" Ever the consummate performer, Henry hailed the tall, silver-haired man in the bowtie as if he had not noticed the film crew, bright lights, camera cables or curious bystanders.

His friends in Montreal had ordered him to get out of town. They all knew this was the morning the Supreme Court would release its verdict. One way or another, Henry should not be available when word hit the street. So he, Mireille and his daughter, Goldie, were in the air somewhere between Montreal and Toronto when the decision came down. It was left to Ratcliffe, an engineer of few words, all plainly spoken, to deliver the blow.

"The appeal is rejected." Ed shoved an oversized yellow daisy at Henry.

"What appeal is rejected?"

Behind his dark-rimmed glasses, Henry's eyes darted fearfully. Goldie's hands shot up to her face as she pressed against her father's back. Mireille's gum-chewing grin faded quickly. Someone gave her a white carnation, which she gripped as the horrifying news sank in.

"That's all I've got," Ratcliffe replied.

"Whose appeal is rejected?" Henry couldn't believe it.

"Your appeal is rejected."

"Do I have to go to prison?" Henry's voice cracked; the courageous facade finally slipped. He was frightened and confused. This time there was no talk of outrage, anger, justice and his fight for the women of Canada.

"More news coming," Ratcliffe said. "I thought I ought to tell you that much. I couldn't do anything else."

Still Henry didn't seem to comprehend. Then he pulled himself together and shrugged. "Yeah, well, okay."

In a six to three decision, the Supreme Court of Canada had upheld the Quebec Court of Appeal's decision. Henry was guilty of performing an illegal abortion and he would have to go to jail. At Wright Pelrine's Toronto house he prepared for the press conference CARAL had previously scheduled at the Westbury Hotel.

"My conscience is clear. My only regret is that, at this time, women in this country are still suffering. They are exposed unnecessarily to anguish, stress and danger of death and injury because of a restrictive law, which in theory tells them they can have an abortion if they need to, and in practice denies them this right." At the packed press conference, he said all the right things, but the fire was out; his voice was weary.

Goldie, long, blond hair falling over her shaking shoulders, wept and hugged her father as he patted her back. She stroked his damp forehead as he got out a folded cloth handkerchief, took off his glasses and wiped his face. Later, as newspaper photographers took their close-ups, Goldie stood beside her father, one arm hung protectively over his shoulder. But she was angry. "I just don't understand how a thing like this can happen. If a jury's decision can be turned over just like that, there's something wrong and we're in trouble. I don't want to live in a country that can do such a terrible thing. Maybe I'll apply to the States for political asylum," she told one reporter.[1] As she spoke, Mike and Trudy were flying in from Montreal, Bamie from Boston. The next day they would all return to Montreal so Henry could turn himself in.

On the front steps of Police Station No. 4, Henry was his public self again. As women hastily assembled by Gertie marched and sang "We Shall Overcome," he smiled and waved a bouquet of flowers. He announced he'd spend his time usefully, writing his memoirs (which he never finished) and reading *Civil Disobedience* by Henry Thoreau (which he never started). His lapel button — Why Not Repeal Section 251 — had been designed and paid for by Ratcliffe. Henry said, "I hope this will spur people into action. I hope enough people will feel indignant about the decision." Later Bamie would say, "This isn't an abstract idea. There's something real going on here."[2] But his father had never been able to differentiate the two. The abstract was his reality. And Henry knew he was going to jail because he hadn't played by the rules — either set of rules: not only had he performed abortions without the say-so of a committee, but he had persisted in going public and political with it. Henry's clinic had, quite literally, attracted the best clientele in the city. The wives and daughters of some of the politicians and police officers responsible for the situation he was in now had availed themselves of his services. He knew it; usually they knew it. And that's the way it might have remained had he not pushed the envelope. Henry hated the hypocrisy for all the right reasons, but also because it demeaned him and what he was doing. And Henry had to believe that what he was doing was noble.

"There was a sadness [about him], but I can't remember any fear," said Gertie. "I remember we hugged at the police station. I wanted to shake him [and ask], 'How could you do this to us?'"

At the station Gertie kept a protective arm around Bamie, who seemed lost. Eva Morgentaler was out of the country; no one was at Barton Street to go home to. "He was hurting a lot," says a family friend. But Bamie was also a resilient young man, accustomed to looking after himself, turning what might be construed as neglect into a plus, becoming independent, popular, a leader, although only with the help of the families of some of his closer friends. Since the age of fifteen, he had usually been alone in the big house on Barton. "After the fact I can see it might have been a hard time. It's not something I would recommend for my own kids," he said later, "but then I wasn't aware of any hardship. My parents were having their troubles. Both were busy and travelled a lot. My mom was in Australia, and I took care of myself a lot and I got a lot out of it. I coped very well with it."

Henry was the one most of the people at the station that cold and wet afternoon were worried about. How would he be able to withstand prison? Later, he shook with fear as he was being driven away to prison. While his father had been incarcerated outside Lodz, his mother had visited him weekly, but Henry had never accompanied her. As a member of the youth branch of the Bund he might well have been arrested, "but I never asked to go with her.... I was scared. I know now I was scared.... [A]nd my father was taken from prison and shot on my birthday."

It took almost another decade before Henry would admit to his fear. He did it when re-enacting his ride to prison for the National Film Board documentary-maker Paul Cowan. *Democracy on Trial* was a docudrama in which Henry, Mike and Sheppard played themselves with a certain gusto and a certain number of liberties. Inexplicably, and despite Henry's objections, when Cowan recreated the scene at the airport in which Ratcliffe tells Henry the news of the Supreme Court's decision, he moved the locale to Montreal and changed the messenger to Mike. Mike somewhat overplays his part of protector as he dismisses the media horde and leads Henry away. (Ratcliffe said he ducked out of the film by deliberately going out for a sandwich when they were filming that part.) But Mike was restrained compared with a grinning Henry, dressed in striped prison pyjamas, waving his push broom in the air for the camera, as he recreated the ten months he spent incarcerated. Because of his experiences in the concentration camps, Henry had never again worn anything striped. "But this was acting, which is never as hard as reality. I was out of it. I had freedom of action," he said. So, for the sake of the story and because he loved the acting, he wore the striped garb for the scene. The truth was the prison system nearly broke him, although not initially. He sent out pages of badly typed single-spaced letters to friends, which were widely circulated, as he had anticipated and expected them to be.

To Gertie, Henry wrote:

I'm late in answering, but better late than never... I got your letter to the paper [to the editor]. I thought it was terrific. June Callwood drew my attention to it. I'm slowly settling into prison life, not without difficulty. It is as if you have to develop a whole new set of reflexes almost the same way as when you arrive in a concentration camp, where almost all the rules of civilized behaviour have been thrown overboard and you have to start from scratch and learn new techniques of survival. You have to keep your dignity and self-esteem intact at the same time. You have no right to kiss your wife here — you have no right to pick up the telephone — you have no right to go anywhere without a pass. Here are a few rules as an example of the kind of new convict society we have to live under. Of course you are familiar with the oppressive atmosphere prevailing here. My sense of humour is a great help occasionally. I even composed a hymn devoted to the institution, entitled "O How I Love Bordeaux Jail," to be sung to the tune of "O What a Beautiful Morning."

I'm gratified at the tremendous response from people across the country but am rather pessimistic about the success of the campaign to release me.

I've been screwed by the system a bit too much to have much faith in the responsiveness of the powers in place to public opinion. I think only something really strong and sustained might have an effect. I'm mentally digging in for a long siege and hardening my soul and my feelings to be able to withstand the little and big indignities that are part of prison life here.

Could you send me some selected books of poetry? I will let you be my guide in that area . . . I do write the occasional poem and it is a wonderful release.

. . . Give my best to all our friends, especially those devoted to our cause. By the way, I received a beautiful letter from Sally McLaughlin [a member of the Committee for Neutral Schools], which gave me quite a lift. All the best to Carl, Shary and Linda. I'm sending a poem by an inmate here. Tell me what you think of it.

> Cordially, affectionately
> Henry

Ed Ratcliffe still has copies of the letters sent him from Henry. He reprinted parts of them in CARAL news bulletins and sent them to everyone he knew. He was outraged by Henry's incarceration and how he was being treated; he knew Henry wrote the letters to fuel widespread public indignation:

> ...It is obvious that my only hope is that public opinion will sweep away both this iniquitous law and the sentence by forcing the Government to commute my sentence; occasionally I am quite sceptical about this; from time to time I get my hopes up — the eternal optimist, always hoping for the best inspite [sic] of evidence to the contrary — Mireille thinks I am a dreamer and Eleanor [Wright Pelrine] thinks I am naive in believing that if my cause is right and my motivation noble nothing bad can happen to me. They are both partly right. It is true that in spite of my intimate knowledge of Evil (concentration camp, vendetta of reactionary forces here against me) I have retained a belief in the basic goodness of Man, or at least in the potential for Goodness and a feeling that we have to cultivate this potential. I do trust people too much in general; occasionally I get burned, but on the other hand it permits me to develop easy and very friendly relations with most people. In prison here I am getting along splendidly with most prisoners and many guards. There are only a few of the brass who do not like me because I insist on my rights and on my human dignity and I have already had a number of conflicts about this. 2 days ago I was put in solitary confinement for 4 days in my cell on denunciation by 2 guards. After I wrote an indignant letter to the director and asked for a hearing to present my case I was released after 24 hours. The atmosphere here is really oppressive. It must be one of the worst prisons in Canada; even in penitentiary they have better conditions than here. Everything here seems designed to break the morale and spirit of the prisoner; the limit on visits, the separation by a thick glass from visitors, the listening in by guards into your private conversations on the phone (limited to two per week), the rags they think is prison garb (unpressed, torn and bespattered by paint), the hurried eating of food (average of 10–25 minutes per meal — if you have not finished the guard

hurries you along even though you still have food on your plate.)
I could go on listing the things. As you know, Mireille's health is
not very good. One evening I asked for an additional telephone
to call her as I was worried about her. One of the chiefs flatly
refused me.

...I am getting a lot of mail from all parts of the country;
many wonderful letters that help me keep my spirits up; up to now
I have only received three mildly abusive letters. In spite of all the
support I sometimes get the sinking feeling that somehow all this
might be of no avail; people will get tired of writing letters of
protest; the summer months are coming and I will have to linger
here behind these terrible walls and fight every day for the survival
of my soul and dignity.

It does not help that I am in the power of my sworn enemies,
Jerome Choquette and Otto Lang — I do not expect much from
them, only the worst.

I am also worried about my ability to ensure a continuing education for my children — the Quebec Revenue Dept. seems determined to choke me by refusing to deal with me, my lawyers are
confronted with a brick wall and stalling tactics all the way — in
the meantime my assets are frozen and it looks like personal bankruptcy might be the only way out eventually.

Two days later, on May 3, Henry wrote another letter, this time
of a more direct nature, addressed generically to "Dear Friend" and distributed by Ratcliffe to everyone on the CARAL mailing list, media
and beyond:

...My only hope is that my friends outside, the public, public opinion, will help me. My morale and spirit are not broken and they
will not easily break; but I am worried and concerned about the
immediate future. I know I could ease the situation and plead
guilty so that I might get concurrent sentences. This would save
me stress, expense and aggravation. But it is against all my principles to plead guilty to something which is not a crime.... If you

believe, as I do, that the right to a safe medical abortion is a fundamental human right, and if you want me to continue to fight
for this right and to help me personally against all the forces of
reaction who want to destroy me, I appeal to you to help me
financially so that I may be able to defend myself in court. Should
a situation arise that I may not need the money thus offered me
I promise hereby to transfer it to the appropriate organisations
fighting for women's rights or civil liberties... I must say I am
reluctant to make this appeal. If I do it, it is because I am pushed
to the wall by your enemies and because I am not fighting for
myself alone.... Please help me to continue the fight for justice,
humanity and sanity.

> Henry Morgentaler, M.D., Prisoner #118658,
> Bordeaux Jail, Montreal.

Along with the letter Ratcliffe sent a plea for funds for CARAL, and
got a favourable response.

Other public figures of the day were making known their outrage
over Henry Morgentaler's imprisonment. In April the council chair for
the Ontario Advisory Council on the Status of Women, Laura Sabia,
declared, "Dr. Henry Morgentaler wouldn't have been sent to jail if
he had been French — but he's a Jew."[3] She urged members of the
National Council of Jewish Women to each send a letter of protest to
Lang, Trudeau, Choquette and Marc Lalonde, who was the minister
responsible for the status of women.

Nevertheless, Henry was becoming desperate. After the first few
days back in the Parthenais, he had been transferred to Bordeaux Jail, a
fortresslike, grim structure resembling the Pentagon from the air and
patrolled by machine gun–wielding guards. Bare light bulbs shone
overhead twenty-four hours a day and the cells held an uncovered toilet and a hard, narrow bunk. Henry believed he could handle the physical hardships. What rankled him most were the small indignities —
when authorities confiscated his chess set [the pieces had metal strips],
removed his radio [because of its built-in cassette player], limited his
phone calls to two a week and in-person visits to only once weekly.

The prisoner routines were "deadly." Henry worked in the library, where he wanted to be, but "having to ask permission to ask permission" was galling, and he had already signalled to those in charge he was not going to be a compliant model prisoner. He hypnotized a couple of the prisoners, more for the entertainment value than anything else. But that pleased him, because the subject has to trust the hypnotist for the process to work, and Henry wanted to be trusted by these men. (He himself has never been hypnotized — "I trust, but only to a certain level. I need to be in control.") He circulated a petition, signed by every man inside, calling for "contact visits," in which the prisoner and visitor could be in the same room, not separated by glass or mesh; private telephone conversations; even conjugal visits. "The officials didn't like me. They thought I had too much influence and they didn't like my constant badgering."

The imprisoned men inside did. Henry gave them medical and psychological advice. They respected him for that and for his attitude. Once, after his release, when he ran into a couple of his fellow cons at a gas station, they said to him, "You walked around as if you owned the prison." He must have made his mark: years later, prison authorities turned down Paul Cowan's request to film scenes for *Democracy on Trial* on the actual premises. So they shot Henry re-enacting his incarceration in a derelict prison facility. As the cameras swooped in, Henry hissed at the actors playing the guards he had so despised back then, and beat them off with a furious, scornful swing of an arm as they closed in on him to remove him to solitary confinement. In the film, Henry lay naked on a cot in solitary (one leg strategically bent), glaring and unbroken.

But that was not exactly how it had happened. Prison authorities had pounced on Henry at their first opportunity. An argument Henry had with a supervisor in the library prison gave them their opening. Admittedly, Henry had goaded the man. "I think all I said to him was 'You are going to be here forever, but I'm going to get out of here.'" Henry was brought before a kangaroo court of three officials, who found him guilty and put him in deadlock, confining him to his cell for twenty-four hours. Henry immediately snapped off a letter to the warden, saying the charges were fabricated and unless he was immediately released from deadlock he would go to the media. He was out that evening.

The media were keeping a close watch on Henry, who was out of sight but still a headline maker. His friends and followers were making sure of that. Former prime minister John Diefenbaker had called on cabinet to release Henry. The National Advisory Council on the Status of Women asked Parliament to grant Henry a full pardon. The American Humanist Paul Kurtz organized a petition calling for Henry's release. And a Toronto-based group, Amnesty for Dr. Morgentaler, comprised of writers (Callwood, Berton), members of Parliament (Tory Flora MacDonald and Gordon Fairweather), the Toronto mayor David Crombie and the Ontario Federation of Labour president David Archer called for Henry to be freed, as well. Meanwhile, CARAL had stepped up its lobbying. Ed Ratcliffe had personally sent Trudeau a telegram asking for Henry's release, and published two editions of a pamphlet featuring Henry's picture and prison number. "The first was to get sympathy and the second was after he was moved [to Waterloo, another prison facility], to get money and tell people where to write," Ratcliffe said. An international defence committee for Henry had been set up, as well as a trust fund, administered by lawyer Clayton Ruby, to collect donations for his legal defence.

But Prime Minister Pierre Trudeau and Justice Minister Lang refused to consider any action. The authorities also wouldn't release him from jail to allow him to receive the American Humanist Association award for the Humanist of the Year, to be presented on May 24 in St. Louis, Missouri. (He shared the honours with the feminist author Betty Friedan.) Henry "was no hero. He got what he deserved," Choquette snapped to reporters. Lang was as disparaging: "Anybody can form a club." Trudeau hailed Henry as a "fine humanitarian" and told reporters in Belleville, Ontario, he'd known Henry personally for twenty years "and he's a humanist in the good sense of the word. But I don't agree with his views on abortions."[4] In fact, Henry and Trudeau had corresponded on the abortion issue until 1970, the year after Section 251 was passed, when Trudeau stopped answering Henry's letters.

Then, even though Choquette had told a reporter from Canadian Press that Henry had "been humiliated enough. I don't plan to press the other charges for now,"[5] he was hauled back into court. Again he refused to plead guilty, even though Sheppard urged him to, believing it would be in the interest of deal making. After another court summons, a court date for a second charge of performing an illegal abortion was set: Henry's trial would commence May 26 and he would be again tried by a French-speaking jury. The Saturday before Henry was to appear in court, the Ottawa chapter of CARAL held one more huge rally on Parliament Hill, demanding freedom for Dr. Henry Morgentaler. Representatives from CARAL, the Humanists, DRAL, Carleton University's School of Social Work and others met at 1 p.m. on May 24 in front of the Supreme Court of Canada building at Wellington and Kent and marched through the Spark Street Mall to the Hill. Rita McNeil sang, and overhead a plane buzzed, trailing a banner with the words "Justice Now for Morgentaler and Women." Betty Friedan, author of *The Feminine Mystique* and one of the founders of the American group the National Association for Abortion Rights, came to Montreal the Monday of the court date, along with some Humanists, in a foiled attempt to present Henry with his Humanist of the Year award in the courtroom.

Less than two weeks before the award was to be presented, Henry had suddenly been transferred to Waterloo, a minimum security rehabilitation centre. This seemingly benevolent act was out of context, given that Choquette had recently renewed the legal attack on Henry. But June Callwood had received a letter from Henry in which he sounded so besieged, beleaguered and physically ill she had become alarmed. "I was surprised when Henry wrote because I hadn't thought I was very close to him but then there was a crescendo of letters from Henry. The letters began to be almost deranged," Callwood recalled. "He wrote about taunting the guards. I became so worried about him in prison as a Holocaust survivor; I had the impression [from the letters] Henry was determined to push his jailers into hitting him. I hardly knew Jim Coutts but I called him and said I was afraid Henry was going to taunt the guards into beating him." Coutts was a Trudeau aide.

The next day Henry found out he was moving. In a May 17 letter he wrote how he

> had gotten used to the stinking old place [Bordeaux], and it had
> become home to me — I had my friends there, my work, if
> you can call it work, my battles fought and won. My status as
> a celebrity, confidant to many, medical and psychological advisor,
> hypnotist, gadfly, Ping-Pong champion, chess champion, fighter
> for prisoners' rights, my pet enemies among the medical staff and
> some of the brass. Everything, you might say to endear the
> place to me. And then there is always the stress of the moving,
> as described by Solzhenitzyn in *[The] Gulag [Archipelago]*
> when the trauma of moving from one camp to another is so
> vividly described.
>
>   Inevitably you have to go through some invasion of privacy
> again when you move.... Just the day before I left a friend had
> made me a sort of filing cabinet for all my papers and letters,
> and I had to leave it behind. The big problem was to move all
> my books. The guards were amazed at the number. Intellectuals
> must have books, I said....[6]

By this time Henry's petition [for contact visits] had 105 signatories and he wanted to deliver it to the prison director before he left. The man was too busy to see Henry; he gave it to another prisoner to deliver. "I think [it's] a good humanist manifesto, even if the author thinks so. Let the shame of Bordeaux be exposed. My campaigns are what I am."[7]

In the beginning Henry was delighted to be at Waterloo. "It was out in the country, there was grass, you could move around. And no cells — it was dormitory style. There were contact visits — Mireille and I could walk around and hold hands." But Henry bucked their system from the first day and he never stopped. The day he returned from Parthenais, where he had been held during his second trial, a recreational boxing match turned nasty when one opponent was knocked practically unconscious. Checking for a pulse and other vital signs, Henry told — not asked, not suggested — the guard to take the man to hospital right away. Instead the guard called the warden, who said to Henry, "You're not a doctor in here. You're a prisoner like everybody else." Many of the guards were openly hostile — he explained that away by telling himself they were staunch Catholics and he an abortionist exhibiting no remorse or shame. The warden treated all the inmates like children — badly behaved children. He was a stickler for demeaning details. Henry had to keep his shirt tucked in; he wouldn't. "Fuck you," he swore at the guard. Recalling this, Henry said, "I know you shouldn't talk like that, but…"

The constant sniping at his dignity and independence wore on his nerves. They treated him like the school troublemaker, and Henry reacted like an adolescent. He rarely admitted it, but he was worried about the course of the second trial. This time the prosecutor was René Dominique, but his case was no more skilful or successful than that of his predecessor, Robichaud. Police photographs of Henry's clinic may have been meant to create the impression of an abortion mill, but instead were presented by Sheppard as clean state-of-the-art lab facilities. (This description greatly amused the staff, who confided to one journalist, "What lab? That's a storage room. We don't do lab work.") The young witness police had found had been seventeen when she had gone to the clinic for an abortion, but she testified she and her lover were now married, were hardworking and were saving money. It took the jury less than an hour on June 9 to find Henry not guilty. Even then Henry was returned not to Waterloo, but to the hated Parthenais Detention Centre, from which he was shuffled back and forth to court on several more occasions. Several days elapsed before he was allowed back to Waterloo.

Meanwhile, a Gallup Poll found that 77 per cent of Canadian adults had heard of Henry, and of those, 46 per cent believed the Liberal cabinet should set him free.[8] The Criminal Lawyers Association of Canada, comprised of 250 Ontario criminal lawyers, stated in a press release June 18 that Canada's Supreme Court had destroyed a fundamental principle of democracy by upholding Henry's conviction. "We ask the public to recognize the seriousness of this blow to our Canadian system of justice and to urge the federal government…to intervene immediately," said the association president and Toronto lawyer Arthur Whealy. Choquette had already stated the government was appealing Henry's second acquittal, when a letter bearing the names of 850 people willing to take Henry's place in jail for at least one day landed in his office. It contained the signatures of television personality Laurier LaPierre, economist Dian Cohen and Montreal councillor John Gardiner.

———

At Waterloo, Henry was prevented from going back to his old job in the laundry. He had to wash floors. Henry well knew the symbolism of that chore. As Ed Ratcliffe, who had visited Henry in Bordeaux on several occasions and thought him "calm and coping," noted: "People feel strongly about washing floors. I know that from my work in industry. It is the second most degrading thing you can ask people to do. Cleaning toilets is the first. Ghandi picked that out." Saying he had been acquitted by two juries, Henry refused to wash the floors. The prison authorities threatened to bring him in front of the discipline committee and Henry said, truthfully, he didn't care what they did, but people across Canada might be interested to know.

Then, late in the evening of June 15, Henry was lying on his bed in the dormitory, listening to his radio through his earphones and writing his memoirs shortly before lights out. He had had a pleasant day. Mireille had visited and he had picked her a bouquet of wildflowers, which a guard had insisted on confiscating. One of the guards was pacing back and forth, watching Henry suspiciously but saying nothing, so Henry continued with his writing. Suddenly, six guards bore down on him. "Why aren't your feet under the covers?" It was summer — it made no sense. But Henry knew well why the rules at Waterloo were invoked. "Nobody told me that," he replied. One guard insisted that Henry had been told and that, once again, he was flouting authority.

When the assistant warden arrived, the guards moved in and Henry shattered. "Bastards, you bastards," he screamed, over and over, as he fought and kicked out at the men dragging him downstairs into solitary. "Let me walk," he shrieked. "Tomorrow all of Canada will know about this."

They made him undress completely. Body heaving, his head splitting from the anger and hate inside, Henry wadded up his underwear and threw it in the warden's face. Henry remembers the man starting to move towards him, body tense, fists balled as if to strike him. But he stopped, retreated, then slammed the solid steel door shut with a brutal thud. Naked on the cold floor, heart thundering, head pounding, guts heaving, Henry beat on the door with bruised hands, calling and sobbing for maybe half an hour.

Another guard looked in on Henry, who was still heaving but calmer. Henry knew something terribly wrong was happening to his body. "I have a pain down my arm, in my chest. I feel faint," he said. The guard called his superiors, who, suddenly worried and hushed, summoned a car. Shortly thereafter it streaked through the night, taking Henry to intensive care at Shefford General Hospital in Granby. Even in his fear and misery, Henry was aware of finally being treated with compassion, respect. He overheard a nurse tell a doctor on the telephone that his blood pressure was 80 over 50 — low — his condition was poor. His fists were still clenched, as they had been for months. "I was in a condition of rage and humiliation." He had suffered a prethrombosis heart attack and he honestly believed it was the end for him.

Word leaped out that Henry Morgentaler had suffered a heart attack in prison. A letter written by Henry and smuggled out earlier to June Callwood hit the headlines with new relevance. On June 17, 1975, the *Toronto Star* stated that in his letter Henry had accused prison officials of denying him his medicine, nitroglycerin, which was used to treat his angina, to punish him for hypnotizing a fellow prisoner to help conquer the prisoner's insomnia. Their actions had caused his heart attack. The *Star* followed with a considerably shorter article on June 23, stating that a new letter written by Henry had been smuggled out. The television host Carole Taylor had read it the night before on CTV's "W5." In the latest letter, Henry claimed he'd been left for fifty minutes "in the hole" after he'd asked for help for his heart attack symptoms. This time, according to Henry, he'd been reading via night light at about 11:30 p.m., when the assistant chief director, Jean-Yves Desrocher, appeared in "a menacing pose." He said, "We'll show you who's boss around here," after Henry apparently stated he would never be broken — "after the whole power of the state had failed to bring me to my knees." Prison officials denied there was such a thing as a "hole" in Waterloo Rehabilitation Centre. To prove it, they took reporters on a tour of the facility, showing off an open-air swimming pool and a nicely furnished aboveground room where, they insisted, prisoners were sent for solitary. "That was dishonest," Henry said. "The room they put me in was subterranean, with a naked toilet bowl and a light bulb." A representative of the Canadian Medical Association then toured the facility and announced in Calgary that he found no evidence indicating Henry had been mistreated at Waterloo: "A review of the manner in which Dr. Morgentaler has been detained and treated...indicates Dr. Morgentaler is receiving the same treatment as other inmates. There is no evidence that he was being mistreated so as to create a serious health hazard. Nor has he been denied appropriate medical attention," the statement said.

Years later Henry denied he ever needed nitroglycerin. He said that during the trial he was rushed from Parthenais to St. Luke's Hospital complaining of chest pains one evening. An electrocardiogram found nothing conclusive, so he was sent back and the trial continued. The only prescription Henry said he had was for Percodan, to alleviate the tension headaches the trial was causing him. Although his pill bottle was on his lawyer's table in the courtroom, he couldn't take one because he did not have permission from prison authorities to do so. (He said he did manage to sneak half a tablet one day.) He said he was even denied the standard dose of Valium given prisoners dealing with the stress of undergoing a trial.

By June 18, Laura Sabia had lost all patience: "There is nothing more stupid than that Morgentaler is in jail, when men and women who have done things a hundred times worse are running around.

"Two juries have acquitted him, but they are still after his hide. [Quebec Justice Minister Jérôme] Choquette wants his head, and those stupid, spineless creatures in Ottawa are doing nothing because it's happening in Quebec," she said to an audience in St. Catharines, Ontario.[9]

Choquette fought back, telling reporters outside Quebec City's National Assembly the next day that the entire incident had been fanned into flames by Henry's supporters, then blown out of proportion into a raging bushfire by media. "It's a real joke as far as I'm concerned. The lies people are telling would be sad if they weren't plain funny."[10] He had told the Assembly there was an "orchestrated newspaper campaign to degrade the administration of justice in Quebec."

The roiling battle in Quebec over abortion rights had spilled out from the confines of the political arena into the personal for both protagonists. Choquette's and Henry's animosity towards each other was visceral; each loathed the other, beyond what the other represented. Henry believed Choquette had pulled every string he possessed to run him in and run him down. It wasn't the federal income tax department that had come after Henry, but Quebec Revenue. Even though they often work in tandem, the federal government never acted on that front. And it was the provincial revenue office that stated that if Henry wanted to resolve the situation of his assets being frozen, then he would have to sue them.

A journalist said he once sat in Choquette's office long past the end of the working day, ruminating and talking abortion war stories.

"Long after you and I are gone, Morgentaler will be on a stamp," the journalist predicted.

Choquette was outraged. "Never," he shouted. "Never."

"But that's the way things work," the journalist persisted.

Choquette paced in front of the window in his office, the lights of Montreal behind him. "But he's a criminal."

"So was Louis Riel."

Sometime later, Choquette joined a group of charismatic Catholics and became mayor of Outremont, an affluent French-speaking area of Montreal. Sometime after that, Henry said he ran into him in a clothing store, the only time the two have ever encountered each other in public.

"The chief of the Gestapo himself," Henry said by way of greeting.

"Know what I think of you?" Choquette replied.

"No, what?" Henry taunted.

"I think you are an assassin."

"Well, I think you are a cretin and an idiot."

―――――

As Tory leader Robert Stanfield was calling for an independent inquiry
into the alleged mistreatment of Dr. Henry Morgentaler (later ruled out
by Lang), the patient-prisoner himself was being transferred to the car-
diac unit of the University Centre Hospital in Sherbrooke, Quebec. As
soon as he was able, Henry began to phone his supporters from his hospital bed. He could not go back to prison; he was afraid for his life; they
simply had to help. He found Linda Rapson at the Acupuncture Foundation Clinic Toronto office. "He was a little hypomanic. He was calling
everybody. He was in the hospital, had had the heart attack and was yelling that I had to get hold of Wendell [Watters] — we had to get him out of
jail. He was really pushing us, told us we had to do another plea for help."

On June 19, a few of the 150 people at the inaugural meeting of the
Toronto chapter of CARAL at St. Paul's Avenue Road United Church
decided to pitch tents on the concrete concourse between city hall and
the law courts for a vigil they intended would last until Henry was
released from jail. While Callwood told the new organization its "primary goal is to stop the rollback of abortions in hospitals because Right
to Life (anti-abortion) people are taking over control of the hospitals,"[11]
others planned a mass rally of support. The Toronto Board of Education voted to back the Amnesty for Morgentaler committee, joining those
such as financier Edward Bronfman, politician Dalton Camp, editor
Robert Fulford, former cabinet minister Judy LaMarsh, businessman
Harry Rosen, lawyer Clayton Ruby and physician Morton Shulman, who
had affixed their names to another full-page newspaper advertisement
demanding Henry's release. And the Tent Vigil vowed to move on to various plazas and other public venues throughout the city after camping out
for ten days at city hall.

Henry wrote an open letter to Trudeau requesting "an immediate,
unconditional pardon.... My acquittal by two juries on charges of
performing illegal abortions was the verdict of the people and must
be honoured."

Henry was not pardoned, but he never went back to prison. Under doctors' orders, he was transferred to Villa Mount Royal, a convalescent home in Montreal, where he lived among the aged, frail residents. "I hated the place. It was a place of decay and impending death."

Richard Cleroux, a reporter who had covered Henry's court cases since 1973 for the *Globe and Mail*, dropped by the nursing home one afternoon. He said it was comfortable, even luxurious, "but it's hardly the place for someone leading a crusade, someone who's been in the spotlight for years."[12] Later in the same article, Cleroux remarked, "It was in this comfortable but stifling setting that Dr. Morgentaler spent the last seven months of his detention, completing the breaking-down process that had begun in jail.

"He became grateful for the privileges he got. Bit by bit he had bargained away his indignation and freedom to speak in return for small favours that helped him survive," Cleroux wrote.

Esmond Choueke, a freelance photographer, found Henry sitting on a piano bench, atop a pile of magazines, practising a trill study on the piano one day. He started when he saw Choueke, whom he had known since the early days of his clinic. Choueke had interviewed Henry during a walk on Mount Royal with his mutt, Beebee, and Goldie's collie, named Pasha, for articles he wrote for the McGill newspaper and a Winnipeg newspaper. He also lived near Henry in the Town of Mount Royal. And he was a supporter. "Henry was a lifesaver in those days — literally," he said. "Women were dying from abortions then. Our family knew of one. A Concordia student had died from a botched abortion. People at McGill knew the Morgentaler Clinic was the safest, and used to phone it giving a secret number — G62 — so the clinic would know we weren't the police or anything." Henry begged Choueke to leave, saying he wasn't allowed to speak with journalists. Choueke did leave, but returned another day and through a window photographed Henry sitting inside in a wheelchair. Choueke later attempted to photograph Henry working out in the gym at the Young Men's Hebrew Association. Henry convinced staff to bar the photographer. But there was nothing in Henry's agreement with prison officials allowing him to spend the remainder of his prison sentence in a nursing home about

photos being taken of him in a public place. Choueke took them anyway. Some were used in Dan Garson's film *Morgentaler.*

Henry admitted that he was far from happy. In Bordeaux when he
had realized his hatred and resentment of the prison authorities and the
Crown attorney were harming him more than them, he'd vowed to
control his emotions. On his cell wall he'd scratched the words "Love is
stronger than hate" and swore he would live by that credo. But little
things still rankled him. He berated himself for having entrusted his
dog to Eva to look after, because Eva had given away Beebee. "I was
attached to that dog, but underneath I must have believed I was never
coming back from prison. I wasn't thinking I would go to prison for ten
months, maybe twelve months, and then get my dog back. My feeling
was that this was the end of my life, basically." Proud to be allowed the
freedom to roam the streets while still officially a prisoner, he let himself into the Barton Street house. Henry considered it a friendly visit —
he was happy with Mireille and accepting that Eva was equally content
in her new relationship — but when he tried it a second time he found
the locks to the doors had been changed. Insulted and very angry,
he instituted divorce proceedings on the basis of Eva's adultery. They
were easy to prove, since her Australian lover had been living with her
in what was still officially the Morgentaler matrimonial home. Later
Henry reconsidered. "I had committed adultery many times before, so
it was a bit sneaky and hypocritical that I should accuse her of adultery."
(He subsequently changed the grounds to marriage breakdown out of
respect for both of them, and the childhood sweethearts were officially
divorced in 1977.)

His heart attack had also taken a toll, and he was worried about his
health. He was going to rehabilitation sessions at the YMHA three times
a week — he made his own way there, walking through the streets of
Montreal, dressed dowdily, grateful to be unrecognized. "I was just trying to survive. I wasn't happy — actually, I was depressed. I couldn't
speak freely. I was a prisoner, and I didn't want to make waves, since I
had relative freedom. I couldn't bear the thought of being confined to
my room with all those dying people. I thought it would just be a question of a few more months."

On September 9, three months to the day of the second acquittal, the National Parole Board announced it had turned down Henry's request for parole, even though he had completed a third of his eighteen-month sentence. Henry's "unacceptable behaviour" within the institutions was the reason. That fall, Lang introduced legislation to prevent any other jury verdict from being overruled, but the government showed no signs of being in a hurry to act on it. By the beginning of November, Sheppard was telling reporters that Henry was financially ruined. With eleven months still to serve of his sentence, Henry stayed in the nursing home, "in very bad shape physically." The sheriff's office announced on October 31 that he owed $11,628.13 in back taxes on an apartment building on Sherbrooke Street, and $5,898.13 for a twenty-unit building on Dudemaine Street. The buildings were to be auctioned off December 1 if the money wasn't paid — news that sent Mike scrambling. He showed up with a cheque one day past the deadline, but in time to prevent the sale.

All over the country Morgentaler Defence Funds had been scrambling for donations. New CARAL groups had begun in Kingston, Calgary, Thunder Bay, Quebec City and Stratford. CARAL had held rallies in places such as Edmonton and Winnipeg, where invariably the hat was passed. In Toronto, Pierre Berton hosted a rally and benefit concert featuring Stringband, the songwriter Nancy White, plus the then-ubiquitous Flo Kennedy (who alone cost $1,305.29 in fees, airfare and hotel expenses, which left a balance of $1,424.97 from the night). A newspaper ad placed by CARAL in London raised more than two hundred donations and as many letters to members of Parliament. The results of CARAL's letter-writing evenings in Ottawa, Kitchener-Waterloo and Guelph poured into MPs' offices. Mireille Lafortune spearheaded the ACALA (the French abortion rights organization affiliated with CARAL) questionnaire sent to one thousand Montreal area doctors about their involvement with abortions performed in Quebec. As a result, more than 140 doctors signed a public declaration that they, like Henry, had performed, recommended or assisted in abortions. CARAL's Montreal chapter worked up sixty thousand signatures on a petition destined for Choquette calling for amnesty for Henry.

A cause had become a movement that had become a crusade. Public pressure was incessant, intense. But the federal cabinet seemed immune to the outcries, the rallies, the petitions, the speeches, marches, vigils and letters. Henry was so depressed he believed he was abandoned, the cause usurped by other issues of the day.

Then, on January 20, 1976, the tide began to turn when the Quebec Court of Appeal upheld the second jury acquittal, making it a point to validate Sheppard's defence of necessity in the process. Three days later Justice Minister Ron Basford announced they were starting all over again. Henry's convictions in the Court of Appeal and the Supreme Court on the first trial were being set aside, and Henry would have a brand-new trial on the original charge against him. In Quebec, Choquette had been removed abruptly from the justice portfolio to take over education. In his place was Fernand Lalonde, formerly Quebec's minister responsible for the status of women, who reacted to Basford's news by slamming Section 251 as "unworkable and unenforceable." Nevertheless, the Professional Corporation of the Physicians of Quebec suspended Henry's medical licence for a year just a few hours before Basford made his announcement. The weekend pass Henry had asked for and previously been denied was suddenly granted. On Monday, January 26, he was back in court for a bail hearing, but the Crown had already told Sheppard he would not oppose bail and didn't intend to ask for any special restrictions. It took all of fifteen minutes.

Technically, Henry was a free man.

"I won't practice any abortions for a while," he told reporters meekly that day. "I'll just wait and see how the situation goes." In an article called "The bitter symbol of abortion wars," published February 16 in the *Globe and Mail*, Richard Cleroux noted that "the last time he was released in November 1973 he had rushed off to his east-end clinic and whipped off twelve abortions to celebrate.

"He is no longer willing to provoke the authorities into sending him to jail.

"He is no longer the indignant, outspoken advocate of abortion who proudly trotted off defiant and unbowed to jail March 27, 1975, promising to fight harder than ever."[13] Cleroux also noted Henry had lost about fifteen pounds and aged considerably during his ten months of incarceration. "Today he is bitter, disillusioned. He believes he was a victim of a great injustice and lost ten months of his life for something that was not a crime."

Henry hated the article. "He made it look like I had given up. It was just a question of lying low so I could fight again."

Gertie and Carl Katz accompanied him to the nursing home to pick up his things. They stood by the elevator, waiting to leave. Henry was angry, impatient. "Let's get to work," he said to them. "I've wasted a lot of time here."

CHAPTER 10

THE PRIMAL SCREAMERS

IT WAS NOT A BRAVE, NEW BEGINNING. Locked out of the Barton Street home by Eva, Henry went first to Mike's apartment, then moved in with Mireille and her young sons. He had his own room and he paid her rent. It was almost week before he again spoke with any reporters. He had a lot to face.

First, he had been wrong. Eleanor Wright Pelrine's book *Morgentaler: The Doctor Who Wouldn't Turn Away* had been published in November 1975. In it she noted: "Henry never probably realized he would actually go to jail. He was the most surprised person I had ever seen when he learned he lost in the Supreme Court. He always had this childlike naïvete, an unshakable faith that he stood in a charmed circle and that no harm could come to him because he was honest."

Now his medical licence had been suspended. Publicly, Henry bluffed, "If there's any expert on the subject [of abortion], it's me."[1] Privately, he agonized. He was a good doctor, an important fact that had fallen by the wayside as he became more of the political symbol his followers needed, but something that had never lost its importance to him. He would do whatever it took to regain his licence and professional reputation. There was also the matter of the Supreme Court. This time it was the prosecution that had applied for a hearing to overturn his second acquittal after it had been upheld by the provincial Court of Appeal.

And still to come was his court date on March 1, on which his trial date would be set. Henry continued to want a pardon, not a new trial. He was convinced he deserved one after all the injustices meted out to him. Instead, the government showed every sign of starting all over legally, as well as stalling politically. One of Otto Lang's last acts as justice minister had been to announce in September 1975 the formation of a committee to study how the abortion law functioned. This was anything but a conciliatory move. The Badgley Committee was the creation of a justice department responsible for the implementation of that very law, and headed by a minister who had issued a memoradum in October 1974, later leaked to media, declaring that the abortion law had to be applied strictly, without consideration for social and economic conditions. As St. Francis Xavier University professor Larry Collins commented:

> Many wondered why Lang so openly tried intimidation. The reason will probably never become clear; he was accused of allowing his personal beliefs to interfere with his ministerial duties. But it is clear that his department was taking the political heat generated by Morgentaler's trial. It is more likely, therefore, that he over-reacted and confused his role as a member of the government and his role as a department head. As a Government member his job was containment of the issues, but as head of the Justice Department he had to respond to the legal challenge raised by Morgentaler.[2]

Word of the contents of the internal justice ministry memo were leaked at the same time as Alliance for Life handed over to Parliament a petition of one million signatures — the largest ever in Canadian annals — demanding that the government protect the unborn. This spurred the president of the Canadian Medical Association, Dr. Bette Stephenson, to lodge an immediate complaint directly with Prime Minister Trudeau. Doctors wanted an official definition of what exactly "health" encompassed in the context of therapeutic abortion committees, or they might disassociate themselves from the committees, she said. Trudeau was unmoved, and reminded doctors that the existing law was influenced significantly by CMA recommendations made back in 1967. But Stephenson did not back down, either, and called for Lang's resignation unless he clarified government policy. Lang was forced to concede that "health" in this context included mental as well as other factors. To further appease the doctors, he established the three-person Badgley Committee, chaired by Robin F. Badgley, a sociologist from the University of Toronto, to determine whether the abortion law was operating fairly across Canada. Statistics at the time stated that Canadian women had 43,136 abortions in 1974, up 11.4 per cent from 1973, and that fewer than half of Canadian hospitals had set up therapeutic abortion committees. DRAL (Doctors for Repeal of the Abortion law) completed a survey of the 258 hospitals in the country that had therapeutic abortion clinics, according to Statistics Canada. The results showed serious inequities. Fourteen of the hospitals surveyed did not have therapetic abortion committees, ten hospitals had committees but had performed no abortions in 1974 and sixteen hospitals had performed fewer than five abortions that year.

Lang was careful not to give Badgley's committee free rein. It was not allowed to analyze or to make recommendations on the underlying policy of the law, thereby ensuring that "the final report would not condemn the government," according to Larry Collins. This was the same government, Collins noted in *The Politics of Abortion*, that had created the family planning division of its health and welfare ministry in 1972 "as a lightning rod to channel political controversy into a bureaucratic agency which spread a message of concern while doing little." The Family Planning Department also "helped maintain the dominant view of abortion as an unacceptable form of birth control, and propagated the myth that abortion and birth control were two different things." Everything was going along relatively smoothly according to this plan until "the political issues raised by Dr. Morgentaler, however, redirected the controversy squarely back to the federal government via its Justice Department."

A week after his bail hearing Henry told the *Toronto Star* that Lang had a "vendetta" against him and had headed "a concerted effort to get me." On February 1 Henry, along with the other members of CARAL, was on Parliament Hill, lobbying members of Parliament for the legalization of abortion. In an updated paperback edition of her biography, Wright Pelrine commented he was "noticeably thinner and quieter since his incarceration."[3] However, as the centre of media attention, he was anything but quiet about what he had just experienced and what he thought about the current law. That may have motivated the Quebec justice department to announce that only the Quebec Court of Appeal could decide bail conditions. None other than Henry's old foe, Crown Attorney Louis-Guy Robichaud, asked the Court of Appeal to impose a gag order on Henry, whom he persisted in addressing as "the ex-Dr. Morgentaler." Mr. Justice Laurent Bélanger complied by ordering Henry not to discuss his past or future trials, or to do any abortions. Sheppard told the media Henry was now the only person in Canada unable to speak out on abortion. The Canadian Civil Liberties Association was outraged; its general counsel, Alan Borovoy, vowed to take action. "The purpose of imposing conditions of bail is to ensure a person's appearance in court," he said. "I have difficulty believing how muzzling Morgentaler would ensure his appearance in court." But Sheppard was uncertain whether to appeal this latest ruling. "It depends on how long a wait there is before the new trial," he said.[4]

The *Globe and Mail*'s Cleroux had already found the young woman from Sierra Leone who had been the Crown's reluctant but star witness during the first trial. He reported her to be happily married, living in west-island Montreal and pregnant. "There's no way I'm going to court in my condition," Verona Parkinson told Cleroux.[5] "That's all in the past. I don't want to bring it up again." She had not been approached to testify anew. "I feel sorry for [Henry]. . . . He has already served 10 months. Why don't they let him go?"

A month later the Supreme Court of Canada refused to allow the Crown to appeal Henry's second acquittal, but Henry still faced a new retrial. Sheppard was jubilant, saying that the Supreme Court's support of the Quebec appeal court ruling meant that the defence of necessity [an abortion is acceptable if a doctor considers it necessary in the interest of a woman's health] had become part of the law. Henry was silent.

Wright Pelrine told a reporter from the *Montreal Gazette* she wasn't sure Henry could make it through another trial. In many ways, Henry's situation was worse than it had been when he'd first entered prison.

While he had been fighting prison bureaucracy about the right to give flowers to his lover, the Right to Life groups had been proliferating (mushrooming from seventy-five to more than 230 groups).[6] Their members dominated the boards of many hospitals where, not coincidentally, abortions were no longer being carried out.

Henry had to be talked into travelling, even into coming to Toronto for the launch of a book written by Humanist colleague and supporter Wendell Watters. Henry had nowhere to stay, Linda Rapson remembered, so he went to her house after the event and stayed with her family. "I didn't know him that well, but he needed every shred of support he could get at that time." Her husband had already introduced himself to Henry during his first Supreme Court hearing when Morris Manning's colleagues Eddie Greenspan and Clayton Ruby were intervening on behalf of two organizations that supported Henry. Like many others, Rapson had made it a point to write to Henry in prison and she had continued to work on the co-ordinating committee of DRAL. But she was surprised to see how lacklustre and listless he seemed. "I'll always remember the look in his eyes then. He had the look of a trapped animal."

The next time Henry was in Toronto he attended a huge fundraising dinner on February 26, 1976, when more than four hundred supporters gave him a "standing and foot-stomping ovation" at the Sai Woo restaurant and then paid $25 each — $17 of which went for Henry's legal fees. "The diminutive doctor stood on a chair, hands upraised giving the V-for-Victory signs with both hands as the tumultuous applause laced with shouts of 'Viva' and 'Viva, bravo' shook the air," wrote Toronto Star reporter Anne Carey. He could only speak on a personal level about being in detention for ten months; others, including Linda Rapson, addressed the issue. But his financial support was growing. By the end of April 1976, the Toronto-based Morgentaler Trust Fund, administered by Clayton Ruby, had $10,561.01 in its account. In Montreal a group of supporters worked long, hard hours organizing another fund-raising Chinese dinner for Henry's defence. Touted as a major event, it was supposed to raise enough money to make a significant cut into Henry's legal debt, which was well above

$200,000, even with Sheppard reportedly having reduced his fee and having involved three or four of his firm's juniors on a pro bono basis.

According to reporter Richard Cleroux, the women were shattered with how little money they raised and how much work it took. Quietly they put the word out that money was needed for Henry's legal bills. "Everybody knew Sheppard was a good guy, and all this money started coming in," said Cleroux. The cheques and cash arrived in square envelopes between the folds of thick vellum notepaper. They were from the uppermost reaches of society, and they were accompanied by notes saying, "I wish there had been someone like Henry Morgentaler when I was eighteen."

"They sent $50, $100. You could tell by the notes they had suffered and no one knew. They were wealthy women who were not particularly known to be spokespeople. These weren't feminists — they were low-key women. If they had lent their name to the cause they would have taken it a lot further. They were not strident in any way, but they were there, at least moneywise," Cleroux said. Without any real effort, more than $40,000 was raised. When it came to the abortion issue, women from every social group gave what they could as often as asked. They did not need to attend dinners or fund-raisers to show their support.

Cleroux said that when he understood the breadth and depth of the support for legalized abortion, he realized Henry Morgentaler was going to win his battle. "It made me think, the law is gone." Yet it would take longer to win the battle than Cleroux might have expected. Henry's retrial was postponed from May until September. Henry resented being a pawn in this "waiting game." He resented how kind and understanding Mireille Lafortune was being to him. Although suffering from serious health problems herself and on cortisone treatments for lupus, she supported him and carried on for both of them. She was active in CARAL, a leader among French-speaking feminists and intellectuals. She was a tower of strength, both for the movement and for him, but those were supposed to be his roles, and even though he was unable at that time in his life to fulfil either of them, he chafed at her abilities and all her kindnesses. When they had met he had just been

acquitted the first time and he was jubilant, "full of victory and pro-
jects," he said. "In the beginning she depended on me. I was the one
who was more exuberant then. After a while I started depending on her
for support. I didn't like it. She was very warm and affectionate and caring and I depended a lot on her. Things started to go wrong. She was
there during the time I was in jail. She would visit. The person I called
would be her. But afterwards, as far as I was concerned she was too pos-
sessive. I needed more freedom, more room for myself." He felt guilty,
but not enough to stay. "I was beholden to her and I couldn't do it anymore. She reminded me of the awful period in my life." She reminded
him that things were out of his control, as they had been in the camps,
as he had vowed they would never be for him again.

He moved back into Mike's apartment for a couple of weeks, then
into the twenty-room house that he had purchased back in 1971, situated across from Westmount Park. He had let the Humanist Fellowship of Montreal use the house for meetings for a number of years, but
now he needed it for himself. The house at 381 Melville Avenue is the
only one Henry ever became attached to; it is also the only one he ever
lived in by himself, if only for brief periods. But by the time his trial
started on September 9, he was involved with Joyce Yedid, a young,
articling law student. Henry had met her through his friend Mauriello
when she'd told the psychiatrist she admired Henry and supported his
cause. She visited Henry at Villa Mount Royal as an acolyte, and their
relationship progressed from there. She was interested in literature, and
there was much Henry could guide her to. She was just starting on her
intellectual journey; Henry appreciated being her leader for a time.
Then the relationship became like chess for him. He needed a challenge, someone to provoke and engage his wits. He began to notice that
Joyce never ventured her own opinions, only those of others. "That's
what people tell you. What do you think?" Henry would say to her.
It was a "dangerous time" for him, too quiet, too slow and still, when it
was too easy for the negative, despairing thoughts to catch up and
crowd into his mind, jangling his core. But without an income, doctor's
licence or public platform, he had no political diversions, no cause
as shield.

He was acquitted for a third time on September 18, but he was only going through the celebratory motions at the post-trial party. Eight other charges of performing an illegal abortion still hung over him. Despite the fact that former prime minister John Diefenbaker had said further prosecution of Henry "would be making him a martyr and would degrade the jury system," a view echoed in many of the editorial pages of newspapers across the country, the Quebec government announced swiftly that Henry would face another trial on December 13. As chairman of the Canadian Bar Association's criminal justice section, Morris Manning said he agreed with the Quebec Bar's suggestion that all abortion trials be postponed until Parliament reviewed the law, but Justice Minister Ron Basford replied that he would not intervene.

It happened that he didn't have to. On November 15, Robert Bourassa's Liberals were thrown out of office and the separatist Parti Québécois was elected. At the PQ's first cabinet meeting, Marc-André Bedard, the new justice minister, said he would decide within two weeks whether to drop the charges. He said the decision was a priority. On December 10, the Quebec government halted all prosecution against Henry and recommended that the federal government amend the abortion law. Prosecuting Henry had cost the Canadian taxpayer a minimum of $500,000, but at least the proceedings had been stopped. Henry was in Florida visiting his former nurse, Joanne Cornax, and at the home of her neighbour, a former patient of his, when Bill Cornax loped across the lawns to tell him he had a phone call. It was his receptionist, Trudy Martens, with the news. "I felt liberated. It was weighing very heavily on me. Every trial was a lot of stress, always hanging over, taking up a lot of emotional space. It blocks everything out. Everything is under this cloud. You can't plan for anything. Your fate is not in your hands. It was like that with every trial. This was quite like liberation. It felt like the first bit of good news in a long time."

He flew to New York and talked to reporters from Goldie's apartment, saying he wasn't sure whether he would start performing abortions again. His licence was still officially suspended, but his appeal was being heard the next month and he had been allowed to practise until then, so that was not the reason for his hesitation. He was bored with the procedure. It had become tedious to do because of his own improvements and modifications to the technique. Yet he and every other doctor who performed abortions had to stay alert because of the variations in the human body and the potential for perforations and other complications. Months earlier, when he had first been released on bail, Henry had announced, "I intend to teach abortion methods — which I developed — across Canada.... I am willing to forget all the injustices that have been done to me and am willing to co-operate with the federal government in establishing methods of abortion which I have pioneered." Since May he had been allowed to operate a general practice pending his appeal to the provincial doctors' professional association, but he had worked fitfully and had not been entirely successful, and he had two children in expensive American universities.

Quebec Revenue officials had put a "privilege" on his assets back in 1974, laying no charges but leaving it up to him to prove he hadn't made as much as they said he had. (At that time, the properties — seven apartment buildings, two houses and the clinic — were worth about $1.5 million, but had mortgages on them totalling more than $1 million.) The department was claiming Henry owed them $354,799.14 in unpaid taxes and interest between 1969 and 1972, inclusive. They estimated Henry had grossed more than $1.4 million during that time, which they came up with by multiplying the seven thousand abortions Henry had stated in court he'd done by $300, the top price. A department official later publicly stated the amount was "an arbitrary figure," chosen to encourage Henry "to come round to negotiate."[7] But Henry never took the bait, and always claimed he'd averaged $110 per abortion before expenses and that he'd paid all the taxes owing on gross revenues of $704,000. It took years to settle: Henry prevailed upon a friend, Education Minister Camille Laurin, author of the reviled Bill 101 on the French language, to intervene on his behalf with the man who was then revenue minister. Under Jacques Parizeau, the amount was knocked down to $220,000, which was better, but not good enough. Henry had other bills to pay, including $100,000 to Sheppard, who insisted Henry take out a mortgage (at interest rates then nearing 20 per cent) on one of Henry's buildings as payment. "I thought that was excessive," Henry said. It took him five years to pay it off and he didn't want to get himself into the same financial squeeze over a government debt he was convinced was fabricated. He waited it out a few more years, until a junior minister took over the revenue portfolio. Then he asked Laurin to make another approach. "I told Camille we may have more influence on this guy. He came up with a figure of $101,000. I told my lawyers to accept." He sold his clinic to one of his companies to get the money and again took five years to pay off the full amount. "Good riddance. I didn't have to spend time in court. I didn't have my patients being quizzed about how much they paid. It was worth it."

Henry had always been a careless bookkeeper because the business of business had never interested him. Also, women often paid what they could for the procedure, some promising to pay more later, money that sometimes never materialized. It never mattered to him because he genuinely was not doing abortions for the money. But as flexible about fees and casual about cash as he was, Henry was making a very good living. He never denied that; however, it didn't help further the cause of legalizing abortion when those opposed to abortion referred to him as Morgentaler the millionaire. In his last court battle the prosecuting lawyer, René Dominigue, had made much out of the income derived from the ten to twelve abortions Henry said had been done daily at the clinic. And in suspending Henry's medical licence for a year, the disciplinary committee of the Professional Corporation of the Physicians of Quebec commented on "an attitude which is primarily directed to protecting his fees. No really valid interview is held before proceeding with the abortion. This behaviour confers a mercenary character on the doctor-patient relationship. This committee is incapable of reconciling this behaviour with the humanitarian concern that the accused invoked throughout his defence."[8] Mindful of his socialist roots, Henry may even have been subconsciously trying to sabotage some of his substantial income, as he was not as oblivious to money as he tried to believe. He had never become addicted to the finer things it could buy — he dressed perfunctorily and serviceably, never expensively and never well; he drove good, but not flashy, cars. He loved food and good wine, hardcover books and music, but a sofa would have to be sprung before he would notice it, and the nuances of status symbols — whether a holiday destination was accept-able with a certain crowd or whether it wasn't, for instance — escaped his notice. Mike functioned as his business manager but Henry always had the final say on all the dealings. He knew the power of money. He was very aware of the big cash-flow picture, tax shelters, the pros and cons of various investments, and especially the $300,000 he now owed for legal fees and court expenses. "I'm a practical idealist. I knew I needed money to do what I wanted to do. Money is good to have because it gives you the power to do things."

So five days after his charges were dropped, Henry announced he would resume abortions at the Montreal clinic, with one caveat — he would get one or more doctors to give a second opinion on the need of a patient to have an abortion to avoid "future and possible accusa-tions."[9] He told Cleroux his plan was to work with a team of doctors in the clinic who would function as a therapeutic abortion committee, and reiterated his offer, originally made in 1973, to turn over his clinic to the provincial government so it could be accredited as a hospital, and would therefore fall within the letter of the law. He planned to join medicare; previously he had been one of very few doctors in the province who did not belong to the Quebec Health Insurance Plan, because what he did was illegal and he had never wanted to report the identity of his patients to any government body. Again Henry said he wanted to get out of the actual work of performing abortions and into teaching others his technique.

He was restless. Winning had meant he had lost his cause, and without his cause he no longer had an identity. He was a private citizen without a purpose, living safe and flat; he was ordinary. Always a lover of women, he pursued them now with pent-up, redirected passion. He fell wildly in love with one woman the instant he saw her from across a crowded room. They were both at a party. A therapist, she, too, knew Mauriello. "I was madly in love. Louise was married with a son. I had this enormous love to give. I wanted to marry her, adopt her son, do anything for her." He left Joyce Yedid. "I couldn't see enough of Louise. She was stringing me along. She said she would come, then she wouldn't, or she would, but only for half an hour and then say she had to get home." There had been, and would continue to be, many women in his life, and with one exception — criminologist and Le Dain Commission member Marie-Andrée Bertrand — Henry was always the one who left. "I think each woman would believe she was the final stop, but the train had a lot further to go," said Gertie Katz. "Once he left Chava he got on that train and it just kept going. For a long time there was no stopping."

His breakups with women were often abrupt and careless. Many times his liaisons overlapped, making the women feel betrayed as well as abandoned. In Toronto and Montreal, there was talk that Henry Morgentaler was a chauvinist, insensitive to individual women. But Henry was still raw from his crusade and ten months in captivity; Gertie believed his bravado, his cool replacement of one lover with the next, was emotional protection. His tightly focused world had fallen wide-open. Mike had become ill while Henry was in the nursing home and helpless to do anything. Originally, the illness was thought to be pleurisy, but the diagnosis was later revised to viral myocarditis, an unusual, progressive disease that attacks the heart muscles, causing the heart to pump at increasingly less than 100 per cent capacity. Mike had sat through all Henry's trials with him and looked after his business, fussed over him, acting like an older, not younger, brother, even though Henry signed his paycheque. Mike could and did act the man of the world to Henry's naif; Henry could and did play up the part of forgiving, long-suffering father to Mike's many and spirited fits of temper. Gertie watched it for years. "They could push each other's buttons." But Henry knew he was alive because of Mike, and Mike always believed his brother was "the bravest man in Canada," Gertie said.

His clinic had barely been open a month, but Henry had long been bored with the repetitious nature of his work. He was also somewhat troubled by his frantic love life and continued to fight his fear that the quiet, anonymous life was all he would ever have now. He bolted for some primal therapy. He had read *The Primal Scream*, Arthur Janov's 1970 bestseller that described one of Janov's patients appearing to be in a comalike state, writhing on the floor, screeching, convulsing, then finally releasing a "piercing, deathlike scream that rattled the walls of my office." Janov called this the "primal scream" and explained it as the product of all the original unconscious pain we all carry within, in body organs, muscles and in the way we behave. Unlike Freud, who believed man was born neurotic, Janov believed, as Henry did, that a person's neurotic process begins in childhood when needs may not be fulfilled for a period of time and the child instinctively separates his self from his needs and feelings, thereby shutting down the pain. "A loved child is one whose natural needs are fulfilled," Janov wrote.

Janov believed fear to be the signal that pain is nearing the surface. Fear is a defence mechanism, part of our instinct for survival, and anxiety is "felt but not correctly focused fear." What primal therapy does, he said, is return fear and pain to their original states, the emotional states in which feeling has not been severed from reaction and dislocated into forms of compulsive action.

In his book Janov described his technique. Deprived of alcohol, cigarettes, drugs, other people, television and often sleep for one or two days before therapy begins, a patient is deliberately thrown off guard. When therapy finally begins, the patient must lie on a couch spread-eagled for his body to be as defenceless as possible. Using deep breathing and other techniques, the therapist attempts to get the patient to surrender any remaining defences. The patient's throat often becomes tight; his chest might feel as if it is constricted by a band, and the patient may be convinced he will vomit until something comes out — words such as "I hate you" or "Mommy be nice" or "Daddy, help."

"This is the primal scream," Janov wrote. "It comes out in shuddering gasps, pushed out by the force of years of suppressions and denials of that feeling." The scream is felt all throughout the body. "As the days go on, the patient goes further back into his childhood. It is common to hear the exact voice of the age being relived — the lisp, the baby talk and eventually the infantile cry."

Janov refused to go back beyond infancy, but his theories did give rise to rebirthing, in which its many advocates believed they re-experienced being in the womb and being born. Then, in *The New Primal Scream*, which Janov wrote in 1991, he revised his original belief that experience starts only in infancy. "I know now that birth trauma is indeed coded and stored in the nervous system. A whole cottage industry of rebirthers has grown up around my discovery, leading to the most dangerous kind of charlatanism," he wrote. But he also added, "One of the most striking aspects of imprinting is that it can begin before conception. ... [A]fter 12 weeks of gestation, the fetal nervous system is fully organized and can fully react to, code and store trauma." Not surprisingly, Henry rejected all of the rebirthing lore and Janov's subsequent theories, and clung to the "attachment theory" that if children are loved and nurtured and comforted in the first three years of life, they will develop a sense that "the world is a good place, they can trust it, and they will relax." As for regression into the womb? "It does violence to my intelligence," Henry said.

The goal is to feel, not necessarily to feel happy. "If someone is exactly what he is, he cannot be hurt and has no need for anxiety. The function of fear, real and unreal, is to keep us from being hurt. The only way to conquer fear is to feel the hurts. As long as hurts are unfelt, fear remains," Janov wrote. Henry knew he was numb. He had just won in Quebec, "but I didn't feel satisfied with myself personally. To feel good about yourself you have to feel in harmony with yourself, with other around you, people close to you. You have to feel peace. I didn't." He didn't like that he was so afraid of authority and that he automatically assumed authority would be hostile to him. This was understandable, given his past and present circumstances, but Henry also understood that he was projecting this feeling onto any authority, often inappropriately. That kept him closed down, unable to trust or react spontaneously. He simply had to be in control at all costs, and one cost was his inability to make any permanent connections with women.

He went on a weekend in Quebec's Eastern Townships with other middle-aged men from Montreal; he went for a week to Mays Landing in New Jersey, to a place run by a therapist named Bill Swartley. In that age of inner exploration and experimentation, primal therapy was attracting a lot of characters. Among the more colourful was Swartley, whom Henry only met up with in New Jersey, although Swartley also operated the Centre for the Whole Person on College Street in Toronto, a centre at the "wild end of primal therapy," according to a writer who used to frequent it. Swartley, who died a few years ago of lymphatic cancer, had many lovers from his coterie of women followers and once celebrated all that was natural and instinctive by jumping on top of (but not out of) a birthday cake, clad only in a red jock strap with a strategically placed heart. But what Henry recalled about Swartley was that he was a descendant of Pennsylvania Dutch (Henry never forgets anybody's antecedents) and that he was full of verve and humour. Swartley was the first person who ever pointed out to him that he had brought on many of his battles himself. In one of the groups, Swartley told Henry that in his experience, concentration camp survivors always believe that horror and persecution are going to recur. In Henry's case, the persecution had recurred because he had decided to fight the government. The terrain of the battle had been his choice; it was not something imposed on him as if he were powerless. His action had precipitated the persecution.

Henry was taken aback, and mumbled a noncommittal "You may be right," but he realized Swartley was essentially correct in his analysis. "Before, I was a member of an anonymous mass and didn't count for anything. Here I counted for something. I did something that I considered important. I challenged authority and I survived. Before, I survived by chance, by a random thing." That insight made it easier to connect to the feelings in the group. Some members, "sitting on a mountain of anger," became violent, shouting and screaming and pounding pillows, although the primal process had built-in verbal safeguards and controls that everyone complied with. The first couple of weekends, Henry was not among those shouting, crying or beating their fists. He remained aloof and controlled, but he was intrigued by the group process and impressed by Swartley, who had also warned him that if he went into primal therapy he might decide not to fight anymore.

He went back to Swartley's Mays Landing several weekends. There was a pool, where the water was kept at body temperature, and always at least a dozen people round it. All their stories fascinated Henry, who told himself he might well become a therapist, that he was there in therapy because he was "adventuresome and had a lot of faith in myself"; only occasionally did he admit to "patches of my personality I didn't want to look at, maybe I'm not completely okay." When Henry did decide to have an "intensive," as recommended by Janov in his book, Swartley suggested he do it with Nina Lee May because, he told Henry, he needed a therapist at least as intelligent as he was. Henry had only seen May once before when she'd cochaired a group with Swartley at Mays Landing, but he agreed to go to New York City for a week-long intensive therapy session. May was about fifty then, divorced, the mother of four, intuitive and very bright and very serious about her work. Like all primal therapists, she had been through the primal process, and like most primal therapists she continued to do work on herself. May had a padded room in her apartment in the Village, where Henry spent three hours each morning, weeping, talking, raging, banging his arms, legs and torso against the walls, pacing, screaming. He was completely free to do, feel or say whatever he wanted.

Gradually, grudgingly, his anger with his parents emerged. But they were victims of the Holocaust, steadfast martyrs for their socialist cause till the end. How could he resent them? Because every child has anger, he was told and told again; because it is all right to feel. He relived his life, this time feeling his fright when his mother was short-tempered with him, his jealousy when Mike was born, his anger with his father for never being there — "He was nice, but it wasn't enough." And running alongside the entire time was his guilt for feeling such despair, loneliness, grief and regret over his lost, hopeless childhood. He would emerge, blinking, into the afternoon sun, his muscles aching; some days he felt as if a truck had run him down. Distracted, he would stride down the streets of the Village, lost in making shreds of sense out of what was emanating from his raw nerve endings, then would drop onto a park bench to scribble something down, a line or two. He wrote poems all the time; he was compelled to explain this anger of his, give it concrete expression, then push it away. He stayed at Goldie's apartment, on Charlotte Street, also in the Village. He was by himself that time; there was nothing or no one to interrupt this process. By the week's end, he was depleted and elated and certain he was better. He invited Joyce Yedid to come down for a celebratory weekend in New York City. They went to see an Israeli comedy show and Henry laughed and laughed.

But it wasn't the end and it wasn't enough. For years he had night-mares of being surrounded by German soldiers, or being in prison, or just being in peril; dreams that woke him up sweating, fear in his throat, fight-or-flight adrenaline coursing through his veins. When Henry went down to Philadelphia for the first ever session of the Ark, a forty-day and forty-night training and therapy experience run by therapist-guru Bill Smuckler, he came face to face with the rest of his past. Henry and nine others each paid $4,000 to sleep seven to a room on mats in the basement of a home called Carriage House and do intensive work with five therapists, and hours of work with one another. Most days Henry cried for hours, so hard the therapist said he was "a river of tears." Henry called it "the watershed experience of my life."

There were no other Holocaust survivors in the group, but there was one German man. Henry was terrified of him, so Smuckler forced the two to role-play, to re-enact Henry's concentration camp experiences so that Henry would re-experience all the dread and fear and anxiety and despair. All Henry will say was "I cried a lot. I went back to normal mode, sure — eventually." But after the role-playing experience he avoided the German — hard to do in a place with deliberately no pri-vacy, and group interaction morning, afternoons, even during the eve-ning lectures. One other member of the group, a Norwegian, was furious with Henry, who reminded him of his grandfather. The man admitted to his homicidal feelings towards Henry, a phase that lasted for two nerve-wracking days, before he worked out that he was projecting feel-ings onto Henry that had nothing to do with him. Even more than with the German, this tore through all the layers of Henry's protective coat-ings. He was frightened to his core of the Norwegian, and truly believed he would be killed or hurt. Once again he was impotent, worthless, helpless. But this time, with the therapy, he realized exactly what he was feeling, and that he was not in the same situation as before — that he was free to decide that he never wanted to feel that way again.

For Henry, that meant a promise made to himself after forty days and nights: he would never feel that afraid of anyone again.

Gertie noticed the difference in Henry immediately. "He was more tolerant of discussion. He is a very impatient man, you know. He seemed to be calmer internally. There wasn't that tight lid on him that I used to perceive all the time, which you couldn't get past. He had lifted that lid with primal therapy."

Mike mocked Henry. "Look where he's going. To the screamers," he would say to Gertie.

"Mike, you could use that, maybe," Gertie sometimes replied. Mike never avoided or skirted the past the way Henry did, but she knew he was as tightly wound and as affected by the past as his brother.

"I can scream well enough without them," Mike would shoot back.

"Okay, there you are right," Gertie would answer with a laugh.

Other friends thought Henry appeared "lighter," very much a different person. Henry said, "I had shoved off a lot of unnecessary baggage. I had felt I was responsible for the world. There was a big obligation to do something positive, to keep the world civilized." He had a diploma in primal therapy from Ark, and a vacant basement downstairs in his house. He padded the basement of 381 Melville for weekend primal groups. Charlie Ashbach from Philadelphia often came up to help Henry lead them. He returned to Nina Lee May for more intensive weekend work every six weeks to eight weeks for the next five to six years. In April 27, 1977, under a photo of Henry, the *Ottawa Citizen* ran the headline "Psychiatry New Practice for Morgentaler?"

All the signs seemed to indicate it was. His sessions at Melville went well. "They were very intense, lots of group interaction," he said. Following Janov's advice, Henry and Ashbach selected the participants; they would ask people to write in and express their backgrounds and problems so they could "avoid psychotics." But at times Henry worried about people losing too much control, exhibiting too much rage. He says he relied on Ashbach for these crises. However, Henry was the one who was asked to Quebec City to guide a group there in French. He attended meetings of Montreal's primal association. It met regularly, often on a social basis. He began to have some individual patients come to him for solo therapy. But his abortion practice was also growing. Henry was the best-known abortionist in Canada, and now that it was clear that no one in Quebec would be prosecuted for performing (and by extension having) an abortion, the clinic was operating on overload. Henry

soon realized he could not do both. He had to commit to either performing abortions or doing primal therapy. He chose abortions, ratio-
nalizing it as the more important in terms of helping people: "If you
figure most people have problems because of their childhood, if you prevent childhood problems in a sense by preventing unwanted pregnancies, in a way you could say abortion was preventative psychiatry." True.
However, it could also be said that therapy is tedious and progresses by
fractions of centimetres before backsliding, and Henry was always an
impatient man. "Although abortion practice was not a challenge, to
have a patient go out half an hour, an hour later, feeling well — that was
great," Henry decided.

But only in Quebec was the way so clear. In the rest of Canada, the
abortion battle was in full cry. The Badgley Report, released in February 1977, confirmed that "the [abortion] procedure provided in the
Criminal Code for obtaining therapeutic abortion is illusory for many
Canadian women," specifically the poor, the young, those with less education and those living in smaller communities. No consistent definition of criteria allowing abortions existed. One in six Canadian women
obtained abortions outside Canada, possibly because only one in five
Canadian hospitals had TACs.[10] And most of these hospitals were in the
cities, which meant for two out of every five Canadians living in smaller
communities, abortions services were not available.[11] Women who did
have access to abortion facilities experienced on average an eight-week
wait for the procedure. The report, however, concluded that all this was
not the fault of the government or its laws, but of the country's medical
institutions and people's ignorance of birth control methods. The report's solution was to recommend more effective family planning, co-
ordinated on a federal and provincial level. A month later when federal
Health and Welfare Minister Marc Lalonde said the family planning
division would be more aggressive in distributing birth control information and the provinces should think about establishing women's clinics that provided many services, including abortion, more than 500,000
angry letters poured in. Lalonde scrapped the suggestion and the Badgely
Report was never acted on.

Henry did speak up, but he was not in the headlines as often, and his speaking engagements were not as frequent. When he was asked to speak, he tended to tell his own story, heaping scorn on the politicians but reserving the full frontal attack for the Catholic church. He thought the church had effectively used his legal and political battles as camouflage and he wanted people to understand what an active and powerful player it had been in the abortion battle. "Fanatics and Catholics... brought their immense weight to bear to reverse the jury's acquittal," he said to two hundred members of Toronto's First Unitarian Congregation.[12] In Winnipeg he noted that it was the Roman Catholic church that represented "99 per cent of the drive against safe abortions for people."[13] He kept his faith in humanity by blaming their faith.

Nevertheless, Henry refused to let any politicans off any hook. He wrote Marc Lalonde on December 22, 1978, to congratulate him on his appointment as minister of justice, remind him the abortion law was unjust and ask him for compensations for the cost of his trial. "The government is aware of the findings of the Badgely Committee that in many instances the procedure provided in the Criminal Code for obtaining therapeutic abortions is not being made available on an equitable basis," Lalonde replied February 20, 1979, "...but as you know the provision of medical services is a provincial matter." Henry underlined this statement on the letter and wrote three huge exclamation points and one question mark beside it. "As for the other matter you have raised, I see no reason to re-examine your request for compensation," Lalonde wrote.

Henry had not expected any other response from a federal politician, even though Lalonde was from Quebec where the abortion issue was no longer contentious. Even as women's coalitions were forming in that province in 1971 to protest Henry's arrest and the charges against him, there were some feminists who resisted supporting the man rather than the movement. A key group was Le Front de libération des femmes, the founder of the Montreal Women's Centre, which provided birth control information as well as an abortion referral service, often to Henry's clinic. But in 1973, when Montreal police again raided the Morgentaler clinic, they also swarmed the Women's Centre, arrested their workers and confiscated their files.

The Comité de défense de Morgentaler was created after it became

clear in a heated meeting of more than six hundred that many francophone women wanted to fight for abortion on demand, not to focus
only on defending Henry Morgentaler. Members of the subsequently
formed Committee for Free Abortion on Demand forged strategic
alliances resulting in the Quebec-wide Coalition for Free Abortion
on Demand and a strong commitment from the women belonging
to the Parti Québécois. Despite the disapproval of leader René Lévesque,
the women of the PQ fought on behalf of a proposal endorsing free
abortion on demand, which the party approved. That endorsement
proved crucial.

When the PQs pushed the Liberals out of power in the 1976 provincial election, they didn't back down from their promise to the women.
They dropped all existing charges against Henry and announced they
would refrain from prosecuting any other abortion clinics that were
operating under good medical conditions. "If the PQ said it wouldn't go
against the clinics, it was because they owed their election to [pro-
choice] women," said Pauline Gingras, founder of Quebec City's first
women's clinic. "They didn't owe it to Morgentaler."[14] Maybe not, but
Henry, along with all abortion-on-demand advocates benefited from
the new benign provincial government.

———

When supporter Jeanne St. Amour asked Henry to train her in the procedure later in 1979, he was delighted. She was a doctor who worked
in one of the provincially financed community health services centres,
centres locaux des services communautaires (CLSC). Henry eventually
trained fifty doctors, some of whom worked in the province's hospitals as well as in clinics. It was all unofficial and free. One or two other
doctors opened clinics like Henry's. Eighteen months later, when La
Presse newspaper reported that illegal abortions were being performed
at the CLSCs, the government again did not back down. The minister of
health at the time, Pierre-Marc Johnson, stated it was more important
to protect women's health than enforce a federal law that Henry Morgentaler had three times been acquitted of breaking. The issue faded,
abortions continued to be performed but women favouring abortion on

demand took a hint from the politicos and kept a low profile for some time after that.

Health Minister Denis Lazure, an acquaintance of Henry's who was also a colleague of his friend Mauriello, freed up some money for hospitals to use to improve existing facilities or set up new ones. Few hospitals instituted new therapeutic abortion committees and the money went to about a dozen hospitals that already did offer access to abortions. Henry said Lazure "was an enlightened minister of health," but not, he insisted, enlightened by him. "When they become ministers they're harder to reach." But Henry didn't really try that hard to contact them. "I'm a bit shy when it comes to people with a lot of power or who become ministers." He was comfortable only as an outsider, lobbing ultimatums, keeping a good distance from the system he was out to beat. He had never worked from the inside out, even though, with his increasing fame and connections, he most probably could have. He knew three PQ cabinet ministers reasonably well: Lazure, Laurin and Lise Payette, who had been "a friend and fan" for years. But when he wrote her and asked to meet to discuss the issue, she never replied.

While things remained calm in Quebec, Henry wrote a book on abortion and contraception in French — and fell in love. Carmen Wernli was a translator and teacher. Having been raised in Chile and having worked in Switzerland, she was very cosmopolitan and very dramatic. She knew radicals; she knew revolutionaries; she knew artists; she played the guitar. Henry was dazzled. Mike and Gertie were not. Gertie saw Carmen apply "womanly wiles" with almost comic effectiveness on Henry. Henry was so intelligent that she couldn't believe he was being taken in. "It was the old story. She chased him until he caught her and then she would talk about how he went after her." Carmen was clever with opinions on almost every subject and in particular on the Quebec separatist scene. Gertie had them over for dinner one night with friends who knew first-hand how highly charged the emotional split between federalist and separatist was. "She didn't have the brains to ask the right questions. She told them what Quebeckers were feeling. Can you imagine, with all the high emotions running then? A teacher from South America is telling them what they think? That did it. My friends contained themselves as well as they could but told me later, with people like that, what is the use?"

Carmen was pregnant; she and Henry were married January 19, 1980, in a civil service in Longueil, across the river from Montreal, followed by a party at the house on Melville. Mike, Gertie and Carl were at the ceremony, sitting, aghast, in the back row with Bamie, then interning in Boston. Gertie remembered him looking "stricken." Goldie had dropped out of journalism and then out of a master's program in literature. She was at loose ends, but she wasn't at the ceremony. Ed and Elinor Ratcliffe were, although they had left CARAL in 1976 to fund the construction of abortion clinics in Third World countries. Carmen was in her element; she was married and hosting her own wedding party. And she loved to hold parties. For Henry's birthday that year she had it catered and hired a butler. She wrote a song for Henry, which she played, accompanying herself on guitar, many times that evening. Gertie, Carl and Mike sat at the far end of the table, and Mike laughed at, not with, the proceedings, his voice growing louder and louder. "It was such a pretentious show," Gertie said. She was embarrassed for Henry, but angry at Mike for not hiding his reaction and — once again — trapped in the middle between the brothers.

Yann was born June 2, 1980, five weeks premature. At forty, Carmen had suffered placental insufficiency; her placenta had not been providing enough nutrients to the fetus. At fifty-seven, Henry was again a father, and deliriously happy about it. Mike and Gertie went to the hospital room with champagne. Henry was so excited he waved it in a stream around the room. Yann was in an incubator for five weeks, and when he came home, Henry said he did everything for him, from changing diapers to feeding him bottles. "I was a very happy father and he was a very happy child," Henry said. When Yann was four months old, they hired a twenty-year-old Chilean nanny, Marisol, recommended by Carmen's family. Henry would come home early from work to be with his baby and didn't realize, he said, that Carmen was ignoring Yann during the day. "She would pretend she had looked after him all day when I came home. But the baby was on the third floor of the house, and if he cried, it was Marisol who took him into her room with her." According to Henry, when Yann was eight months old, Carmen wanted to go to a yoga camp for three weeks to get away and "deepen her spirituality," she told her husband. Henry couldn't understand. He thought to himself, "a Jewish mother wouldn't do that." Carmen was not Jewish.

She began building a house in the country, on a lakefront lot in Morin Heights that Henry had bought as a favour to a developer friend thirty years earlier. Henry had never wanted a house on the property; he would only go there with various women companions to enjoy nature, picnic on the rocks and watch the sun set. But Carmen dreamed of a log home, and definitely had a flair for decorating. Henry left her to work with the contractor. Other than signing the cheques, he wasn't involved, but the house consumed Carmen. Elinor Ratcliffe remembered asking her once what it was like. "Substantial," Carmen replied. She very much appreciated the lifestyle a doctor's salary bought; she so enjoyed being the lady of a rather fine house that she began to cast an eye on the business that made all of it possible. "She treated Mike like a messenger, I was a hireling, Henry was inefficient and she could organize things much better," Gertie said. (Gertie had been working in the office of the clinic one day a week ever since 1978, when Mike had asked her for some temporary help.) Gertie remembered another dinner at her home — this time with Mike and Trudy and Henry and Carmen — during which Carmen again brought up how inefficient and badly organized things were. "Part of it was due to my lack of organization, and if I could just be replaced ... She was talking around it, but that's what she said. At that point Mike was laughing so long and hard he was doubled over. I was flabbergasted. Henry got her coat and said, 'Carmen, we're going to leave now.' He rushed her out of the house."

Henry was discovering Carmen was not as he had thought her to be. "She appeared to be liberal minded. She had many friends who were homosexual. She was for freedom of choice. In many things she was on the right [correct] side of the track, but when you dug a little deeper, there was a very conservative attitude," he said. Her parents were extremely conservative, supporters of the Pinochet military regime and concerned about their position in Santiago's very class-oriented society,

Henry discovered, when he visited them while Yann was an infant. Carmen's father, an employee for the Swiss-based firm of Nestlé's, was middle-class, but her mother was an heiress to a family going back five or more generations in Chile that had built an industrial complex based on iron and steel. Henry saw that what Carmen wanted was not much removed from the life her parents led. When pre-election polls in 1981 were showing the Parti Québécois behind the Liberal Party, led at the time by the staunchly Catholic Claude Ryan, Carmen asked Henry if he would still continue doing abortions. "Of course," said Henry. "Just because Claude Ryan is in power doesn't mean I give up."

"Yes, but that means there'll be more trials, and I'm not willing to go through this," said Carmen.

"Well, too bad, you know," replied Henry.

It was all theoretical. Henry was not fighting laws or societal standards — he was simply running a prospering medical practice — but he understood what Carmen was saying. She wanted the quiet life; she didn't want to be in the storm. If he indulged in civil disobedience, she wouldn't be there.

That's why he never bothered telling her when he changed tactics. It happened about a year later in February 1982, at around six o'clock one night when Henry was in Times Square, grabbing something to eat before his 10 p.m. flight to Chile. Carmen and Yann were already there visiting her family. Henry had stopped in New York to see an immigration lawyer for Goldie, who was unemployed and no longer a student, and worried she would be asked to leave the country. In the restaurant, Henry went down a flight of stairs to the urinals. He heard footsteps behind him, but there was another urinal and he wasn't alarmed. Suddenly, he was being choked with a force so strong he thought it might be two men attacking him. He wanted to say, "Take my money and go," but he couldn't get a sound out. The man twisted Henry down to the floor. Henry looked right at him. He was young, about twenty-eight, with "very dispassionate, cool eyes, like a hunter looking at prey." Henry strained with every ounce to resist, thinking he would never see his little baby again and how sad it would be to die in a place like this. Then he passed out.

When he came to, his watch and wallet were gone. He still had his ticket, $1,000 in traveller's cheques in his breast pocket (normally he never used traveller's cheques) and another $1,000 he had inexplicably put aside in an envelope addressed to Mike. The envelope had been overlooked because it appeared to be a letter. He notified the police who prowled Times Square, but they found no one matching the description of his assailant. Still, he had money and he had his life. However, he had no voice, and when he phoned his office in Montreal he was so hoarse that his secretary didn't recognize his voice. Henry was concerned his throat might swell and constrict his breathing during the flight, and he took a taxi to a hospital emergency room for some cortisone. No one would help him. The staff at a pharmacy wouldn't help, either. He decided to have a Valium and take a chance. "I'm a risk taker," he reminded himself as he boarded the flight.

He had a lot of time on the plane to think. He wasn't a risk taker, not anymore. For the past five years he had been a bourgeois doctor, not a crusader. Reporters didn't call anymore; they had moved on to people like his Manitoba abortion foe Joe Borowski, who, the Supreme Court had just ruled, was allowed to challenge the abortion law. Yet at CARAL meetings and from other individuals and organizations across the country all Henry had been hearing was that the best they could expect was to hang on to what they had. Anti-choice groups had successfully taken over hospital boards in British Columbia and Prince Edward Island. In Moncton, New Brunswick, anti-abortion group pressure convinced a therapeutic abortion committee to suspend requests. Hospital boards in Moose Jaw and Prince Albert, Saskatchewan, were persuaded by similar groups that it was illegal to perform abortions without an obstetrics department. Only one doctor in Newfoundland did abortions — and he did only seven a week. "It was time to go in and open another clinic. It was the only way we knew at the time to break the back of the law." Close up, it looked like a win-win situation to Henry: the issue needed him to come alive and he needed the issue to feel alive. Somewhere above the clouds, between North and South America, Henry Morgentaler made up his mind to finish the fight he had started in 1968. He'd spend the summer writing the English version of his book *Abortion and*

Contraception. He'd promote it coast to coast in the fall, meet with supporters, get them primed, drop the red flag via letter to a couple of politicians and, if everything went according to past form, go to court, face a jury, get acquitted and win. He just wouldn't tell Carmen, Mike or Gertie for the moment. They would think he was on a suicide mission.

CHAPTER 11

HIJACKING A MOVEMENT

O N THEIR OWN AND INDEPENDENT OF HENRY, the women working on the front lines of this issue had been coming to the identical
conclusion. They had not gone away; nor had they been sitting around.
In 1977 and 1978, the Ontario Women's Health Organization (WHO)
and the Toronto Women's Health Clinic had each presented a brief to
Dennis Timbrell, then Ontario's minister of health, proposing to establish free-standing abortion clinics. His answer was the same each time:
no. His successor, Larry Grossman, also thought about it and said no.
Yet the situation was worsening. By the early 1980s almost all the doctors performing abortions had opted out of OHIP (the Ontario Health
Insurance Plan) to set their own fees, usually high (at least $300, when
Henry charged $225) and usually payable in advance. The ministry did
condemn this cash-up-front business as unseemly and unethical, but it
never bothered to reprimand or prosecute anyone for doing it.

Nevertheless, Metropolitan Toronto was described as a veritable
mecca for abortions. About sixteen thousand had been performed there
in 1980, almost twice as many as the 8,940 performed in Quebec's clinics and about one-quarter of the 65,751 legal abortions performed
throughout Canada that year. Between 1979 and 1980, the number of
abortions in Canada increased only 1 per cent, but in Metro Toronto
the figure shot up by 9 per cent. It may have looked like the promised
land for women in need of an abortion, but three thousand of those
abortions were performed on women who had come from places outside Toronto, presumably because abortions weren't available in their
own communities.

But there were other signs the demand outstripped the supply. In 1981, 181 Ontario women travelled to Henry's Montreal clinic for abortions. In August of 1982 alone, twenty-four of his patients were women from Ontario. About 10 per cent of the patients at Buffalo's clinic were from Ontario. Fewer and fewer provincial hospitals had therapeutic abortion committees, down nine from 1980 to 1981. One hospital — Toronto Western — had stopped doing the procedure for women more than fourteen weeks pregnant. At Women's College Hospital, three abortions were performed a week and no more. When requested by the Family Planning Network Subcomittee on Abortion to double their weekly quota, the hospital refused. Then, for the first six months of 1982, none were done there because the chief of the gynecological clinic, Dr. Gregory De Marchi, a member of a Catholic order of brothers, refused to allow abortions.[1] Toronto General Hospital did continue to do abortions — but only on Thursdays, and only six — and it was receiving, on average, seventy-five requests for abortions a day. Only gynecologists performed abortions in Toronto, and the women working in the birth control and abortion referral clinics were constantly updating their phone lists as certain doctors stopped doing abortions and others replaced them. Appointment calendars would immediately become booked. "It was a Russian roulette type of thing. You had to dial and dial and you couldn't get through for half a day oftentimes," said Carolyn Egan, a worker at the Birth Control and Venereal Disease Centre on Bathurst Street. Also at the clinic was Janis Tripp, who remembered always feeling as if she were calling into a radio station contest, because only the first six callers could get an appointment with the Toronto General. "We used to sit at the clinic with a chart of the women we wanted to refer and dial all the numbers except the last one, wait for the right time, and dial the last one and hope to get through. If you had three women, you knew they weren't going to take them all, so it was a case of prioritizing. None of us wanted to be in that position of making that decision for somebody else. It was just awful."

At times it was worse for the few women admitted for an abortion. Tripp talked one woman through an entire saline procedure (necessary because the fetus was more than sixteen weeks) via the phone. "They just left you in a room by yourself once they started the saline installation. They just left you there to go through your labour and deliver your dead fetus. The nurse would come in every once in a while and check you out, but nobody was going to stay with a woman for the whole time. It was horrifying. We were on the phone for hours. I told her I wouldn't go anywhere. I would be there for her. We took breaks when she got tired. I would tell her, 'Phone me back. I'll be here.'" Often the Toronto women working at the clinic would refer women to the abortion clinic in Buffalo, where they knew the women would be well treated and where they knew there would be no waiting for some committee to approve them. Tripp began to believe some hospital committees were deliberately delaying so they could say to the media that they were doing abortions, but in reality were using any and all excuses not to. In Toronto, women were waiting three to four weeks to be processed by a therapeutic abortion committee; in Northern Ontario, women were being made to wait six to eight weeks.

Along with the limited access to the procedure, some of the women had endured insults and abuse from their physicians — some had been called "sluts" to their faces. Tripp and the other clinic workers used to warn the women to take a friend along to the appointment with one physician, who would do inappropriate breast exams, supposedly to confirm a pregnancy. Another doctor used to wiggle nipples to wake women from the anesthetic after the procedure. "We really needed somebody to do good procedures and treat women well, even though none of these women complained. They were too vulnerable. They were never in a position to make a complaint."

Nor were the clinic workers. They were being overwhelmed by the daily scramble of trying to help all the women who were calling in. "Every Wednesday night we would get together to commiserate, share information, figure out what we were going to do next," recalled CARAL member Ruth Miller, who volunteered at the Women's Liberation Birth Control and Abortion Referral line.

On February 5, Henry had written Miller a letter: "I just got back from Calgary, where I had been invited to address the Calgary Birth Control Association. The situation there is bad. They send out 50 per cent of their women to the States for abortion. I'm getting more and more ready to start battle again to spread the benefits of my achievement in Quebec to the other provinces and establish clinics across the country." Then he added, "I think CARAL should get more militant. Will discuss it with you when I get back from vacation." Miller had laughed when she'd first read those words. "That was typical," she said. "Henry had a plan of how things should go, and if we weren't doing it or what ought to be done, he took the opportunity to let us know." It was at CARAL's eighth annual general meeting, in the University of Toronto's Hart House on April 24, that Henry announced he would open an abortion clinic in Toronto if the law wasn't changed to make obtaining abortions easier — and that he had already written Justice Minister Jean Chrétien, saying the law should be changed. "It came out of the clear blue sky," said Norma Scarborough, by then president of CARAL, which had renamed themselves the Canadian Abortion Rights Action League to encompass their broadened mandate and to fall in with their sister American group, NARAL, the National Abortion Rights Action League. "Our idea was then that it would have been nice if Henry had talked to us first. This wasn't a case of Henry having talked to us and then going off in his own direction, but an announcement of what he had done. We found out that this would be typical of Henry."

Equally typical, Scarborough added, was that Henry was right. Miller agreed: "We had tried to get services through hospitals until we were blue in the face. We thought it was time to get a clinic established here." She had spent many evenings listening to women debate whether they wanted a clinic to provide an abortion service only or a range of services for women's health. Then on July 15 Miller met with Egan, Tripp, Tripp's colleague Michele Dore and eight other women. They called themselves the Committee to Establish Abortion Clinics (CEAC). One of them telephoned Henry to clarify things. No, no, he told them, he was not the doctor who would be starting up a clinic in Toronto; another doctor, who was just back from Australia would be; he was the one Henry thought should have a clinic in Toronto. The women had never heard of this doctor, and Henry had just recently met him, as well, but thought he would do fine.

Les Smoling had worked in a legal abortion clinic in Sydney. From 1965 to 1968, he had operated an illegal clinic in Toronto called the Toronto Free-Standing Abortion Clinic, which was the main place of referral for the Women's Liberation Abortion Coalition and the University of Toronto Advisory Council, the CEAC women discovered; he had been charged three times, they also discovered. Smoling had literally skipped the country, returning only after the statute of limitations on his charges had expired in 1979.

The CEAC women checked out his background. He was a member of good standing with the College of Physicians and Surgeons of New South Wales, and sister groups in Sydney said he was a competent physician. But when they met with him July 27, they were decidedly underwhelmed. Tripp couldn't comprehend the man they were meeting. She thought Smoling awkward, and noted that he bordered on pudgy, his voice was high-pitched, his hair was dyed and his social skills were nonexistent. The women could not envisage him offering comfort to a woman during a procedure.

Maybe he was just burned out, they said to one another. He did know his stuff when it came to the issue. He knew he was risking arrest, he had $15,000 to put towards a clinic and — the real deciding factor — he was willing to take direction from a group of women. With Smoling, the women could finally have their dream: a woman-oriented, woman-run clinic. He was willing to be the technician; he was willing to say nothing, stay low and let Henry remain the main spokesman for the issue. "There was something attractive about having Smoling as an underling. Then we could work with him much more easily. And all some of us wanted was a technician. All we wanted was the assurance he could do [the procedure]," said Diana Majury, a lawyer who had been among the women presenting proposals for free-standing abortion clinics to Timbrell, and an early member of CEAC. "I was certain the women in the room with him [during procedures] could monitor him if he were, say, a sexual abuser. I was sure we could control every piece except, could he do the abortions? We were desperate and we felt we could have women around him constantly."

They turned to Henry, who was acting as their advisor and mentor, for the final say. Tripp has notes from a CEAC meeting on July 23 in which Henry had reported having "mixed feelings" about Smoling, that Smoling appeared to be under some stress when he was with the patients and he was nervous with the nurses. Henry said it was probably because he was working with new equipment and that the man could obviously do therapeutic abortions. They would need good support staff, Henry warned them; that would make or break the clinic. "Smoling did not inspire confidence, but Henry recommended him and said he could do the job," said Michele Dore, who quit work to scout locations for their new clinic. "The idea was, once we were open and operating perhaps other doctors would be available."

Henry flew into town to meet with them about the clinic, strictly as an advisor deep in the background, he assured all the women. They gathered at his hotel by the downtown Toronto waterfront. It became a brunch for Henry and the "gang of twelve," as they sometimes referred to themselves. Norma Scarborough has never forgotten that meeting, because just as the bill came, Henry had to take a call. Norma ended up putting the entire lavish meal on her credit card.

The women had plenty to tell Henry and one another. "We knew we would be doing all the work. And we did. Lots and lots of it," Tripp said. "Michele [Dore] had seen every progressive real estate agent in the city. She was very upfront about what we doing, but only if we knew the agent or if he or she was recommended." They looked at houses, old nursing homes — "they were depressing," said Tripp — storefronts and an apartment on the Danforth above a popular East Indian restaurant. "We tried to make every space work. Michele wasn't going to give up on any of them." Finally they settled on 300 square metres on the twenty-second floor of Lucliff Place, a high-rise medical building, ironically less than a block from the offices of the province's attorney general. Smoling agreed that two women from CEAC would hire staff, along with Henry and him, as Tripp and Dore went out and shopped for equipment from the blankets on up. "It was all up to us. The whole time Smoling sat in his apartment and did nothing. He didn't seem like other doctors — he was so passive, uninvolved," Dore noted.

The women knew they also needed community support. They

decided to build a coalition of individuals and organizations endorsing the venture. CEAC would work on getting the actual clinic up and operating; the new organization would work on creating community momentum to keep it going. The first meeting of the Ontario Coalition for Abortion Clinics (OCAC) was held September 28, 1982, at Trinity-St. Paul's United Church in Toronto's Annex area. Tripp was one of three speakers. "We looked upon the development of a clinic in Toronto as the biggest breakthrough in the abortion struggle in the history of Ontario," she told the people from seventy organizations there that night.

CEAC had already sent one more brief to the minister of health, calling for approval for abortion clinics. As always, it was ignored. CEAC had also previously contacted lawyer Morris Manning, who agreed to represent the doctor; fobbed off a reporter from the *Globe and Mail* reacting to the rumours a clinic might be starting up; and been told by Henry they should start up a defence fund. Those at the founding meeting of OCAC that night were not totally apprised of the situation — organizers worried that anti-abortion infiltrators might have attended the meeting and they did not want word to leak that the clinic was anything more than a theoretical group goal. But it was clear from its onset that OCAC was going to be crucial. It would educate, politically organize and mobilize the public around this one Toronto clinic — "Otherwise it would open up and be shut the next morning, and we'd be in court for years," said Carolyn Egan.

They changed the syntax of the struggle, labelling themselves prochoice because it fit their broad socialist political agenda as well as took much of the sting out of the anti-abortionists' attacks. Even women who would not have an abortion themselves could support the notion of having access to abortion within the list of options available to others. "When we said choice and we said it everywhere, at every rally and at everything we ever put out, what we meant by choice is the whole range of women's issues.... And abortion was part of that and we decided we had to fight for abortion because we really felt it was under attack," said Egan. The political right had made the struggle for abortion, and by extension women's reproductive rights, a basic tenet in its action strategies.

OCAC's own strategy was modelled after the successful movement in Quebec and was to build alliances and a ground swell of favourable opinion before the clinic opened its doors, to create a united social movement centred on the abortion clinic. They became the women who could hit the pavement running, pulling together and pulling off a demonstration in hours, the ones who believed in guerilla theatre, mass actions of the fist-waving variety. They deliberately never held official positions of leadership, although Egan was always front and centre. With her thick braid of prematurely white hair over one shoulder and alert blue eyes, she was easy to pick out in any crowd or meeting. More of a standout, however, was her uncommon ability to turn radical political rhetoric into slogan-chanting group actions and still emerge sounding sensible and reasoned on all the television news sound bites that evening. Egan's wide streak of pragmatism gave her more credibility with media and the mainstream than many of the other counterculture lefties, as they were then labelled. Egan never lost sight of the movement's political mainframe — her subsequent analyses of the pro-choice movement and OCAC, written and otherwise, rarely if ever mention Les Smoling, for instance — and she was more comfortable in the line of women inevitably standing behind the speaker at the microphone.

More and more that speaker was Judy Rebick, now an outspoken feminist, television personality and writer, who arrived in the pro-choice movement from the activist ranks of the League of Revolutionary Workers. Rebick always said that's where she crafted her rhetorical skills, which were impressive. She knew how to say it dramatically and swiftly — and unrehearsed — for the benefit of all the radio and television reporters, who had only thirty seconds allotted in their news items for a talking head to make the point. She once told Norma Scarborough that the Revolutionary Workers had taught her to speak well "and use small pieces of paper you can fit in the palm of your hand," a skill she was to use often when, as president of the powerful feminist umbrella group, the National Action Committee on the Status of Women (NAC), she crisscrossed the country, leading the No side during the Meech Lake debate. Rebick was a member of OCAC's co-ordinating committee, along with women from the International Women's Day

Committee such as Linda Gardner and, later, Cherie MacDonald, whose stints at the loudspeakers during demos and rallies were as much stand-up comedy as sit-down revolution.

OCAC held public bimonthly meetings from that September meeting on, but the power and strategy plotting happened behind closed doors at the in-camera meetings of the executive committee. They considered CARAL middle class — and everything that entailed. Cherie MacDonald once told Norma Scarborough, clad in blazer and knee-length blue skirt, that by dressing "respectfully" Scarborough was giving in to the system. MacDonald favoured the message inherent in torn jeans and military jackets. Clearly, the two groups did not always get along, but they worked together effectively. Their territories were sharply delineated — CARAL would continue to lobby politicians to press for legislative reform and educate the citizenry about the issues in boardrooms, meeting rooms and classrooms; OCAC would hit the streets with banners and bullhorns.

One of OCAC's first converts was the Ontario Federation of Labour. OCAC attended their annual convention that fall. "We put together five hundred kits on why abortion was a trade union issue. We went to every caucus. When the motion actually came to the floor, OFL president Cliff Pilkey was wearing a Choice button. We framed the motion that if a woman in truth was going to have equality at work, then she had to have the right to control her reproduction, and that was pivotal. We had women and men at the floor mikes, talking about what it means. We won handily, but not unanimously," said Egan.

The woman who swayed the union members was one of their own. Joyce Rosenthal had been fighting for freedom of choice in family planning for more than thirty years, ever since her second child, Ron, was born a hemophiliac. Joyce and her husband, a sculptor, decided they should not have any more children. She stood up in the crowded hotel ballroom and introduced herself as a member of Local 343, the office and professional employees' international union, member of Organized Working Women and "loving friend, comrade and mother of the late Ron Rosenthal, militant hospital worker, who was discharged, along with thirty-four other hospital workers in this province,

for participating ... in an illegal strike. Unfortunately he did not live to
see his vindication — twenty months after being fired, the arbitration
board changed the discharge to a short suspension." In a voice quiver-
ing with outrage, her nervousness at speaking in front of so many evident, this small woman with abrupt gestures and grey hair cut in bangs
straight across her forehead changed the meeting's tenor from the political to the personal. "In spite of taking all birth control precautions
available, on three different occasions I became pregnant," she said.
"Each time I pleaded with physicians and hospitals to give me an abortion. Each time I was refused. Each time I had to resort to a woman who
didn't have any medical training to induce an abortion. Each time I had
to go to the hospital to recuperate from infection, brought on by a well-
meaning woman who worked in a less than sterile environment." As
a result of fighting for treatment for her son, Rosenthal and her sister
had started the Canadian Hemophilia Society. Rosenthal wanted to win
on this front, as well. "I am sure each and every one of us, sisters and
brothers, know women who needed an abortion and had difficulty getting it. Abortion is not only a woman's issue. It's a family issue. It's an
economic issue. It's a social issue. Because it affects all people, it's a trade
union issue."

It was a tough sell. But after much debate, the resolution the OFL
adopted stated:

> WHEREAS it should be the fundamental right of each woman to
> choose when and if she will bear children, and
> WHEREAS present Criminal Code restrictions affect the legality
> and availability of abortions, and highly organized campaigns are
> underway to further limit the right to choose and
> WHEREAS two-fifths of the population of Canada lives in com-
> munities not served by hospitals eligible to perform abortions and
> WHEREAS there is not a safe and effective method of birth con-
> trol for each woman;
> BE IT RESOLVED, that the O.F.L. endorse a woman's free-
> dom of choice by supporting the right of women to full access
> to abortion

BE IT FURTHER RESOLVED that the o.f.l. demand the removal of abortion from the Criminal Code

BE IT FURTHER RESOLVED that the o.f.l. demand that free-standing medical clinics providing abortions fully covered by provincial medical plans be established

BE IT FURTHER RESOLVED that the o.f.l. reaffirm its policy on sex education, family life education and birth control.

With that, the women had succeeded in broadening the issue beyond the purview of the women's movement. Theoretically, things were looking up, but in the real world of landlords and leases, disaster had struck. Everything was ready at Lucliff Place. All the instrumentation and sterilization equipment were there, a new bathroom had been built and a little lab area installed to do pregnancy testing and blood work. The clinic even had an opening date: November 2, 1982. Henry flew in to have a look, and gave the clinic his stamp of approval before he, Smoling, Dore and Tripp went out for a celebratory lunch. It was an unusually hot day, sunny except for the hazy layer of smog hanging over Toronto. Later that afternoon, just as Tripp walked into her east-end apartment, the phone rang. It was Henry calling from the airport. A reporter had just asked him when Lucliff Place was opening.

"Oh, God, now what!" Tripp gasped.

"Somebody has leaked it. The landlord is reneging. It's all for nothing," Henry told her.

Smoling lost all his money; he withdrew to his apartment, appearing for all the world a defeated man. Henry moved to take up the slack. He came to the Toronto for "a very stormy" meeting with CEAC, OCAC and CARAL at the Park Plaza Hotel:

Basically I said I was taking over the whole thing. They were mad at me because I was taking away their baby, in a sense. Carolyn Egan was there. She was a moderating influence when some of the others were saying, "We have this organized and you are taking over." I said to them, "The only reason I am taking over is [that] I have a sense of responsibility. If I open something it has to be well

done. If it is not well done the whole cause will topple. And if
it is not up to high standards it would be terrible if we had complications or a death. It would be the end of the ideal that clinics
could provide these services." My reputation was on it and I
might as well take a more direct approach. But there were
some hotheads there who couldn't be convinced, although the
majority were.

Among the "hotheads" were Tripp, Majury and Dore. They knew
too well they would never be able to find another place to rent in the
city, let alone soon, and that neither CARAL nor OCAC had the money
for a down payment to buy a property. The women had lost their
dream. "It was going to be Henry's clinic, not run by women for
women. That is what we've got now. We were going to have to deal
with it," said Tripp. "It's still going to be for women. We had to keep
focused on what this clinic was going to serve, and it was going to serve
women, and that was a hard vision to keep focused on, because some-
days you felt you were losing that focus [on women]."

Henry alerted Morris Manning, who contacted Bruce Bussin, a
neighbour and a fellow lawyer. Bussin was the one who found space in
a restored, red brick building with large, deep-set, arched windows that
abutted the sidewalk. It was at one end of an enclave of bookstores —
including Toronto's first feminist bookstore, the Women's Bookstore —
relaxed restaurants and one of the most popular and fragrant bakeries
in the city. Students hung out there; the feel was bohemian. Tripp and
Dore had settled on Lucliff Place for many reasons, all of them practical. But the location found by Bussin was political, dramatic and sentimental, perfect for all of Henry's complicated, unacknowledged, as well
as upfront needs and motivations. True to his form, Henry had already
gone public. The fact that there would be a clinic in Toronto was out in
the open and the centre of a huge campaign. The women scrambled to
keep up. By November 12, 1982, a full-page ad appeared in the *Globe
and Mail*, signed by six hundred supporters, who had paid to be counted
in (and had helped to pay for the advertisement, as well). It announced
a public meeting the next week, on Thursday, November 18, at the

Ontario Institute for Studies in Education (OISE) "in support of the legalization of free-standing abortion clinics."

This was going to be the pro-choice workers' litmus test. CARAL had released the results of a Gallup Poll it had commissioned — 72 per cent of Canadians now thought abortion a matter between a woman and her doctor — but Ontario's attorney general, Roy McMurtry, had vowed to close any abortion clinics as soon as they opened. This was a chance to show Queen's Park that many voters supported a clinic.

It turned out to be one of the best political meetings any of the women of CEAC, CARAL and OCAC had ever attended. OCAC had enlisted women to act as marshalls. By the time they'd assembled upstairs on the second floor of OISE, the seats in the auditorium downstairs were full and the line of people wanting in snaked along Bloor Street and north along St. George. Despite the anti-abortionists on their knees praying fervently in the institute's lobby, the air was thick with excitement, full of possibility. It was joyful; everyone knew then that the poll was right. This is what people wanted; this was something more than a thousand people paying $2 to come out and line up and be counted. Henry spoke about opponents as "fanatics acting out of revenge," but when Judy Rebick announced, "We are going to change the laws," the auditorium erupted into wild cheers.

Janis Tripp sat next to Les Smoling in one of the small pockets of calm in the auditorium. The man who would have been the hero was ignored — deliberately. "I remember protecting him like hell at that meeting. I told him to sit by me. I think I even picked him up and drove him home. I didn't know what he might say to people," Tripp confessed. "When Henry was going to buy the clinic and hire doctors, there was no use for Leslie anymore. We knew he wasn't the greatest. Henry knew he wasn't the greatest. There would be a short time in which he would work at the clinic, but he knew it was until Henry could recruit other progressive doctors who weren't afraid of the ultimate prosecution."

Were the women naive? In retrospect, Norma Scarborough thought they were. "Henry had the power to [open a clinic] because he had the money to do it. And the women didn't have the money to do it. We couldn't have done it." Scarborough said the women "had begged"

Henry not to come to Toronto. As much as they respected him and admired his Montreal clinic, they didn't want a clone of it. They wanted a woman-centred, woman-run clinic and "there was no way Henry could have let that happen. He wasn't going to go through what he went through in the seventies to have sat back. He couldn't have done that. He was too driven to be the centre of attention of this cause. He had made this cause his cause. He was not going to sit back and let a clinic open in Ontario or wherever and not be head of that struggle."

Of course Henry had been thinking of establishing a clinic in Toronto. "For prestige reasons, I wanted Toronto — sure," he said. He and Smoling had cut a deal and Henry had a partnership contract drawn up: Henry would be medical director; Smoling would be the employee. As far as payments and income went, it was fifty-fifty, but as medical director, Henry had the right to dismiss Smoling for incompetence. Henry would not have recommended Smoling to the women in Toronto otherwise. "It was clear to me it was necessary. I was putting my reputation on the line." Henry was also concerned that Smoling was allowing the women to do all the work and make all the decisions. Here seemed to be a man who wanted no responsibility, yet, curiously, was willing to risk jail and persecution. He definitely looked upon Henry as his leader.

"Smoling was my Trojan horse," Henry said. "He didn't make a move without me. He had the idea that if he hung with me nothing would happen to him. He had ideas of my importance and power."

Yet many women wondered why they had ended up with Leslie Smoling in the first place. "I certainly have wondered many times," Scarborough admitted. Judy Rebick believed Henry was "naive. If he likes you, he thinks you are a good person." Smoling ultimately did work at the Toronto clinic for a short time, but at the nurses' request was sent to Montreal for more training from Henry. Henry assumed Smoling was reacting badly to the stress and death threats his job elicited; his nurses refused to extend Smoling the benefit of the doubt. "If you want a class clinic," they told Henry, "get another doctor in." Eventually Smoling faded from the scene, re-emerging in 1987 when a hospital medical advisory committee in Woodstock, Ontario, revoked his two-year-old hospital privileges because of numerous incidents of "inadequate patient care."[2] In 1993, Smoling, then practising in Windsor, Ontario, lost his medical licence for overprescribing drugs. "He simply hands out drugs...that is the extent of his practice," lawyer Alan Gold said to a three-person panel of the College of Physicians and Surgeons.[3]

But in 1982 Smoling was essential to Henry, who had plans that affected, Henry believed, the whole of Canada. He had written the attorneys general in nine provinces, stating his intention to set up abortion clinics on their home turf. He requested they follow Quebec's example and refrain from prosecuting. As he'd expected, nobody jumped at the bait, so this was not a deterrent. If Henry's first rebellion was a knee-jerk reaction to authoritarian laws, this second offensive had "all the trappings of a well-oiled political campaign. Legal strategy, media strategy, finances and co-ordination with both national and local pro-choice groups were all carefully mapped out in advance," according to University of Calgary associate professor F.L. Morton.[4]

Or so Henry wished. The reality was that Henry acted and CARAL, OCAC and other pro-choice groups reacted. Groups operating on a consensual basis are by nature sluggish, and Henry was a man in a hurry, who anticipated and expected advocates of his cause to fall in behind and move swiftly. He wrote the CARAL executive from Montreal on November 21:

> After my two-week tour of Canada promoting my book and our cause, and especially after 4 enthusiastic meetings in Vancouver, Victoria, Saskatoon and Toronto, I am more than ever convinced that the tide is running strongly in our favour and that the only way to break the legal impasse is by building free-standing abortion clinics in the major cities as they now exist in the Province of Quebec.
>
> At this moment in our history, it is essential that CARAL become as strong, vocal and efficient as possible, and follow the very successful tactics used by the National Abortion Rights Action League (NARAL) in the States.[5]

At one time, NARAL had fifteen paid field workers; in 1982, CARAL had a small office on St. Clair Avenue in Toronto and a core group of a half-dozen people who met there every Monday evening, summer and winter. CARAL had testified before the joint parliamentary committee on the proposed Charter of Rights and Freedom, stating that anything in the charter for the purpose of extending the rights of the fetus should not restrict the rights of a woman to a medically safe abortion — precisely what the Coalition for the Protection of Human Life was requesting. Nevertheless, the charter proclaimed on April 17, 1982, was "scrupulously neutral" on the abortion issue.[6] By that time, CARAL was very concerned about the Supreme Court hearing scheduled for the spring of 1983 in which Manitoban Joe Borowski would challenge the 1969 Criminal Code allowing therapeutic abortions.

Borowski was as much a renegade as Henry, the counterpoint to his point, alike as only two opposing forces of nature can be. As passionate and obsessed with the rights of the unborn as Henry was about the rights of women, Borowski, a devout Catholic, had spent time in jail for his beliefs. He had fasted for eighty days because there was no right to life for the unborn in the charter. Only the intervention of Ed Schreyer, who contacted the Vatican's Canadian emissary, stopped the fast. Borowski had been a popular cabinet minister in Schreyer's NDP government until he resigned in 1971 to protest public funding of abortions. He was as adept as Henry at stealing headlines, and he was also as clever in choosing his lawyers.[7] Morris Shumiatcher was an intellectual, a board member of Alliance for Life with extraordinary legal credentials, including a doctor of jurisprudence and an appearance before the British judicial committee of the Privy Council. Ironically, he believed, as did Henry, that lawyers must use ingenuity and creativity. They must be innovators. He would argue that according to Section 17 of the new charter, the "everyone" guaranteed rights to "life, liberty and the security of person" included the fetus. Henry refused to publicly or privately take seriously Borowski's challenge. But CARAL did, and had mentioned it in one of their more recent fund-raising letters. This may have prompted Henry to suggest CARAL redirect any money he believed they were raising to fight Borowski's Supreme Court hearing.

"It is my opinion," he wrote, "that the money collected for the Borowski case should be used to defend doctors challenging the law in other provinces, in case they are prosecuted. If we win the right to establish free-standing clinics everywhere because no juries will convict, then the Borowski challenge will evaporate into the air. The people who donated the money obviously did so because they wanted abortion to be maintained...I am still paying my own lawyer for another year in monthly instalments on the debt remaining after my legal battles were over 6 years ago."

Henry usually dredged up the $100,000 he still owed Sheppard for legal services when he wanted to push CARAL to do more fundraising. "We were trying to help Henry," Scarborough remembered, "but sometimes his thinking about us getting money was less than realistic. He always was bringing up his lawyer's bill." He then suggested they hire a paid executive director (he also recommended a woman who was living in Victoria, British Columbia, who ultimately moved to New Zealand), reminded them they had to raise money for it and also to pay "for the running of an efficient office...A letter should be going out asking for additional funds in view of all those additional foreseeable expenses."

Scarborough agreed with Henry — CARAL would benefit from a full-time staff member; in fact, CARAL would love to have staff, lots of them — but that was going to take time, and money. In the meantime, CARAL remained a wholly volunteer organization already committed to worked on repealing the abortion law, educating the public in Henry's and their own way of thinking and helping establish the Toronto clinic. Henry's "suggestions" were simply not appreciated by everyone. Even Henry knew that. "It was brought to my attention that some Caral [sic] members felt badly about the comments I made to the media that they were poorly organized," he wrote. "I wish to assure you I fully appreciate the work done by so many volunteer people, but that we must improve our organization and efficiency in order to reach the enormous potential support which is out there, needing only to be tapped."

If Henry sounded abrupt and impatient, he was. People had told him that winning in Quebec was one thing, but English Canada was a whole other matter — different and important. To Henry, English Canada was Ontario — Toronto, specifically — because "it was the centre of Canada, the CBC was there, all the news organizations were there. Toronto is the metropolis of English Canada, so if we could establish a clinic there that would work, it would be a model for the rest of the country."

In the meantime, Manitoba was the one province with an NDP government. To Henry, that was as good a welcome mat as he would ever get. About the time Les Smoling's clinic should have opened, Henry was in Winnipeg, phoning the local CARAL contact, telling her to prepare for a clinic there. Ellen Kruger was astonished, but that was nothing compared with how the women in Toronto felt. Still reeling from the loss of their clinic, they were cringing from some of the reaction to Henry's announcement about a Toronto clinic. A *Toronto Star* editorial on November 4, 1982, for example, berated Henry for his "ill-considered arrogance" and said he was "offensively presumptuous" in thinking he could predict what a court would decide. "When Henry went off to Winnipeg it was 'What's he doing? We're in an uproar here. Why is he going there?'" Ruth Miller said.

———

The May 5, 1983, opening of the Winnipeg Morgentaler Clinic, the first clinic west of Quebec, was a triumph; "a historic event," according to Henry. Carmen drooped kittenishly against her husband at the press conference, modestly deflecting the praise for the beauty and grace of the wicker- and plant-filled clinic she had decorated. Henry proclaimed himself "dazzled." To his tape recorder he confessed: "I didn't realize that Carmen had such tremendous talent for interior decorating." In Montreal, Gertie was grimacing over Carmen's latest bill — $40 for a moose caller — but there was little she could do or say anymore. Carmen Wernli had decided to jump feet first aboard her husband's bandwagon. They had marched hand in hand in a rally in Toronto; she was jetting between Toronto and Winnipeg, shopping for furnishings for the two new clinics. Gertie continued to work one day a week, spending her lunch hour listening to Mike, who chaffed at and railed against

Carmen's free-spending ways until May 3, when he had told Henry over the phone that he was quitting. Henry rationalized Mike's behaviour in the memoirs he was tape recording at the time:

> For whatever reason, I think the strain of the last few months was obviously maybe a factor in that, but also the fact that I'm sort of not giving in completely to him and he puts up all kinds of petty objections about money and other things that are necessary for the building of the clinic. Well, it's just too bad. I mean, I told him that if he wants to quit and if he wants to quit by the first of June as administrator of the buildings and president of Habal [Henry's holding company], I said, "Well, you can quit, but I think you should consider this carefully. I can give you a leave of absence for three months and [you can] take a rest." The fact of the matter is I have been bending over backwards the last few months not to frustrate him and not to go against his objections except when I couldn't do otherwise, because he is a sick man now.

Mike didn't quit, not that time, but despite his brave front, Henry might not have been able to handle his brother's defection had it occurred. That summer Bamie had married Susan Edbril, an attractive dark-haired psychologist he had met in an elevator in the Boston Hospital where he was in residence. "You have to make a date with me before this elevator stops," he had said to her. She was from a wealthy New York family and the wedding was lavish and large. But some of Bamie's friends from Montreal were uncomfortably aware of the cold front between the tables of the father and mother of the groom. "It was such a schism," said one guest about Henry and Eva. Henry danced to a fast, exuberant song with his daughter, which ended with them both perspiring and grinning. The dance has special significance for Henry, because it is the last time he can remember Goldie being happy in his company. Not long after the wedding, she began to be cool and remote with him.

Goldie's behaviour was another reason that he threw himself back into the abortion cause — almost recklessly, some watchers at the time

thought, because Henry's run to Winnipeg had been arduous, dangerous and exhausting.

He'd barely known Ellen Kruger when he'd telephoned her at her
work the previous fall; they had met only superficially at CARAL's
annual general meetings in Toronto. That was enough for Henry. "Hi,
it's Henry Morgentaler. Remember me?" he asked Kruger. "I'm thinking of establishing an abortion clinic in Winnipeg. Do you think it's a
good idea?"

Kruger's mind leaped ahead — Manitoba was not the socialist paradise Henry had assumed it to be. This Prairie province was progressive
on economic issues, but Kruger knew first-hand that the provincial
New Democratic Party had a conservative core that reflected the social
values of the province's rural areas and its many and strong religious
groups. As far back as April 1977, CARAL-Winnipeg had proposed that
the government of Manitoba establish a pregnancy counselling service
(which would include "adequate facilities for performing abortions on
an outpatients basis") that was connected to or within a major hospital
facility, and would therefore be within the federal law. Of Manitoba's
sixty-four hospitals, only eight had therapeutic abortion committees,
they noted, and in Winnipeg three of the major hospitals — St. Boniface, Concordia and Misericordia — had no committee. Most of the
province's abortions were being done either at the Health Sciences
Centre (where bed space was limited) or the Victoria General Hospital
(where there was a quota of ten procedures a week). Every year hundreds of Manitoba woman travelled to Dr. Richard Leigh's abortion
clinic in Grand Forks, North Dakota (who later lowered the U.S. $250
fee for Canadians by 20 per cent because they constituted about 30 per
cent of his business, he said. Leigh also said the only difference between
Henry and him was "I do it quietly"[8]). But women often encountered
trouble crossing the border, even though Winnipeg's Women's Liberation Group had a system of volunteer escorts to accompany them. This
led some doctors to write letters saying the women were going into
the United States for a "medical procedure," never specifying which
one. Another local clinic, Mount Carmel, referred women needing
abortions to New York because Mount Carmel's indomitable founder

and director, Anne Ross, had a personal connection there. All this may have partially accounted for Manitoba's relatively low abortion rate of 8.2 per 100 live births in 1974, compared with 28.3 in British Columbia, 20.2 in Ontario (although only 1.8 in Newfoundland).

About three years later, two doctors at the Health Sciences Centre, one of them John Tyson, the newly appointed ob-gyn head, announced their proposal for a new reproductive health centre, and included their endorsement of a free-standing, hospital-affiliated clinic for abortions. The women rallied around the proposal, fanning community support, but when the doctors received one million government dollars for a new neonatal unit with no mention of a reproductive health clinic, they not only dropped their issue, they also stopped performing second-trimester abortions. "I think we were sold down the river," Kruger commented. "Not another public word was said."

Later in 1981, the Women's Health Clinic had started up, but they would not do abortions for fear of losing their government funding. The feeling was the same among staff of the progressive and large store-front health clinic called Klinic where Kruger then worked. All in all, the women's community was somewhat depressed and inactive. Henry might be just what they and the cause needed. "It's a marvellous idea, but we have a lot of planning to do," Kruger had told him the morning he called.

Nevertheless, Henry flew into town on November 30, 1982, expecting a huge community clinic kick-off meeting to complement the press conference, a meeting with Attorney General Roland Penner and the radio talk-show appearances he'd arranged for that day and the following one. Kruger had assumed he'd want to meet quietly with a few supporters, discuss the Manitoba climate and strategize. She'd been careful to keep word of the proposed clinic under wraps. Instead, Henry threw a no-holds-barred press conference announcing he was setting up a clinic as soon as he could find a building, and "it's not hard to find a good site in Winnipeg."[9] At the same conference he was shown an anti-Semitic cartoon recently published in *La Liberté*, the French-language weekly in Winnipeg. Henry was depicted as a knife-wielding Jewish butcher with pointed ears, standing next to trash cans out of which small legs protruded. Ravens pecked at the human remains. And in the background was Auschwitz and its telltale smoke from the gas ovens. "The people who are against abortions are the spiritual fathers of Auschwitz and the spiritual descendants of Hitler," Henry snapped. The cartoon remains the "worst" he has seen; but he was equally appalled by a letter from the bishop of St. Boniface (Winnipeg's French-speaking area). Published on the same page as the cartoon, it decried "the abortion action of a foreign doctor." Nor did any of the Right to Life associations distance themselves from the cartoon or its sentiments. "Anyone who can kill 116,000 innocent babies and receive $225 for each one has a nerve calling anyone else a descendant of Hitler," Right to Life president Laura McArthur was widely quoted as saying. Henry stormed onto an open-line radio show on CJOB hosted by Peter Warren, ready for a verbal brawl with Borowksi. He told Borowski he was "demeaning" himself. "You have used terms such as 'abattoir' which demean you. I'm not running a butcher shop. It's an excellent clinic that provides an essential medical service that is not being provided by hospitals in Manitoba."[10] Then he blasted Health Minister Larry Desjardins as "prejudiced" because he refused to meet with him.

However, Attorney General Roland Penner was amenable to meeting with Henry. At Penner's office, the reporters and even Penner's secretary were sent away and the two men agreed to call each other by first names. Henry settled himself in for a cordial, productive meeting with the former law professor and defence attorney. Penner told Henry about his father, who had been a Communist (as had Penner in law school). He said he was sympathetic to the ideas Henry represented, but reiterated that he was hampered by the obligations of his office. Henry mentioned that by not prosecuting him, the attorney general of Quebec had set a precedent Penner could follow. Penner did not seem to agree, and took a stand he would stick with for the months ahead: he could not stay any proceedings which might be taken against Henry Morgentaler. Henry asked Sheppard to talk with Penner. On January 20, 1983, Sheppard wrote back: "I had a long telephone conference on December 6, 1982, with the attorney general of Manitoba, Roland Penner. He explained his position. I informed him of the attitude which had been adopted by the Attorney General of Quebec. Although he was familiar with it, he did not feel he could follow it and my efforts to persuade him were not successful."

This was not at all what Henry had expected. Before returning to Montreal, he hurled a final insult at Penner and the other Manitoban politicians for their "lack of courage" and for caving in to a "fanatical minority."[11] He departed Winnipeg in an uproar, leaving behind a dazed Kruger attempting to build a coalition to support a clinic. The best she could do was announce a week later at a pro-choice rally that CARAL was starting up a Morgentaler Defence Fund for the legal costs everyone expected Henry would incur because she hadn't been able to pull together a supportive coalition. Or rather, she had been able to pull together a Coalition of Reproductive Choice (CORC), consisting of pro-choice organizations and individuals, but hadn't been able to elicit unconditional support from them for Henry's clinic. Many had been neither impressed nor amused when Henry Morgentaler had blown into town and made his announcement, obviously assuming Winnipeggers would all fall in line behind him and the cause. In an initial meeting, the group voted not to support a Morgentaler clinic, according to notes handwritten by Wendy Land, a teacher who was home at the time with her elder daughter. "It took a month or two to get the group on board," Kruger recalled.

A later Coalition meeting in January 1983 in the basement of a piano store was "contentious and successful," Kruger remembered, as a majority was finally convinced that supporting a Morgentaler clinic was the best way to support the pro-choice cause. But in attendance were those who didn't want to support a private clinic, especially not one owned by Henry Morgentaler, an outsider, a man and a brash and egotistical one at that. Others weren't willing to support anything illegal to get it. The NDP members wanted to give the government more time to meet the need. There were many pro-choice women in the Manitoba cabinet — Mary Beth Dolin and Deputy Minister Muriel Smith, for instance — who were working on the issue from the inside.

Kruger, a small, calm woman who became the major spokesperson and worker for the cause while holding down a full-time job as an administrator at Klinic, as well as meeting the needs of her husband, an IBM executive, and her children, saw clearly that Henry was the leader of a movement in the eyes of the media. And she was determined there would be a movement in Winnipeg for him to lead. "It was Henry's actions, commitment and courage which were the catalyst. Henry crossed the line and people were inspired."

People were also enraged and frustrated. When Henry agreed to debate Borowski at the Festival of Life and Learning at the University of Manitoba that year on January 28, Kruger and others in the Coalition thought Henry was hitting "a new low," dignifying a man they believed had often lied to attack their cause. They were wary but respectful of Pat Soenen, a Catholic nurse and head of the three thousand–member Manitoba League for Life organization, who was organized, efficient and effective in getting her message out through the media. "Holy Joe" Borowski was a caricature, ludicrous even to some of his followers, they thought, and Henry should ignore him.

A bomb scare was telephoned in while Henry was midway through his opening remarks and the packed hall evacuated. When everyone returned, Henry dropped his own bomb: staff at his clinic had performed an abortion on the girlfriend of the son of a Canadian attorney general who lived in a province where he was planning to open a clinic, he stated. The father of three sons, Penner was understandably outraged, and subsequently tore into Henry's ethics and motives in front of the press. He reiterated his support of a woman's right to an abortion, but Henry Morgentaler's manoeuvring had been "shamefully exploitive." Henry had been referring to a New Brunswick politician, but he had not made that clear. Nor did he later attempt to apologize to Penner in private; he figured the damage had been done, knowing as he did that it had started a week or two earlier when Henry had spoken to a group of law students at the University of Toronto a week after Penner and had criticized what Penner had said to them.

Henry didn't look back. He was focused on opening his clinic. A building had been found, a former house at 883 Corydon Avenue, the street where Winnipeg's hottest new restaurants and computer cafés are now located. Then it was a quieter neighbourhood of small local businesses and hardworking, house-proud residents. But before anything else, Henry had to obtain a personal licence to practise medicine in Manitoba and an occupancy permit for Corydon Avenue, and meet the Manitoba College of Physicians and Surgeons' standards of quality control, none of which was easy. "I don't think Henry ever imagined how many hurdles there would be. I mean every step of the way hurdles were put up — for getting the renovation licence, getting the facility approved, permits for all the different kinds of work that had to be done on the building. I don't know how many times the opening was delayed," said Kruger.

Lawyer Arne Peltz, a Coalition member, worked behind the scenes to convince the province they had the power to legalize the clinic — "all the province had to do was sign a letter that it was a provincial responsibility and then the whole thing was legal." Later that year he wrote a paper — "The Role of the Attorney General in the Morgentaler Case" — that concluded that the attorney general could decline to prosecute, could stay any charges already laid and could act personally on these matters, and in theory and practice controlled Winnipeg's police force.

Another CORC member, Linda Taylor, was a powerful and influential NDP organizer and member of their executive, who was lobbying the politicians and party insiders. She held a breakfast meeting at her house for all elected NDP women — five MLAs, three city councillors — plus every woman on the federal or provincial party executive who was pro-choice. "I had an idea that as they were all pro-choice they could en masse say they would quit if the NDP didn't change its policy. But the women finked out. They had other causes, they weren't sure...we didn't have the nerve to do it."

The vehemently anti-abortion Manitoba health minister, Desjardins, was a savvy politician who wielded enormous power adroitly — when he crossed the floor from the Liberals to the NDP fold he brought the sought-after voters of St. Boniface, Manitoba's major francophone riding. "The party would give him anything he wanted," Taylor said. Yet the Coalition hoped that the NDP cabinet would do right by them. They pleaded with Henry to give the government more time to approve his clinic as a hospital. "[Wendy Land] is a girl who is supposed to be a

supporter of mine, and [she] declared at one meeting that I was her hero
and then she proceeded to upbraid me for not co-operating with that
group and doing it all my way and being stubborn and not listening to
anyone, and yesterday she proceeded to do the same thing for more time
before opening the clinic," Henry complained in his taped memoirs. He
told them he would wait for the cabinet to hold two more meetings, but
that was all. A Winnipeg clinic was becoming an expensive proposition
and CORC was not fund-raising as aggressively as Henry expected them
to. "We were initially all behind him," Land said. "It wasn't until he
went off on his own and made all those assumptions that all the money
we were raising was going to his legal defence, even though we had no
say in his legal strategy, that we began to object."

What really appalled the Coalition was the man Henry hired as his
lawyer. CORC had submitted to Henry a short list of lawyers who were
skilled and devoted to the cause. "But he ignored it and hired this man
with this horrible reputation among us for the kind of cases he took on,"
said Land. "He defended murderers and rapists. He was...also the
most expensive lawyer in town."

Greg Brodsky had defended 163 murderers when Henry hired him
(it's five hundred now and climbing). He had a reputation as a driven,
obsessive, workaholic insomniac, who had learned Dutch to help him
understand some crucial evidence in one of his cases. As arrogant, gutsy
and successful as Henry, he, too, preferred to remain a relative outsider.
Brodsky may have had the corner office, but he had not made the letterhead. The firm where he worked was called Walsh, Micay and Company. "I was definitely not a popular choice," Brodsky said. "Henry hired
me for negative reasons. He didn't want to go to jail." Brodsky took the
case, he said, "Because Henry was in trouble" (technically, Henry wasn't
yet, but charges were inevitable as he kept moving down his deliberately chosen collision course) and because Henry didn't ask him how he
felt about abortion. "I don't audition for the job. I didn't agree to represent him as an agent. I was his lawyer." He also took it because Henry
Morgentaler was the biggest news in town, and as the legal moves un-
folded, it was Brodsky, not someone from the Coalition, who was quoted
by the media.

"We almost did kill each other in the beginning, but that's the reason it worked out. I trust him and he trusts me, but it took a while," Brodsky recalled. It was a point of honour for Henry that Brodsky considered him a "difficult client," because it meant he was never pliant. "I know exactly what I want. I know how to go about it and I am not easy to manipulate." When Henry called his enemies "jackals" or "hyenas," it made the papers; when Henry told the *Globe and Mail* he gave the instructions to his lawyer, not vice versa, it was also reported. When Brodsky protested, Henry rationalized, "I was bleeding, wounded, on the ground, and they [the Manitoba College of Physicians and Surgeons] came in to attack me then."

Somehow, he and Brodsky ended up liking each other. When he was in town, Henry used to call him from the Delta Winnipeg Hotel, where he always stayed, to drop by for one of their many postmidnight meetings, which would last hours and sometimes get personal. "I *know* him," Brodsky said. A religious Jew who observes Shabbat and at the time was president of his synagogue, Brodsky invited Henry and Carmen to his home for the Friday-evening meal.

"I know he likes to be around his people," Brodsky said. But Henry refused to put on a yarmulke, even when Brodsky insisted. That was April 23.

Henry opened the clinic unofficially Saturday April 24, 1983, by performing three abortions. He had mentioned earlier to Brodsky, almost in an offhand way, "Well, you know we're doing a few cases today."

"I'm sure they're all emergencies," Brodsky replied straight-faced.

"Well, sure," Henry countered.

They both laughed too loudly at Brodsky's weak joke, each too proud and stubborn to let on to the other that they knew just how gruelling the battle looming ahead would be.

CHAPTER 12

GURUS AND GARDENING SHEARS

Soon after the anticlimactic opening of the Manitoba clinic, Henry left for Oregon to follow a guru.

Baghwan Shree Rajneesh, the "sex and Saran Wrap swami," as he was swiftly labelled by media pundits, had set up an earthly and very earthy paradise of spiritual followers outside Antelope, a small town in Oregon. Along with a fleet of ninety-three Rolls-Royces, the guru had managed to amass thousands of red-robed devotees, most of them white, middle-class professionals, 60 per cent of them college grads, who changed partners as often as a square dancer. David Marcus, a writer for the Knight-Ridder newspaper wire service, described Rajneesh's blend of "laid-back California-style sensory therapy and Eastern mysticism" as an amalgam of the "spirituality of Buddha and the materialism of Zorba the Greek."

Henry said he first heard the swami's East-West fusion on tapes belonging to people he'd met on primal therapy weekends at Mays Landing. "He dealt with science and technology in a way that would enhance society. He used (the Western world's) problem-solving knowledge along with the Eastern way of going deep into the soul, of meditating. I thought it was a tremendous idea. I thought it would create the kind of person who had knowledge and a deep understanding of soul and self."

By this point, the union with Carmen would have been shaky even if Henry hadn't subscribed to the "wife and mistress" school of marriage, so Henry went to Antelope alone. As a neophyte, Henry was given a band with one bead, signifying he was untested — and that meant medically. Anyone having sex with Henry was on her own. "Rajneesh was ahead of his time about AIDS and diseases," Henry explained. "He had his followers wear rubbers. He even had married couples wear condoms and rubber gloves during sex. I thought *that* was stupid."

He was one of a handful of guests in a hotel Rajneesh owned, where the rooms were $90 (U.S.) a night. The television broadcast only speeches by the guru and the room service wasn't. Instead, steak-and-potatoes-loving Henry got coupons for vegetarian food served up in a communal dining area. But he liked the guru's brand of dynamic meditation where he and others moved freely to music; he approved of the advice he heard others get in some of the counselling sessions; he liked the chanting, the massages; he agreed with them that sex was important; he figured all the Rolls-Royces weren't.

He tried to meet Rajneesh, but the guru's guards stopped that. He only saw the great man at two o'clock each afternoon, driving down Zen Road in a Rolls, with machine-gun-toting bodyguards in trucks in front and behind. This may not have been all paranoia. By November of that year, Rajneesh was involved in more than a hundred lawsuits, and so many sexually eager visitors had flooded the Rajneeshpuran commune-compound that Ma Anand Sheela, the guru's principal advisor, had to officially announce to the women followers they were not obligated to have sex on request. (Two years later, Rajneesh was arrested on board a plane he had chartered with some followers, trying to avoid some immigration charges. He was fined $400,000 and ordered never to return to the United States; his fleet of ninety-three Rolls-Royces were put up for auction. He died in India in 1990.)

After three days Henry was bored. "I had never intended to become a disciple," he said. "The way they talked about Rajneesh, like he was a living god." He left early, eager to get back to where he was a leader.

He was in Montreal again, when in Winnipeg the police pulled up in six police cars at the trim, white-stucco clinic building on Corydon Avenue shortly after 9 a.m. on Friday, June 3, 1983. They pushed past the Right to Life protesters already out front as they rushed the building. Four officers stationed outside prevented anyone from following or from leaving. Inside, Dr. Robert Scott and head nurse Lynn Crocker were in midprocedure. It was their habit to lock the door to the second-floor operating room. After this raid they began to lock the door at the foot of the stairs, as well. When police knocked on the OR door, Crocker had the presence of mind to ask them to shove their badges under the door as proof of their identity. "They were so upset when I opened the door, but it gave us some time to get the patient up and off the table," she said. About forty minutes after they had come, police escorted Crocker and Scott out by the front door. The others in the clinic, including patients, were led out the back, heads covered with blankets. By the time Borowski arrived at the scene to congratulate the police, the women and staff had all been questioned and released from the police station, without any charges being laid. The staff returned to the clinic because other women were booked for that afternoon. But police had scooped up the equipment from the operating room, and Crocker spent the time lining up alternative appointments for the women, as Bob Scott slipped quietly out of town on an already scheduled flight back to his home in Alexandria, a town near Cornwall, Ontario.

A quiet, almost taciturn man, Scott had trained with Henry in Montreal. Henry hailed him as intelligent, dedicated and not afraid to risk criminal prosecution when he'd announced Scott would be doing abortions in the Winnipeg clinic. A 1978 McGill grad, Scott was six-foot-five, bearded, with reddy blond hair and hard to miss. The son of the surgeon general of Guelph, Ontario, and a nurse, he'd studied mathematics, philosophy, botany, anything but medicine when he'd first gone to university. He was twenty-eight when he went to medical school. But he never became a pro-choice spokesman, and always refused to be interviewed by media. "I was the leader and he was the follower," Henry said. Scott was so private some people in Alexandria, where he was a family practitioner three days a week, thought he had been in Toronto taking courses on his days off when he was in Winnipeg performing abortions. He presided at the home births of his daughter and son; for a time his wife, Maria Corsillo, did counselling for La Leche League. Their children were still toddlers when Corsillo read a column written by Michele Landsberg about a fifteen-year-old girl who had become pregnant after being raped and had been refused an abortion. That night at home Corsillo's husband called it "inhuman" and the next day she was on the telephone. Her calls led her to CARAL and Norma Scarborough — their friendship has strengthened over the years — and her offer of her husband to perform the abortion for the young teen. They were to pay a price for their compassionate action; Corsillo still believes raising their children within the ensuing abortion struggle was "a terrible thing to do to a child." They were often hounded by abortion opponents, once on a busy Saturday in a sportswear store in Toronto's Eaton Centre, when Corsillo, her seventy-year-old father and her children were accosted by one zealot, who leaned over her five-year-old son and screamed, "Is this how you spend your father's blood money?" An off-duty police officer happening by escorted the man out of the mall, but not before considerable time had elapsed and harassment had occurred. "That stuff is not something you forget," Corsillo said. Their house was sprayed with tomato juice almost as soon as her husband's occupation became known. Late-night phone calls of death threats had become a regular occurrence by the time Scott and Henry, along with four nurses and two counsellors, were charged with conspiracy to procure an abortion in Winnipeg. That happened on June 6, the day before Morgentaler announced he would be opening a clinic in Toronto the following week. He expected to be prosecuted by the attorney general of Ontario, Roy McMurtry, Morgentaler told reporters the following day as they toured the two-storey, plant- and wicker-filled Winnipeg clinic, which had been renovated and equipped at a cost of $100,000.

———

At least one hundred members of the media were already gathered on Harbord Street a half hour before Henry's Toronto abortion clinic was set to open at 9 a.m. on June 15, 1983. "I must have walked up those stairs and opened the clinic at least fifteen times for the camera," Judy Rebick recalled. Despite OCAC's morning and afternoon support pickets, things were pretty uneventful. No abortions had been scheduled; no Right to Life picketers had appeared. Henry was flying in from Winnipeg, where he had appeared in court after being fingerprinted, and then had held a press conference to say the Corydon Avenue clinic was back in business. His plane was due in at 3 p.m. About forty-five minutes later, a blue airport limousine pulled up. With another supporter, Rebick jogged across the street to greet Henry and lead him by the arm through the media horde. "The next thing I knew there was a guy grabbing him in front of me," Rebick said. "I pulled the guy off [Henry] and I pushed him back. That's when he pulled out the garden shears. I blocked his arm, but I could see in his face he thought better of brandishing the gardening shears. I was enraged. I wasn't scared till later."

The television cameras were on Rebick as she pushed the attacker away from Henry and waved a hectoring forefinger at the man. Henry looked startled, then confused, as the other escort grabbed his left arm and they ran to the clinic porch. Henry tried to laugh it off. "Well, he was obviously not in favour of abortion," he said when asked by reporters if he thought his attacker belonged to an anti-abortion group.[1] (Augusto Dantas, fifty-five, was subsequently charged with possession of a weapon dangerous to the public peace and assault and released after questioning. In November, a judge found Dantas had been drinking and gave him a conditional discharge, stipulated he had to do one hundred hours of community work and ordered him to stay away from the clinic.) Inside the clinic, Rebick sat down and cried, then pulled herself together for another round of interviews. When she watched herself on the CBC's national newscast that night, she realized she was shaking inside again. Henry called her after the newscast to say, "Judy, you saved my life."

"He was serious. I don't think he knew what had happened during the day until he saw it on TV. I had noticed that Henry hadn't said anything. I had thought he would have at least commented [at the clinic] that I had stopped a guy from hurting him, even if I hadn't saved his life, but he didn't say anything. He may not have been aware the guy had a weapon."

It had upset Henry more than he let on, even to himself. He feigned nonchalance: "She happened to be there. He was drunk. It was a reflex action. She just pushed him away. The guy didn't persist," he said in retrospect. He was not comfortable being seen on national television as vulnerable. He implied Rebick had overreacted. "She has a lot of anger, which she directs to the cause. It is very good to have an outside enemy." And what he dictated that night into his tape recorder started off jaunty and typically positive, even cheerful: "...tonight is sort of a special night in the sense that for the first time in history I have been physically attacked by a man wielding shears, gardening shears, in front of the clinic in Toronto, and I must say it didn't upset me too much. I'm really surprised at myself. It may have shaken me up more, but it hasn't, and in a sense I feel good about myself." Except "I'm tired. I'm sort of down. I take the occasional Valium in order to sleep. I've started taking Inderal, which Dr. Reisler prescribed for me so that my heart rate wouldn't go too fast and my blood pressure wouldn't shoot up too much. I find myself under too much stress. Today in particular I feel quite good about myself in the sense that the struggle is hard, but I'm so confident we are going to win. There are things that worry me, of course. The Winnipeg clinic is losing money. People don't come out because they are scared of the pickets or of the police action or police raids."

In Winnipeg the police came back on June 23. Suzanne Newman was filling in for the receptionist on a day off. Newman has since graduated from medical school and now works at the Winnipeg Morgentaler clinic, performing abortions, but then she was a mother of four young children, who lived near the clinic. She had joined the Coalition when she saw the picketers out front of 883 Corydon with their signs, "which were so awful, so full of lies about the Holocaust and baby killers." She kept notes about what happened the second time the police bore down on the clinic:

> [Clinic employee] Devon began describing the scene outside. One of the patients remained in the waiting area. I remained typing.... Then she yelled: "They're coming. This is it. Briefcases. Walkie-talkies." As she was relaying this, I sounded the alarm. Seconds later they...pounded on the door. Christina, who was a patient, stood up...I stood up and tried to say to remain calm, that nobody had to answer any questions, that a lawyer would

come and talk to us... [M]eanwhile Devon was opening the
door, which they pushed open and actually pushed onto
her body.

That scene has been freeze-framed in her memory. It was Newman's turning point. Like almost all the clinic supporters, she was middle class, respectable, brought up to believe the policeman was her
friend. "But [Devon] wasn't obscuring. She wasn't trying to lock the
door. She was trying to open the door for them. Their adrenaline was
awful," Newman said. "They were so excited, these cops. They literally
stormed the building." When Newman asked to see their search warrant, a detective slammed it down on the desk. Before she could look
at it, the detective ordered the others to get upstairs. Robert Scott was
unable to finish the procedure; his patient had to go to the hospital.

"The room filled up quickly. People were being let in the back door.
Others charged upstairs pounding on the door," Newman noted. She
phoned Brodsky, who wasn't home. When she tried to call his office, the
detective told her she'd already had one call. "They frightened everybody," Newman remembered. "Many of the women there [as patients]
spoke little English and were terrified. There were TV cameras — the
press had been waiting for something to blow. That was the hard part
for the women who were there for the service, not for political reasons.
They wanted their faces covered. This is the most personal of decisions,
and to have their faces broadcast over the evening news..."

The staff were herded into the kitchen, the patients into the waiting
room. Police ordered the partner of one of the patients to sit down.
"Well, arrest me then," he yelled back at them. While the police were
diverted, Newman told Devon to join the patients in the waiting area so
she could remind them to remain silent and could help calm them.
"Somebody had to be strong for them, because the patients were upset."
In Newman's purse was about $950, fees collected that day, which she
managed to covertly hand over to Brodsky when he arrived. While each
staff person was individually questioned in the kitchen for about twenty
minutes, the patients were taken to the Public Service Building, Winnipeg's remand centre and also, at that time, its jail. The patients were let

free, but the staff's bail was set at $1,000 on condition they not go within
a one city block of the clinic.

"We said this was crazy," head nurse Lynn Crocker recalled. Crocker,
Scott, Newman and three other staff had been arrested. Only one had
accepted the bail conditions. "Suzanne [Newman] would be breaking
the conditions if she even went home. Plus we were not doing anything
wrong." Crocker was incensed that the Crown had used as a precedent
conditions given to prostitutes about not returning to their street corner.
"So we went to jail."

"The usual way of doing it is to sign the recognizance, and then dis-
agree and argue with it when you are back on the street. You get your
bail, then tell your lawyer to challenge your provision, but from your
home, not from a jail cell," Brodsky commented. But at this stage none
of the players in this evolving drama was following a script. Henry had
publicly pleaded for the charges against his staff to be dropped; Brodsky
thought he had hammered out a deal with police that they would notify
the clinic in advance of any raids in return for access to up-to-date clinic
records, but that hadn't happened. Charged with conspiracy, Henry had
been robbed of an opportunity to address the whole issue of abortion in
his defence.

Scott was led to his own cell, content with a supply of books he
always kept at the ready. The four women were put in one part of a
compound on the fifth floor. They were strip-searched, not allowed
a comb or toothbrush, had their belts and shoes taken away and given
nightshirts. To shower, one woman had to keep flushing the toilet to get
hot water while another held the door closed. They hoped to make political points by their imprisonment, but there was little coverage of their
plight. On Sunday, Kruger organized about two hundred supporters to
come out to a rally in front of the jail. By climbing on another's shoulders, Newman could look out a small window and see the supporters
below, including her four-year-old son, Jesse, who had dressed in his
Superman outfit and come to rescue his mommy. "We got teary then,"
Crocker admitted.

The clinic staff were locked up from the Saturday to the following Monday morning, when a judge threw out the bail conditions but

charged Scott, Crocker and another nurse, Pat Turczak, with two charges of performing an illegal abortion, as well as conspiracy to procure an abortion. Newman and two other nurses (Barbara Burr and Lynn Hilliard) were charged with conspiracy to procure an abortion. "I remember sitting there as we were charged, and all the women were sitting way in the back, and Bob and the lawyers were sitting in the front at the table. I felt like Lynn Crocker should have been there — she had the same charges as Bob and Henry — but she was herded into the back with the girls," said Suzanne Newman. "Here we were, fighting for women's rights, and who was fighting for them? All these men. All the lawyers were men and all the doctors were men, and it hurt so. It was just something that when you saw it you either had to laugh or cry." For the second time police confiscated clinic equipment; Henry vowed to buy more and hire more staff to keep open the clinic. "The clinic is open ... we're on our way back to work," Crocker nevertheless announced on Monday, June 28, 1983.[2]

That afternoon, about three hundred marched to the legislature, demanding that Penner explain why the police had raided the clinic again. Instead, their friend and fellow pro-choice advocate Muriel Smith was sent out to speak with them. They expected to hear "I'm with you." But Smith was a government apologist, who propped up Penner and reiterated how the laws must be obeyed. "It was one of the most horrible moments I remember," said Kruger, who had been a leader of the march. "We couldn't believe what we were hearing. Then people started to boo, and here was our friend up there. We were saying, 'Stop it, Muriel. Stop it.' I was crying. Muriel was crying. Many women were screaming and yelling. Muriel should have never done it." Smith was booed off the stage; she was still crying when interviewed by a CBC reporter. "It was shameful," said Wendy Land. For many it was also the last straw, the shattering of any illusion that the provincial New Democrats would ever act on their pro-choice stance, even when their federal counterparts would reiterate their pro-choice position a few months later. That night, Kruger sat at home writing a letter to Pawley and Penner, drinking brandy and sobbing, saying to herself, "Did I really believe this was the party of my dreams?" Many other women quit the party; some wrote to say they would now donate to the Coalition. "They lost big-time," said Kruger. The NDP almost lost the next election, eking out only a two-seat majority, but in 1988, the election after that one, they lost it all.

The Coalition lost their faith and what was left of their political innocence. What they were fighting for had not changed, but the battle plans had. They now knew the Manitoba government would never be persuaded to turn a blind eye on the Morgentaler clinic, the way the Quebec government had. There would never be hospital-affiliated abortion clinics as long as Desjardins was health minister, and Desjardins would be health minister for as long as he wanted (he resigned before the 1988 election). The battle was going to take much longer and be much harder than they had ever dreamed. And now it was about much more than keeping open a clinic.

Crocker told Henry the staff didn't want the clinic reopened. "He was so angry with us. He just wanted to keep going. But there were women waiting in the wings to have the procedure done and it wasn't fair to them. If we had thought for one minute the government would say, 'Fine, let him do what he will,' but there was no indication of that, and the police made it really clear that if we kept breaking the law they would keep raiding." The women had talked it over in the cell. When they got out they listened carefully to the comments of others. "People were saying, 'Come on, Henry. Enough is enough. You've got the charges. Take it from here. Don't flaunt it in their faces,'" Crocker said. "Politically, people knew the politicians were saying Henry Morgentaler is not going to tell them what he can and cannot do. It was a battle of male egos here. That is what we were into. It wasn't political anymore. The more we talked the more we knew there was no reason for us to continue anymore. And what were we going to say to the women? You may get hassled the day you come? You may have police burst in the day you come? You may get thrown in jail? You may get your name in the paper?"

"I was taken aback," Henry said. "Up to this time they were pretty steadfast and determined." Others still were: Newman lent him $4,000 to keep the clinic running as a referral service. The rest of the staff left and Crocker scaled back her hours by half. Ed Ratcliffe wrote another generous cheque, and with the Coalition's support, Newman encouraged some general practitioners to come in and do routine examinations at the clinic for a time so it could profit from the billing. For a few years, the Childbirth by Choice Trust, an independent pro-choice education organization created by CARAL, paid the modest salary of a person to staff the referrals-only clinic. That, too, was Newman, who also tried to get women to go to their bank managers and borrow $1,000. If fifty women did it, there would be $50,000, she thought. "I feel embarrassed about the idea now," she said. "Nobody lined up, not one person. I was the only one. I couldn't understand why the others didn't think it was a good idea. I had complete confidence in Henry, and I actually thought this issue wouldn't last very long. I was so convinced of how right it was I thought it would last six weeks, maybe."

Mike Morgentaler flew in to help get the clinic expenses under control, and in Montreal, a somewhat sheepish Henry approached Gertie bearing a carton of receipts and ledgers of incomprehensible bookkeeping initiated by an accountant-bookkeeper hired by Carmen. "Give it to Carmen," Gertie told Henry. "She's hired an accountant and paid thousands to a business consultant. You don't need me." Henry picked up the carton and left. Gertie remembered Mike laughing because of his dislike of Carmen. But that evening at home, she thought about it and wondered if Henry was in trouble. "I picked up the phone and asked if he was and Henry said yes. So I told him to bring the box to my place, not the office, because of Mike, and I had a go." Gertie became the business administrator of the Toronto clinic as well as the Winnipeg clinic.

Carmen took it personally and exploded. She had hired the consultant to advise her on running three clinics; she had very much wanted to be in charge. She had not always been onside. Judy Rebick remembered one meeting in Toronto at the Park Plaza Hotel when "it was pretty uncomfortable because it was obvious [Henry] didn't want her there and she had nothing positive to say about what we were doing. She was a real drag." But Carmen had also made a strong and positive impression on others. Lynn Crocker was in awe of her collection of expensive suede suits in vibrant colours, made expressly for her by a

New York City dressmaker. In Toronto, clinic employee and pro-choice activist Pat Hacker thought of Carmen as being like one of the warm, fleshy, loving characters from the film *Bagdad Café*, with the sensitivity and sensibilities to create a clinic of contentment and caring that was filled with lovely things, like the perfectly shaped vase or the joyfully patterned floral sheets in the recovery room bedroom, that soothed and reassured. "She simply adored Henry, was totally smitten, thought he was brilliant, wanted to be there to do everything she could for him," Hacker said.

But Henry was not as appreciative as Carmen wished, because he wasn't as cavalier about money as he made himself out to be. Carmen had racked up huge bills on behalf of both clinics, but especially with Winnipeg. She did love to shop — she once told Crocker in a girlish giggle that she had been forced to cut up her credit cards while married to her first husband, a schoolteacher — but shopping was her one and only way into her husband's all-encompassing world of clinics. The clinic infrastructure was not well delineated: Mike Morgentaler assumed she needed his approval for all her purchases. When that usually wasn't forthcoming — Mike was always cautious about expenditures — Carmen would go to Henry, who would "break down and give in," Mike said, which made him feel powerless and frustrated. Then, inevitably, Henry would panic about the mounting clinic costs and complain to Mike. But when Henry told Carmen, "Look, [the bookkeeping] wasn't working. There's no point," he was unconsciously speaking about more than Carmen's business acumen or lack thereof. Carmen may have realized that; she did become "very emotional," Henry said.

As far as he was concerned, he told himself, it was all about the Winnipeg clinic — an infuriating reminder that he had put himself in a position to lose money with it open or lose face if it closed. In his mind he connected this clinic with the internecine battles being fought among his inner circle, and the out-and-out nasty business being played out between him, the Winnipeg police force and Howard Pawley's NDP government. "Winnipeg really was a drain. Mike and Carmen were feuding. Carmen and Gertie were feuding. They were draining me. It looked like it was going to be a catastrophe." He kept sweating the small stuff: "I continued to pay her salary for some months. I should have cut her off after two weeks," he said about Lynn Crocker's $500 a week full-time salary, which was soon halved.

The Coalition were also concerned about costs, and worried that every time Henry or Mike flew into town it was to say the clinic was being closed for good. They worked hard on fund-raising, and soon had a mailing list of three thousand. Many Winnipeggers who were outraged by the police raids voluntarily wrote cheques. Many wealthy Winnipeggers wrote big cheques. Nobody in the Coalition was too thrilled about a clinic opening in Toronto, because it meant they couldn't count on any defence-fund dollars from the East, but through-out the next few years, plenty of wine-and-cheese parties were held in the fine, older homes of River Heights with women who had paid $25 to attend, and at one point, Kruger addressed a forty-five-minute rally every Friday after work at the legislature, where the hat was always passed. More than $1,000 was collected after the staff were first arrested. And the Coalition sent lawyer Arne Peltz to talk Brodsky into cutting back on his fees. "I remember sitting in his backyard by his pool, telling him the Coalition could not afford his fees and that we had a list of other lawyers who would do the work for much less," Peltz said. "And he capitulated."

But the Coalition never stopped trying to tie Henry to their purse strings. "Is this an acceptable compromise?" began one draft of an agree-ment between them. "We will commit ourselves to $7,500 (depending on our having it or being able to raise it) plus our effort to help organize primary care delivery plus our continuing effort to lobby for control of the police. . . . In return Henry will not open to do procedures until we indicate that the political climate is acceptable." Henry crossed out the latter sentence and replaced it with "In return Henry will consult with the Coalition as to the political climate."

Finally, after one particularly heated battle over money with Henry, the Coalition decided to set up two funds. One was the Morgentaler De-fence Fund and the other was for public education around the issue. In 1984, a group of media professionals led by Randa Stewart devised a huge multimedia, issue-oriented, communications campaign that generated more than $190,000, of which only a small portion went to Henry. "I remember saying to Henry that there was no way we were paying off his legal bills, that this was our money and we would spend it as we saw fit," said Wendy Land. "If we decided to spend the money on your defence we will spend the money on your defence, but you should not assume the money you are raising is for your defence. It's for a public education plan we had already begun to establish before you came on the scene. He was furious. Around the table were those who supported me and those who supported him."

From then on, some fund-raising events supported the clinic and some supported the education program. "We felt we couldn't win this issue on just the legal case alone," Kruger explained. "We felt that this issue was broader than just the legal case. If we were going to win the clinic and hang on to it and win support for the women who were using it, we had to educate the public."

But in Toronto, police were planning a major swoop that would ultimately and irrevocably change the direction and up the stakes in this struggle for reproductive freedom. When the police raided his clinic this time, Henry was in the hot tubs of Esalon, California's high-priced hippie haven of transactional analysis and feel-good mud bathing. A cross-Canada warrant for Henry's arrest was put out even as he was chartering a truck to get to San Francisco to make his connection to Toronto, "which cost me a lot of money," he recalled. But by the time he touched down at Toronto's Pearson International Airport, his colleagues, Scott and Smoling, had been sitting in the Don Jail for two days and nights.

It was up to clinic spokesperson Judy Rebick to do the public sputtering: "If you look at the number of police and ambulances, you would think they were raiding Bonnie and Clyde, not a group of people wanting good health care."[3] Police had hauled out two huge ambulance buses and a smaller ambulance and were blocking eastbound traffic on Harbord Street. Two plainclothes police officers, posing as an out-of-town couple needing an abortion, had already gone into the clinic to book an appointment. According to Rebick, who had not been there at the time, the woman asked to use the bathroom, from where she signalled police outside the building to start the raid. Once again Scott was at work in the operating room when police bounded up the stairs and demanded a key to the locked OR door from a nurse. The raid occurred at about 11:30 a.m., about ninety minutes before an Ontario Supreme Court justice rejected Henry's bid for a court injunction to prevent any police raids. Rebick said police forcibly took the key out of the nurse's pocket and opened the door themselves. Newspapers reported that fifteen plainclothes officers, as well as uniformed policemen, took part in the raid.

"Harbord Street was yellow — cop cars were yellow then. The street was solid. They took over the whole street. You couldn't move. The yellow cars were like a tidal wave." Doctoral student and OCAC-trained marshall Andrea Knight had deliberately come to the clinic early that day — about 7:30 a.m. Representatives of the media were already there. Somehow, and nobody remembers how, everyone knew that was the day of the raid. "I was there, on the steps, helping these nice people into the clinic. We didn't know the undercover cops were inside," Knight said ruefully.

OCAC's policy was that every woman entering or leaving the clinic was accompanied by two escorts, to confuse police about the identity of the patient. Health worker and OCAC stalwart Linda Gardner had trained about a hundred volunteers as escorts and set up a complicated system of safe houses, where women could be met and where they could be taken after leaving the clinic — again to confound police. They had a phone tree so they could alert up to two hundred women and get down to the clinic within the hour.

When the raid began, Knight ran to the phone in the downstairs Women's Bookstore. "The fire escape was right by the window and all I could feel was the banging of endless cop boots running up the fire escape. It just went on and on. It was unbelievable. You got a real sense of state power and force. In our culture we don't live with that military presence."

Scott was quickly escorted out to a waiting police car and driven to the downtown 52 Division. Police took several boxes of patient files and the clinic's vacuum aspirator. By the time many of the police were leaving the clinic, they were met by more than a hundred pro-choice people, crowding the clinic steps and linking arms to prevent, or at least slow, the progress of the police. "I just remember the front steps were completely blocked," Knight said. "It took only a few minutes for one or two hundred supporters to get down to the clinic and be out front. I can still see those cops trying to move through to bring out cartons of evidence, and the women just wouldn't move. There was just this solid mass of people from the clinic, and the cops were trying hard to pick their way through. They didn't want to provoke anything, but they couldn't move." The women who were outside had no contact with those inside, but they knew that four patients, heads covered in towels, had been taken out by the back. At the same time, Smoling, who was not working at the clinic, was arrested at his Scarborough home, which was searched. Police found a document they later produced in court. It was the old contract between Smoling and Henry, in which Henry was to receive $2,165 monthly as a consultant for the Toronto clinic and had the power to hire or fire Smoling. (Henry was embarrassed when this was revealed in court. "I think that any time money is discussed I feel a bit uncomfortable. It's as if something within me still feels bad about making money or making arrangements about money," he said in his memoirs. "It's still this old kind of proletarian socialist upbringing that comes back and then the fear that I will be accused of trying to make money, that this would be my main motivation.") The police, however, were more interested in the contract as a basis for charging Smoling (and Henry) with conspiracy to commit abortions between 1982 and 1983. Smoling, Henry and Scott were also charged with two counts of procuring miscarriages, the legal terminology for abortion.

The next night, then provincial New Democratic Party leader Bob Rae, CARAL's Norma Scarborough and labour representatives addressed a Queen's Park pro-choice rally of four thousand as Henry was met by his lawyer, Morris Manning, in a secured section of the airport and escorted through the baggage section. Henry did not join Scott and Smoling in jail, but went to a hotel, after promising not to speak with media and to surrender to Metro police first thing the following morning. The next day the Canadian Press wire-service story that ran in many newspapers across the country reported: "Judy Rebick, spokesman for the Ontario Coalition for Abortion Clinics, received one of the loudest cheers of the night when she told protesters just before the rally ended: 'Henry Morgentaler was not arrested tonight.'" But Rebick also promised they would raise money to replace the confiscated equipment and pay for the legal defence, and within the pro-choice circles that statement was much more explosive. It tore apart and ultimately destroyed CEAC. "There were always two opposing factions within the pro-choice movement," Rebick rationalized. "There was a wing in the women's movement that wanted nothing to do with Henry." In fact, Rebick had become a spokesperson for the clinic and OCAC because many quickly understood it would be the only way the women's movement was going to get a voice in the struggle. Rebick relished her role — "Not to undermine Henry," she made clear, but to keep the struggle focused on women's agenda. "Henry was a very strong-willed person, very stubborn. He's not a feminist but a humanist, which is different. He does understand the equality of women is one of the central social issues of our society, but he is very much an individualist," said Rebick. "I still don't think he understands the role of the women's movement in it all."

But he did understand the role of individual women like Rebick, Scarborough and others. As Rebick put it, "What he does is glom onto individuals he sees — he would describe them as energetic, powerful people — that's how he would see them. The first time he met me he was onto me right away because he saw I was powerful, I was passionate and I was energetic, and so right away he honed in on me and paid a lot of attention to me and asked me to be the spokesperson for the clinic. He very much relates to individuals, not to groups." Rebick definitely had the gift of the quotable quote, but the media were so focused on Henry that some of her best statements ended up coming from Henry's mouth when they made the next-day editions. "Henry wasn't a great speaker, but he was a great man. That's what people responded to," Rebick believed. Henry was always willing to share the microphone and press conference time with Rebick, who built up a large media presence for herself, and therefore the clinic and the women's movement, despite the fact many within OCAC and CEAC hadn't wanted a spokesperson at all because it deflected from their collective cause. But when Rebick announced at the rally that the women would be fund-raising to buy new equipment so the clinic could reopen, clinic supporters and CEAC members Diana Majury, Michele Dore and Janis Tripp were not just angry, they were offended.

"We supported Henry, but we were not in it to invest in his business," said Majury. They were not against fund-raising. Dore and Majury had attended one event in the wealthiest section of Toronto, in the home of a Rosedale judge, where the (male) butler wore a tuxedo and was very attentive about refilling drinks. They were embarrassed at being served by a uniformed male; embarrassed that the guest of honour, American feminist-lawyer Flo Kennedy, expected homage; embarrassed at the awkward alliance of otherwise disparate women united only in this one issue. Both bright, very articulate women, they mumbled a few stock, depoliticized phrases when it was their turn to speak and quickly left. "We were not great," said Majury. Even when the clinic became the Morgentaler Clinic, not the Toronto Women's Health Clinic or any of the names they had been thinking of, and it might as well have been stamped "Property of Henry Morgentaler," they continued to work for it. Majury, Dore and Tripp still wanted a women-oriented abortion clinic, which they dreamed would become the centre of a women-run extended-health-care clinic, but they saw "by that time there was a larger political agenda," as Dore said, and that it was being finessed by Rebick and Egan. And that agenda focused on one clinic and every aspect of its defence. "We couldn't bear to see OCAC turn away from all the public education, all the lobbying. We thought, CARAL is out there. They have defence funds and they're a bigger organization. We thought if we do fund-raising, shouldn't it be for women who can't afford a procedure? For getting transportation for them?" said Tripp. That fall, the issue was brought to a vote at an OCAC meeting. Tripp, Majury and Dore met ahead and decided they would quit CEAC and OCAC if it was decided that all the money would go to clinic defence, which is what happened. They were not even given the courtesy of being allowed to speak to the issue before the vote, Tripp recalled. Majury said she found leaving "really hard." Dore said, "It was terrible." But Rebick said it was one of the hardest decisions OCAC ever made: "I was really angry. They just didn't want to give the money to Henry."

Tripp was devastated. "It was out of our hands now. Basically, it was Henry Morgentaler and his property and his ass on the line." Henry was oblivious to their pain. What he wanted was the endorsement of the women's movement, and that is what he got. The fact that it wasn't unanimous didn't trouble him. Tripp went back to work with Egan, but Dore quit her job at the service. Henry wasn't concerned by Dore's withdrawal, although she had worked on his payroll for a few weeks while locating a new site for the clinic. Dore was aware that Henry didn't like her — she speculated he may have been disturbed by her out-of-the-closet lesbianism, but said she never had any concrete proof of it — and believed Henry made it clear he was not comfortable to have her work in the clinic. Tripp continued to have a cordial relationship with Henry and was on call as a witness for his trial, which was gearing up. She never expected Henry to analyze the issues with which she and her colleagues found difficulty. Tripp said, "He was a very proud figure. And egotistical. He is the centre of his universe for a lot of people and if someone else didn't see him as the centre of their universe it made no difference to him. He was far too busy, and I don't think he would have stopped for a minute to look at the reasons we were backing away. He was in charge — he was doing this — his neck was on the line — he deserved this support. And he did. And he got it big-time."

The only time she and the other CEAC members received any public recognition for their clinic-building work was in a column written in the *Toronto Star* by Michele Landsberg. Tripp and her colleagues were not even mentioned in an OCAC history written by Bob Lee, a pseudonym for several OCAC members. CEAC's plan was the first, but not the last, attempt to have a clinic belonging to women. But with one exception — the Everywoman's Health Centre in Vancouver, British Columbia, which was created much later — any attempts by women to go it alone were doomed. In Canada, the abortion issue belonged solely to Henry Morgentaler. He was the only doctor in the country willing to publicly put his neck on the line.

Then, on July 29, 1983, a fire deliberately set in a closet of the ground-floor Women's Bookstore damaged $25,000 worth of books and caused $10,000 worth to the building. On the second and third floors, the clinic suffered water and smoke damage. Andrea Knight had received a call at home at about 2 a.m. Someone riding past the clinic on a bicycle had seen flames. She called Bob Gardner, and by the time they arrived on the scene at about 3 or 4 a.m. the bookstore was gutted. "By six o'clock when we were allowed to go into the clinic, the entire OCAC executive was sitting on a doorway stoop across Harbord Street, having a meeting, planning a rally, writing a flyer. By 8 a.m. it was printed and distributed," Knight said. Six months later, Agostino Oliveiro Bettencourt, twenty-three, was sentenced to two years less a day in prison for breaking and entering and arson. He was not a member of any pro-life group, but it was widely assumed the clinic had been the primary target. "We're dealing with the fanatic fringe of the anti-choice movement. Only a lunatic would do that," Henry said from Winnipeg. A man sleeping in a third-floor apartment in the adjoining building had been rescued by police at 3:15 that morning; there could easily have been a fatality. All Henry's high-blown rhetoric about fanatics and forces of evil, destiny and danger had come to pass. The battle for abortion rights was no longer a metaphor and Henry could never again be dismissed as some obstinate maverick. He was a man whose cause had put him in danger.

Smoling and Scott had spent two nights and days in prison, but it was the one night Henry spent in there that made the headlines. Running in newspapers across the country, the photograph of the three doctors being ushered into a paddy wagon after their first court appearance spoke volumes: Scott was hurriedly collapsing his huge frame into the safe anonymity of the vehicle. A slumping Smoling looked depressed, dejected. Only Henry was beaming, turned full-faced towards the cameras, arm high and fingers in a V-for-Victory salute.

The issue followed Henry into the courtroom. Activists like Tripp quietly returned to the front lines to try to provide some makeshift help for the real women in real trouble out there, but nobody seemed interested in their problems. On October 1, designated by CARAL as the

National Day of Action for Choice, fewer than a thousand supporters turned out at Nathan Phillips Square in Toronto. Not even announcements of the walk-bike-run Choice-A-Thon in Winnipeg, the speak-outs in Regina and Saskatoon and the mall displays in British Columbia, also ongoing that day, pierced the gloom. It was as if all the energy had been sucked from the bleak concrete city square and deposited on the lawns fronting Queen's Park, where forty thousand anti-abortionists sang "O Canada" and swayed to prayers. In her book *Abortion: The Big Evasion*, Anne Collins described the scene: "Up on the stage Toronto Right to Life Association president Laura McArthur had started to chant out the names of all the Ontario pro-life groups who had bussed people to the rally. As each name was yelled out (Bracebridge, Brockville, Cambridge, Halton) a different part of the crowd roared, and signs were shaken at the sky."

Definitely, the fortunes of the pro-choice movement rested with the fate of Henry's court case. "I know women who still dislike him intensely for that," said Tripp. She didn't. "I still think if it wasn't for someone like him nothing would have happened. We women have got to get over some of the hostility that occurred over the years when we women realized we didn't have it because Henry's got it. It's not something I want to carry for the rest of my life. This is a bigger issue than Henry Morgentaler. If somebody wants to speak of the wonderful things Henry Morgentaler has done for the women of Canada, then the operative phrase is 'women of Canada,' not Henry Morgentaler. That's what I hold on to."

CHAPTER 13

BRODSKY V. MANNING V. MORGENTALER

BOROWSKI HAD LOST IN SASKATCHEWAN. After his pro-life forces spent more than $200,000 and flew in experts from around the world, a Saskatchewan Court of Queen's Bench judge ruled on October 13, 1983, that fetuses weren't protected under the Constitution, that Section 251 remained valid. Still to come was CARAL's date with the Supreme Court of Ontario to argue that the abortion law denied women the right to life, liberty and security, which the new Charter of Rights and Freedom had guaranteed, and a similar action launched in Manitoba by Kruger's Coalition for Reproductive Choice.

In Winnipeg, the battle raged, taking bizarre turns after a summer hiatus and after a stubborn Crown attorney refused to waive preliminary hearings for Henry. Judge Charles Rubin set October 5 to 7 and 12 to 14 for the hearing dates. It was difficult to see what direction, if any, Henry's case, and the cause, was taking in Manitoba. When one judge refused to order the state to give back the clinic's equipment, the Manitoba College of Physicians and Surgeons voted to allow abortions to take place outside a hospital. "Nothing in that action changes the law. It's really a housekeeping change," cautioned the College's registrar, Dr. James Morison.[1] The next day Health Minister Larry Desjardins quashed that: "It doesn't change anything as far as I am concerned."[2]

Oh, yes, it did, insisted Dr. Robbie Mahood, a spokesman for Manitoba Physicians for Reproductive Choice. He was one of thirty-nine physicians who signed an April 15, 1983, statement to the media supporting a free-standing abortion clinic in Manitoba and urging the health minister to approve Henry's facility. Those doctors estimated that 2,300 of the approximately four thousand Manitobans seeking abortions in 1982 obtained one outside the province. "The fact that 55 per cent of women seeking abortions had to leave the province is shameful and shows how poorly the needs of Manitoba women are being met," it stated. Worse, less than 12 per cent of the abortions performed in the province were under eight weeks, compared with 24.7 per cent for Canada as a whole. "Ideally, 5 per cent or less of abortions should be performed in the second trimester."

And the pretrial show did go on. Clinic staff wept when one woman told the court all the reasons she wanted an abortion; Manitoba's chief medical officer testified "small fragments of embryo"[3] were found on a cloth in the clinic during the June 3 raid; a woman said she began hemorrhaging and had to go to hospital a month after her abortion at the clinic. On the first day Joe Borowski sat in the back of the courtroom, and during the morning break went up and shook hands with Henry.[4] It was good political theatre.

"I hope you don't mind, but I'm praying for you to see the errors of your ways," he said.

"No, I don't mind at all," Henry replied. What he did object to, he added, was the language used in protesting the clinic.

"Well, you know the old school saying, 'Sticks and stones will break my bones, but names will never hurt me,'" an unrepentant Borowski replied.

Two days later, NDP MP Svend Robinson sat in on the preliminary hearing. That, too, was effective political posturing. He wore a Co-conspirators for Choice button and slammed all the charges as "ludicrous." But the Crown had decided to drop the charges of procuring a miscarriage or abortion and proceed, instead, with conspiracy charges against Henry and his staff, "actively sabotaging," as Kruger said, the hope of a clear challenge to the abortion laws. Greg Brodsky, the lawyer representing Henry in Winnipeg, agreed. Brodsky's plan had always been to focus on whether it was illegal to have an abortion in a freestanding clinic without the permission of a therapeutic abortion committee. Henry had counted on being acquitted by a fourth jury, which would convince the provincial government to let the clinic operate in peace, the way the clinic in Quebec did. He expected no help from the federal front, since Mark MacGuigan, the new justice minister, was avidly anti-abortion.

On October 12, 1983, in a surprise move, the defence team announced they would be challenging the constitutional validity of the abortion law, but the following day they retracted, saying that argument could wait until the trial. Provincial Court Judge Kris Stefanson did order Henry and seven staff, including Robert Scott, to appear before a higher court on November 7 for the arraignment. But when that time came, the charges were put over to February 1984 to give time for Henry to stand trial beginning November 21, 1983, in the Ontario Supreme Court in Toronto.

Brodsky had lost the horse race — to Morris Manning, representing Henry in Ontario. "Brodsky was manoeuvring to get it settled in Winnipeg first," Henry recalled. "He definitely wanted the national limelight. Actually, he and Morris had a big quarrel because Brodsky was fishing to have the big trial in Winnipeg. Manning was dead set against it. Manning said Toronto should be the setting for a national debate on a national case. I agreed with that, meaning that Toronto was much better, since it was the centre of all the national media. Winnipeg was just a backwater." Although events initially worked against Brodsky, Penner did drop the conspiracy charges against Henry and the seven clinic employees midway through the Toronto pretrial, saying they would be tried for performing illegal abortions. But it was Henry's call, and he had made it in Italy, where he was vacationing, before any trial started. He phoned Brodsky from there. "Are you and Morris fighting?" he asked. He had received a fax from Manning and a phone call from Brodsky. Brodsky said they were not. "Morris may have thought I was fighting too hard to get Henry charged for actually doing abortions," he said later.

Manning was accustomed to fighting — and winning. Toronto city council had hired him to clean up Yonge Street, which he did, forcing more than fifty body-rub parlours and sex shops to close. But he also had defended tavern owners in Mississauga, an outlying city of Toronto, in their fight against a by-law ordering nude dancers to wear G-strings.

As chair of the criminal justice section of the Canadian Bar Association, Manning had long spoken out in Henry's favour. And as reporter Bill Walker noted in the *Toronto Star* on November 19, 1983, his plush Bay Street office had been the site of many press conferences and strategy sessions in the months before the pretrial motion.

"Morris was instrumental in allowing me and Judy [Rebick] to work on the strategy," said CARAL's Norma Scarborough. "It was Morris's willingness to do this, not Henry's." According to Rebick, Manning recognized that the women's movement was crucial to the case. "Morris really understood the relationship between what was happening politically and what was happening in the courtroom." Few have acknowledged the contribution of the women then, she added. "What we did was turn around public opinion and we made it a higher price politicians had to pay to go against [choice] rather than for it. And what we did was create a truly mass movement — in fact, the most effective mass movement we've seen in Canada."

The strategy sessions were often — usually — volatile. "Henry's very dominating if he's concerned about it. If he's got an opinion about something, it's his way," Rebick said. "It's not that he won't listen — he will listen — but he doesn't change his mind very much." And he was often right about those things, she added. But Manning, also, was accustomed to getting things his way. Although his wife, Dr. Linda Rapson, was an early supporter of pro-choice rights and a founding member of DRAL, Doctors for the Repeal of the Abortion Law, and Scarborough was a friend of the family, Manning made a point of later telling another *Toronto Star* reporter that the cases he took on were not necessarily causes. "I believe individual liberty and individual rights are very important and I decide on an individual basis whether I am going to act for people who are oppressed, either in my view or their view. I like to defend people who are subjected to government regulations in a way they don't want to be. Only occasionally do I get involved in a case that is a cause, one that dramatically affects a lot of other people. The Morgentaler cause was one of them," he told Jack Cahill of the *Star*.[5]

Manning was known for the amount of background research he put

into every legal argument. He'd present thirty or forty reasons to sustain his point, culled from legal judgments and arguments from all over
the world, one legal colleague told the *Toronto Star*. They would often
be imaginative, which is why Manning moved swiftly with a motion to
quash the conspiracy charges against Morgentaler, Scott and Smoling.
The charges violated the Charter of Rights and Freedoms, which guarantees security of the person as to freedom of conscience and religion
(Section 2A), freedom of belief and expression (Section 2B), the right to
life and freedom of the person (Section 7), and ensures that all rights be
applied equally to men and women (Section 28). If Associate Chief
Justice William Parker agreed, there would be no jury trial.

Henry wasn't totally sold on that strategy. He believed in juries,
and he wanted to be heard by one. It would lead inevitably, he thought,
to a fourth acquittal by society's stand-ins. As well, Henry was not convinced Parker was the judge they wanted. At the time Parker was one
of the province's three most senior jurists. He had been named an associate chief justice — a position created by the Ontario premier, William
Davis, in 1978. One of the few Progressive Conservative appointments
to the bench, he had been president of the Hamilton West Progressive
Conservative Association, but had severed those ties when he came onto
the bench. "Morris had a high opinion of him when we started out. Said
he was decent, nice, they had been at a couple of lawyer-judge functions
together," Henry recalled. "I thought the guy was a plodder, sort of
average guy. He used to write everything down in longhand despite the
presence of the court reporter, who took every word down. Morris and
the other lawyers had to talk slowly and wait until he had finished writing the end of the sentence. But Morris expected this judge, obviously a
plodder, a detail kind of man, to invalidate the law. You've got to have
imagination for that, some different qualities, instead of being a plod-
ding kind of bureaucrat who has everything doubly written down."

Ontario's first test of the 1969 abortion law was a highly anticipated
event. To prevent any clashes between the pro-choice and pro-life sides,
police were stationed outside the University Avenue courthouse, where
the pretrial was being held in the spacious Courtroom 20 on the sixth
floor. It was a bitter November day, but about twenty-five people from

either side marched quietly but determinedly. The only altercation was minor, and it occurred when Judy Rebick was giving television interviews to a backdrop of "My Body. My Choice" and "Drop the Charges" signs and the pro-life people tried to push their "Stop Killing Babies" signs into the camera range.[6] Inside, the courtroom was packed with proponents of both sides. Those wearing Choice buttons sat on one side of the room, and the members of Right to Life, Campaign Life and the Christian Action Council, identified by the red roses in their lapels, sat on the other side. The judge was stern in his opening remarks: "This case has aroused a great deal of publicity and emotion among various groups across the country. I will have no outbursts or anything that would disturb the solemnity of this trial."

Parker ruled that Manning could argue his constitutional challenge and present witnesses to support his motion to drop the charges. Ontario's Crown attorney Alan Cooper startled many when he announced he would not be pressing the charges of procuring an abortion against the three doctors at the pretrial. Because of the constitutional challenge, the federal government sent its own Crown counsel, Arthur Pennington, to represent Justice Minister Mark MacGuigan. Pennington focused on fetal development, which prompted CARAL's national co-ordinator, Leslie Pearl, to fire off a telegram from CARAL to MacGuigan protesting "the government's leap to the defence of fetuses when women's rights are being argued, while in Regina the government sat silent when fetal rights were being argued. In the Borowski case the government argued that fetal development was irrelevant to the constitutional issue; suddenly it has become relevant. We asked Mr. MacGuigan whether the government was merely hypocritical or actively anti-choice."

Manning knew he was cautiously and laboriously laying out what would become a far-reaching challenge to the Canadian legal system. "One of the strangest memories I have throughout the pretrial motion is of Henry saying, 'Speed it up. Speed it up. We don't need this. This is not the trial.' And of Bob Scott, whose name, reputation and family and life, too, in a very real sense were on the line, sitting there reading that wonderful criticism of the English justice system called *Bleak House*. I'm sure that every day he found parallels," Manning recalled.

Beginning with Carolyn Egan, he called nineteen expert witnesses in a pretrial with ninety-one exhibits and exhaustive questioning. The pretrial lasted almost four weeks; Henry lasted only two. "I had enough. I told Morris I was wasting my time just sitting there. I was going back to Montreal to work. We had a big fight. He wanted me to stay." Aghast, Manning first tried persuasion — Dr. Augustin Roy, president of the Quebec Association of Physicians and Surgeons, social worker Thérèse Venne and Henry's great friend Dr. Jeanne St. Amour, whom he'd taught to perform abortions, would be testifying in a few days; Henry should stay as a show of support for them. "'They know they have my support,' I said," Henry recalled. "Morris even threatened me. If you don't stay, et cetera et cetera. I said, 'Don't threaten me,' and things like that and I left in a huff."

Henry was not present when the trial resumed on January 19, 1984. Neither was Scott, who had sat through the entire pre-Christmas session, often with his wife, Maria Corsillo, always silent and stoic; nor Smoling, whose soul had seemed to shrink as the days passed, and who was struggling one more time to start up another practice. Manning ended up taking eighteen days for his closing submission and ten days to rebut the Crown's arguments. Henry was in Winnipeg when a Manitoba justice announced that the Morgentaler trial there was being postponed until May. Henry had begun to mention his court costs at every opportunity — he expected they would soon reach $200,000, he said on January 25. He predicted out loud that the loser of the Ontario court case would have to go all the way to the Supreme Court of Canada. "The next battle may cost me all I have," he said as the pretrial dragged on until May.[7]

Henry thought Manning was taking too long in his arguments, and "in the meantime I suffered financially. I suffered from waiting and waiting. The clinic was losing money. Public interest was flagging. Everything was going wrong." The Pro-Choice Defence Fund, operated by CARAL as a separate entity to raise money across the country for Henry's case and for other legal battles, including CARAL's constitutional challenges, had collected $101,467 in donations by the end of 1983. It would collect another $84,872 by December 31, 1984, almost all of it going to the lawyers via Henry. But it was never enough. "Henry would come to CARAL board meetings, or on occasion he would write and say he wanted to come and talk to us, and he would say, 'You know, you've got to give me money,'" recalled Scarborough. The CARAL women resented the pressure — they were working hard at educating the public because they knew that was crucial to the court case. And Henry was a well-paid doctor. "He would drive us crazy about this need for us raising money for him, and then he would lavish money on all sorts of things we thought were unnecessary. You were left thinking that for him this need to raise money was to show how important he was to us by doing it for him and setting up the defence fund," said Scarborough. Few ever believed he was genuinely worried about money. "He thought that it was our responsibility to pay, and to a large extent I agreed with him. I did think it was the responsibility of the people supporting him to support him financially." Some feminists, especially in Quebec, had been actively downplaying Henry's part in the abortion rights movement, but "we would be no place without Henry Morgentaler," Scarborough said.

The Montreal clinic was busy and profitable. At the time, Henry was paid $12,000 a year as medical director, and he earned a percentage of each procedure. The clinic was open three days a week, but they were three long, emotionally exhausting days in which as many as seventeen abortions were done — and in which the gross take could easily be $7,000.[8] It cost $3,000 a month to run the Winnipeg clinic, and more for the Toronto clinic. Henry's principles came gold-plated. Small costs were mounting, too: vandals smashed two plate-glass windows in Winnipeg and stole the clinic sign.

And Henry was about to embark on a costly separation. The marriage to Carmen was over — she had packed up almost all the furniture from the house in Westmount and moved up to the Lake Cook country house. "She had taken the plates off the light fixtures. She had taken the bulbs out of the ceiling fixtures, the curtain rods off the windows. I've seen houses for sale that had more furniture in them," said one witness. Henry lived in two rooms in this grand home — the living room and the bedroom — and kept a few pieces of cutlery in the kitchen.

What had begun as a passionate connection ended because Carmen could not accept Henry's need to be a free agent and Henry could never adhere to what he considered to be Carmen's formula for domestic bliss: large city home, gracious country home, beautiful child, wealth, comfort and ease, and erudite, witty dinner parties warmed by candles and fine wine in the company of other members of the privileged class. He was not yet convinced that he was entitled to this good life; the more Carmen surrounded him in comfort and luxe, the more compelled he was to escape — to flee to his work and his crusade so he might one day deserve it. The break was harsh; each was scored by the other's cruelties. Carmen loved the house outside Morin Heights, the way of life it represented, and was determined to keep both. Henry had decided she was not going to have either.

Then, on July 20, 1984, Associate Chief Justice Parker dismissed Manning's motion. Just one week earlier Henry had been named winner of a Distinguished Humanist Award from the International Humanist and Ethical Union, along with Soviet nuclear physicist Andrei Sakharov and the redoubtable Betty Friedan, but unlike his fellow honorees, he would be facing a full trial, along with Scott and Smoling, in the fall. Henry bowed his head when Parker made his announcement and handed out copies of his ninety-six-page decision; some of Henry's supporters hissed as Parker left the courtroom. Outside in the hall, Scarborough wept. Parker had written: "That a person procuring an abortion or the pregnant woman herself may rely upon the defence of necessity or be immune from prosecution by receipt of a certificate from a committee does not derogate from the fact that no unfettered legal right to an abortion can be found in our law, nor can it be said that a right to an abortion is deeply rooted in the traditions and conscience of this country."

Parker also stated: "I am not deciding whether abortion should be permitted legally in Canada. The issue is whether Section 251 of the Criminal Code is valid legislation."

Manning said the ruling was "narrow" and vowed to appeal; at a CARAL press conference Henry threatened to re-open his Toronto clinic. That night, pro-choice supporters held an angry demonstration in front of the closed Harbord Street clinic, at which Rebick called the ruling "a slap in the face." OCAC and CARAL decided the abortion issue had to be front and centre in the forthcoming September 4, 1984, federal election. Scarborough supervised CARAL's massive country-wide mail-out of a questionnaire to every candidate. Her office walls were covered with charts rating every candidate in every riding — from one for strictly pro-life to five for pro-choice. But Brian Mulroney's Tories were re-elected, including a large and noisy contingent of pro-life back benchers. And even Manning's motion for an appeal was rejected.

Henry was relieved when the trial started on October 15, 1984. He'd been in Guadaloupe for a week, at Club Med with Yann, and had come back rested and ready. At sixty-one, Henry was a fan of these highly organized sun vacations where tanned, always smiling social co-ordinators got everybody up and surfing, singing or performing at talent nights, which was Henry's speciality. He invented Dr. Apfel Strudel, part shrink, part silliness, a comic alter ego seeking happiness and — after many groaners and thigh slappers of jokes — finding it either through primal therapy or Eastern religion. He performed his routine about every six weeks, which was as often as he was going to this or other Club Meds, which was as often as he needed to relieve the stress he was living under.

On October 21, 1984, a Sunday night, a week after the trial had started, Henry said in his memoirs: "My morale is a lot better than it's been for the last year and a half waiting for all these legal proceedings and constitutional challenge to be out of the way.... I was glad that finally the jury part of the trial, where I rely on the jury to acquit me, is coming to pass." But he was still fuming about Manning's legal strategy and its results. "The constitutional challenge was a flop. Even the motion for leave to appeal was a flop. It wasn't even allowed. It's obvious now the whole exercise was an exercise in frustration. Lots of time, lots of money lost. Lots of efforts lost. But maybe it wasn't a complete loss in the sense that there had been some public education as to the issues in Toronto, especially, for the country." He resented Manning's having postponed the trial from September 17 to October 15 "without my acquiescence or consent." The pretrial had been so lengthy that Henry believed Manning was maximizing the time in court so he would get paid more. This is maybe an unjust charge as far as he is concerned. I think he was more concerned, being obsessive-compulsive, with having a complete argument, and the best possible argument, and not to omit any possible clue or any argument that might be in our favour, and I think that it's a necessity for him psychologically to do that. In the state of financial insecurity in which I was, where I saw myself dragged into a lot of legal bills, for which in the final analysis I was responsible, I didn't take too kindly to that, and we had a number of fights and relations weren't too good between us when the trial started.

(Manning has commented he never charged Henry his top fee and that he also enlisted for the case the aid of many of his top staff at bargain rates.)

Two American professional jury consultants were working with Manning in the laborious process of choosing twelve jurors. It took three days to decide on the six-man, six-woman jury panel, and Henry was actively involved in the decision making. One or the other of the American consultants made a point of sitting beside him to get his opinion. The defence team privately graded each prospective juror from zero to five. Manning would collect the opinions from the consultants and Scott and Henry before either accepting or challenging an individual. "I told Manning that if I put a zero on somebody, I definitely didn't want him in," Henry recalled.

Henry was fascinated by this process, but wary of some of the choices. He recorded his impressions later. Postal worker Alex Tapley was the second juror chosen; Henry questioned if he and Glenda Scott, when acting as the first jury triers, were deciding to reject or accept based only on gut instinct. He was surprised that Jewish businessman Arnold Naiman made the grade. "I was surprised that [Crown Attorney] Cooper had accepted him. I figured he might have felt that he would be partial to me, but Manning figured that he let him in because otherwise he might have been accused of having an anti-Jewish bias." Another juror (Sharon Ryan) "seemed rather severe in her outlook —

she had her mouth sort of tight," Henry noted. "It seemed like she had had a rather difficult life." Henry had faith in the "reasonableness" of what he was doing. As long as he sensed a potential juror was intelligent, he assumed he or she would learn enough through the duration of the trial to make the rational and intelligent decision and acquit him. He felt that way about Mary Catherine Raica, "a computer programmer and a very intelligent woman and the mother of two children. What bothered me about her was that she declared that she had some opinions about the whole issue many years ago and it wasn't clear to me whether those opinions were in our favour or against us." Despite her surname, Henry thought she might be of Croatian origin, and therefore possibly Roman Catholic.

Henry was worried when Boris Shostack, "Ukrainian or Russian, a tall fellow who is a manager, well-dressed, around forty-five, had said he was a former classmate of one of the lawyers, whom Henry assumed was Manning:

> Morris accepted him, although he didn't solicit any opinions on him and we didn't really know what criterion to go by. Then by surprise the prosecutor accepted him and he became the sixth juror. I was very unhappy about this....
>
> The seventh juror who was chosen was Susan Bishop, a very beautiful young woman, an engineer, self-possessed, obviously intelligent and bright. Looked like a feminist — her nipples were standing out and in my mind she was wearing no bra. Which confirmed me in the idea that she was a feminist. I had the impression that she sort of almost greeted me when she came in, and to my great surprise, Cooper accepted her. I had given her a five and we all thought she was very good.
>
> The next one to be accepted was a fellow called Tom Green. He looked like a fellow of around thirty, thirty-two, very intelligent, bright, and I was also surprised he was accepted. These two seemed to get along very well, Susan Bishop and Tom Green....
> The ninth juror chosen was a fellow called Devoe, which is a Dutch name...and he looked like he was anti-establishment. He

came to court in jeans, had an open-necked shirt without a tie, and he wore his hair long up to his shoulders. He seemed like the right type for us. He was a courier....

The next one was a blond girl, Maureen Daves, who looked like she was sort of spaced out, gave the impression of a little floozy who didn't know anything about anything. Was sort of waving her hips and walking in a very sort of provocative manner, very sexually sort of enticing. We accepted her, I think, because first of all she responded well to the questions and then she was in the high-risk group of women who would need abortions. But on second reflection, I think she is sort of a bit dumb and sort of immature, and in any case I don't think she would vote against a majority or would be strong enough to vote against a majority.

Henry thought the penultimate juror, a young man named William David Francis, was the genuine thing — someone who did not have an opinion one way or the other on the issue. But he was not thrilled with the twelfth juror. "We decided we would accept Anna Syrko in spite of the fact she was Ukrainian, coming from a background that is rather conservative and possibly against abortion. In spite of the fact that the anti-abortion people who were sort of trying to influence her in the corridor during these few days."

Henry gazed at the twelve people who would decide his future and figured his chances were good. Very good:

Here is a group of people, most of whom had less knowledge than myself, possibly less ability than myself, less life experience than myself. And these were my judges, in effect, now. At least five of them are, I would say, if not exactly dummies, maybe of limited intelligence, maybe two or three not even able to grasp the issues involved. But I think there are a few there who are intelligent and open-minded enough, and possibly strong enough, to resist whatever influences might be coming to bear on them, be it from the prosecutor, or from the judge himself.

In conclusion, I think we have a good jury. I am now almost

certain the possibility of a conviction is extremely remote or almost
impossible, that the chances for acquittal are good and that the
worst that can happen is a hung jury.

Henry decided to get along with his legal counsel. "I would not
allow [Manning] to bully me, which I had allowed him to do before," he
said in his memoirs. But he had also re-assessed Manning's style: "He
was sharp — he was good with the jury — he was methodical. He was
standing up to the judge beautifully. He was using every skill and art of
a lawyer to maximize our advantage. It was just a beautiful, perfect performance, and I told him so. I congratulated him on it, and he wasn't
too difficult when we tried to persuade him to shorten things or when
we had strategy sessions. And I was participating very actively, something which they did not allow me to do or something which I did not
do during the constitutional arguments, which had to deal more with
abstract points of law."

This time he had perfect attendance, and he took care to sit so that
the jury could see his reaction to testimony. Mike came down from
Montreal for moral support; Eleanor and Ed Ratcliffe dined with
Henry one night and promised to write a cheque that would cover the
cost of all the witnesses. No wonder Henry was convinced events were
unfolding as they should. He was even magnanimous when Norma
Scarborough intervened on behalf of his former biographer, Eleanor
Wright Pelrine, who needed to cover the trial and interview him for an
addendum she was writing for the paperback version of her book.
Pelrine had been roundly criticized by reviewers for presenting Henry
as a one-dimensional, flawless crusader, yet subject and author had
parted acrimoniously. She complained to her friends and colleagues in
the pro-choice movement that she had pulled her punches for the sake
of the cause. By the end of their working relationship, she had begun to
refer to Henry (behind his back) as "His Lordship." Henry claimed she
had never returned his papers, including the correspondence from
Pierre Elliott Trudeau he'd lent her for her research. Scarborough, who
was a friend to both and functioned at times as their intermediary, said
that was most probably true. After Wright Pelrine died of cancer in

December 1989 at the age of fifty-seven, Scarborough had helped clear out rooms full of papers and boxes of documents. Like many writers, Wright Pelrine was disorganized and had no office system in place — but Scarborough never found Henry's property.

Henry and Wright Pelrine had agreed that the proceeds from *Morgentaler: The Doctor Who Wouldn't Turn Away* would be split down the middle. But, Henry said, after it was published, Wright Pelrine came to him saying she wanted two-thirds because she had done all the work on the book. Henry agreed. "But when it was published I didn't get a cent. When I confronted her, she made excuses about being in debt. I figure she should have told me straight and acknowledged she owed me money. I figured she was taking advantage of me." Henry agreed to co-operate with Wright Pelrine on the paperback addendum if she agreed to pay off her debt to him at $25 a month. She said she would.

But Scarborough said Wright Pelrine probably was telling the truth about her financial situation. The author was involved with the National Action Committee on the Status of Women, the National Youth Orchestra, the Media Club of Canada, the Humanists, Toronto's Rape Crisis Centre, as well as Metro Toronto's YWCA — all prestigious organizations, for which she did volunteer work. Her biography of Henry was not a huge seller. At one time her husband, Dennis, wrote mildly erotic novels from a home they rented in Mexico, but the market for them fell off. "She most probably was broke," Scarborough said. Henry said he was still angry with her about the 1974 article she wrote for *Chatelaine* magazine, in which she stated he was compelled to defy authority. This statement, coupled with the fact that he was an immigrant, was used against him during the Quebec trial, he said. He also remembered watching a television show while recovering from his heart attack, in which Wright Pelrine described him as having an abrasive personality — and he never forgot her words. "The fact that I stand up for what I believe in doesn't mean I have an abrasive personality," he said. To prove it, almost a decade later, he agreed she could witness him once again stand up for what he believed in.

———

Again Manning called on a parade of witnesses, but the brightest moment of the trial, in Henry's opinion, occurred on Wednesday, October 24, when the court admitted as evidence a tape of the speech he gave November 18, 1982, at OISE:

> The speech was a good speech and it contained all the elements of a good defence. It set out the goals, why I wanted to establish a clinic in Toronto, why it was necessary. It set out the situation for the rest of Canada. It gave the history of the struggle for abortion rights, the achievements in Quebec, the fact that I want to extend the benefits that I had achieved for the women of Quebec to the rest of the country, my legal history, the three jury acquittals, the plea to a jury...it was tremendous. I think it was one of my better speeches. There was no repetition, almost very little, anyway, and whatever there was it was relevant, and the diction was good, delivery was good. It was real terrific. I was really impressed by my own speech. At the end I really got carried away, really, with not just the speech but with the courage it took to undertake this whole thing, to take such a courageous step in face of all the difficulties and all the opposition from the fanatics of the so-called pro-life and the governments and whatever. I think it made a tremendous impression of the jury. They now know what it's all about.

Even better, Mike Morgentaler arrived in time to hear the speech broadcast throughout the courtroom. It was one of the increasingly rare peaceful and supportive moments between the two brothers.

By Thursday, November 8, the jury was in its second day of deliberations. They asked Parker for a copy of the Charter of Rights; he refused to give it to them; then they asked him for a dictionary, which he also refused to give to them, probably because he felt he had clearly delineated those matters in his instructions to the jury. Henry wasn't perturbed by their actions — he interpreted both requests as good signs for the defence. He sauntered over to a Canadian Press reporter and joked that he hadn't known the Charter of Rights and a dictionary were subversive documents. Most reporters thought the jury would take hours longer to reach a decision; Henry was about to buy into their betting pool on the jury's estimated time of arrival, when Manning dragged him away, saying it wasn't appropriate for him to bet on his own jury. Another five minutes after that a buzz filled the courtroom: the jury had reached a verdict.

For the first time during the trial, Henry, Scott and Smoling were ordered to stand in the prisoner's dock. This shattered Henry's equanimity. "At that time I realized the gravity of the moment, and although my reason told me that the only verdict in a short time like that was not guilty... I found myself going white in the face and being quite tense. And when the jury filed in they were sort of very serious and they didn't look at the three of us, the accused, which is usually a sign that it's a bad verdict."

It wasn't. Again, Henry's faith in juries was justified. All three doctors were acquitted of all charges. Henry asked Parker if he could address the jury. "It was obvious he was not very pleased with the verdict and he said to me with a finger pointing at me, 'You keep quiet.'" Only when Parker left the court did pandemonium break out. An ecstatic Henry hugged Manning, shook hands with Scott and Smoling, then went outside to meet a wall of television cameras. Rebick gave him a bear hug and Scarborough emerged from the up escalator just as they were going down — she had missed the verdict because she had promised writer Anne Collins she would telephone her the results, but had left Collins's phone number at her home. Scarborough had ordered her cab driver to break all speed limits, but had not made it in time for the verdict. Henry had everybody sing "We have overcome" to the tune of "We Shall Overcome" in the cab back to Manning's office, where there was a round of Scotch before Henry made the rounds of the television and radio stations. Defence lawyer and columnist Clayton Ruby later said Manning's jury address was "spectacular." "It took courage, real courage to do that," he said. "I remember after that victory, Morris came into the lawyers' lunchroom and for the first time in my life — and I have never seen it again, nor do I expect to see it again — every lawyer in the room, about three hundred, stood up and applauded."

At three o'clock that afternoon, CARAL and OCAC held a jubilant press conference. Three men had been acquitted of the same charge, but for weeks it had been known as "the Morgentaler trial" and not just in the media. Scott was smiling, but didn't stay around to savour the win. He decided he should be in Montreal the next day for work and left. Nobody, including Henry, can remember if Smoling was even present. He was neither noted nor quoted in any of the newspaper accounts of the conference. "Of course I was the star attraction," Henry recorded in his memoirs. "I felt so much in touch with my power. I was so calm and self-assured I was really, really content with myself. I talked for a long time. I paid tribute to Manning, which was his due...because he had complained earlier that I had not mentioned too much about him and that Joe Borowski was praising his lawyer. I had never up till that time praised my own lawyer."

Then there were even more interviews, including one with CBC's news magazine program "The Journal." With Henry was his good friend Selma Edelstone, who had taken on the job of arranging his public relations schedule. They had known each other since their Montreal days when she was social action committee chair of the Montreal Humanist Fellowship and Henry was its president. They had gone down to Chicago to hear a speech by Betty Friedan on abortion, which had electrified Edelstone. Edelstone's husband, Gordon,[9] an executive with a large clothing retailer, had relocated to Toronto in 1969 before she could get too involved with Henry's struggles in Quebec. But one day she ran into Henry again in a Toronto hotel elevator. "Whenever you're in Toronto, you have a place to stay with us," she said. Soon he was spending two to three nights a week on the third floor of their Georgian-style stone mansion in Toronto's posh Forest Hill district.

Henry was her "soul mate," Edelstone said. They were like brother and sister. When the inevitable rumours surfaced that they were having an affair, she just laughed: "It would be like incest." He was close with her three daughters and with her husband, too. "Henry sometimes said he was lonely. No one could feel the passion he could feel, even though there were all these groups around him," Edelstone explained. "His whole life was enveloped by the issue. For most people it was part of their life. This was his whole life. His marriage broke up — I never even saw Carmen — he was away from his family. It was the issue of his life."

Henry gave media interviews from the Edelstone house. The times were militant. "Are you sure you want to?" her daughters asked her. "Absolutely." she replied. During the trial, Edelstone was usually right by Henry's side, sometimes to incongruous effect. She was slim, blond, always elegant in expensively tailored and very fashionable suits and coats, a socialite who could have been planning symphony fund-raisers instead of standing on wind-swept courtroom steps behind or beside a man a good head shorter than her striking five-foot-nine height.

She looked after Henry, which he needed. She organized his media interviews, screening requests from less important outlets; she set up a timetable and made sure Henry got to where he was supposed to be. "I enjoyed being taken care of that way, and having someone efficient to do this for me," Henry said. So he decided he wanted Edelstone to replace Rebick as spokesperson for the Toronto clinic. "It became important to have a spokesperson for the clinic who would not be Judy Rebick, who is rather abrasive and militant and a radical feminist and represents this type of . . . radical feminism. I had told Judy that I would choose somebody else, not her, that she should not be the spokesperson for the clinic. I wanted the clinic to be thought of as a calm, serene place where people get good medical treatment. She agreed with it, although it was obvious that she likes the spotlight and she likes to be spokesperson." Rebick stayed on as the voice of OCAC. The organization had never been enthusiastic that she had been doing double duty, believing that the broader issue of reproductive rights had been often lost because of the clinic's higher media profile. The media continued to call Rebick frequently; she was unconcerned and unaffected by Henry's decision. Edelstone turned down Henry's offer — she had talked it over with her family, who thought her husband's position, along with the family's safety and anonymity, could be affected if she took on the job. Undeterred, Henry choose Wendy Taylor-White as spokesperson, a quiet, untested supporter whom Henry had always liked. "I gave her my book to read and she really grew into her role. She was a very good change.

She's more of an establishment type, quiet, more calm than Judy, not as abrasive."

Henry never discussed with anybody his intention to remove Rebick. CARAL had never agreed with him that there should be a separate spokesperson for the clinic anyway, but they had never disagreed with him, either. "He made it clear he wanted the place to be less politically focused and more a medical centre. He did not want it to be the centre of political activity," Norma Scarborough recalled. "It was not an anti-Judy thing. He thinks highly of Judy and Judy was cool about it, a real pro."

Rebick was celebrating along with all the others that night at the party at CARAL national co-ordinator Leslie Pearl's row house on a Toronto side street under the shadow of the Don Jail. Her narrow home was jammed with supporters. "We were all so shocked we had won," Scarborough said. Henry toasted everyone with red wine, stood on the crowded steps and hollered happily about how he'd unwittingly ignored all Manning's pen signals they'd worked out ahead of time when he got his chance to be on the witness stand. Manning's speech was gracious and witty. His wife and two teenaged daughters were there, as were some reporters who had covered the entire trial. Dr. Linda Rapson said she gave a speech that night that brought the house down. "Do you know how many times Morris would come home and say, 'That little prick is going to drive me up the wall?' And Henry laughed more than anybody. I always said I learned the meaning of 'jubilant' that night." Their entire family had been involved. During one photo opportunity, Manning suddenly ducked out via the back into the crowd because he had just heard that an elderly gentleman was involved in an altercation. Rapson grinned. "That was my father. He had hit a Right-to-Lifer with his umbrella. Morris just knew it was him." A friend of their elder daughter ended up defending them in her high school classroom when a nun told them Henry and his lawyer were evil. "I know Mr. Manning and he is not evil," Kate Manning's friend said. A friend of their younger daughter was forbidden to play with her because of who her father was. "But she didn't like the kid anyway," said Rapson.

At 11 p.m. everybody crowded into the television room downstairs to sit on the floor and watch Henry and Manning on the news and cheer. At one point, union activist Joyce Rosenthal and her sister took Scarborough upstairs for a private talk: Scarborough had been seen on so many newscasts and was so closely allied with Henry they wanted her to start wearing a bulletproof vest.

As for Henry, the last time he had felt this good was on November 13, 1973, almost exactly eleven years ago, when there was a big party in Montreal after his first jury acquittal. "I was hugging everybody. I was in such an expansive, nice, sort of quiet victory mood. It really was a pleasure for me to see for myself. I felt this surge of confidence and love for all these people and being involved in a common cause that everybody could celebrate in, and I clearly felt I was the hero of the meeting. They couldn't have done it without me, and I felt vindicated and I felt really good about myself." Late that night Henry called Bamie, waking him up. But he didn't call Goldie, and Mike had left for Montreal two days earlier. But so many other people were there offering their congratulations.

Andrea Knight had worked hard to keep the clinic open for referrals after the raid and before the arson attempt, but had returned to her studies. When she heard the news of the acquittal on CBC radio, she phoned Carolyn Egan and the two drove right down to Manning's office and then to the party at Pearl's. "It was like I never left," she said. "At the celebration it was instantly, 'Okay, now what do we do?' We knew the clinic was going to be open again. It was just a question of when."

CHAPTER 14

SHAKEN AND STIRRED

WINNING DIDN'T CHANGE MUCH. The anti-abortionists didn't go away, the antagonism didn't go away, although Ontario attorney general Roy McMurtry, a front-runner in the race to lead the provincial Tories might have wished it so. McMurtry waited until December 4, 1984, four days before the last possible legal moment, to rise in the legislature and announce he would appeal the jury's decision in the Morgentaler case. Henry was in the gallery with Selma Edelstone that day. It wasn't as though he was surprised; in fact, the day after the acquittal (and one day before he announced the clinic would re-open) Henry made his ritualized offering of the Toronto clinic as a training facility for the province. A familiar game plan had begun: Greg Brodsky tried to get leverage in Manitoba by asking Penner to drop the charges against Henry (and Scott and Crocker) in light of the acquittals. CARAL and OCAC members flooded Penner's office with telegrams and letters demanding the same thing. Desjardins refused a written request to give hospital status to the Corydon Avenue clinic; Penner said he would wait and watch Ontario before making any decisions about the charges. And Ontario refused the offer of the clinic. Henry wrote Ontario Health Minister Keith Norton a scathing letter in response, in which he criticized "the unseemly haste" with which his offer had been refused and suggested it might be due to Norton's lack of knowledge about the issue. Checkmate. Time for the attack.

Henry re-opened the clinic on December 10, 1984 — with brand-new equipment (the equipment seized in the 1983 raid couldn't be returned until all appeals had been dealt with) but without Smoling, who told the media he had severed his connections with Morgentaler (and by extension the performing of abortions) to set up a general practice in Woodstock, Ontario. That was face saving; Smoling would not have been allowed back in the operating room because Scott, among others, had been very perturbed about the quality of his work. It was a new beginning for the clinic, which now boasted an elaborate alarm system, an equally elaborate OCAC escort system to shield patients, plus clinic-hired detectives to guard the entrance and ensure that only those with appointments got in. That, as well as twenty-four-hour surveillance by police after Henry received a death threat and the clinic front door was smeared with tar, signalled the end of any vestigial innocence. After the firebomb, the Toronto Women's Bookstore moved into new and separate premises and the Morgentaler Clinic took over the entire building. The Toronto area Right to Life Association had asked McMurtry for an injunction to shut down the clinic; he refused, even though Toronto's Campaign Life chair, Jim Hughes, said his group would do more than picket if there was no injunction, and Laura McArthur declared, "If he doesn't bring an injunction, it's an open invitation to civil disorder."

Henry was not around for the clinic reopening. After a media skirmish with the Roman Catholic archbishop of Toronto, Emmett Cardinal Carter — Henry had handed reporters copies of a telegram he'd sent the archbishop, asking to meet to "discuss ways to calm the passions and hysteria gripping the anti-abortion movement"; to which the cardinal's office replied, he was "not interested in publicity stunts"[1] — he left for another holiday. Scott would be the doctor working in the clinic the first weeks after its reopening. "I figured they wouldn't raid after I had been acquitted. Public opinion was too polarized," said Henry, who once again made an offer to police through the media that he would provide all the necessary evidence as long as they didn't raid the place.

Police arrested the doctors, instead. On December 19 they picked up Scott as he was leaving the clinic, and on December 20 they issued a warrant for Henry, who was in Montreal. Again the charge was conspiring to perform a miscarriage. Henry flew to Toronto the next day for another session of fingerprinting and press conferences: he told reporters he was going on holidays and the clinic would be closed for two weeks until January 7, 1985. "I wanted to show what was going to happen to women if they had no outlet. It was clear the clinic was filling an important need," he said.

He flew to Puerto Rico, to the Contada Beach Hotel. He was a man transported, and not only by his Ontario legal victory. He was in early thrall to the lush emotions generated by his new relationship with Maureen Reilly, a CARAL supporter he had met at the party the organization always held in the home of Ruth Miller after its annual general meetings. Reilly was not yet thirty, with wavy red-gold hair, and zaftig like many of his women. She was also vulnerable, with an artistic and shimmering intelligence. He had been her hero as a teenager; she found this affair to be "profound," yet she was self-conscious, because he represented so much of what she believed in and what she believed women worthy of. And never had Henry felt so indomitable, so worthy of adoration:

> I feel I have had a tremendous moral victory standing up against
> the power of the state and I've been acquitted for the fourth time
> by a jury, something that many people predicted could not happen
> in Ontario. Basically, I've achieved what I wanted — to convince
> the people and the government that a jury will not convict doctors
> offering safe medical abortions to people who need them — and,
> strong with that conviction, I will continue to build clinics and
> fight for reproductive freedom in Canada.... I feel I have the
> moral stature and the prestige and the know-how to do that
> well now.

This he confided to his tape recorder on December 27. It was his first opportunity for stock taking since the acquittal. He went on:

> I'm over the year and a half of stress and depression and suffering
> which I had to endure until the trial started and until the acquit-
> tal, and I feel just great. I feel all together. I feel authentic. I
> feel strong. I feel in full capacity and power to do the things I set

out to do. I feel the country is with me and I am bathing in a
tremendous bath of popularity with the masses, with the people
who come up to me wherever I go, Ontario or Quebec, and tell
me they admire me, how they think what I am doing is right. In
my weak moments...I get scared that indeed somebody might
pump a few bullets into me and I will die an untimely death,
but I know this will not deter me. I'm determined to fight on
and win. I'm determined to become a martyr, if I have to, but I
wouldn't cherish the idea of dying so young, especially with Yann
being four and a half years old, with my new relationship with
Maureen and everything looking up so bright.... Life is so beautiful, it's a pleasure to be alive, it's a pleasure to feel in full power,
it's a pleasure to have a good relationship with a loving woman
who I love.

Yet Reilly said that what drew her to Henry was "the little guy
thing about him. He's the little Woody Allen, the little *mensch*, the
frightened one who overcomes his fear all the time. He's afraid every
moment." But Reilly was the one who had failed to work up enough
courage to shake Henry's hand the first time she saw him in Ruth
Miller's kitchen. This was the man she had listened to speak on behalf
of the women of Canada when she was sixteen, who motivated her to
work for the pro-choice movement while still a student in grades eleven
and twelve. She had overheard Miller trying to call Henry a cab to get
him back to the Park Plaza Hotel. Reilly and some friends were on their
way to a movie, so she offered to drop him off at the hotel. He got in
the passenger seat; she was driving. "Suddenly he's stroking my leg,
asking, 'What movie are you seeing?' then [saying,] 'I think I'll go to
that movie.'" Later when she dropped him at the hotel he asked her if
she wanted to manage the clinic and if she wanted to come up for a
drink. She remembered thinking, "Do I want an affair or a job?" She
opted for the latter and met him for breakfast the next morning with
her résumé. She sensed she wasn't his first choice, and eventually turned
down the opportunity because she wasn't sure about waiting several
months for a job that "might last one afternoon." (Andrea Knight took

over the position early in 1985, also thinking it would be temporary. By March she knew it wasn't. She quit her studies — she had been working on a doctorate in women's labour history — and gave back her Canada Council grant. She was in it for the long haul. Knight was the niece of Irving Heller, one of the Montreal Humanists who had opposed Henry back in the late 1960s and called for his resignation, as Henry well knew.)

Reilly stayed in touch with Henry; she was considering medical school, and asked his advice (she is a therapist now). He phoned her one evening during his trial and invited her out to dinner. It was not an intimate evening: seated at a nearby table were several women executives from the CBC, who sent over champagne to Henry. His second invitation was to the victory party; his third, to a dinner party with Dr. Linda Rapson and Morris Manning at the Edelstones' home. "A post-postvictory-party party," Reilly said. Edelstone knew Henry well — "When things start to slow down he gets edgy, he gets a little depressed" — and understood he wanted to continue the celebrations, but Reilly began to wonder if there was ever going to be any down time when dating Henry. He was staying with the Edelstones, and asked if he could take Reilly back to his room. "I felt I should assure Selma we would keep the door open. I felt like a kid," Reilly said, laughing. He had his Walkman and some tapes and he showed her some books; when he took her home he asked her to go to Club Med with Yann and him. She met Yann the evening before they left for Eleuthera. He was sleeping, and when Henry introduced them the little boy rolled over and put his arms around her. Reilly instantly loved the child, still does. The next morning she was the one holding the small boy's hand as they boarded the plane. "Henry was walking ahead, doing his head-thrown-back strut so that people would recognize him. And you could see faces turn, people nudging their neighbours."

Reilly learned what anyone who spends any time with Henry knows: he was a popular figure. Every cab driver recognized him; few ever let him pay. Truck drivers saluted him; waitresses insisted the bacon and eggs were on the house. He was the Everyman hero, the respected underdog not afraid to take on the system.

Their holiday was glorious. Yann continued to enchant Reilly, which strengthened Henry's attraction to her. He simply worshipped his youngest child, already personable, outgoing and trilingual (he spoke English, French and Spanish). At the end of the vacation Yann said to Reilly, "I have an idea. Why don't you and I and Mummy and Daddy all live together?" When she explained to him why it would not be a good idea, he adjusted immediately. "Okay, you and me can live with Mummy and you and me can live with Daddy." If only it were that easy. By then Reilly knew she was with a man who was "difficult but compelling." She had watched him play Ping-Pong with a stream of twenty-three-year-olds, defeating every one of them. "They were pitched battles. That will, that drive — he'd outlast them. They would get frustrated. It was the same thing he shows in the courtroom. He'll outlast them. If it's not power or skill, he'll do it by sheer tenacity. I learned a lot watching him play table tennis." She worried about what the feminist community would think of her new relationship. Those who knew Henry understood how impulsive he often could be if he liked someone, which he usually did, being an optimist and a humanist, as well as a man who appreciated women. Judy Rebick had experienced that kind of whole-hearted approval the first time she met him; others had been offered jobs as swiftly as Reilly had been. Standing outside Metro Toronto police's 52 Division one day, she asked another protestor how her fellow CARAL members were reacting to her affair with Henry. "Maureen," she was told, "no one complains when the river flows past their door."

Right from the beginning, Henry warned her he had never been able to be monogamous. It wasn't open for discussion; it just was. She made the relationship conditional on their seeing a therapist together. "He went once. That was all. The joint session was not good. The therapist was impressed with his celebrity client. And he made sure he impressed the therapist," she said. "I sat tapping my foot throughout it." Nevertheless, they endured, Reilly in Toronto, Henry still living in his grand, empty Westmount home.

But he was in Toronto often. They were sitting around the Edelstones' kitchen table, when the idea first came up to fund-raise directly and specifically for Henry through an ad. Selma Edelstone said, "Why don't you just say, 'It's me, Henry Morgentaler. We're having trouble with money. Give me a hand.'" Henry was tentative — compared with the fact-filled, restrained fund-raising letters CARAL sent to their membership, this was akin to holding out a hand on a street corner. Gordon Edelstone came up with the headline for the ad: "I need your help." They all agreed the ad had to feature a photo of Henry, and because he was such a familiar face, it did not have to be large. Selma Edelstone rallied together some stalwarts, such as June Callwood, with her friends and neighbours, wealthy, powerful women who called themselves The Issue Is Choice and ran this and many other national ad campaigns in twenty-two major Canadian cities throughout the next few years. They virtually took over fund-raising from CARAL, which had been cracking under some of Henry's financial pressure. "He made us feel sometimes we were letting him down. He would certainly phone me and say, would I talk to the board about it. And sometimes he would set an amount," said Norma Scarborough. "He would do it really well. He wouldn't come out and say, 'Look, you owe me,' but he would make you feel guilty, and he was very persuasive in the way he did it."

CARAL never stopped fund-raising for Henry's defence and for other actions in the cause, but it was soon apparent that The Issue Is Choice was a cash-generating juggernaut. They began by holding coffee parties where people came, with chequebooks, to hear Henry, Manning and, once, Scott, although never again after Selma cringed through a speech Scott gave in which he lambasted other doctors, the medical establishment and the government. "It was just not appropriate for people who we wanted to give money," she recalled. The Issue Is Choice later brought Gloria Steinem to Toronto for a special evening of champagne and desserts at the Sheraton Centre. In his clinic, Henry still has the framed photo of Steinem and him taken that night. In a bald attempt to reach past the banner-carrying, fist-waving pro-choice supporters to the well-heeled mainstream, tickets were a stratospheric $50 each. People like Judy Rebick swallowed hard, told themselves they would never have another chance to eat all the desserts they could ever want in a night and paid. The concert hall was filled with sleek, prosperous women, professional women, influential women. It was a turning point for the movement and for feminism, and it was a huge financial success. Over the years, The Issue Is Choice was to bring in close to $800,000 for Henry's legal battles. At its peak, Selma Edelstone would drag back to her house two or three large bags of mail for The Issue Is Choice from the post office on Davenport Avenue in Toronto and she, Gordon and their daughters would spend all evening sorting them. About 5 to 7 per cent of the responses were negative, abusive, vicious and sometimes violent. Once a .22-calibre bullet dropped out of an envelope opened by Gordon Edelstone. "The next one is for you, kike," the accompanying note read. Most often the mail held cheques, $20 on average, often with no return address, and poignant, personal letters. Once there was a cheque for $10,000.

The first "I need your help" ad ran on Saturday, January 5, 1985, symbolically, in the *Gazette* in Montreal, where Henry's crusade had begun. Two days later Henry was in Toronto, again symbolically, to perform abortions for the first time in that city. Scott was working in the Montreal clinic. Surrounded by supporters wearing blue armbands with the word "Choice" on them over their bulky winter coats, Henry arrived at the clinic at 8 a.m., about three hours earlier than he would have preferred (he has never been a morning person). Only reporters and camera operators were there.[2] The twenty-five anti-abortion protestors arrived half an hour after that, too late to prevent Henry from starting on the fifteen abortions he had scheduled for that day. (Bob Scott never did as many procedures a day as Henry, Andrea Knight said. "Henry was a maniac. He worked incredible days. Partly because he can't sit still and partly because there's always one more woman who needs an abortion. It's both with him. You simply can't separate out his own personality from the commitment to the cause, because they have become inextricably linked.") That evening Henry told a press conference he would be reopening the Winnipeg clinic in March; two days after that Henry announced that his personal appeal for funds (the "I need your help" ad) had elicited more than 250 letters and $7,000.

Then the Sylvia story, as it came to be known, hit. Sylvia was the pseudonym of a patient who told a Toronto radio station she'd been mistreated at the Morgentaler Clinic. She said she'd been given no painkiller, and when she'd told staff she didn't want an abortion after all she'd been forced back down on the operating table and had a sanitary napkin stuffed in her mouth. It was inevitable. Henry had proudly been engaged in his own count — one thousand, then twelve thousand, then eighteen thousand abortions without a "single death, hysterectomy, complaint or lawsuit," he liked to say, numbers that spiralled from their own momentum, their own power.

Everyone at the clinic knew the police were following some of the patients in cars or on foot, approaching them, Andrea Knight said, "lowering their voice and making it all full of concern and asking, 'Are you all right? Do you need to go to a hospital?' Which of course terrified a lot of women. A lot were immigrants, visible minorities. We tried to make ourselves available to make sure they got away safely, or that they were not accosted or harassed on their way in or out." In Sylvia's case, police had followed her home, then met her as she was getting out of the taxi. Judy Rebick happened to be in the clinic the day a reporter from Toronto's CFRB radio station called with two tape recorders in his hand: one with Sylvia's own story and one running, awaiting Rebick's reaction. For once, words failed her and Rebick fell back on clichés. She didn't know the story, but given Dr. Morgentaler's reputation there must have been some misunderstanding — then she ran upstairs to talk with the nurses. They confirmed that Sylvia had panicked during the procedure, and they had given her a sanitary napkin to bite down on (a standard procedure). Afterwards she had been grateful and happy and had hugged everyone, including Henry.

At the time of the uproar he was in Montreal, and Rebick decided he should keep a low profile on the story. She chose "the most angelic-looking nurse on staff" to tell media the clinic's version. Henry remembered the police chief in Toronto, Jack Marks, seizing the opportunity to state this was typical of how women were mistreated at Henry's clinic. Then a reporter located Sylvia's taxi driver ("much better than if we had," Rebick admitted), who was an actor and who remembered Sylvia's conversation with the escort — she had invited her in for soup — and also recalled police stopping her for questioning after she left the taxi. Next someone from the hospital the police had taken Sylvia to called to say Sylvia had been in fine health; this was followed by another call from someone within the Immigration Department, who stated that Sylvia was in the country illegally. "It confirmed for me the extent of the public support. The police couldn't get away with anything. We even got a call from one of their own people, somebody inside the police department," Rebick said, putting a positive spin on the most serious attack yet on Henry's reputation. The Sylvia incident aimed directly at Henry's ability to be a compassionate physician. If they had lost that publicity battle, they would have lost their cause. Everyone knew that, especially Henry.

He was relieved to swing into action. With Rebick, he took off on a five-day three-city tour to the West, touching down in Calgary, Edmonton and Winnipeg, searing the ground wherever he landed. At the airport in Calgary he was sprayed in the face with ketchup in front of a hundred supporters and media. Police wrestled a man to the ground, later identified as Larry Heather, president of the 350-member Calgary Association of Christians Concerned for Life, but refused to lay charges. Henry could not wipe his face entirely clean; red globs of ketchup dripped down into his beard and dried on the lapels of his tweed coat. Whisked away by security hired for his visit, he sat behind the driver — his dark-red splattered side exposed to the window and the photographers. He knew it was a shocking image. He was furious, and shaken. What if it had not been ketchup? Henry was also hit on the head by a pro-lifer's picket sign when about four hundred demonstrators surged past a police guard towards him as he entered a television station for an interview. In Edmonton he was hit by a wall of words. Alberta's attorney general, Neil Crawford, said criminal charges would be laid if an abortion clinic was set up in the province, no matter what happened in Ontario. Less civilized were the taunts of "queer" and "faggot" when he arrived on Thursday morning (January 17, 1985) for the first interview of a day packed with radio talk shows, meetings and an evening lecture. After the interview was finished, he was followed down the street by a man who asked him over and over, "Is it true you won't do abortions on Jews?" until Henry finally snapped, "Shut up and go away. You're a stupid a —."[3] Security guards checked everyone at a news conference in a classroom at the University of Alberta to ensure they were members of the media, and that night five hundred carried picket signs and candles outside the university hall where Henry was speaking. He was forced to use a back entrance. Once inside, however, he was met by a capacity crowd of 750 who had paid $7.25 to hear him. He got carried away with his own rhetoric and announced to the cheering crowd, "God told me to help women" and "God is all-powerful. If he wanted to, He would have stopped me. I have come to the conclusion that God is guiding my hand."[4] The headline in the *Edmonton Journal* read "Morgentaler Claims Divine Guidance." Two days later Henry won a retraction: he had not experienced conversion on the road to the Alberta capital. When he left for Winnipeg, supporters estimated he had raised $20,000 during his two-day visit to Alberta.

In Winnipeg, the Coalition was taking no chances. They had organized a large public reception for Henry and Rebick January 18 at the Delta Winnipeg Hotel, a private party at Linda Taylor's home at $25 a ticket and the next evening a $100-a-ticket affair at the grand home of Dawn McKeag, wife of the former lieutenant governor for Manitoba. They hired private security for Henry, but he had received a death threat before he even landed. Borowski had told media a man had phoned offering $20,000 to anyone who would get rid of Henry Morgentaler. Rebick was to have stayed at the home of CORC member Lynne Pesochin, but offered to switch with Henry. (OCAC members who travelled with Henry usually stayed at supporters' homes across the country, because it was cheaper and because they preferred it. Henry generally stayed in hotels, always with a pool, so he could swim.) With the clinic's security guard, Pesochin met Henry at the airport and drove him to the clinic for a press conference, then to her home. It was one of the coldest weekends in Winnipeg's history, 33 degrees Celsius below zero, and the supporters had to travel in convoy because cars were seizing up or not starting. When it was time to go to the hotel, Henry asked Pesochin for some warmer clothes. She gave him the only clean thing she had — pink floral longjohns belonging to one of her teenaged daughters. When she called downstairs to check on him (his supporters knew Henry had a habit of catnapping in his baths), she was greeted with the sight of Henry at the foot of the stairs in pink flowered longjohns. "I will take that with me to the grave," she said. "Here is the man who has caused such a kerfuffle in the legal communities across this country and he is standing in my basement in floral underwear." On the way to the hotel, he slumped in the back seat of Pesochin's station wagon, pulled a toque over his ears and fell asleep. "He looked like a crumpled lawn ornament," Pesochin said. "We drove right up the hotel ramp, right past the protestors. They had no idea he was right under their nose." It was so cold the hotel's power blew (a generator rescued the event), but Henry was warm and ebullient and affectionate, hugging everybody. The weekend netted more than $10,500.

Henry was in great demand. The next month he was the featured speaker (on health and human dignity) at Queen's University's prestigious Dunning Trust lecture series, following luminaries such as Oxford academic Cecil Day Lewis, physicist Robert Oppenheimer and economist John Kenneth Galbraith. His fees were all going into his legal funds, but his opposition seemed to sense a rise in the pro-choice fortunes, both financially and in terms of public opinion. In mid-February Emmett Cardinal Carter, Toronto's Roman Catholic archbishop, threw his considerable weight behind plans to besiege the Harbord Street clinic by mobilizing members in 196 parishes for successive demonstrations from February 18 to 21. What began slowly — only about 125 showed up the first day — bloated into a street-blocking demonstration by some of the more than three thousand protestors who marched the last day. Police detained three people. On February 22, more than five thousand pro-choice supporters marched from Queen's Park to the clinic to show they were not going to be intimidated by "pro-life thugs," as OCAC member Cherie MacDonald called their opponents.

Henry missed all the action. He and Reilly were touring India, after Henry had addressed a law and medicine conference in New Delhi. That was a new honour for Henry. As Reilly said, "He was just starting on his university speaking tours and getting paid for it, and had just started the ads in the papers and getting income from that, so this whole notion that he didn't have to be alone in this, that the world would actually pay him to speak on this topic, was still something to get his head around. He was coming into his own and into his expertise."

The trip was not a pilgrimage, although Reilly would have liked it to be. The seeker who slept with a copy of feel-good pop guru Leo Buscaglia's book *Living, Loving and Learning* by their bed reacted vehemently to India's religious spirituality. "To him it was all religious nonsense. He didn't see the spiritual wonder. He saw it as a primitive superstition sitting on the heads of the masses. I tried to let the bus boys, taxi drivers and waiters share the brunt of all those humanist lectures, while I would get out and walk the grounds if possible."

Henry remembered India's "staggering poverty." When he saw hundreds of people "bathing in the Ganges with [all] its filth because of a religious faith," he refused to respect such beliefs. "Why should I respect them because they believe? People believe in all kinds of stupid things." Henry found himself recognized even in India: he was hailed by a doctor from Ottawa at the Goan seaside. He and Reilly also went to Bombay, the Taj Mahal and Kashmir, where one evening they drifted in a sensual haze of marijuana in their own houseboat after consuming a gourmet dinner delivered to them by a waiter in a water taxi, accompanied by sitar players Henry had hired for the occasion. Henry arrived home rested and restored, which he needed to be, because in his absence in Winnipeg two thousand pro-life supporters had marched on the streets at the opening of the legislative session. When the College of Physicians and Surgeons of Manitoba gave Henry back his licence, chief Dr. Patrick Doyle resigned in protest, stating he would order the clinic shut down if Henry opened it March 23, as promised. (In 1983, the day before police raided the Winnipeg clinic, the College had sent Henry a letter ordering him to close the clinic, because by not sending all removed human tissue to a pathology lab, not giving assurances that all patients would be treated in a hospital if the need arose and not supplying the name of the clinic director, the clinic did not meet the College's medical standards.) Doyle ensured that the College would continue to prosecute Henry and the clinic, even though the abortion-related charges against him had been stayed pending the Ontario appeal. "They did the dirty work for the government," Henry noted. The first thing he did upon his return to the country was assure the College the clinic would comply with all medical requirements, even though he said he knew they were not required elsewhere. But League for Life decided to apply for an injunction to prevent the Morgentaler Clinic from re-opening anyway, which was later denied. Meanwhile, an Ontario organization called Choose Life Canada, headed by a Baptist minister, the Reverend Ken Campbell, announced it was moving into 87 Harbord Street, the building attached to Henry's clinic. Henry was blasé: "I hope they are good neighbours," he told the press. The remark appeared in the *Globe and Mail* as the "Quote of The Day." (When Campbell moved in, he presented Henry with a box of chocolates as Henry was coming in to work. "I said, 'Thank you.' What else could I do? But I was wondering if he put poisoning in them," Henry said with a laugh. "Yeah," added Andrea Knight. "Then he made me try one first."

Henry left to speak at universities in London, Guelph and Kitchener-Waterloo, Ontario. At the University of Western Ontario in London, he announced he would set up a clinic in Newfoundland. He told the sold-out crowd of 2,300 he had just received a letter from Justice Minister John Crosbie, saying he wouldn't change the law. "I said, 'If he doesn't want to help women in Newfoundland, I will.' Good line, eh?" as one thousand pro-life demonstrators, including 140 nuns and priests and MPP John Sweeney, marched outside in mournful circles. Henry was oblivious. "I remember I was in great form. I declared pro-choice was pro-life and that I'm pro-life because I was pro-choice." At Waterloo, he was tired but exhilarated by the "big crowds there."

He flew into Winnipeg to open the clinic as announced, and on schedule, on March 23. Other than Suzanne Newman, who was a counsellor, Henry had hired an entirely new staff. At 2:30 that afternoon, police raided the clinic after Henry had performed four abortions. Newman said she recognized some of the officers from the 1983 raid, but their deportment, and hers, was very different this time. The clinic alarm bell sounded; Newman asked to see a search warrant and then requested permission to go upstairs before the officers did. They agreed to that. Henry had just finished a procedure, but the patient was upset and asking for her partner. "I spoke with Henry in his office. He was enraged. His immediate reaction was to fire off a telegram to Roland Penner. His other thought was to destroy the files."

Brodsky arrived at the clinic about twenty minutes after Newman had reminded the staff not to make any statements. The first two patients had left. The police knew about the fourth patient, but patient number three could be protected: Henry tore up her file. Newman went downstairs again as Henry and Brodsky discussed what to do with the fetal by-products. In 1983, clinic staff would examine the fetal tissue, put it in a garboretor and flush it down the drain. "We do not consider it a human being," Henry had said to inquiring reporters.[5] Provincial regulations stated tissue removed from a human being during an operation in a hospital must be preserved, identified and examined by a pathologist. But the Corydon Avenue clinic was not a hospital, so it was exempt. In 1983, police had a plumber take the entire garboreting system apart, looking for evidence. This time the products of conception were kept in a jar that Newman believed had been destroyed. Henry had time to finish his telegram and have the receptionist phone media and read it to them before he and Brodsky were led from the building, about eighty minutes after the raid had started. Police confiscated his equipment again, and that was going to cost another $5,000 to $10,000 to replace.

Kruger and the Coalition had organized a press conference for 3 p.m. to announce that the clinic was open and a number of abortions had been successfully performed. It became a protest as three hundred women marched across the Osborne Bridge right up to Roland Penner's Roslyn Road home. The Manitoba government had taken some steps to improve access to abortion services: the number of procedures done at the Health Sciences Centre was up 34 per cent. "We were pleased. We had always wanted better access to hospitals, where women could use medicare. That had always been our fight. The reason we wanted a free-standing clinic was [the hospitals] wouldn't ever budge," Kruger said. But the Health Sciences Centre did not publicize its services and Brandon General Hospital was the only hospital with a new therapeutic abortion committee. "The government's move is partly to undermine the fight for the Morgentaler Clinic," Kruger had written in the

Coalition spring newsletter. Penner met them outside his home in jeans and a ski jacket, but was jeered when he told them he had done as much as he could to help them by not pressing charges. Penner also said he had asked Henry not to reopen the clinic until his Toronto appeal was heard. At 6 p.m. Henry held his own press conference. He confirmed his arrest, that four abortions had been performed, that the police had been more polite and less aggressive on this raid and that he would be back in one week, provided he could get equipment. That was all the College of Physicians and Surgeons registrar, James Morison, needed to announce an investigation that might result in Henry's licence being revoked for breaking College by-laws by performing abortions.

"The police had instructions from Penner not to keep me over-night," Henry recalled. He left for a previously scheduled speaking engagement at McGill University in Montreal and then one in Halifax, where he announced he intended to set up a Halifax clinic, as well. Meanwhile, police in Winnipeg made their own statement: they were laying three counts of intentionally procuring a miscarriage against Henry. Although Penner said the Crown would delay prosecuting the charges, Henry was ordered to appear in court the following Monday. Borowski was reported to have reacted to the news with a "Hallelujah!" and an announcement that he would continue to break provincial laws, such as not wearing a seat belt, because "if Henry can break the law, anyone can."[6] Even though the College suspended Henry's licence for seven days on Friday, March 29, the next day he was back at the clinic, prepared to perform abortions. For the second straight weekend, police swooped down. They allowed Henry to finish the abortion he was in the process of, and after waiting while he gave a phone interview to a reporter from Canadian Press, demanding that Penner resign, they seized their fourth set of clinic equipment, then escorted Henry to the Public Safety Building.

Once again Kruger led a group of protestors to Penner's home; again he went out to meet them and again he refused to intervene. On Monday, Henry appeared in court, plugged into a portable Walkman tape player. His case was remanded to April and he was released. But two days before three more charges were laid on Henry (causing Henry to call Penner "a hypocrite" and describe the Winnipeg police force as the most "dogged, disruptive and destructive" in Canada), the College decided to seek a court injunction preventing Henry from practising medicine. He launched an appeal, which he eventually lost. Penner fought back, telling a reporter Henry was hurting the pro-choice cause by turning abortion into a personal issue rather than keeping it a policy issue.[7] Then a judge on the Manitoba Court of Queen's Bench ruled that Henry could not practise in the province until the licence suspension was settled in mid-April. Henry offered Manitoba women free abortions in his Toronto clinic. On behalf of the government, the Crown agreed with Brodsky to delay further court action pending the Ontario appeal. However, Henry still had the College injunction to fight. He spent four hours in court on April 18, "in a passionate testimony, peppered with shouting matches with College lawyer Ken Houston."[8] The injunction continued until Henry had Brodsky re-apply in midsummer to the College for approval of the clinic as a nonhospital surgical facility. "My feeling is they are leading me down the garden path," Henry said to media. "I'm going to call their bluff." To which Morison responded, "We don't bluff."[9] Henry found out he lost that bid in October. For the first time he admitted publicly that he had probably failed: "I don't have too much hope. It is like hitting your head against a brick wall. There are certain defeats that you have to accept."[10]

The Coalition was also discouraged. Suzanne Newman reported at an October 10 steering committee meeting that even though Mike Morgentaler had offered to keep the clinic open till the end of the year, its $3,000 monthly expenses were fixed, whether a referral line was in operation or not, and that fund-raising didn't seem feasible right then. The issue was worn out; a recent appeal by Henry through local media had elicited only two donations. By November, however, Henry had bounced back, aided by the $12,000 in pledges that his latest plight had generated. He vowed to keep the Winnipeg clinic open "as a symbol of the fight for reproductive rights."[11] But it would be a long time before any abortions would ever be performed again at 883 Corydon Avenue.

Selma Edelstone had organized everything, from catered lunches to crowd control to security so tight Henry thought it was a bit "cloak and dagger, with two cars, one in front, one in back, walkie-talkies, decisions about which entrance to go in to avoid demonstrators, RCMP and police co-operating to protect my safety. It's uncanny," he said midtrip in Vancouver. He and Carolyn Egan had come to the West Coast that April to bang the drum loudly; that the *Toronto Star* published an article on April 9 in which Henry had estimated his worth at that point in 1985 at $500,000 and the *Globe and Mail* had printed a lengthy description of what appeared to be a Morgentaler abortion clinic empire of interlocking holding companies did not deter them from their goal. Nor did the galling news that Borowski would appear on December 16 in Saskatchewan's Appeal Court to protest a ruling that rejected his 1983 bid to have Canada's abortion laws struck down.

For five days Henry was in a celebrity whirl and treated like visiting royalty. From the moment he was met at the airport on Wednesday, April 10, by television interviewer Laurier LaPierre and whisked to the studio set that night for a two-hour show with LaPierre and a live audience, every need was met and almost every minute accounted for. On the bright yellow pages of Henry's confidential itinerary were the names of the RCMP co-ordinator and the two Vancouver police undercover escorts, plus various mobile phone numbers. There were two drivers on call to get him to all seven interviews scheduled for the next day, which would be followed in the evening by a private cocktail party at the University of British Columbia Faculty Club (tickets priced at a minimum $20), an even more private meeting with sympathetic local physicians and then finish, finally, with a very private dinner at the home of one of the members of Concerned Citizens for Choice on Abortion, the CARAL affiliate that had sponsored his trip. Friday morning, Henry did his first interview with radio host Dave Barrett, the former premier. That night there was an enthusiastic rally back at UBC, but this time in the students' domain, the Student Union Building, followed by a wine-and-cheese party at a community centre. After the obligatory interviews the next day, Henry spent the afternoon at LaPierre's home before heading off to another rally. By Sunday he was in Victoria, for one more press conference, another rally and the inevitable fund-raising wine-and-cheese event in the evening.

What others might have found gruelling Henry experienced as "exhilarating." Egan was shaken by the security measures needed to get her into the hall she was to speak at. Fifteen hundred anti-choice people stood outside. "It became very clear and very stark that moment what we were up against," she said. Nor was Henry immune to the crowds of anti-abortion demonstrators, the elaborate security precautions. "I woke up this afternoon from a little nap with lots of anxiety and palpitations when I imagined that three guys were accosting me outside the public place, accusing me of killing babies and threatening me. I woke up because I felt really threatened.... It took maybe two hours to recover," he recorded on Saturday evening, April 13, in his hotel room. That may be why so many of his thoughts that evening were deliberately positive, spoken more as reassurance than for the record. "I've been received with such tremendous acceptance, enthusiasm, admiration, adulation — it really blows my mind," he said. "There is tremendous response from the public. People shake my hand. They look at me admiringly, express their admiration — 'You're fantastic and keep on fighting. We support you.' The money that's coming in is also an example of that. Tonight they collected $4,700 in a crowd of nine hundred."

After the Calgary ketchup incident, a man approached him on a plane to say that "Not everybody in Calgary is a boor." In Winnipeg, Henry was having a Scotch while waiting for a flight in the airport, when a stranger pressed a $20 bill in his hand. On another occasion a gentleman approached him with a cheque for $500. "When you endorse it and the bank sends it back to me, that will be my autograph," the man said. That day Henry had read a local Vancouver columnist's description of him as the most hated and admired person in Canada, a person arousing more passion and getting more press than former prime minister Trudeau ever had. "Somehow it looks as though I have arrived, I have made my mark on Canadian history, that I've imposed myself as a sort of personality that has captured the public's imagination...I think by now I have accepted the idea that I am a sort of role model for some people, the Canadian hero who does not flinch, who does not give in to threats and who continues on his course of social action, which really is his right."

When he got back from Victoria, he wrote the Saskatchewan government, requesting approval to set up a medicare-funded abortion clinic. "We will be doing everything within the power of this government to prevent him from establishing a clinic in this province," Health Minister Graham Taylor replied within a day of receiving the letter.[12] In New Brunswick, Premier Richard Hatfield was equally as adamant about rejecting a request from Henry Morgentaler to establish a clinic there. Henry had anticipated no other reaction; he, Yann and Reilly were at a Club Med during it all anyway. What was important to Henry, although he wouldn't be attending, was the hearing on his jury acquittal, before a panel of five judges from the Ontario Court of Appeal. Chief Justice William Howland would oversee the proceeding, which would begin April 29. Crown Counsel James Blacklock argued that the jury should never have been allowed to consider the defence of necessity because there was no "clear and imminent" emergency warranting that the law be broken. Morris Manning was "grilled" extensively on most of the arguments he subsequently raised in defence of his defence by three of the five judges, and four of Manning's arguments were tossed out by Howland — meaning the panel did not have to respond to them in coming to their legal decision. By May 7 it was over, the judgment reserved, as it happened, until October 1, when the appeal was allowed, the jury acquittal set aside and a new trial ordered. Henry had one card left to play — he immediately announced he would appeal to the Supreme Court of Canada. At least the government of Ontario had backed down on one thing: it would not shut down the Toronto clinic while the last appeal was pending.

With the Montreal clinic running smoothly and the Winnipeg clinic closed, all the attention zoomed back once again to the red brick building on Harbord Street. Ken Campbell's Emmanuel Baptist Church in Milton, Ontario, had a prayer dedication at the Way Inn, the next-door coffee shop cum drop-in centre and Christian counselling centre and reading rooms. There always seemed to be picketers out front of the two buildings, many of them so regular they become well-known to the women working inside the clinic. The summer of 1985 was tense. "There were days I felt I worked in a war zone," Andrea Knight said. The picketers had become bolder, louder. They pleaded with women entering the clinic not to kill their babies, screamed "Killer" and "Remember Auschwitz" to staff, sometimes sang "Happy birthday to the baby you just killed" to women leaving the clinic. In late June when demonstrators blocked four women trying to get into the clinic, Bob Scott came outside and tried to pull away the arm of a man holding on to a railing and very effectively blocking off clinic entry. In the struggle Scott's nose was broken. Two men were charged with assault. They countercharged, but they were convicted, fined $400, put on probation and ordered to stay away from the clinic. By the summer, pro-life protestors were regularly being dragged away from the premises by police, who began laying charges of trespassing. A sixteen-year-old was charged with possession of a dangerous weapon and three counts of pointing a firearm after she began shouting "I'll blow your head off" at anti-abortion demonstrators from the second floor of a next-door building where she was staying. Unnerved by the constant picketing, she had pointed a shotgun at a group that had included an eleven-year-old boy and a Jesuit priest.

Henry was in Europe with Reilly, touring Greece and Rome before stopping over in Brussels to visit some of his extended family. At a family dinner, Reilly recalled the wife of Henry's cousin looking over at Henry "as if to say, 'Henry, Henry, when will you settle down? Who's she? What happened to Carmen?' That look that said there was no point in getting to know this one's name, when in another two months there would be another one there. Boy, if I didn't know then, I knew after that. It was not a moral judgment. I could have tried to win a place as an individual, but I could see they had more history on the truth of the thing than I did."

Henry and Reilly's relationship was winding down. The disparaging remarks had begun: Henry recalled Reilly saying, "What do you know? You're just a little abortionist," during a discussion on a non-abortion-related topic. The relationship never recovered from that insult. He never forgot the time she left Yann alone in the park across the street from his Montreal home. Reilly said she felt lonely in "Fortress Henry. I felt so isolated. He didn't have time for me." At the same time, his battles with Carmen were monumental, raging affairs. When Carmen would come to the house on Melville Avenue for more negotiations, Reilly would huddle in the kitchen with Yann, trying to distract him with crayoning, which never succeeded. "Mummy and Daddy are fighting again," the child would say — a statement, not a question.

And what Reilly called "the phone calls taken in the other room" had begun. During his time with Reilly, Henry was casually involved with Jean Rankin, a therapist he had met at the 1982 Labour Day primal weekend. Henry and Rankin became friends instantly, and after their brief interlude became friends again. Rankin had trained at the Primal Centre for Personal Development in Toronto under Marsha and Dr. Herman Weiner, Americans from New York, and Herman's Weiner's son (Marsha's stepson), Eric, who also became Henry's close friend. Eric Weiner later married Andrea Knight. Rankin's affair with Henry was "nothing serious," said Rankin, twelve years younger than Henry and newly divorced when they met. "Once when he stayed, in the morning I was in the kitchen and he said, 'I'll have two boiled eggs,' and walked into the living room, put up his feet and picked up a magazine. I decided at that point this was not the man for me. I was right. We are much better friends." Later when she told him about that realization, he was dumbfounded. "Why didn't you just say something? We would have gone out for breakfast," he said.

Rankin valued the friendship more — "which is open and honest and we go back and forth to get good counsel. He has a wonderful creative intelligence. He can really let go of this world and think about ideas." She is one of the few people Henry has allowed to see how deeply he can feel events. "He can get frightened, very, very frightened. People send him hate letters, holler at him on the street — that affects him very deeply. It is terrible having people out there hating you, but he is not going to let that stop him." Henry has told Rankin he can say anything to her, that she may know him better than anyone. "The man with the gardening shears?" she said. "He was very taken aback by that, but he's not going to come out and say that to the media. He'll say it was scary and he was shaken, but he won't say that then he gets anxious and he can't sleep properly. Sometimes he can get depressed, and part of the depression is having these feelings and not wanting them to bother him because he wants to get on with his work and won't let anyone stop him. Sometimes he has to do it in spite of being scared. He is able to talk [to me] about being scared at a very deep level." They acted as each other's therapists and playmates, tossing around ideas with the abandon of Frisbee players on a long, empty beach. "Sometimes Henry's so full of himself that he's unbearable and then I think he's hilarious, I love it," Rankin said. "He'll come and pick me up and say, 'I'm full of my-self. I'm a hero,' as I get my coat, and I will laugh and laugh. At first I thought, 'What an egomaniac,' but there is something charming about it. If you can allow your negative feelings — I'm hurting, I'm weeping — why can't you acknowledge when you feel wonderful? I remember when it dawned on me. I said to him, 'I would love to feel like that. It must feel wonderful to just feel full of yourself.' So we worked on that. It was good for me to be even able to say that." She said the therapy sessions helped her understand why her friend always seemed to be wanting more. "He was a high addict, everything he talks about has to be exciting." He needed continual stimulation because he was able to swiftly synthesize ideas and facts, process and integrate them and move on. His broad streak of hedonism motivated him even more to chase those highs. Rankin began to understand that to Henry, sex was simply another of life's pleasures, "like another glass of wine."

Reilly could not. That summer she had moved in with Henry in Montreal, but prudently had kept her apartment in Toronto. Whether she would stay past September was always in question. She did not know then that Henry had already met her successor, Arlene Leibovitch.

Arlene had worked for Henry in the clinic for three weeks at the beginning of 1985, when OCAC and CARAL had decided Henry should handle the Toronto clinic and Bob Scott the Montreal clinic to make sure the police wouldn't close down the Toronto operations. Arlene knew Rebick, who worked at the Canadian Hearing Society, but she was also an OCAC member in her own right. An adventuresome teen-ager, she had been at the Banff School of Fine Arts, and was attending

an alternative school in Toronto and dreaming of a career as a concert
pianist, when she quit everything to work at a posh Bloor Street clothing store for the six months it took to earn $2,500 and to buy a $200 one-
way airline ticket to Amsterdam. "At the airport my mother burst into
tears and said, 'I know you are never coming back.' She knew. I met
some incredible people [in Europe] and lived there for ten years," said
Arlene. Nine of them were in Italy, where she married, taught English,
worked in hotel management and became a radical. It was the time of
the Red Brigade and the Bader Meinhoff in Germany, when European
society was rocked by terrorist tactics from these bands of intellectual
radicals. "I learned not to believe in the state obediently," she said. When
her marriage broke up, she returned to Canada, but she had missed the
decade from 1972 to 1982, and Henry's public battles. "I never had to
bridge the hero gap," she noted wryly.

She and Henry had spoken Italian for one and a half hours during
her interview and she got the clinic job. But she left after three weeks
because she was in demand as an interpreter, and Scott, who had returned to the Toronto clinic, preferred to do things himself and his way.
In June, a filmmaker friend wanted to film an interview with Henry, so
Andrea Knight arranged the evening, which she dubbed "My Dinner
with Henry." Arlene, a superb chef, was there to poach the salmon. The
filmmaker told Knight that Henry was thoroughly distracted watching
Arlene. Six weeks later he called Arlene, who said, "He broke up with
Maureen. He took a chance. He didn't know whether or not I would be
available." Reilly said she and Henry never discussed their breakup; on
the day in mid-August that she was about to go back to Toronto she
asked if they could talk about it. Henry said, "Not now." But, Reilly
said, she was proud to have left without being goaded into a fight. She
said she realized she had been a "sycophant in the inner ring," but "like
a bull's-eye" there was another ring and another ring, and probably
there would be many more.

Minutes before Reilly left the house on Melville, Carmen came to
fetch Yann for what she told Henry would be an extended vacation.
Reilly kissed the little boy goodbye, knowing she would never see him

again. What Henry couldn't know was it would be the last time he would see his son for months. When Carmen left with Yann that day, she vanished.

CHAPTER 15

THE PRESSURE COOKER

CARMEN CALLED ONCE to say she and Yann were so enjoying their Greek holiday they wanted to stay longer. Henry readily agreed. He had never been a twenty four hour a day parent; his life was his work, and when he wasn't out in restaurants or at a cinema, there were always evening meetings, trial strategies to discuss, friends and colleagues from the cause to call. The evenings that Gertie Katz came to the house with a business file for Henry she remembered a four-year-old Yann not leaving the room, no matter how much Henry asked, cajoled, pleaded with — but never ordered — him to. It was obvious to everyone how much Henry adored this child, but the boy needed reassuring that he came first with his father, Gertie said. He was very clever, the bright spoil from a soiled marriage. He knew it; he could and did manipulate his doting father. Henry would never have sent Yann away, but extending the boy's holiday with Carmen gave Henry more time to know Arlene.

He took her to the annual IPA (International Primal Association) convention in Philadelphia in September 1985, on the Labour Day weekend. All Arlene knew of Henry was what she had seen in the clinic — his gentleness with patients, his good-humoured patience with staff. But she wasn't impressed with the others at the primal weekend: "I found a lot of them were very needy people. By the end of the weekend I actually felt very sorry for a lot of them. I thought they came specifically to get their yayas out, that this was the only time they could be who they were. It was obvious to me they didn't have the kind of support network around them around them that enabled them to be who they needed to be."

Henry was not like that. That weekend she realized "he would go away and see the people he wanted to see and do what he wanted to do. And it would not be all just the cause, either." Like Maureen Reilly, Arlene was three decades younger than Henry. She was also stylish, forthright, possessed of a tough intelligence. She said she admired and accepted Henry's independent streak. "I wanted time and space alone, as well." She deliberately had not been involved in a serious relationship the previous five years so she could learn about herself. She grew up strong and secure, attending Jewish schools and living in a predominantly Jewish area of Toronto, but in a secular home. Although the younger of two daughters, she had been the organizing force in her family. "It wasn't upsetting for me my parents were deaf. It was just a fact. As far as I was concerned they were the same as everybody else except they were deaf." She was still a take-charge personality, "but Henry and I take charge of different things," she said. She was content to live in separate cities; Henry wasn't.

Later that September they went away on a Club Med vacation in Ixtapa, Mexico. It was the week that an earthquake virtually destroyed Mexico City. Even the aftershock a day later registered about 7.5 on the Richter scale. The Club Med complex was built to withstand earthquakes, and so they stayed on even when others in Ixtapa were evacuated because huge cracks in sidewalks and balconies had appeared. By the time they returned to Canada, Henry was eager to see Yann. Mike called that night, so Henry asked if there was any news. Nothing that couldn't wait till the next day, after he'd had some sleep, Mike said. That's when Henry found out Carmen had sent her first ex-husband a letter, which he had given to Mike. She was taking Yann away forever, Carmen had written from Greece. Henry shouldn't bother coming to get him; they were going to live in a Spanish-speaking country in Europe. "Overnight Henry went from a man full of spirit and life to a depressed, lifeless, defeated man. He was devastated," said Arlene.

"It was hell. This was the worst time of my life," Henry admitted.

He hired a detective. He knew a Greek doctor living in Montreal who still had many connections in his homeland. But neither of them could find a trace of the mother and child. At the house at Morin

Heights, Henry came across a telephone bill with two phone numbers from Greece. They didn't pan out — they were probably red herrings planted to send Henry careering and flailing about the wrong part of the world. He had immediately called Carmen's brother in Chile, but he said he had not seen his sister. "It was a lie. The brother said to me later, 'She is my sister. What could I do?' But I was put off the trail," Henry said. For six cruel months he had no idea of the whereabouts of his ex-wife and his son. "Henry became physically ill over Yann's kidnapping. I remember bringing him soup," said Gertie Katz. "[Losing Yann] destroyed him. If anything brought him down, that was it. He couldn't think. He couldn't work. He couldn't do anything." His health broke down. Bamie Morgentaler flew up from Boston to comfort his father; Goldie did not, and in fact, Arlene never met Henry's eldest child. For several months Henry was listless and weepy, until his strength and resolve returned. Gertie telephoned all the major international shipping companies until she located the firm holding Carmen's possessions. They were awaiting further instructions, they told Gertie. Henry decided Carmen and Yann had to be in Chile. He sent Marisol down to look for them. Marisol had been Yann's nanny, a Chilean hired by Carmen. She would know where to look to find them.

He confided in Rebick over dinner and relied on the strength of his new relationship with Arlene and his old ties with Gertie, Mike and the Edelstones. He pulled himself together because he had set too many things in motion: the abortion issue would not leave him alone in his grief. That summer and early fall, there were minor irritations. Everybody, for instance, on Harbord Street was getting fed up — the prochoicers were angry at the police for not clearing out the pro-life demonstrators; the pro-lifers were angry at the police for arresting some of their numbers for trespassing; and the beleaguered local storekeepers were angry at both sides for obstructing day-to-day commerce. Already two restaurants had gone out of business; others were cutting back hours. A notice in the building next door to the clinic read "For the protection to our patrons and our own, La Bohemia will be closed for lunchtime today. You will understand the circumstances."[1] A plea from Emmett Cardinal Carter to limit the numbers of picketers brought no reduction in the tensions. And a secret meeting in August between Henry and a half-dozen fundamentalists (but not Ken Campbell) resulted in statements about mutual respect and little else.

When the Ontario Court of Appeal ordered new trials for Henry, Smoling and Scott in the beginning of October, OCAC reacted with another of their rallies. Henry announced he would appeal to the Supreme Court, but he did not speak to the cheering and chanting crowd of three hundred at the University of Toronto, as he otherwise might have done. When the Manitoba College of Physicians and Surgeons refused to approve the Winnipeg clinic as a nonhospital surgical service, Henry admitted that "occasionally I'm exhausted and weary," but only a handful of the people closest to him knew how weary and soul racked he was — and why. He continued to go through the motions, answer calls from the media, react for the record. When it was discovered he had submitted more than two hundred claims on an OHIP billing code, he had to explain it was for pregnancy tests and checkups, not abortions, and then he filed two notices of motion with Manitoba's Court of Appeal to quash the College's order suspending his medical licence and to roll back the injunction preventing him from practising medicine. "That he could continue to act as a spokesman, go to courts during this, is the essence of Henry," said Gordon Edelstone. Like his wife, he admired Henry and was genuinely fond of him; like many men, he was not part of the passionate centre of the cause. But as a businessman, he was skilled at accurately assessing motivation, context and content. "For Henry [the cause] is an obsession. He saw unbridled force and brutality against the helpless people in the concentration camps and he found a cause right up his alley. The irrational unfairness he experienced as a child — he will never rest until he can destroy that ghost." But as CARAL organized abortion tribunals across the country during the first months of 1986, in which the abortion law was put on trial and women testified about their abortion experiences, Henry was uncharacteristically absent from the newscasts.

Then Marisol called. She had seen Carmen and Yann playing in a park near the home of Carmen's family. Henry immediately made plans to fly down. Marisol hired a local lawyer, who ran into Carmen at a news kiosk (she recognized her from the photo Henry had supplied) and told her Henry was arriving the next day. Carmen was calm when she heard the news; she had already retained a lawyer, and knew she was well protected by Chilean law. She had appeared before a judge, saying she'd returned to her birthplace with her child after her husband had abandoned them. The judge granted her custody, and Carmen had immediately applied for Chilean passports for her and for Yann. Henry knew he didn't stand a chance in the Chilean legal system. "All she had to do was say I do abortions in Canada, in front of a Catholic judge," he said. Carmen drove a hard bargain, and for once Henry was in no position to dictate or demand. "I was desperate." They met at his hotel. Although Carmen lived in the mountains overlooking Santiago in an attractive house with a swimming pool, she took no chances. She told Henry she was renting a house (in fact she owned it) and whisked Yann off to stay with friends who lived eight hours away. Then she negotiated. Henry was rueful: "She trusted me enough to know I wasn't going to kill her, although I had the desire to strangle her." Yann would spend eight months a year with her, four — two in summer and two in winter — with Henry. Henry would pay her $1,000 a month support all year and make no demands on funds from the trust Carmen received from her mother's wealthy family. And Carmen would make no demands on his Canadian assets, including the Lake Cook country home she loved. This was not the victory it seemed for Henry, because it was her lawyer who had counselled Carmen to keep their assets separate in their wedding contract, lest Henry claim a part of her substantial inheritance. Henry agreed to everything. "I knew I couldn't do any better." When he asked her why she had run off with Yann, she just shook her head and said she didn't know.

He was allowed to see his son the following day. Carmen calmly announced, "Yann, c'est papa." The child remembered Henry, but he hung back; Carmen had told him his father was trying to kidnap him, Henry said. Henry had brought a toy, something wooden with lots of colourful pieces, which helped break the ice. But Henry had to be so careful and initially cautious with his boy, as if he were taming a skittish colt. By the next morning, Yann was relaxed with him. Henry's heart soared when he said, "You smell of Daddy" the next morning, in Spanish because he had forgotten all his English. Arlene flew down and the three went for a two-week holiday in Villarica, a southern resort in Chile's volcanic area. "Henry was exhausted and slept long and late and had naps, and I ended up entertaining this little boy who would not speak English," Arlene recalled. "By the end of the holiday he was speaking it with a Spanish accent."

They made plans to see Yann in Canada that summer of 1986 and flew back to Toronto, not Montreal. There was a crisis in the Harbord Street clinic. Bob Scott had issued an ultimatum: either Henry fire Nikki Colodny, the other doctor on staff, or he would quit. At the request of his wife, Scott no longer worked at the Winnipeg clinic — another nail in the coffin of the Corydon Avenue clinic. (In May 1986, the College again refused to licence the clinic.) He was the physician in charge in Toronto. Henry had professionally wooed Colodny for almost two years. The first time she met him, during his Toronto jury trial, he asked her to work at the clinic. Initially, she'd preferred to join OCAC and work for the pro-choice cause as an escort. A single mother of a young son, she had very real reservations; as a doctor, she knew additional physicians were needed to do abortions; as an American-born activist, idealist and feminist, she knew that many in the women's movement had long wanted a woman abortionist.

Henry was training her in Montreal and she was working at the clinic only a half day a week but becoming an increasingly vocal and public spokesperson for the cause, when Scott made his demands. "Scott is unable to work with anyone unless he is the boss. I had given him so much power in the clinic because it was impossible to do otherwise, and he was believing himself to be indispensable to the point I would never replace him. At the end he gave me an ultimatum, which I could not accept. The ultimatum was that I dismiss Nikki Colodny, that I not allow her to work and that he be allowed to dismiss the whole staff, which he felt was plotting against him," Henry stated in memoirs he dictated in September 1986.

Clinic administrator Andrea Knight blamed "pressure cooker" working conditions. "It was hard to wrest anything from [Bob]. For

instance, they had a problem with the sterilizer, which was constantly
going on the fritz. We wanted Bob to get a new one and Bob didn't
want to get a new one. They're stupid things, but when people are
working under that kind of pressure, some things can really build. His
inflexibility made it difficult for the staff to cope." Knight thought he
may have been tired of trying to stay on top of everything, knowing it
was always Henry's clinic and his cause. Henry said he tried to talk
Scott out of the ultimatum telling him that it was only half a day for
Colodny. Some patients prefer a woman doctor, so what? Don't take it
as a personal insult. He even thought he had succeeded. But eventually
Scott resigned because Henry would not cave in to his demands. "I
don't like ultimatums," Henry said. Colodny began working two weeks
on, two off at the Toronto clinic, and Henry began working fulltime in
Toronto. He stayed with Arlene in her small apartment in a downtown
high rise. It was "a wrench" to leave Montreal, and at first they went
back almost every weekend.

   In March 1986, Colodny publicly announced she was doing abortions at the Morgentaler Clinic; by April, her home in Toronto's River-
dale area was being picketed. Campaign Life members even attempted
to disrupt her son's eighth birthday party. Colodny took it in stride and
said most people told her they deplored the other side's tactics. "It's the
way I met the neighbours," she said. In May 1986 Scott opened his own
clinic. Mike did the mediating between the two abortionists, keeping
things cordial. Although Henry worried about the competition, he also
believed it was important to the cause and beneficial to women to have
two or more clinics in Toronto. But he heard rumours that David Peter-
son's Liberal government believed the Scott clinic was a front for some
kind of Morgentaler franchising empire. Clinic staff noticed police beginning to follow them and photographing patients. Henry knew he
was being followed back to Arlene's apartment. He presumed it was so
police would know where to go when it came time to arrest him. He
told the head of Metro Toronto police's morality squad it wasn't necessary to photograph patients for evidence, that he would sign a statement
saying he was performing abortions. At a July strategy meeting with
Scott and Norma Scarborough in Morris Manning's office, Manning

warned Henry he might be arrested soon, and very likely a condition of bail would be that Henry stop doing abortions. "I was worried
about that. I would never agree to that. I would rather stay in jail. And
if I did go to jail, I thought that would mobilize the whole country to
force them not to do it. But I was really worried I might have to go
to jail again."

In August Henry wrote to Attorney General Ian Scott, saying that
if the Ontario government moved to arrest and charge him or Scott
before their Supreme Court of Canada appeal, the provincial government could be construed to be in contempt of the country's highest
court. He also reminded Ian Scott that the clinic had helped out during
the doctors' strike that summer when hospitals had referred abortions
to him. Even doing up to twenty-five procedures a day, the clinic was
swamped with patients, and Henry had sent the overflow — sometimes
as many as ten a day — plus women who were fourteen to sixteen
weeks pregnant over to the Scott clinic. "Bob Scott would have gone
broke without the doctors' strike," Henry said. Before the strike, Scott's
clinic had had few patients. Norma Scarborough acted as an emissary
for Scott, asking Henry if he would refer some patients to him, which
Henry did. Nevertheless, both clinics had helped out. "It would have
looked bad if they had arrested us immediately after the strike," Henry
believed. He also wanted to avert, or at least postpone, any arrests until
after Yann had gone back to Chile. Carmen had kept her end of the bargain and had sent Yann to Henry for a month's vacation.

"Yann is bright and sweet and full of energy and full of zest, very
adaptable. It's surprising, in spite of his mother and in spite of all the
bad influence she might have had on him and the disruption in his life
she has caused, that he's adapted so well. I attribute it partly to the
nature of [the nanny], who took such good maternal and good care of
him, and to me, who has always given him so much love, and partly
to Carmen, too. I guess she has a good side of her and occasionally it
comes out. He's attached to her — there's no doubt about that," Henry
recorded in his memoirs on September 17, three days before Yann left
to return to Chile for three months.

By then Henry was convinced the police would arrive any day.

Rumours of a police raid were so intense that Henry thought it might be affecting his work. "I sort of psyched myself into believing the next day I was going to be arrested, and although I hadn't taken any sleeping pills or anything else, I don't think my sleep was very calm and... I had a very tired day. It affected my concentration. I kept thinking about it and my work suffered.... If I graded myself [on Wednesday] at A plus, then on Thursday it was B minus. I hadn't hurt anyone. It's just in order to do a good job you have to have relaxed muscles, and feel what is going on inside while I operate, and it was much harder as I, being conscious of it, just limited myself not to do any damage. And with my knowledge and experience I can do that. But it wasn't a type of superartistic excellent job I was doing on Wednesday."

Protestors at the clinic had become more vociferous. One of them slammed shut the door of a cab as Henry was alighting, narrowly missing his foot and fingers. "They were really obsessed and they were there day in, day out. I was tensing up every morning going to work. It would take me ten to fifteen minutes once inside just to relax. I never knew if any of them had a gun or a knife and would shoot me or stab me. These were very hostile people and I had to go through them, even in the back lane." There were days he took half a Percodan tablet for his tension headaches.

Yet he and the others were prepared for police action. CARAL had made provisions to take women to Montreal if or when the clinic was closed, and he and Scott had long before decided they would not accept bail on any condition that would prevent them from performing abortions. Colodny seemed desirous of political martyrdom. "I had a conversation with Nikki today [September 17]. Apparently she's quite eager to get charged. I don't know whether she wants the glory and everything it will do for her public [image]. Maybe she doesn't realize all the shit that goes with it and the suffering and disruption of her life. [Or] if she just says she wants to be charged to appear courageous and brave. In any case, I like her," Henry noted in his memoirs.

Colodny got her wish in the very early morning of Wednesday, September 26, 1986. As she was getting into her car to drive her son, Daniel, to school, two plainclothes officers emerged from the car parked in

front of her, knocked on her car window and flashed their badges.
"There was just a moment there when I thought, 'I'll just roll the window back up and drive away. It can't really be happening. This is a
movie and I'm not the right player,'" Colodny recalled. It was two
weeks before the opening of the Supreme Court hearing on abortion,
and for ten days she'd had an overnight bag packed, with knitting and
reading. She had told Daniel the longest she'd be gone would be a few
hours, maybe overnight. But he was still frightened and worried when
it actually happened. Police also arrested Scott at home as he was readying himself for a third straight day in court. He had been countercharged by the man who had broken his nose in an altercation outside
the Harbord Street clinic in June of the previous year. (He was acquitted later that day.) Norma Scarborough called Arlene's apartment at
about 8:30 a.m. to tell Henry of Colodny's and Scott's arrests. "I thought
I'd be next," Henry reported matter-of-factly in his memoirs, "and
about ten minutes later the police rang the bell downstairs. Arlene went
to open, and three cops were there and they asked for me. I told Arlene
to ask them to let me finish my breakfast. They did that. I made a number of phone calls to my lawyer, to Selma, to June Callwood, who I
wanted to invite for supper for Thursday, and I told her husband I was
just being arrested."

Arlene remembered they had to walk down a long corridor from
the kitchen to the living room, and Henry stopped to choose a tie. He
asked her, then he asked the police, which one he should wear to police
headquarters at 52 Division. In the living room he hugged Arlene and
reminded her about taking his shirts to the cleaners. "Arlene was quite
nervous about the whole thing and I was a bit excited, too, but I tried
not to show it. It seemed like a big operation. There were police cars
almost everywhere. In the middle of the road there was another police
car. It's as if they were hunting for the big fish or for some kind of big
criminal who might resist arrest and produce machine guns and violence and what not. It didn't make any sense." Later that morning
Arlene was out running errands, and learned there had been police at
every corner of her apartment building "as if Henry were going to take
off and run away. I thought it was a bit of overkill."

The media, along with supporters like Rebick, Egan and Edelstone, were already at the police station when Henry arrived to be finger-printed, questioned and charged with performing illegal abortions. News of the arrest had spread quickly — at the clinic two nurses, one of them the head nurse, quit when they heard of the arrests, probably fearing they would be picked up next and charged. "I made my usual declaration, which would have been good for the jury, stating that I was proud of what I was doing," Henry recalled. "I thought it was the height of hypocrisy to arrest us after the doctors' strike, after we averted a catastrophe for the province, that I believed that what I was doing was not only morally right but legal, as well. After that I said I [would] not answer any questions without my lawyer. The policeman seemed to be relieved, because my monologue lasted for half an hour or twenty minutes and the guy wrote it down verbatim." Henry saw Colodny at the police station and noted she had a "Freedom of Choice" button pinned to her red dress. "She was a bit nervous, but quite composed. I sort of like Nikki. I think she's a great girl. She has her foibles, but who doesn't on the whole? I admire courage and she has that. It took her a long time to get onto the public stage and risk so much, and now she is being tested, and she had declared before that she wanted to be charged. People were holding this against her, as if she was seeking publicity. In my mind she was saying it publicly to appear courageous and give her-self courage, but deep down I believe she was afraid and apprehensive about what she might face — with good reason."

But three hours later, when the doctors appeared before Judge Jane Bernhard in Provincial Court, Crown Attorney Paul Culver announced the charges were stayed until the ruling from the Supreme Court of Canada hearing, on orders from Attorney General Ian Scott. (Scott said later it was the hardest decision he ever had to make — certainly it was one of the most baffling, since it was Metro police chief Jack Marks who had personally ordered the laying of the new abortion charges.) "Ahhhhh! There were big smiles between Manning and myself, and Scott and a few of our friends . . . we were brought in as arrested people. Now we [were] free again, and I faced a big crowd of reporters. . . . I enjoyed the spotlight again. I was well dressed. On the way to Morris's office we were mobbed by reporters and cameras and passersby and our supporters. It was like a procession," Henry recorded.

Colodny had made a point of hiring Marlys Edwardh as her own lawyer. In a June 10, 1986, letter to the CARAL board, she said she was "critical of the role that Morris Manning has been playing in the use of the Charter against the union movement, and in the case of the Visa strike against working women. My grandparents spent their adult lives working to achieve what Mr. Manning is attacking. I am personally uncomfortable having him represent me and this is a fundamental reason for my choosing another lawyer. In addition, there are many who share my concerns about Mr. Manning's actions. The decision to use another lawyer, a woman lawyer, will bring support in several crucial sectors."

Manning was representing Merv Lavigne in his fight not to pay the Ontario Public Service Employees Union (OPSEU) union dues. He had also acted for a Hamilton, Ontario, company boss who had contracted outside labour during a strike. "[The Lavigne] case was key," said Marilyn White, now working for Canadian Union of Public Employees' airline division. She is also married to Canadian Auto Workers union president Bob White. "We knew it could open up the floodgates and we had been working so hard to get labour onside [with the pro-choice ranks]."

White met with NDP leader Bob Rae about it. "It was unreal. I went nose to nose with him. The NDP had ratified [a pro-choice stance] at their last convention, but Bob Rae refused [to speak up]," she said. His decision caused a 10-year rift between the previously close White and Rae families, she said.

She and Judy Rebick then met with Norma Scarborough and other CARAL members in Toronto to try and convince Henry to change lawyers. "He flat out refused," White recalled. "That was an eye-opener... we decided to keep [the disagreement with Henry] low profile."

Judy Rebick and others in OCAC were none too happy about Manning's past, either. Rebick and two others, Julie Davis from the Ontario Federation of Labour and Jane Armstrong from the Canadian Auto Workers, went to Montreal to ask Henry to replace him. "[They] were supposed to be the [union] hardliners, but they were so awed at meeting Henry Morgentaler they were soft," Rebick scoffed.

"I was awestruck being in his company," Julie Davis recalled. "Henry held such respect [within] the UAW, from the president on down." At the OFL meeting where union support of the issue of freedom of choice was put to the test (and to a vote), OFL and OCAC pro-choice women had stacked the microphones. So many supporters lined up to speak at the floor mikes "the lines filled both aisles and went out into the hill," Davis said, as Cliff Pilkey openly and passionately pushed for members not only to endorse women's freedom of choice, but also the decriminalization and full funding of abortion. "I know he got death threats; once someone sent him thirty pieces of silver [covered chocolate coins] in the mail. But he was influential in convincing other leaders [to support] the motion."

Pilkey readily authorized payment for Davis' trip to Montreal. The three women met Henry at a hotel near Montreal's Dorval airport where Davis said she and Armstrong presented their unions' perspectives. "I'll never forget that meeting as long as I live, and how tough Judy was," she said. Rebick admitted she was

very emotional about this. It was probably the thing I was most upset about.... At a certain point in the discussion I said to Henry, "What if Manning defended [Alberta Holocaust denier James] Keegstra. Would you get rid of him then?" [The other two women] were totally amazed I said that to him. Henry said it is not the same thing. I said it is to me. He wouldn't back down — I mean he would not budge. He is so stubborn. It was really heavy and they were totally freaked out that I would talk to him like that. Henry asked if I could have a drink with him alone. We went and he said, "I know you are doing this because you believe this is the right thing for the movement, and I don't want this to come between us as friends." And I was very moved, because we had had a serious political difference and I have been quite tough on him, and yet he could separate that not only from our working relationship, which I would expect because you don't give up allies, but also that it mattered to him that I still cared about him, that I wasn't mad at him, that I wasn't rejecting him as a friend.

So it made me realize how much he cared for me as a person.

And also how much I care about him.

Henry did subsequently disassociate himself publicly from Manning's other cases, which mollified some — not all — within OCAC.

Henry was angry when Colodny rejected Manning for another lawyer, whose fees would have to be paid by CARAL's arm-length Pro-Choice Fund or by The Issue Is Choice. He had at times described Colodny as "hard to work with" and "stubborn" and he knew the staff complained she made them wait to start procedures if she had political phone calls, but he needed her services. And he did understand why she was drawn to the cause of reproductive rights. "I became a doctor to do this kind of thing," she said. She knew she wasn't everyone's heroine. "There has always been an undercurrent within the pro-choice movement that saw attempts of mine to have a [public] profile as somehow a bad idea. I should go and do my work and be quiet. So it has been quite difficult to come out in Henry's shadow. As a matter of fact, I don't believe I ever have." Yet she said she decided to risk her medical future for feminism. "I thought it would help build the movement. A woman doing this for other women would be very empowering for women, just in their own lives. If people don't know there's a woman doing abortions, why do it?"

But the media still expected the statements to come from Henry, and many supporters believed the fate of the issue rested on him alone. The fact that Smoling and Scott were also participating in this historic Supreme Court hearing was often glossed over. Henry had been the only doctor in Canada doing abortions who was willing to talk with media and adept at it — until Colodny. It had been easier, although not necessarily accurate, for journalists to portray Henry's legal battles as one small man against one very large system — again until Colodny. She was an ungainly suitor attempting to cut in on the very smooth, well-rehearsed pair on the dance floor, and often it was not a pretty sight. When Edelstone organized the Gloria Steinem gala, Colodny complained vehemently that she, a woman doctor doing abortions, was not asked to speak to the women that night. Nor was Henry asked, even though he was on almost every podium these days.

"Henry wouldn't notice that it might be a good idea if someone else spoke, but if I jumped in, he would move aside. He's better now about that kind of thing, not just around me but around lots of women. Then he would never say, 'Here's Dr. Colodny,' but if I jumped in he would be very gracious. It was not Henry. It was the pro-choice movement and the women around him who were overprotective, frankly," Colodny said.

Henry said he was more concerned about the monetary effect of Colodny's beliefs and actions. "She threw a monkey wrench into our thing by choosing a lawyer different than Morris Manning and writing an open letter against [him], which to a certain extent damages the defence fund, which is at the crisis point. We don't have money to pay the lawyers. I think that at the present time, we owe Brodsky and Manning about $120,000 and there is no money," he recorded in his memoirs. After the charges were stayed, he explained to Colodny and to Edwardh, whom she had brought to the meeting at Manning's, that there was nothing for either of them to do until after the Supreme Court battle was over, which he predicted would be in six to nine months. In the meantime, he would be placing another round of fund-raising ads in the Saturday editions of the newspapers — "People have sort of fallen asleep" — and the only defence the movement was concerned with was the one Manning was working on for doctors Morgentaler, Smoling and Scott.

Henry knew how important this hearing was. "Well, today is Tuesday, October 7, the day that the Supreme Court of Canada again, after twelve years, has been hearing the abortion case which bears my name," he blithely announced in his memoirs. "It is billed as one of the big cases before the Supreme Court."

Morris Manning planned to reiterate his argument that the abortion law was unconstitutional. "Canada's legal community will be holding its collective breath to see what happens to one of the new issues Manning will raise — whether the Crown should have the right to appeal a jury acquittal. In both the United States and England, a jury acquittal is the final ruling and cannot be appealed," William Walker wrote in the *Toronto Star* on October 4, 1986. Manning had filed a sixty-page factum

with the Supreme Court, in which he argued that Section 11 of the
Charter of Rights and Freedom guaranteed the right to trial by jury, but
"judges [can] second-guess and usurp the power of juries" when they
hear a Crown appeal, he told Walker. "There are those with rigid views
who argue the Toronto jury's verdict was an unjust defiance of the law,"
Manning wrote in the magazine *Canadian Lawyer*. "They have questioned the integrity of that jury and have called the entire jury system
into question. They are wrong."

In that same article he added: "Judges, as we all know, are subject
to far more subtle controls than juries. They face at all times the pressure of their peer group and the reviewing eyes of the appeal courts.
They have institutional controls that limit their independence."

In his presentation Manning also planned to stick with the defence
of necessity and to continue to argue that Section 7 of the Charter guaranteeing "life, liberty and security of the person" included a woman's
right to choose whether or not to terminate a pregnancy. "Such decisions are deeply personal, private decisions about how one wishes to
lead one's life and are fundamental to one's control over one's body and
the ability to lead one's life free from interference," Manning stated in
his factum.[2] He had other Charter arguments. Because hospitals were
not required to have therapeutic abortion committees, the law was
applied unequally; therefore the Charter right that all people be treated
equally was violated. Section 2 guaranteeing freedom of conscience
and religion was violated because women cannot make the decision
on their own.

Hearing it all would be eight men and one woman. The *Star*'s
Walker categorized as the moderates Chief Justice Brian Dickson and
Bud Estey, both from Saskatchewan; Gerald Le Dain, from Quebec;
Scottish native Bertha Wilson; and Saskatchewan-raised William
McIntyre. Among the conservatives he counted, Jean Beetz, Julian
Chouinard and Antonio Lamer, all from Quebec; and Gerard La
Forest, of New Brunswick. Henry noted that Beetz and Dickson were
the only two who had heard his case twelve years earlier. When Mr.
Justice Chouinard took ill, Mr. Justice Gerald Le Dain was removed
from the hearing to ensure a majority verdict. By Henry's reckoning

that was "three for us, three against us, and Brian Dickson down the middle." His hunch was that McIntyre, Beetz and La Forest would vote against him, but that he could count on Bertha Wilson ("she has good civil libertarian credentials and apparently represented Planned Parenthood at one point"), Antonio Lamer ("who I know personally from having been on a panel with him about fifteen years ago on TV in Montreal, at which point he was very much in favour of freedom of choice or so it appeared to me, but he may have changed"), and Bud Estey ("probably on our side, he is a civil libertarian from Ontario, but he appeared to be quite new to the whole issue of abortion. His questions [on equality] demonstrated that"). Chief Justice Brian Dickson was "the enigma in the whole thing," Henry noted in his memoirs.

When Henry arrived at the country's appropriately grey and austere high court, he was besieged with journalists and photographers. "It was a media blitz. I felt again quite happy about this, being the articulate spokesman for a cause and being recognized as such. In a sense it was my day." And so with the cool detachment of a professional assessing a protégé, he rated his lawyer's performance — and found Manning "excellent." "He's really sharp on his feet. His manner of presentation is mature, responsible," Henry stated in his memoirs after the first day. "He goes through his points well. His diction is good. In answer to questions he is brief and to the point. He's really excellent. He seems to have an excellent grasp of the issue and he's presenting it extremely well. I called him last night to tell him he should insist more on the danger to women, the real danger of complications and death due to the delay in providing abortions under the Code as it exists now. I still hope he will stress that."

As for how he felt, he admitted only to "some kind of inner tension," but pardoned himself. "This was an issue, of course, with which I had been identified over so many years. It wasn't easy to fight for, when I look in retrospect. I have achieved tremendous victories for the movement, in the sense that I brought the issue to the Supreme Court for the second time now. Victory is achieved in the Province of Quebec, where women have access to free abortions now in clinics, and government-operated clinics, and we almost won half of it in Ontario, where women now are being provided this kind of service." What he was not going to say, even to himself, speaking into a minitape recorder at 11:45 p.m., Tuesday, October 7, in Ottawa, "fifteen minutes before a new day starts," was that everything he had worked for for close to two decades was on the line. Better to accentuate the positive, even — *especially* — when alone at midnight. "I think it was a good day, reminding me of the good old days when I felt I was the centre of the world. I was defending a good cause. I was acquitting myself well. I realize again that over the years it took a great deal of tenacity and courage and perseverance to do what I've done, and I'm sort of proud of myself."

The arguments from both sides were heard in four consecutive days when the justices agreed to sit on a rare Friday session to complete the case. Henry told some reporters that if he won, he would like to be a consultant with the Ontario Ministry of Health and help to train doctors in his safer technique. But he was going to have to wait more than a year for a verdict from the panel, and waiting was one thing he had never been good at.

CHAPTER 16

WINNING IT ALL

IT WAS A QUIET YEAR. Nineteen eighty-seven was either the calm before the storm or the post-apocalypse blues. When Henry thought about what had just transpired, his outrage was rekindled. "What struck me after all these years was that judges have complete disregard for what happens to people.... We need a system of law — no doubt about it. But laws should be rational, responsive to people's needs, based on good reasons, should have acceptance among the people. And obsolete laws must be changed or turfed out." But for the first time in more than a decade, there was nothing he could do about it. He had to wait and try to stop chaffing at the ordinary, routine cycles that now patterned his life. He and Arlene moved into a larger, more comfortable apartment on the third floor of a house in the Annex area of Toronto. "Much nicer than the one Arlene had before, overlooking a parking lot. We called it our love nest." He was happy, and because Arlene wanted it, monogamous.

Henry was also pleased with recommendations made by Dr. Marion Powell, director of the Bay Centre for Birth Control and a member of the panel that had produced the 1977 Badgley Report. Commissioned a year after the Liberals had been elected in 1985, her report, a review of access to therapeutic abortions, was tabled in the Ontario legislature on January 29, 1987. Powell urged the government to establish independent regional abortion clinics with their own committees, affiliated with but physically separate from hospitals. She recommended that these clinics offer a full range of family planning services. The report noted the geographical inequities of services in Ontario and that women often face "outright hostility" from medical authorities and are stereotyped as "promiscuous and sexually irresponsible." CARAL's Spring 1987 edition of the newsletter *Pro-Choice News* pointed out that one of the Liberals' election promises had been to improve access, especially in Northern Ontario. It stated: "There was also the embarrassment of the Morgentaler Clinic, a constant reminder that women in Ontario (and other parts of Canada) were not able to get abortions through the hospital system." Two months later Health Minister Murray Elston announced that $2.5 million of a $9-million women's programs package would go to help hospitals provide better abortion service. While there were 27,274 legal abortions in Ontario in 1985, at least 5,000 women from Ontario received abortions in Quebec or the United States every year and the two Toronto clinics performed 3,700 abortions in 1986.

The government hired Dr. Powell to start implementation of her report recommendations. *Toronto Star* columnist Rosemary Spiers said Powell's report had finally stated "what women know and politicians don't want to hear: Contraceptive failure, not carelessness, is the foremost reason for unwelcome pregnancy, so no amount of birth control counselling will eliminate the need for abortion services."[1] OCAC's Cherie MacDonald was not impressed with Elston's reactions to the report. He "used a lot of words to say nothing about improving access," she said after the announcement. CARAL's Norma Scarborough was more optimistic: "If it is possible to do it, Dr. Powell will get it done."[2] Some analysts interpreted the government's pot of money as a move to knock the Morgentaler and Scott clinics out of business.[3] Still Henry stayed quiet.

In June, the Reverend Ken Campbell lost his Supreme Court bid to appeal Ian Scott's staying of the Morgentaler court proceedings, but that same month the indefatigable Joe Borowski won the right to a Supreme Court hearing about including fetuses among those with a constitutional right to life. Then, as Ontario geared up for an election on September 10 and women from the National Action Committee on the Status of Women demanded from each party leader a promise to drop the charges against Henry (which a re-elected Scott did September 23), the improbable happened in Montreal. Henry was ordered to go before a court of law for arraignment on August 3. The charge was performing an illegal abortion, one on December 13, 1977, and another on

July 14, 1980. It was initiated by former boxer Reggie Chartrand, who had hired a criminal lawyer to privately prosecute Henry. Chartrand's evidence against Henry was the National Film Board documentary *Abortion Stories: North and South*. Henry didn't even bother hiring a lawyer until a former patient was called to testify. "She was a nice woman. My brother Mike was in touch with her. She was in tears because a judge threatened her with contempt of court if she didn't answer the question as to whether I had given her an abortion. She was afraid of going to jail, but she refused to answer. The judge said she had a week to reconsider," Henry said. That's when he called Michel Proulx, "one of the best lawyers in Montreal" and a Westmount neighbour. Henry walked over to his house and asked him to take the case. Proulx told the judge the obvious: there was no point in pursuing the matter, which was before the Supreme Court, but if they did, they would provide the judge with copies of all the documentation currently before the high court, "which would fill the whole room." There were arraignments and postponements, a pre-inquiry. Eventually the charges were stayed by Quebec's attorney general because the matter was before the Supreme Court, but not before Henry had spent $40,000 on legal bills. Henry refused to debate Chartrand, and forced one radio station to interview Chartrand and him separately. It was too annoying even to be a diversion, as much as he needed a break from all the waiting.

His world was in limbo, a smooth, efficient limbo, but still a loathed state of suspension, like the moment before a fall or an ascension, in which everything is infused with a timelessness and a grace that replace purpose. There were no crises. The clinic in the Beaugrand bungalow hummed; the stucco two-storey in Winnipeg stayed shut for abortions; even in Toronto, the protestors came and went every day, as predictable as the letter carrier, and as familiar. The clinic workers knew them — Dan McCash from Etobicoke; his teenaged son; Helen Burnie, a retired nurse not above good-naturedly chiding Henry about his clothes. She once told him his shoes were disgraceful and she was sure he could afford a new pair. Every now and then there were flare-ups and another handful of anti-abortion picketers would be arrested. Some were charged; some were not. By May 1987, Metro police had spent $451,920 on the salaries of the police guarding the clinic during the previous two and a half years. "It was waiting, waiting, a year of consolidating and waiting," Henry said with a sigh. He was having horrible dreams. Arlene said he would wake up exhausted, with his entire body covered in sweat. "I couldn't get near him."

She was pregnant. She said it was her decision and the baby would be her responsibility, although Henry was delighted. The pro-choice slogan — "Every child a wanted child" — was more than a motto to him; it was a credo. He believed in the goodness and wonder of the newborn, and often quoted Swiss analyst Alice Miller. Murderers, rapists and Nazi officers were not born as such but had evolved because they were unloved children. This was the crux of his humanism, his faith in people and in juries. It was why he believed women should have full access to abortion on demand. It was the only way he knew he could fight the evil, black acts in some men's souls. And whenever Henry was with a child, something inside his own soul unlocked. "I become child-like," he said approvingly. He believed he reflected back to them their selves — playful, innocent, charming. Gertie has said Henry was happiest then. Bamie Morgentaler remembered his father always took "a childish glee in minor things, from a nature walk to an ocean panorama. He plays silly games and makes funny faces to entertain the little kids at the dinner table. He's a fun person. He's been like that all the way through my growing up. As a child, having somebody like that was a wonderful role model. It's given me licence to be absolutely silly with my kids and they love it."

Henry's third son was born on January 9, 1988. The doctors suspected Benjamin Yosele (or Joseph) had a brain lesion when he went into convulsions. They told Arlene and Henry the baby had an infarct in an artery of the brain, which had damaged some cells, and there was a possibility he could be permanently weakened on the right side of his body. "Arlene started to cry and I was near tears, but I had to comfort her," Henry said. The baby was hospitalized for five days and given medications to prevent further seizures. There was nothing more that could be done, no operations that could be performed. They simply had to wait it out; it would resolve itself or it wouldn't. It did, and six days after he was born, Benny ("I started calling him 'Yosele,' after my father, but stopped. Benny was good enough," Henry said) was home with them, healthy and hungry. Then the word went out: the Supreme Court had reached a decision. It would be announced on Thursday morning, January 28.

―――――

Henry took the 7 a.m. flight to Ottawa, an early start to any day, but especially after a restless night only partially explained by a newborn at home. So he tried to catch some more sleep before the plane landed in Ottawa. His optimism was based on instinct, not fact, and definitely not on insider information. "With so many people working in translation and offices, we could have expected a leak, but there was absolutely no leak," Henry said. At ten that morning, an ermine-robed Chief Justice Brian Dickson began reading the text of the decision. Henry heard him say they had found, based on Article 7, that the law wouldn't stand up ("and oh, I was starting to be really ecstatic"), but Dickson continued his careful reading. What still had to be decided was whether or not it was justified within a democratic society. Henry began worrying. "So I tiptoed from the gallery for the spectators to the front, where Morris was sitting with all the lawyers, and asked him what it all meant. Did we win or didn't we? Some of the judges looked at me, whispering in the middle of their big pronouncement." Manning put a finger to his lips, gesturing for Henry to be quiet, and motioned him back to his seat, the way a parent would an unruly, inquisitive child. "He looked stern, upset," Henry admitted. "I guess I was very anxious to find out what was going on."

It was a landmark decision. By a 5 to 2 vote, the Supreme Court of Canada struck down as unconstitutional the country's abortion law as defined in Section 251 of the Criminal Code. Key to the majority opinion (written by Dickson and supported by Mr. Justice Antonio Lamer) were the following words:

Forcing a woman, by threat of criminal sanction, to carry a fetus to term unless she meets certain criteria unrelated to her own

priorities and aspirations, is a profound interference with
a woman's body and thus an infringement of security of
the person.

The opinion also stated:

A second breach of the right to security of the person occurs inde-
pendently as a result of the delay in obtaining therapeutic abortions
caused by the mandatory procedures of S.251, which results in a
higher probability of complications and greater risk.

The harm to the psychological integrity of women seeking abortions was also clearly established:

Any infringement of the right to life, liberty and security of the
person must comport with the principles of fundamental justice.
      These principles are to be found in the basic tenet of our legal
system. One of the basic tenets of our system of criminal justice is
when Parliament creates a defence to a criminal charge, the
defence should not be so illusory or so difficult to attain as to be
practically illusory.
      The procedure and restrictions stipulated in S.251 for access to
therapeutic abortions makes the defence illusory, resulting in a failure to comply with the principles of fundamental justice.

In closing, Dickson wrote:

. . . the procedures and administrative structures created by S.251
are often unfair and arbitrary.
      Moreover, these procedures impair S.7 rights far more than is
necessary because they hold out an illusory defence to many
women who would prima facie qualify under the exculpatory provisions of S.251 (4).
      Finally the effects of the limitation upon the S.7 rights of many
pregnant women are out of proportion to the objective sought to

be achieved and may actually defeat the objective of protecting the life and health of women.

The dissenting judges were Mr. Justice William McIntyre and Gerard La Forest, who wrote, in part:

Historically there has always been a clear recognition of a public interest in the protection of the unborn and there is no evidence or indication of general acceptance of the concept of abortion at will in our society.

The *Toronto Star*'s William Walker noted it was the only woman on the bench, Madam Justice Bertha Wilson, who wrote movingly of the emotions and thoughts of a woman facing the decision:

It is one [decision] that will have profound psychological, economical and social consequences for her. It is a decision that deeply reflects the way the woman thinks about herself and her relationship to others and to society at large. It is not just a medical decision; it is a profound social and ethical one as well.

She noted it would be "probably impossible" for a man to respond to this dilemma, even in his imagination or mind,

not just because it is outside the realm of his personal experience (although this, of course, is the case) but because he can relate to it only by objectifying it, thereby eliminating the subjective elements of the female psyche, which are at the heart of the dilemma.

Henry regarded Wilson's arguments as "inspiring" — and there were portions in which she sounded as tough and indignant as he felt:

The right to liberty contained in s.7 guarantees to every individual a degree of personal autonomy over important decisions intimately affecting his or her private life.

Liberty in a free and democratic society does not require the
state to approve such decisions but it does require a state to
respect them.

A woman's decision to terminate her pregnancy falls within
this class of protected decisions.

She continued:

Section 251 is more deeply flawed than just subjecting women to
considerable emotional stress and unnecessary physical risk. It
asserts that the woman's capacity to reproduce is to be subject, not
to her own control, but to that of the state. This is direct interference with the woman's physical "person."

Wilson also stated:

The state here is endorsing one conscientiously held view at the
expense of another. It is denying freedom of conscience to some,
treating them as a means to an end, depriving them of their "essential humanity."

Everything Henry had ever said and believed in now was being
intoned by the country's highest legal authorities and moral guardians.
Inside him there was an eruption, a blinding explosion of joy. Yet he sat
decorously in the huge, ornate hall and listened to the steady, sturdy
voices of the seven who held his future and all his past within the
sheaves of papers from which they read. He can't remember who was
there with him. Mike? Carolyn Egan? Bob Scott? Selma, yes, because
he hugged and hugged her, then Manning, before he was swept outside,
beaming, jubilant, into the shouting, excited mass of journalists who
were going to record that Henry Morgentaler had made Canadian history; Henry Morgentaler had won. "Bravo for the Supreme Court of
Canada! Bravo for the women of Canada!" he shouted, curious, arcane
words more suitable for a night at the opera. He didn't know why he
spoke those words; they just detonated inside him. On newscasts that

night and in newspapers the next morning he saw himself making the V-for-Victory sign. He had had no intention of doing it, especially after one of his staff had made him promise not to, because they all thought it might look like gloating. "I didn't actually mean to, but the media asked me, and it [was] sort of appropriate," Henry remembered thinking apologetically.

At 12:35 p.m. they were on Air Canada Flight 453 back to Toronto. A white limo was waiting for them. As usual, Selma Edelstone had arranged everything. From Manning's office, Henry did a pair of radio interviews before a 3 p.m. press conference during which he thanked everyone who helped him "throughout this long struggle," but forgot to include Manning. (Norma Scarborough sent him a note about his omission and he hastily tacked on a thank-you before the end of the conference.) Then there were more media interviews, in English, in French, live, taped — it seemed reporters from every national and local news outlet wanted some time with a grinning Henry. It was well after 9 p.m. when the white limo pulled up in front of Morris Manning's low-slung home that backed onto a ravine and Henry went inside for the ultimate victory party.

Clinic staff had popped champagne when they'd heard the news that morning. Outside, about a dozen OCAC supporters had screamed and leaped in the air as OCAC spokesperson Lynn Lathrop shouted over them, "We're completely thrilled. It appears to be a tremendous victory for us." Judy Rebick, who had resigned as OCAC spokesperson the year before to run as a provincial NDP candidate in Toronto's Oriole riding (and lose) was in the crowd. A reporter told her they had won, but Rebick refused to believe her "until it was official." It was another fifteen minutes before Rebick, a woollen toque pulled low over her face, found out. When asked how she felt now, Rebick jumped in the air, with arms wide-open, and shouted, "I feel great." Bob Scott was so convinced they would lose he had stayed in Toronto. Hours after the news he told reporters, "I'm still depressed now. I got so prepared to be depressed I can't get out of it. I figured, rather than spending $500 to go to Ottawa to get kicked in the teeth, I'd stay in Toronto and get kicked in the teeth."[4] As for Les Smoling, the other doctor whose fate was in

the offing, few were in contact with him; and even fewer thought of
him. He had borrowed $10,000 from CARAL to start up in Woodstock,
Ontario, a small, prospering town a half hour from London, Ontario.
They never saw the money or him again. He never claimed any part of
the win; it all belonged to Henry.

OCAC spokesperson Cherie MacDonald had taken the train from
Montreal, where she had been staying, to Toronto, because she knew
the Supreme Court decision was coming and she wanted to be at the
clinic. She was still on the train when the decision came down, listening
to the radio with her headset. She took off the headset, waved her arms
and announced to the whole car "that the Supreme Court had decided
for Dr. Morgentaler, and that I had been working on this since 1971 in
Edmonton, and everybody was congratulating me and talking about it.
There was not one person in the railway car who was pissed off about
it. An elderly woman sitting beside me didn't say much except that she
had never felt strongly about abortion but 'hated the idea of all those
men telling us what we can do with our bodies.'"

After all her years of work, Norma Scarborough missed the party.
She and former CARAL executive director Leslie Pearl were in Florida
and oblivious until the next day, Friday, when they were in a small gro-
cery store and deli in San Hemon Circle in Sarasota. A friend of theirs,
not at all involved in the abortion debate, said suddenly, "Oh, for God's
sake. Here's your Toronto paper. The Supreme Court decision came
down yesterday." Scarborough and Pearl read the headlines, saw they'd
won "and nearly destroyed this little store," Scarborough recalled. "For-
tunately, a European couple owned it and they were very supportive of
us when they realized why we were excited. There was not a word of it
in the American news."

In Winnipeg, Henry's former nurse Lynn Crocker was driving
down Portage Avenue, listening to the radio newscast. "I was crying so
hard I had to pull over," she said. "I learned a lot from Henry. He was
right all along. I had wanted to believe. I didn't have the faith that
Henry had." Ellen Kruger had already left Winnipeg for Grenada,
where she was meeting Linda Taylor and her partner, Marty Dolan, the
next day. The Coalition had the celebratory party that night at Ellen's

house in Winnipeg without Ellen, because she was in Toronto on an overnight stopover. "I knew there would be a big celebration. I walked in [to the Manning home] and Henry said, 'Oh, Ellen, how nice of you to come for the celebration.' I said, 'Yeah, Henry, I did.' I was thrilled to be able to be there." The next morning she took with her a copy of the *Globe and Mail*. When she disembarked, she held up the paper so Taylor and Dolan could see the historic headline.

The large Manning-Rapson living room was overflowing with revellers, the youngest being Benjamin, then two and a half weeks old. The photograph of Henry, tie loosened, tenderly holding his beautiful sleeping son, was the one most newspapers chose for their front pages the next day. Beside him, Arlene smiled at her men, both fighters; that day, both victors. Nikki Colodny was right behind Henry, her face softened, her fight for recognition forgotten in the victory for all women.

All the staff of Manning's law firm were there. They knew how significant this was to the constitutional expert. It was not Henry but Manning who had telephoned the CARAL office that morning with the news, speaking so quickly and with such animation its then executive director Robin Rowe couldn't write down the gist of what he was saying fast enough. "Which section? Which right?" she kept asking the euphoric lawyer, trying to get straight all the arguments of the decision.

Henry had asked that everyone from the Montreal clinic fly down for the party, and Mike had complied. Bob Scott was there; even Eleanor Wright Pelrine was there, hesitantly offering her congratulations. "I wasn't very happy to see her," Henry recalled in his memoirs. "I said, 'You know there are things between us and maybe we can clear it up another time.'"

Yann was there, too, not yet eight but polished and comfortable in the company of adult strangers. Henry phoned Bamie, who was genuinely thrilled; he thought about Eva and how nice it would have been to be friends or at least friendly, without resentment or hostility cutting the air between them. And he wanted to telephone Goldie but knew she wouldn't take his call. Bamie told her sometime later, and reported back to his father that she had been very happy at the outcome. The last time she had really been on his side, caring and protective as her father hurtled after a cause to benefit women like her, was thirteen years earlier when she had stroked her father's cheek and run nervous, shaking hands through her long, blond hair at the press conference where he'd announced he was prepared to go to prison the next day. Now she would not share his triumph, witness it or even acknowledge it.

Emotions collided within Henry at all that was happening. "Imagine, single-handedly almost, I abolished a restrictive, cruel, barbarous law which caused so much suffering to women across Canada," he noted in his memoirs. "At the same time it was a great victory for the Charter of Rights, for human rights in general, an affirmation of liberty, security of the person and freedom, freedom for people to choose what they want to do with their lives. It's a blow [on behalf of] a caring, loving society, which has always been my aim, and I got so overwhelmed by the feeling I, me, myself could have achieved that; I who could have been crushed, annihilated, by the German Nazi machine in the concentration camp, I who could have been by now a piece of dust, had survived and had withstood the whole barrage of forces against me, the state, the police, the courts, the anti-abortionists, the fanatics, and stood my ground and eventually had become victorious." And everybody wanted to talk to him, congratulate him, or thank him — except some important members of his family.

His supporters gathered on Harbord Street outside the clinic that night. "We were all waiting endlessly for Henry and freeezing our toes," Cherie MacDonald remembered. "The masses were freezing. We had speakers from every organization you can imagine speaking and we were so happy. And finally Henry came and we were even happier."

The media-celebrity whirl lasted days, which became weeks. Everybody needed to interview the conquering hero, who was happy to oblige. The political fallout began that same day. Justice Minister Ray Hnatyshyn spoke of "a new reality," but also said he might wait to see what the Supreme Court had to say about Borowski's challenge on the constitutional rights of a fetus; the Ontario government dropped all further legal proceedings against Henry, Scott, Smoling and/or Colodny. Attorney General Ian Scott handed everything over to his federal counterparts. "If the issue is whether there should be a criminal law, the

Supreme Court of Canada has said that is squarely a question for the Parliament of Canada. They didn't say there couldn't be one. They simply said that this one wasn't adequate," he said.[5]

The doctors just as quickly and eagerly passed the ball. The Canadian Medical Association, which opposed abortion on demand because it wanted doctors to have some input into the decision, sent telegrams to its forty-six thousand members the same day the ruling was announced, urging them to continue as if the law had not been struck down. The Ontario Medical Association said provincial hospitals were already too busy to take on the load of performing more abortions. It supported creating abortion clinics. But eighty hospitals in Ontario alone, including seventeen in Metro Toronto, indicated to the provincial health ministry they were prepared to carry on abortions without hospital committees. Ontario Health Minister Elinor Caplan announced that the province would fund abortions outside hospitals. It would pay $100.30 per procedure, but had not decided whether to reimburse doctors working outside a hospital more than the OHIP rate. Henry decided to charge the province $100 (plus $97.40 for a general consultation, pregnancy test and ultrasound) and the patient the remaining $200 of the full fee, and advise all his patients to submit their receipts to the government to be reimbursed. Caplan's counterpart in British Columbia, Peter Dueck, refused to pay for any abortions done outside a hospital. Then, on February 9, B.C. premier Bill Vander Zalm won cabinet approval for a plan to cut off abortion funding unless a woman's life was in danger. Concerned Citizens for Choice had already announced it was opening a clinic in Vancouver. The Alberta Health Insurance Plan continued to cover only committee-approved abortions (and only twenty-two hospitals had committees). But because extra billing was banned there in 1986, many doctors no longer did the procedure. Saskatchewan showed all signs of continuing to be resolutely anti-abortion — in 1986 only 955 abortions were done in its seven approved hospitals. Manitoba dropped all its criminal charges against Henry, and the College of Physicians and Surgeons stated it would restore his medical licence if the Corydon clinic met their inspection. Henry was not impressed. Twice before, the clinic had been inspected and passed approval on medical grounds. The legal barriers had always been cited as the reason the College had refused to grant a licence. Nevertheless, he immediately sent off the $510 the College decreed another inspection would cost. "I hate the bastards!!!!" he noted in his memoirs. "Over the years I've suffered the humiliation of defeat at their hands, their abusive power, the arbitrary abuse of power and denial of medical rights to the women in Manitoba.... Now I think they will have to come around. At least I now have the higher ground, and before I criticize them and knock them down, I'll wait until the situation clarifies itself, because I am motivated by a lot of anger and resentment against these officials and doctors of the College."

Henry had another, smaller, victory in Manitoba. A woman from Winnipeg's Women's Health Clinic called. They wanted to move into Corydon Avenue and share space. This was the same group that had refused an identical request from Henry in 1982 because they were afraid any association with a Morgentaler clinic might lose them their government funding. "The irony of things is never ending. However, I am not one to keep grudges," he noted magnanimously.

Quebec announced it was increasing the amount it paid to private clinics for the abortion procedure to $125 from $84. It had already been covering abortions fully in forty hospitals, twelve community health centres and three women's health clinics, and partially in three private clinics, one of which was the Morgentaler Clinic. Nova Scotia stated it would not pay for any abortions done in private clinics. In 1985, N.S. premier John Buchanan had threatened any member of his caucus with expulsion if he or she took a pro-choice position, and nothing had since softened his position. One week after the Supreme Court decision, New Brunswick's government had not made any move to change the law stating doctors must do abortions only in accredited hospitals. No abortions had been performed in Prince Edward Island since 1982, when Right-to-Lifers took over the boards of the two main hospitals there, and the government announced it would pay for out-of-province abortions only if approved by a three-doctor committee.

It was a free-for-all. The absence of a law left everything wide-open, and the lawmakers rushed in. Even as Henry was updating his "I need your help" fund-raising newspaper ads to "This battle is won, but the struggle is far from finished" and running them coast to coast, Ottawa announced it would soon introduce a law to regulate abortion access, and Ontario began its struggle to impose some regulating standards on the procedure. Henry was not oblivious to all the political machinations his victory had produced. One of the first things he did after the victory was write letters to all the provincial health ministers, offering to be a consultant and train their province's doctors. But he was still in a state of euphoria, riding the victory high. He fell to earth on February 9 at Global Television Studios in suburban Toronto. It was just one more debate, but Ian Scott, Elinor Caplan and Dr. Marion Powell all pleaded prior engagements, and Henry was left facing his neighbour and neme-sis, Choose Life Canada founder, the Reverend Ken Campbell, "the religious fanatic who has been bugging me and bothering me and the clinic for the last few years . . . who is despicable really, and his lawyer, Angela Costigan, who doesn't seem very bright." Siding with Henry were University of Toronto medical ethicist Dr. Bernard Dickens, who had become a friend after being at the law and medicine conference in India with Henry, and Joan Wright, "a very nice woman" from the Bay Centre for Birth Control.

The program began with Paul Cowan's documentary film *Democracy on Trial*. The panelists watched along with the audience. In his memoirs Henry said:

> After the concentration camp, the re-enactment of that and the jail
> scenes, I became so overcome by emotion that I started crying and
> I couldn't contain my crying, although I tried hard, and then I
> started sobbing, and eventually I decided to leave the podium,
> where we all sat. So Selma came over and she escorted me through
> the hall. I took a few minutes in the washroom to wash my face
> and compose myself and then I went back. Then the debate started
> and I felt rather aggressive towards these no-choicers, or anti-
> choicers, or anti-abortionists, or fetus fetishists, or whichever way
> you want to call them. I imagine for the viewers it was good televi-
> sion because there was a lot of conflict and controversy. I ripped

into Ken Campbell a few times. I called him an ayatollah, then he
called me an ayatollah.

After the program he and Campbell continued arguing — it could
no longer be dignified as a debate — in the corridor. Campbell eventually told Henry the abortions he was doing were a Holocaust. Henry
said he

> whirled around at [Campbell] and was really angry and I told him,
> "Don't you talk to me about the Holocaust. I am a survivor of the
> Holocaust, and as far as I am concerned you could be a guard in a
> Nazi concentration camp." Basically what I wanted to tell him
> even more — but I didn't want to pursue the thing — is that I
> think that he is of the same mind-set as the Nazis — that is, intol-
> erant, semifascistic, totalitarian, disrespectful of any other opinion
> but his own, [with] the kind of fanatical religious fervour which
> is dangerous to civil liberties and to freedom in general ....
> Apparently Morris Manning called Arlene after the program, and
> he said to her that he had never seen me so angry. So my explana-
> tion is the fact that I had been overcome with emotion and sadness,
> and expressed some of it ... confronted with this kind of religious
> fanaticism on the part of Ken Campbell and Angela Costigan. It
> really got to me and I had to lash out at them, and I don't regret it.

It was the first time Henry had dared expose his private face in public, displaying feelings and vulnerability instead of his usual rational,
impervious front. He felt safe enough, finally, and accepted enough.
"It's not like I want to sit on my laurels and enjoy all the public acclaim
and adulation. I do enjoy it, soak it in, take it in, which I didn't do many
years before. I would dismiss that as not really belonging to me or as
an aberration or I really wouldn't let it into my heart. But now I do."
Everyone everywhere he went was telling him he was a hero. Finally he
agreed with them, but only because he could now understand that what
made him a hero was not undiluted bravery but the fear he had never
before acknowledged. "The ability to work in spite of all the stress, all

the anxiety — to me that is heroism," he said. "I did try to give the impression I was on top of things. It was not to give in. Now I can say, why shouldn't I admit, 'Yeah, I was scared, but I did it anyway.' Why do I have to posture and have an image?" Now that he was a hero, not a martyr, he could tell himself what was important was that he tried to do the right thing. "There's a Yiddish song my mother used to sing which says, 'It doesn't matter if I reach the shore / the important thing is to walk on the sunny road / which is the right journey.'" He had reached the shore. He was not a failed martyr.

Three weeks later, he took eight-year-old Yann for a week's vacation at Club Med in Sandpiper, Florida. Henry felt he was breathing in deep, letting go, allowing his shoulders to drop, permitting himself simply to be — no striving, no more overcoming. Father and son flew kites, visited Disney World and Cape Canaveral and went to yoga classes together. Yann made many friends, but near the end of their holiday began to spend all his time with his father. Henry savoured every minute together. He had a new tape recorder; he wanted to summarize his historic victory, the profound changes happening inside him and the happiness he was experiencing being in Yann's company. "Yann has become such a delightful child that I said to Arlene in jest I'm having a love affair with him," he noted. He was determined to change his visiting rights to Yann in the divorce agreement with Carmen. He had accepted her terms because he'd been afraid. Now he wanted new terms — either Yann staying six months of the year with each parent or, for the sake of schooling, living alternate years with his mother and then his father. He simply had to see more of his child. Henry was honest with his son, and talked to him of his own father, Josef Morgentaler, and how he still resented the two spankings he'd received from the otherwise loving, gentle man. "I haven't felt so happy for years," Henry said in his memoirs. "...[S]uddenly everything came together, my relationship with Arlene which is beautiful, the birth of Benjamin and the Supreme Court victory." Was this, finally, contentment?

For the first time in a long time I stayed away from Arlene for nine days and I wasn't even tempted to have sex with another woman.... This is a change of enormous proportions for me, because usually whenever I was away from the major woman in my life I would always look for someone else to provide me comfort, and sex and warmth and tenderness. I need a confirmation of my existence and...having sex with a woman was a confirmation that I'm still worthy of being received by the woman.... It's really the first time in my life that I've had a relationship like this where I did not think...it's necessary for me to have other women around...I'm proud of it and I'm glad that I sort of evolved beyond the need...I think I'm going towards that stage in my life and I'm quite happy with that.

He was still troubled by Goldie's silence. "She keeps a lot of anger and resentment against me, unfortunately...I regret the fact we've become sort of strangers.... I have written her a few letters where I have said I have a lot of love in my heart for her and she has only to come and get it or partake of it...so far she has rebuffed all that." As for Eva, with whom Goldie lived, Henry decided he was past feeling resentful, although he knew she wasn't, and he acknowledged that her feelings stemmed "from our bitter alimony fight." And he and Mike were fighting again, this time over Henry's not inviting Mike's children to attend his sixty-fifth birthday party in March. Mike said that if his children weren't invited, he would not come. "He has this kind of ultimatum power on me where he knows he can do that, and I sort of resent it," Henry admitted, but he capitulated, calling Mike to tell him he had made a mistake, that he wanted Mike to be happy and that all his children were invited. Mike didn't let Henry off the hook easily. Why hadn't Henry invited them in the first place? he wanted to know. Henry exploded. He had just performed a humorous skit that evening; all at the resort had said they loved it. "I was feeling wonderful about myself and I wasn't going to take this shit from him.... I accused him of wanting to make me feel guilty, of spoiling my vacation."

The truth was neither Mike, nor Goldie, nor Eva could have spoiled his Florida vacation. Henry had brought with him the entire Supreme Court verdict. Although he had read the judges' conclusions, he hadn't yet read the thick tome elaborating all their rationales for their decisions. "As I was reading it," Henry said in his memoirs, "and

> reading Brian Dickson's verdict and his reasons for the verdict and
> savouring every minute of it [I was] listening to Debussy. [The verdict] made me so happy and so elated that when I switched tapes
> and started listening to Beethoven's violin concerto, which I love,
> this violin concerto sounded so beautiful, so absolutely beautiful,
> that I stopped reading and started moving with the music in
> rhythm as I usually do. As my body moved with the music — and
> it was so indescribably beautiful — I went into sort of a primal
> trance. I talked to my parents. I told my mother that this victory
> was for her and because of her. I talked to my father, telling him
> how, because of him, I became the man I am, gentle, caring, concerned about social justice, able to work for social justice, able to
> sacrifice, if necessary, the way he did. It gave me such a feeling of
> integrity and of beauty and of accomplishment and ecstasy that I
> started to cry for joy. Even though it was raining outside, the
> world was beautiful and life was beautiful. I started reflecting
> on my life and how happy I am, and I discovered that I am a
> happy man.

CHAPTER 17

POST VICTORY BLUES AND UTERINE WARRIORS

T HERE HADN'T BEEN TIME to celebrate in the clinic. The telephone never stopped ringing, and soon half a dozen doctors were on the payroll.

Andrea Knight was hard at work at her desk one morning a month after the victory, when Henry dropped by. He wanted to have a conference, an international conference, and the next month, March, seemed like a good time for it. The event would also mark his sixty-fifth birthday.

As efficient and hardworking as his staff were, Knight couldn't fathom organizing an international conference in one month. Knight shook her head. Henry was not only her boss but a close friend. She and her husband, Eric Weiner, a therapist with whom Henry was comfortable and candid, socialized with Arlene and Henry. Knight knew Henry was always rushing on to the next goal, careless and dismissive about details. His exuberant faith in the ability of the clinic workers to do anything, and almost everything, offset any obstacles. "I've worked with a lot of other doctors subsequently at the clinic and there's a reason none of them are Henry," she said. "Lots of them are wonderful, but it's that combination — that relentless drive to 'justify his existence one more time' is the phrase that leaps to mind. He always is doing one more thing, until he drives you crazy. He is not the easiest man to work for, which is not surprising."

He was the kind of boss who would announce in the morning that he was holding a press conference at noon. "I would say, 'Henry, what is it going to be about?' He didn't think he needed to tell me," Knight said, laughing. "Half time he didn't. I would call media and say that Henry was having a press conference and everyone would come. And he always had a reason to do it, even if I did have to worm it out of him."

But it was April 1988 before a press conference was held announcing a conference on abortion, to be held in Toronto in May. "I sincerely believe the medical profession is behind the times. I hope they are humble enough to learn," he stated.[1] From this inauspicious beginning — none of the prestigious doctors from either the United States or Canada whom Henry had asked would co-chair the conference — to the sluggish ticket sales, the conference seemed destined to fail. But Henry was relentless; he would will or bully it into existence. He advertised in medical professional journals throughout North America; he even dropped the conference fee to $350 from the original $750. "Everyone said it was too much, but it was a conference not only on how to do abortions but on how to open a clinic and make a lot of money," he complained. He wanted doctors to know his safer, easier abortion technique as much as he wanted recognition from the medical establishment for his expertise. But in Canada gynecologists had traditionally been the prime abortion providers — Henry was "just" a general practitioner — and abortions were considered a low-skill procedure. As Elinor Ratcliffe used to like to say, "It's a muffler shop technique." But like everything else, it was evolving. That's why American abortion providers had banded together to form the National Abortion Federation (NAF) to provide the medical education on the procedure, which doctors were not getting from the other medical associations. (Although NAF soon had a loosely knit Canadian caucus, a Canadian Abortion Federation has never been established.) Henry had already taught his method to many doctors; the rest of his colleagues may have had their backs up. "Henry has been publicly very scathingly critical of abortions done in hospitals — often for good reason — but [that] doesn't lend itself to an invitation to come and hear what he has to say and pay money," said Nikki Colodny. "First I bash you on the head and then I want you to come and listen to me? It doesn't work."

Only forty doctors signed up for the conference, none of them from east of Quebec. Even more damning, only a half-dozen were from the States. He lost $75,000 — which, if he cared to dwell on it (he did not), signified more than a financial wipeout. It was a professional snub. Henry had lost very few battles, but he knew when to refocus.

Almost immediately, he contacted prominent Toronto lawyer and civil libertarian Clayton Ruby. He wanted an end to pro-life advocates slashing the tires on his nurses' cars, gluing the clinic locks, breaking windows and every day, all day, harassing patients. He wanted an injunction to keep them away, maybe forty-five or sixty metres away. To get that, they decided to ask for 150 metres. One of the busiest trial lawyers in the country, Ruby took on the case. His grandfather "and all the people before him" had come from Lodz. Henry knew the street where they had lived. "I've always been fairly touched by the connection," Ruby said.

The women at CARAL, and especially OCAC, couldn't understand why Henry was so concerned about an injunction. They had other priorities. Under Norma Scarborough, CARAL was hard at work getting out the word that no new abortion law would benefit the women of Canada. Each organization had a roster of speakers, who went wherever they were asked during the next year and a half. Cherie MacDonald had a blue "demo" bag, big enough for a couple of banners, t-shirts and buttons to sell, and a megaphone. When Laura McArthur spoke in Collingwood, a ski resort town to the north of Toronto, MacDonald unfurled her banner outside the church where she was speaking. "It was Collingwood's first feminist demonstration." MacDonald spoke to women in Port Elgin in the conservative heartland on the shores of Lake Huron, and in picturesque Picton County, where she met with a group of farm wives in the basement of one of their homes. "The women who owned the house said that she couldn't get the dishes done and hold the meeting, so her husband had kitchen duty. He agreed, but only if she drew the curtains so no neighbours would see him at the sink." This group later did a tree planting ceremony in memory of women who had died as a result of illegal abortions.

CARAL and OCAC were exhausted and they were broke — any money that came in went directly to pay off the legal bill — but they knew there would be some government initiative that fall, and that it would be noisome for them. Yet Henry seemed oblivious to their fears.

He had won; the Supreme Court had ruled. That should be protection
enough, although he was beginning to realize his next battles would be
on provincial fronts, and Supreme Court decision or no Supreme Court
decision, they would be fiercely fought. Since the American Supreme
Court had ruled on January 22, 1973, that states could not bar abortion
in the first six months of pregnancy, one president (Ronald Reagan) had
called abortion on demand a national tragedy, and the issue had been
brought back before the Supreme Court another eighteen times,[2] and to
the state courts much more often than that. The cases involved whether
or not parental or spousal consent had to be obtained, whether federal
medicare dollars could pay for an abortion and whether a woman had
to seek advice from a doctor. Opinion in favour of enabling individual
states to set their own guidelines about abortion had been gaining
ground. And on July 3, 1989, the U.S. Supreme Court voted 5 to 4 to
allow states to bar public employees and public hospitals from being
used for abortions. "I don't think it will have a great effect on Canada,
where equality for health care service is guaranteed across the country.
We don't have any abortion laws in Canada and we don't need any,"
MacDonald told Canadian media.[3] By that time Henry was less san-
guine. He worried that the American decision would motivate Canadian
anti-abortionists to increase lobbying Brian Mulroney's Conservative
government, who was working on a new abortion law.

But in the late spring of 1988, Henry was distracted. His comrades,
the ones he would have known were right behind him had he cared to
look over his shoulder on his march to the Supreme Court, were falling
away. Not too long after the victory, a trusted doctor in his Montreal
clinic prefaced telling Henry that he was leaving to start his own clinic
with the words "I hear you have a new baby. I want a new baby, too."
Michel Soucy had been a charmer, eager and quick to learn and apply
Henry's technique, and a welcome and appreciated addition to the
Montreal clinic and the Toronto clinic, where he substituted on occasion.
In his own clinic Soucy started off charging $50 a procedure (Henry
charged $250), raised it to $75, then $100, $150 and eventually after a few
months to $175. "I lowered our rates to $175 to match his," Henry said.
He had to. Soucy spread the word in Montreal that he was using

Henry's technique — and some of his staff. It was all true. Two of Henry's staff had gone with Soucy — Lorraine, a competent head nurse whom Henry valued highly, and Denise, a well-liked and respected counsellor. Even though Henry had sold Soucy some clinic equipment, he was enraged when he realized the extent of Soucy's raid on his Montreal clinic. The loss of a good, and he had believed, loyal head nurse, was especially vexatious. Henry was convinced Lorraine had left because of his brother. "She never said anything, but I heard Mike berated her for twenty minutes to the point where she was shaking. He was in a state of rage," he said.

Mike was becoming more difficult. "He interfered with medical decisions and personnel decisions, especially in the Montreal clinic. He was irritable — he had the heart condition," Henry explained. He also had a vague, shifting job description — even Henry admitted that — and duties that didn't correspond with his official titles. Mike was president of Inbram Inc., the company operating the Montreal clinic, and an officer of Gestion Habal Inc., the company managing all the real estate. But according to Henry, Mike was in charge only of the Montreal clinic's day-to-day operations — "banking, the small decisions I didn't want to be bothered with." Their styles were different. Henry was the risk taker, adventuresome, impulsive, but he didn't have a head for business. Mike was cautious, fiscally conservative, a self-styled business authority. "He had a poorly defined kind of role, but basically he knew I had built things up and he was just there to administer," Henry said. "He claimed he was a fifth wheel, which to a certain extent was true, but so what?"

The sympathies of many, including Henry's former lover, Maureen Reilly, were with Mike. She viewed Henry's relationship with his brother as a power struggle that robbed Mike of his dignity. "They would have a fight, then patch it up again. Mike quit his job to work for his brother, then Henry would breeze in and overrule every decision made, on a whim. That didn't help Mike's heart condition."

For years they had played the game, both of them pushing and pulling; one the big brother to the other's kid brother, and not necessarily based on chronological age. Gertie Katz had witnessed every stage.

She had seen Mike be thrilled that Henry was in town and that he was
actually having dinner with him, then she'd listen to Mike bluster about
how Henry was incompetent and was nothing without him. She saw
how deft Henry was at the digs. "Henry can definitely push Mike's buttons," she said, making a gesture of twisting a knife. But Henry had also
broken down and cried on her kitchen table about his brother, who was
so sick and would become so tired and so angry with him. Mike could
never overcome his paranoia, the legacy of the death camps. "Sometimes I think Mike would look for an excuse to pick a fight with Henry
so he could quit — or else get Henry to show him how much he loved
him by convincing him not to quit," Gertie said with a sigh. "I was always
the arbitrator."

Henry wanted the Montreal clinic phone system updated; Mike
didn't. That's what it came to. According to Henry, Mike quit, saying,
"If you want to run the Montreal clinic from Toronto, I resign." He had
threatened to resign many times, but this time Henry said, "I accept
your resignation." According to Mike, "He fired me. My own brother."
According to Gertie Katz, "Henry was angry. You could interpret the
fact that Henry didn't get down on his knees and plead with him for
the hundredth time as firing. I was in on the negotiations. Believe me,
Henry never fired him."

Mike was very upset, Henry recalled. "Suddenly when he felt he
wasn't necessary anymore, all the hostility he kept bottled up — he was
never analyzed — came out against me." Mike said, "He took me to the
lawyers. What am I to do? After we agreed to meet, just the two of us,
the lawyers come in with the papers. For no reason." Henry phoned
Gertie to tell her he had accepted Mike's resignation. "I'm drained,
Gertie. I can't keep going through this," he told her. He asked if she
would handle it. Mike was ill, exhausted; Gertie and Henry could see
that. Mike had ended his decade-long relationship with former clinic
receptionist Trudy Martens. Mike often said to Gertie, "Ghitel, I am so
tired." And she would look into his ashen face and say to him, "If you
quit, then I'll quit." But that just was to bolster his confidence, make
him believe nothing would run without him, because she knew Mike's
life would be vacant if he didn't have his job. She was working three

days a week for Henry and held many titles, including comptroller. But she didn't quit — "I couldn't leave Henry." Then Mike turned on her and Carl. For years Mike and Gertie had talked every single day; now Mike referred to Gertie as "the perfidious one," part of a conspiracy initiated by his brother. "Someday I always knew he would turn on me, because this is his pattern. He had turned on his closest and his dearest, including Henry," said Gertie. "I never thought it would be as painful as it was when he did turn on me."

Mike had told Henry he didn't have the "equality" he wanted and Henry knew he was right. "He didn't have the equality. It was I who built [everything] up. I just needed his help. I felt my decisions and my advice were of more value. Did I respect Mike? To a certain extent, but probably not enough. I realize that now." But Henry appreciated Mike and his loyalty. "People said he would walk through fire for me and I believe that." Henry used to promise Mike he would try to change his style to allow Mike more input, but he admitted he never could. He never asked Mike's advice on either legal, media or medical matters. "Some of the major decisions I made exactly on my own. I didn't consult anyone. Or I may have consulted them, but it was after the decision. The decision to go ahead and challenge the law in the rest of Canada after I won in Quebec? That was my own decision. In a sense I am proud of that. I knew what I wanted. I felt I could do it. I felt I was in the unique position that only I could do it."

Henry was always in charge. "Mike was under the impression he was the chief of the clinic in Montreal and I always knew that was not the case. I had a very personal relationship with all the people who worked there. We had been through a lot together." But many times Henry had given in to Mike, even if it were just to circumvent another threat to quit. They fought often and they fought about many things, but Henry said he was surprised at the depth of the hostility Mike bore him. "I knew there was a lot of love, but ... " His voice trailed off. Mike believed Henry had never fully honoured their mother: "We had two mothers. Mine was fine — his was bad. Whatever he is he owes to our mother, yet he considers her in a bad light. She said to me, 'Look after your brother.' That is why he owes her." He believed their mother was killed on August 23, the same day he and Henry arrived in Auschwitz. Mike had been back to the silent camp several times to honour her, never with Henry. For her, Mike said he stole the potato scraps for his brother — "I got into a Lithuanian commando unit [in Lager Eins], into a place where it was clean and nobody stole, and got to work in the kitchen. I would wait a little down a ways from the gate and every day Henry would walk by when his night shift ended. Every day it would be a big kiss, then [he would ask,] 'What have you got for me?' right away. 'Go to the bag,' I would tell him, and there would be a potato or something — every day." Henry realized that when telling his life story he hadn't given Mike as much credit as he seemed to need — he began to make it a point always to say his brother had saved his life in the camps. Mike could not be mollified. "You're in the camp and somebody stabs you in the back," he said dramatically, also metaphorically, "and it's your own brother." He believed Henry had betrayed him when he would not leave the camp the time Mike was ill and had asked Henry to go with him. "I had typhus fever. I was sick — whatever touched my lips went through me. I knew I was going to a sick camp, a little camp in Dachau. We had an agreement we go together. He broke it." Mike said he would never forgive him.

The lawyers worked on the division of assets. Henry offered Mike $100,000 a year to be a figurehead, but Mike refused, perhaps because officially he owned half of everything — clinics, Henry's consulting company, real estate, everything. By June, it was over. Mike was a wealthy man and the brothers were officially estranged.

But there was no peace for Henry. At the Toronto clinic, the staff had decided to unionize. "I felt like I was stabbed in the back," Henry said. Another betrayal, from people he had also thought of as his family. He fought back like a wounded beast, wanting to fire everyone, suggesting early tactics that repulsed Andrea Knight. For the first time, she refused to do Henry's bidding, although with her ideological background, she admitted she should have supported the unionization. But she didn't. "This was Henry's clinic and he had been very clear about how he wanted to run it and I didn't think it was right to take it away from him." Working conditions were good — that was never in dispute.

The staff were well paid. Henry picked up the cheque for lavish dinners. Many Fridays there would be champagne in Knight's office —
"just for the hell of it," she said — after the last patient (and picketer)
had gone. Henry paid for Club Med vacations for some longtime staff.
Knight went to Guadaloupe, along with Henry's office manager and
right-hand, Sharon Broughton. "As an employer he was generous, but
he liked to do it on his own terms. He liked to give out the bonuses or
the raises. He liked to hand out the goodies," Knight explained. He was
hurt that more of his children had turned on him after he had been the
good father, the benevolent father. But his own father, Josef Morgentaler, whose memory and martyrdom he worshipped, had risked much
to found a textile workers union. "[Henry] was not without his contra-
dictions," said Knight.

Henry saw no contradiction: "[My father] fought for good conditions. I did offer good conditions."

Yes, he did, agreed clinic worker Janet Mawhinney, one of several
who nevertheless wanted Henry to instigate changes now that the battle had been won in the Supreme Court. "Sometimes you would get
phone calls from people booking appointments and you are the first
person they've told. Imagine the complexity, and you have five minutes
for them. This was brutal prioritizing. The priority was book 'em, get
'em and send 'em home. Pre-1988 I could see the political necessity of
that. Having access alone and providing the procedure was an amazing
achievement." Now the battle was no longer about access to abortion. It
was about the quality of care women received, treating them respectfully, hooking them up to services. "Henry was warm and caring, but
it was the way the whole thing was set up," Mawhinney said. "You
couldn't see twenty-five women a day and offer them more than six or
seven minutes for counselling, including a description of the procedure."
Some of the newly hired doctors were "fabulous." Others were not at
the clinic for the cause but for the money, which, at $100 per doctor per
procedure, was substantial. They could make $1,800 in a day.

The women appointed a spokesperson to ask Henry to initiate
fewer patients per day and better screening of doctors, hire more counsellors. They were surprised he seemed so resistant. They asked for staff

meetings. He said he had no time and it wasn't necessary. Things were fine. He wanted to go on thinking everyone was happy working for him; he hated hearing any complaints, and meetings made him restless unless he had a grand announcement to make. Typically, he didn't say he was tired, that he was still recovering from a recent hernia operation and not up to a meeting. To the women, Henry appeared a man on the move, who was pumping up the volume, riding his own momentum, never stopping to breathe in or assess. They met on their own. "We felt shunted to one side. We were pissed off. We had done hundreds of hours of overtime with no pay. Why were we sacrificing our basic labour rights?" Mawhinney remembered. Better to have things businesslike, they thought, than another round of Henry's good-morning kisses to all and sundry staff. All of them, not just nurses, were paid well, but some even better than that. Mawhinney was one who benefited from Henry's largesse. "But why was I making more than the person next to me? We were sick of this paternalistic shit. We're working. We deserve it. Forget bonuses. There were weekend and evening shifts now at the clinic. Pay us overtime."

Then somebody at the meeting suggested they form a union. "Everyone was shocked, but there was no resistance," Mawhinney recalled. They picked the Service Employees International Union and, when they met with Henry, presented their unionizing as a fait accompli. "This is crazy," Henry said he told them. "There will be two groups here, one as management, and it will be a terrible atmosphere. I think of you as collaborators and you have always been well treated." Henry was shocked to hear one woman's reply: "After the Supreme Court, we have to treat you like any other employer." Mawhinney recalled Henry saying, "I can't believe you are doing this to me. How could you do this to me? I'm like a father to you. I'm your parent. We are like family," and one of their number answering him with "You are not my father. We are not family." The women believed Henry was trying to "guilt us and shame us," said Mawhinney. "That was a big mistake. I just watched those faces in that room that day and they were not vulnerable to his anger. We had a lot of anger ourselves." Including part-timers, the staff numbered about twenty-five. Henry figured only eight were the main instigators.

"Henry felt it personally and took it personally in terms of individuals," Knight recalled. "The lawyer told Henry to back off because he was too emotionally involved."

In the subsequent months, many staff left, to be replaced by people Mawhinney called "Henryists," not feminists or activists. In classic labour relations strategy, many were part-timers, which broke the union momentum. "There was such a reaction against the union, people had broken hearts and left," Mawhinney explained. The union was created and Henry ended up spending $40,000 on legal fees to do it. When he calmed down, and when a union appeared inevitable, he said he didn't want to think he would ever fight a union. But one union activist was accused of stealing medications and fired, another quit in solidarity and a third left for health reasons. "New people were hired who were competent but not necessarily ideologically inclined," Henry explained. "The ideological [staff's] interests were more important [to the unionized staff] than the women they were serving." In less than a year, the union was decertified. Its death blow had come months earlier, when Nikki Colodny and four others, including Mawhinney, had handed in their notices. They were starting their own Toronto abortion clinic, to be called Women's Choice Health Clinic and to be run by women as a nonprofit collective.

"Unionizing and the decision to set up a new clinic were extremely related," Mawhinney said. "We went to the wall. We went the distance to force some of the structural changes. For a lot of us it was like a light bulb going off. Henry had done this incredible job. It's our turn. Let's stop fighting Father. Let's move into our own house and do what we want to have done. And we have a historical opportunity because of what happened in Canada's legal system."

Colodny said they first talked about starting the kind of clinic they wanted April 1 of that year, at a birthday dinner for her. Canada's newest abortion clinic and its only nonprofit worker co-operative opened on September 27, 1988. On December 28, 1988, Colodny locked out the staff. For ten months after that they fought it out in court, until the workers, unemployed and on legal aid, ran out of money and credit. "Poetic justice," Henry said. "When Nikki left it was a blessing in disguise,

since she took all the staff who wanted the union." Neither he nor
Knight had known of Colodny's intentions. At the press conference
announcing her clinic, Knight thought Colodny fired off "some cheap
shots" by stressing that this clinic's doctor was not a man and implying
the Morgentaler Clinic was overcharging. Colodny has since stated she
always considered the Morgentaler Clinic "a model of efficiency and
excellent medical care" and that it was hard to leave (even though she
was only working there one day a week). She admitted she and Henry
have never re-established a fully cordial relationship, the way he did
with Scott. "He's warm and cordial when we see each other and we
have had a good heart-to-heart talk," she said. "But I'm still 'the bad
girl.' I'm still 'ungrateful.' I've just hurt him somehow and I think it is
very gender based."

Colodny had often been contentious and disruptive during the coop's
long, gruelling meetings attempting for consensus on everything from
the clinic's fee structure to the colour of its walls, Mawhinney wrote in a
forthright article in the Summer 1991 issue of the feminist quarterly
Fireweed. Mawhinney and the others ascribed to Colodny "difficulty
with fundamental co-op principles, including the principle of one
woman, one vote."[4] What hurt her more, Mawhinney said, was how
OCAC abandoned the women, and how the radical, pro-union Coalition
did nothing to help them in their struggle to unionize. Mawhinney had
been active in OCAC for three years. She had expected more from the
group. "We asked them for help. We said this was not personal but it is
about what is happening to the model of abortion services. This is your
struggle. But from the beginning the OCAC executive referred to the
clinic as 'Nikki's clinic.' We had huge arguments." Mawhinney also
thought OCAC did not want to upset Henry. OCAC never announced the
creation of a clinic union to their general membership (neither did
CARAL, she said); everyone agreed they didn't want anything that could
be construed as labour-management difficulties to get out to the media
and, Mawhinney said, "OCAC disappeared entirely when we were in
court. From the lockout on, they vanished."

But Carolyn Egan said OCAC supported the unionization and that
she was the one who reminded Henry to stop being hurt by the action

and remember he had supported trade unions all his life. As for the Women's Choice in Health Clinic, "they had already started, so it was difficult to know how we could support them.... We didn't not support them." As political activists, those in OCAC weren't involved in the clinics' internal structures, she added. "Our political support is for the issue. It is not attached to the particular personality of the docs. When the workers at Nikki's clinic were having problems and the lockout, we did speak out, but we first tried to mediate," Cherie MacDonald said. OCAC was also more concerned about lobbying for full clinic funding at the time, Linda Gardner said. In *Fireweed*, Mawhinney wearily concluded: "There are several factors which can explain the pro-choice movement's lack of leadership regarding the lockout and takeover, including fear of bad publicity and the fear of the appearance of a lack of homogeneity within the movement. This perspective was equally evident with the union struggles at the Morgentaler Clinic.... The result was a silencing, which precluded the possibility of community mobilization and in general, cloaked significant and productive differences within the movement."[5] Once again, women in Ontario had a chance for their own abortion clinic — and lost it. Ironically, the women who were successful were those from British Columbia who met with Mawhinney and the others when they were still on staff at Henry's clinic. They had been planning to build the clinic around a doctor until they talked, Mawhinney recalled. "Then the women in B.C. went back to the drawing board and decided to have doctors on a contract basis. It was a big shift, which gave them more protection from being another traditional medical model."

Henry thought the women were short-sighted. The Everywoman's Centre, run by the Concerned Citizens for Choice on Abortion, limited their caseload to about eight a day. "I said, why can't you do fifteen? They did counselling lasting forty-five minutes, then the doctor talked to the patient for an hour and half. And they had a waiting list of three or four weeks. There were women who couldn't wait so long, so they would fly to Seattle," Henry said. "I said to them their counselling was much too long and if they were the only clinic they would have to do everything to reduce the waiting list and accommodate more women. I couldn't convince them.... A woman being counselled for an abortion is often in such a state of anxiety and tension the counselling doesn't even penetrate. They want to make each woman a pro-choice protagonist, this feminist propaganda, but this wasn't the right time or place for it." Henry had no patience when "ideology interferes with good medical practice," which he says had happened in some feminist clinics reluctant to give the women painkillers or afraid of medicalizing the procedure too much. "But let's face it. It is a medical procedure and it is important women not be made to suffer." Despite idealogical differences, when Everywoman opened in 1989, Henry sent them an aspirator.

In the meantime, members of Parliament struggled to find something they could agree on to fill the void created by the Supreme Court decision. By late July 1988, as pro-life activist Kurt Gayle fasted for nineteen days on Parliament Hill and CARAL passed out a coat hanger to each parliamentarian and a button saying "Never again," the MPs torpedoed the five of the twenty-one amendments permitted to be tabled, including one from Conservative backbencher Gus Mitges banning abortions unless two doctors say the woman's life is in danger. Then they defeated the motion itself, which had tried for a two-tiered abortion system: one for early pregnancies, requiring one doctor to state the woman's physical or mental health was threatened; another for later pregnancies, when two doctors would be needed to state the pregnancy would endanger the women's life or health. And with that, everybody understood, there would be no more talk in the House of Commons of abortion until after the November 21, 1988, election. CARAL was pleased. "The longer we can go without legislation, the more we can show people that nothing disastrous is going to happen," said Norma Scarborough.[6] Ontario's health minister had proposed a law for health facilities, which promised public funding for the Morgentaler Clinic and the other clinics but set up a strict government-administered regulatory system.

One small but not insignificant victory was the June 1988 decision of the Ontario College of Physicians and Surgeons to stop insisting that abortions be done only in hospitals. The College had sent a committee to Henry's Harbord Street clinic and been impressed. Henry's Winnipeg clinic quietly re-opened for business on June 27, 1988 — with Dr. Robbie Mahood and without Henry, whose injunction against performing abortions was only lifted the following April.

One extraordinary bid for publicity came up short. Upon being stopped by his own lawyer on October 10 from bringing two fetuses in vials in an air travel bag into the Supreme Court of Canada, Joe Borowski said, "What we want protection for is not blood, as Morgentaler would call it. It's a perfectly formed human being." The court reserved its decision. Borowski used his media time to boast that the pro-life movement would elect 150 pro-life Tory or Liberal MPs, which would give them the majority in the newly redistributed 295-seat Parliament. Even Campaign Life Coalition president Jim Hughes admitted later only seventy-eight pro-life MPs were elected.[7] But it was a pre-emptive strike on the clinic — an entirely different and unforeseen tactic — that forever altered the rules of play and the relationship between the two sides.

———

At 8:30 on any Saturday morning Harbord Street would have been still and clear, free of the vehicles and people that clutter and galvanize the neighbourhood for long after the city has shaken itself awake. But by that time on Saturday, October 29, 1988, about two hundred people had stealthily, efficiently positioned themselves at the front and back doors of the locked and empty clinic. Many of them were Americans, in Toronto for the sixth annual Human Life International (HLI) conference. One of them was pacifist and human rights activist Joan Andrews, freed just eleven days earlier from serving two and a half years in prison, much of it in solitary, for her attempt to unplug a suction machine during an abortion in Florida. *Time* magazine described her as "the one authentic [American] hero of the pro-life movement."[8] Another HLI conference attendee was the powerful president of the Washington based HLI, Roman Catholic priest Paul Marx. Participating local pro-life heroes included Borowski, Kurt Gayle (no longer fasting) and Anne Packer, wife of a Metro Toronto police constable fired in January 1988 because he had refused to guard the Morgentaler Clinic. Linking arms, pressing shoulders together, they were impenetrable. They prayed and sang hymns and rejoiced for the babies they were saving.

Canada's first Operation Rescue Mission was a success. "The spirit here is just terrific. At this point, we're stopping the killing. For how long I don't know, but right now they're not killing anyone," Gayle announced from the clinic front steps.[9] They had closed down Morgentaler's clinic, taking everyone by surprise. Although similar "rescues" were happening in thirty cities across the United States to mark this National Day of Rescue, few in Canada had ever heard of the organization. Cherie MacDonald was getting ready to go to a Toronto disarmament rally at Queen's Park that day when she heard a radio news report that hundreds of people were blocking the Morgentaler Clinic. She had to phone the radio station for details — "We had never heard of Operation Rescue" — before she rushed over to the peace demonstration to ask for volunteers to go to the clinic. The demonstration organizers told her to round up however many she wanted. "We just hollered, 'Anybody here want to go to the clinic?' And so we went. And we weren't shy when we got there." MacDonald said the peace demonstrators and pro-choice supporters tried to "pull them off the clinic. They fought back and it was a real melee." MacDonald's cohorts had arrived at about 12:30 p.m., but it was 4 p.m. before police cleared everybody away. They arrested thirty-nine pro-lifers, Marx included, who chanted prayers or sang hymns as they were led away,[10] uplifted in their victory.

It had been a long time coming. Almost twenty years earlier, the pro-life Coalition for Life had drafted guidelines in Ontario laying out some circumstances — cervical cancer, certain diseases — under which they would agree to abortion as an alternative. But the militants within the movement abhorred this moderate stance and formed Campaign Life Coalition, the political lobbying arm of the movement, the pro-life equivalent to CARAL in its purpose, although not its tenor. They demanded from politicians a law protecting all unborn children and banning all abortions, with no exceptions. Because they believed they had convinced governments, such as the one in Ontario, that they represented the majority opinion of Canadians, they deliberately kept their picketing and protests of clinics, such as Henry's on Harbord Street, to a minimum. But when the Harbord Street clinic continued to stay open, Cardinal Carter put out a call for a week of protests. That was an "unmitigated public relations disaster," author Michael Cuneo later said on a CBC radio program.[11] The protests were a numerical flop and the pro-life cause looked like a fringe obsession inextricably linked with the retrograde, or at least nonprogressive, element of the Roman Catholic church. As more hard-liners affixed themselves to the cause, the more militant it became. The imported American-style confrontation led to inevitable violence.

The man who had transformed the American pro-life movement from the "decorous undertakings"[12] of proper and respected groups such as the National Right to Life Committee to the brash, street action from pumped-up "uterine warriors"[13] was a small-town son of a hippie. Randall Terry left upper New York State at sixteen to be a rock and roll star. He became a born-again Christian instead, and went back to enrol in Elim Bible College near Rochester. Terry was only twenty-seven when he met others in the movement who believed in what they called "direct action." Two years later he was in charge of Operation Rescue headquarters, which had a staff of thirty-six to handle sales of their rescue instructional video (as well as *The Silent Scream*) and his nation-wide appearances and was funded by donations from the likes of television evangelist Jerry Falwell. At every press conference he displayed Baby Choice, a nineteen-week disfigured and discoloured fetus in a jar of formaldehyde, lying in a satin-lined tiny coffin. He came to Canada only once and spoke in Toronto at the huge Queensway Cathedral — a strategic visit, according to the *Interim*, a Roman Catholic publication, because Randall Terry signalled the "providential arrival of Protestant evangelicals to the pro-life battlefield."

Operation Rescue's Canadian branch blanketed clinics in Toronto and Vancouver and, later, Montreal for the following eighteen months. Their next action extended over three days in mid-January 1989, and culminated in a square-off on the steps of the "abortuary," as they called the Morgentaler Clinic, when hundreds of pro-choice demonstrators jammed the clinic entrance for five hours against the phalanx of as many pro-life protestors. About 160 were arrested and the clinic stayed open. "We found out about [many of] their rescues," MacDonald said. "It was spy versus spy stuff." But frightening, serious, real. "We were literally fighting hand to hand," said Egan. OCAC members began staying overnight at the clinic when they thought there might be a rescue, getting up at five or six o'clock in the morning to ensure the doors weren't blocked. "The police were not moving at all. It was up to us," remembered Linda Gardner. "We would have cordons of supporters five deep so that when they started to push in we would be able to stop them. It was very terrifying." Carolyn Egan remembered being caught with two colleagues inside a wedge of more than a hundred Rescuers. Her colleague fainted and had to be carried out. When Egan escaped, she said her right side was bruised "as if I had been beaten." Gardner recalled, "As much as they tried to look like they were peaceful they were not. They would attack women, pull their hair. They were punching and kicking. I got punched in the face." Some mornings the nurses had to run a gauntlet to get to work. Police often created a corridor with their bodies, through which the nurses would dash, while Operation Rescuers grabbed at them from between the police. One nurse, Peggy Misener, remembered making it inside the clinic, where Andrea Knight waited for them. "Patients this way, staff in my office," she commanded. Misener said her knees buckled as she headed for Knight's office, where the manager had a big bottle of Bailey's. "She would slap it down and she would say, 'Okay two ounces maximum for everybody, then back to work.'" Without protestors, the job was already stressful. Misener felt faint her third day on the job as she was checking the fetal remains to ensure all body parts were there and none had remained in the uterus. A senior nurse understood immediately. "I fainted flat out, boom, on the floor, my first day. It gets to you," she told Misener.

OCAC marshals had walkie-talkies to alert everyone when a patient was coming. "I was always so amazed that these women were so desperate and so strong that they would go through this," Egan said. Yet OCAC was very opposed when Henry stated he was going for an injunction. Crowds at a clinic — even if they were clashing — were concrete proof to the world that the pro-choice movement was alive and well and in the majority. They were an integral part of the strategy to defeat the pro-life movement. Demonstrating, the escort service and front-step rallies were also the lifeblood of OCAC. "I'm not sure Henry would see the importance the same way I would," MacDonald said. She was not one of the trio OCAC had designated to be the "Henry handlers" (they were Egan, Gardner, Rebick), but they couldn't sway him, either. The battle itself may have become the issue for OCAC — to lose one was to lose the other — whereas Henry had put everything, including his faith, in the courts. The Supreme Court victory was all he needed — except some peace and quiet for himself, the nurses and, of course, the women. He was fed up with the street theatre of demonstrations and slogans and police protection. They had accomplished little: the rescues had continued unabated. Ninety-four people had been arrested outside the clinic on February 23 ("but never charged," Henry noted). Two weeks earlier, forty-four people at an Operation Rescue in Vancouver were sent to jail for two weeks (another twelve sentenced to successive week-ends).[14] When the Supreme Court decided on March 9, 1989, that it didn't have the legal authority to determine if the unborn child had any constitutional rights, Borowski called for country-wide sit-ins and protests and more Operation Rescue tactics. And two days later, more than a hundred pro-life demonstrators were arrested outside Henry's clinic after the by now inevitable scuffle with pro-choice people turned ugly. MacDonald said the other side had jumped barricades and tried to grab patients. Henry was appalled. "There should be peace and quiet in front of the clinic," he said. He had been personally hounded by Dan McCash, who had screamed at him during intermission at the symphony and harassed him in restaurants. McCash had also damaged the car of one clinic worker and harassed others, when he wasn't literally on his knees begging women, "Please don't kill your baby." Henry filed an injunction against specific people — Packer, McCash — as well as John Doe and Jane Doe. On the first anniversary of his victory he had been forced to admit that the pro-life movement had "succeeded in slowing down progress." He'd had to resign as president of the Humanist Association of Canada; he had intended to make known the low-profile association as a respected source for all ethical and religious matters, as

well as pump up its stagnating membership roster. But he couldn't do it
and tend to the newest abortion crises. "I felt so guilty. People had a lot
of hope I would revitalize the movement and I promised myself I
would do it and I just couldn't do it."

The notice of motion was filed April 13, 1989, the same day Henry
won an interim injunction. It was good until May 2, when Henry received permission to proceed with his $1-million lawsuit against the five
anti-abortion protestors he had named in the injunction. Henry was
awarded a 150-metre civil injunction on May 5, but not before being
asked in a preliminary pretrial hearing by the pro-life lawyer Angela
Costigan whether he had ever aborted a Jewish child, if he had documents proving he was really at Auschwitz or Dachau and if he saw sim-
ilarities between photos of aborted fetuses and Jewish corpses in the
Holocaust. Two days later, a pro-life protestor was charged with breaking the hard-won injunction. After Henry complained publicly about
the breaking of the injunction, about fifteen hundred pro-lifers made
a point of marching from Queen's Park only to Spadina Avenue and
Harbord Street, the closest the law said they could come to the clinic.
They moved on, turning their full wrath on Scott's clinic, where some
chained themselves to the clinic fence to obstruct being led away.

Then into the sluggish days of summer rushed a beautiful twenty-
two-year-old deaf woman, fifteen weeks pregnant, whose boyfriend had
won an injunction in the Ontario Supreme Court forbidding her to have
an abortion. Mr. Justice John O'Driscoll gave no reasons for his decision.
As she walked beside her lawyer, Clayton Ruby, out of courtrooms and
into the waiting web of news cameras, for one week the delicate, up-
turned face of Barbara Dodd represented everything a movement could
want — sweet, shy, stymied but strong. Hours after a judge threw out
the injunction forbidding her from having an abortion and hours before
another notice of injunction was filed, Henry performed her abortion.
Arlene Leibovitch interpreted; Rebick, whose day job was at the Canadian Hearing Society, was beside her the whole time. Henry executed
the abortion perfectly and painlessly. "She didn't pay a cent. She didn't
offer and I didn't ask." Peggy Misener's husband drove her away from
the gathering pro-life crowds out front.

A week later, Henry received a call from Ruby: "He said, 'Henry, what are we going to do? [Dodd] has just had a press conference saying she regrets having the abortion, that she was influenced by the pro-choice movement.'" Henry was "stunned" Dodd could have joined the pro-life side just one week after hugging him in gratitude. The Reverend Ken Campbell presided over the marriage ceremony for Dodd and her boyfriend, Gregory Murphy, and in 1990, very pregnant and on a pro-life publicity tour, she made sure she was photographed full-bellied in front of various abortion clinics.

But that same summer of 1989, a composed young woman from Quebec gave the Supreme Court its second chance in five months to consider whether or not a fetus was a human being. From afar Henry watched Chantal Daigle progress through the courts fighting an injunction her former boyfriend had received to prevent her having an abortion. Henry's only involvement was when he recommended three doctors who do late second-trimester abortions to one of Daigle's doctors at Sherbrooke Hospital. But thousands of women across the country took to the streets in her support (Henry carried a symbolic coat hanger during one march in Montreal) and her case was widely credited with reviving a flagging pro-choice movement.

On July 26, the Quebec Court of Appeal voted 3 to 2 to uphold the ban on abortion. Daigle was twenty-one weeks pregnant. Hospitals in Quebec would not perform abortions after the twentieth week and the Supreme Court wanted to solve her case without commenting on the rights of the fetus. Before her case was heard in a special emergency session of the Supreme Court, she quietly went to Boston, where abortions were performed up to twenty-four weeks, to have an advanced pregnancy abortion. The Supreme Court ruled unanimously that the fetus has no right to life until it is born. Daigle's situation had been troublesome, if not messy: how much easier it had been to defend the fourteen-week-pregnant Dodd. At that time Henry didn't do abortions beyond sixteen weeks (now he terminates eighteen-week pregnancies). "When you talk to reasonable people it is not whether abortion should be granted but up to which point it should be granted, because there is a point at which you could say this is a human being now — or, using a pro-life term, a preborn baby — and after this point it should not be allowed," Henry noted. "I think it should be around twenty-four and twenty-eight weeks on the basis that [fetuses] have viability within the uterus and they have brain waves." But most people just believed the turmoil caused by Dodd's and Daigle's dilemmas pointed out how much Canada needed a new abortion law.

In the heat of the summer (and the chaos) Prime Minister Brian Mulroney promised there would be new proposed legislation when the House reconvened in September. It took a little longer than that. On November 3, what would become Bill C-43 was introduced to a near-empty House of Commons. The proposed new law left decisions on abortions to a woman and her doctor, provided the doctor agreed that continuing the pregnancy threatened her mental, physical or psychological health. If it didn't and she had an abortion anyway, the woman and the doctor would be subject to up to two years in prison. Both sides reviled the intended new law.

CHAPTER 18

EAST COAST STORM WARNING

T HE AIRPORT CAB LURCHED TO A HALT as it rounded the corner
of Robie onto McCully Street. Ever since the motorcycle gang had
moved out, this street of plain plank homes in Halifax's north end, only
one block long and too short for speeding, had been quiet and respectable. Now it was full of furious people bearing signs, Haligonians
who believed the small, dark man in the back seat hastily thumbing bills
to pay his fare was a baby killer. Workers at the Morgentaler Clinic still
wonder whatever possessed Henry to get out of the cab that day, October 23, 1990, at that spot, when a hundred feet — and as many angry
people — lay between him and his clinic.

The women of ACCESS — Atlantic Coalition for Choice Escort
Support — standing in cold groups on the side porch of the clinic overlooking the parking lot where the cab was supposed to have dropped its
fare watched helplessly as Henry's bald spot bobbed in the crowd like
the tip of a lobster trap adrift in a fierce Maritime storm. The people
who hated him were four or five, sometimes more, deep, all around him.
And all around them, like plastic watertight casing, were the media,
with their vicious, black-boxed tape recorders, overhead microphones,
deadly cables. Henry was being pushed and grabbed, as these angry
people tightened in on him, the way a coiled cobra squeezes its trapped
prey. One of the escorts, Nadine McNamara, soft-spoken and quick-
thinking, streaked through the crowd, ducking, feinting, pushing her
way until she could reach out and grab Henry. Her colleague, Debbie
Mathers, ran around and broke through the crowd from behind. With
both hands on Henry's back, she pushed him forward as McNamara

pulled, making his body the wedge that forced the frenzied crowd to falter or drop back a small step, enough for escape. Had Henry fallen, he would have been crushed. Other ACCESS volunteers hauled him into the clinic, where the staff waited anxiously. Clinic administrator Sandra Lanz had ensured all staff and volunteers had arrived before 8 a.m., almost two hours earlier than the pro-life demonstrators.

Henry had come even later, straight from the airport, and had alighted from the cab before it turned into the clinic driveway. Lanz has never understood why Henry decided to try to make the dash through the crowds to get inside the clinic. And she has never forgotten how white, shaken and shattered Henry was. He had been pushed and screamed at by people inches from his face. Safely within the clinic, he'd dropped into a chair as Sharon Broughton from his Toronto clinic took his pulse. He had needed about half an hour to regroup, before he could throw back his shoulders and tell staff, later media, that he had shrugged it all off as more religious fanaticism.

Two weeks later, Henry rationalized the incident as good for his public image. In memoirs dictated while on a Puerto Rican holiday, he said:

> They started shoving me and started to get ugly and many were shouting "Go home, Henry. We don't need you here." I kept my composure at the beginning. Eventually some of the women came and they grabbed my hand and I just followed them and they made a chain and I went through the crowd. I was shaken up because the crowd was really getting hostile and I was completely unprotected against mob violence, and I was apparently very pale when I came in.... It was shown across the nation on television screens by all the media. I appeared to be the one composed in the face of danger and in the face of hostility and I think that was great for my image. In fact, it was true I was sort of daring these people to let me work and to offer help to people who needed me. They came across, of course, as bigots, prejudiced, uncon-cerned about the health and safety of women.... It was a very interesting image.

His clinic manager could only shake her head. "It was terrifying," said Lanz, even though it was neither an isolated, unexpected nor even one of the first incidents indicating the extremes to which many in Halifax and Nova Scotia would go to ensure Dr. Henry Morgentaler not only never succeed in their province, but also that he never again set foot on their turf.

———

The line in the sand had been drawn for years, beginning when Henry had announced back in 1985 that he planned to open a Halifax clinic. Some of the province's pro-choice people learned then from an inside source that Premier John Buchanan had threatened his cabinet members with swift explusions should any support a Morgentaler clinic. How could Henry have retreated after that? In 1985 Dr. Wilkie Kushner wrote to Henry asking that he stay away from Nova Scotia. Kushner was then chair of the therapeutic abortion committee at Halifax's Victoria General Hospital, where the majority of the province's abortions were performed. "I dare say if Dr. Morgentaler makes his promise and does come here...the battle lines will be drawn," Kushner stated.[1] And if people began protesting a Morgentaler clinic, they could just as easily broaden their outrage to include protesting legal abortions, he added.

But Henry had always considered his announcement of taking on the province of Nova Scotia to have been a sensible one. "If I had given in to the superior might of the [Progressive] Conservative government in Nova Scotia, it would have meant that basically I have withdrawn from the fight just because they have more power and I'm scared, and the experience of being scared of higher authority, of course, goes back to the Nazi concentration camp, where I was helpless in the face of a crushing, hostile, murderous machine and where resistance in any overt way meant instant death."

This time, no action followed his announcement. His return to his Ontario clinic could have been easily interpreted as a retreat, but the reason was more basic than that. Nova Scotia had refused to grant Henry a medical licence to practise in the province. Not even Henry Morgentaler could do much about this. What he could do was fight the law in the courts, the country's highest courts. But after his 1988 Supreme Court victory, Henry had been distracted by events in Ontario, especially the recent resignation of Andrea Knight from the Toronto clinic. Henry and Knight's final battle had been protesting Ontario's pending Independent Health Facilities Act. Henry said the Act was "dangerous" legislation that gave the government too much arbitrary power. Also known as Bill 147, Henry believed the Act had the potential to limit the number of, or even ban outright, abortion clinics in Ontario. It meant the government would be in charge of a wide range of medical clinics, not just abortion, and have the licensing power, which was considerable: any unlicensed person owning and/or operating a clinic could be fined up to $50,000. "It could roll back all the gains," a discouraged Henry warned.

Knight was just plain tired. She told Henry she was leaving the clinic because she was burned out. "It is time for me to do something else," she said.

"I wish I could do something else," Henry had replied wistfully.

She'd tried to tell him he could. What about that dream of a television series, "My Dinner with Henry," where he could meet all the powerful, prestigious people he'd always wanted to debate? But they'd both known Henry would never change careers; he'd been typecast and he had already decided Halifax would be the site of his next clinic. "Most people don't deal with most issues in their daily life. You push papers in some office and have few occasions to use your moral compass," Bamie Morgentaler said. "Maybe once a month you can speak out for the underdog, but my father has made his version of morality into a daily event. His passion is very real and he actively seeks it. The drive to it is very powerful."

Yet, for once, Henry was not eager to get into a new set of court battles. But he was restless, and he needed a diversion, and he did want to open another clinic. In his October 29, 1989, memoirs he said:

I'm going to pay a heavy price for taking on this fight. However, I feel good about it. I feel good about myself. I feel again in the role of David against Goliath, the defender of important human rights against the reactionary, ruthless, powerful enemy, and it's a good position to be in. On the one hand, it gives me a great deal of integrity and what you could say is courage in the face of tremendous odds, but courage is tempered, of course, with a great deal of anxiety about what is going on.

Those in the Nova Scotia health ministry would be surprised to hear themselves described in terms usually reserved for a dictatorship, but Henry's vision of the province was scathing:

It appears [that] in Nova Scotia people are very inbred. They are still very dominated by the church. People are very submissive and obedient to authority. There is almost no one to challenge authority except possibly some people in the media.

As for the province's rulers, a.k.a government, Henry compared them to Maurice Duplessis, Quebec's Union Nationale strongman of twenty-five years earlier.

They think they can do anything they want and nobody is going to protest or do something about it. The opposition is very ineffective. It's still a very Conservative area. There is a high level of unemployment. The government had a lot of power to give away handouts and contracts so it's very hard to find people who will directly challenge the government.

But such people did exist. What Henry didn't know and couldn't understand were the tough tendrils of Maritime life and the cautious civility with which people there challenged authority. Andrea Knight had lived in New Brunswick and Prince Edward Island for five years and had tried to explain to him the subtle but indestructible dynamics of how people lived there together. Their conservatism was innate; however, it was not because they were a downtrodden people, but a people with a strong sense of place and self. When Knight was asked "Where are you from?" it was not to ascertain in which New Brunswick or

Prince Edward Island town she lived, but in which province she was born. "When you work in a clinic where people go in clutching their rosary, you just know the reality of life is different from dogma and ultimately women will have to deal with their own lives and they will find a way to reconcile what they need to do and the reasons for them needing to do it," she said. Knight had other reasons for trying to discourage Henry. The women in the movement everywhere were tired; fund-raising had degenerated to burden from chore. She knew Henry "had always had a sense of the motor running. He gets energized by it," but fund-raising wasn't invigorating. It was slogging work — from the bake sales to the t-shirts OCAC sold at every rally, every meeting — and it had been done because (and in spite of the fact) the money kept Henry running ahead of them.

But it came to a head in Halifax. Nobody was ready for another clinic — not yet, anyway. CARAL's Halifax chapter and pro-choice supporters wanted to consolidate the Supreme Court victory and they were worried they would need their energy to fight the upcoming Bill C-43 the federal Tories were talking up as the new abortion law that would fill in the blank on the country's law books left by the Supreme Court decision. While not optimum, the situation in Halifax was not desperate. Doctors at the Therapeutic Procedures Unit (TPU) at the Victoria General Hospital performed more than 80 per cent of the province's abortions, which in 1983 had amounted to 1,701. Abortions were now also performed at eight other provincial hospitals. With the federal law on their side, CARAL had been consistently lobbying for better access. Many doctors and psychiatrists were supporting them, but quietly, discreetly. There was an element of politesse in the Nova Scotians' reticence and if ignored or disturbed, as invariably would happen just with Henry's presence, the goodwill created by CARAL-Halifax over the years could vanish. CARAL-Halifax had long been battling local media: the *Chronicle-Herald* published anti-choice opinion on its religion pages, while refusing to accept paid announcements for the Morgentaler Defence Fund or to carry notices of any CARAL meeting, chapter representative Nancy Bowes noted. CARAL vice president Kathy Coffin remembered when the organization couldn't even find meeting space and when they were banned from all future health fairs at Mount St. Vincent University. Coffin was also on the executive of Planned Parenthood. "I really just pushed the envelope with them and made them be pro-choice," she said. "It wasn't as if they weren't giving out abortion information, but they were scared to death to say [pro-choice] or be [pro-choice]." The Victoria General Hospital didn't start doing legal abortions until the mid-1970s, long after the law was passed specifying under what conditions abortions could be done. By 1986, Nova Scotia's abortion rate was 8 per thousand women, the nation's 10. But it was lower for the other Maritime provinces: 2.5 per thousand in Newfoundland, 2 in New Brunswick, and .4 per cent in Prince Edward Island. Every year about five hundred women from the Maritimes travelled to Henry's clinics in Montreal or even Toronto for abortions, because women under nineteen needed parental consent in Nova Scotia and many rural women could not get a physician's referral. In Antigonish, Right to Life offices were in a storefront on the main street. In Cape Breton there was little call for sex education in the schools, Bowes noted. "People still thought the more you talk about sex the more pregnant teenagers will get," she said.

The Halifax chapter of CARAL consisted of a very small group of middle-class professionals. Although Coffin was a Maritimer, more members were like Bowes, born and raised in Ontario or elsewhere. Almost all were affiliated or loyal to the New Democrats, who held two of the fifty-two seats in the House, and who were officially pro-choice but not in favour of Henry's private, for-profit clinic. Bowes was a sociologist, university teacher and radio commentator, who had not then begun her family, but Coffin, a government health professional, and her architect husband had two young daughters. One of the few women not afraid to publicly associate herself with the pro-choice cause, Coffin had represented CARAL in front of every commission on health and met with every health minister. For years CARAL-Halifax had operated AIRS, the Abortion Information and Referral Service phone line — most recently as an answering machine in a closet in Bowes's home. Coffin would argue with Henry over just about everything he was doing and how he was doing it. "Tone down the bravado. Maritimers don't like

that" she'd say. She advised Henry not to call Buchanan a fascist or com-
pare his laws to Nazi laws. That kind of language didn't go down well
here. And she cautioned him that he shouldn't count on shows of support on the street or at rallies. Maritimers still believe abortion is a private matter and they don't think private matters belong in the public
domain. Henry, she said, would have to try to do abortions quietly, without media fanfare. Haligonians respect that.

Henry was exasperated. "Instead of finding support, I found this
carping criticism." He confronted Coffin. Was she a friend or foe? he
asked. "Friend, of course," a flustered Coffin told him, but Henry
admitted he was neither convinced nor satisfied.[2] He understood Coffin
was criticizing his methodology, not the cause and not the clinic. But he
wanted total support, especially since he believed even the doctors performing abortions at the Victoria General Hospital were opposed to
him. "They were afraid. They were working in relative obscurity and
without being bothered by the anti-choice people, and now I was going
to raise the issue and would become front-page news. They didn't want
me to rock the boat," he said. He thought it was indicative of their
"parochial attitude. We're okay in Nova Scotia. The women in P.E.I.?
Who cares? In New Brunswick? Who cares? The Halifax hospital had
a waiting list of three to four weeks, and therefore many operations
were second trimester because people had to wait so long, and there was
more danger of complications. My clinic really was necessary." And so
Henry's march on the Maritimes followed his pattern, although he did
try to keep word of the clinic purchase under wraps — he did not want
another Winnipeg on his hands with council by-laws and building codes
to overcome. In January 1989, word leaked that Henry was licensed to
practise in Nova Scotia, and Buchanan immediately reacted. "We certainly don't support him in any way, shape or form," he declared.[3]

Henry made his pro forma offer to turn over the clinic to the provincial government anyway. He had done it in every province and never
had any takers. It was a smart tactic that usually deflated talk of Morgentaler self-aggrandizement or profiteering and kept the focus on the
issue and the needs of the area women. But in Nova Scotia, the fight for
a clinic was always personal. Henry Morgentaler was an outsider, an

interloper, a Jew. Among the comments in the letters sent to him were these: "He must be a Jew trying to get even with the white people because of Hitler trying to kill as many Jews as possible"; and "I want you out of my town now. The nerve of you foreign people coming into my town and doing this. Get out now. You are not wanted. You are not going to decide the fate of my young women, men and children. Get out now. This is an order"; and "The face of the devil incarnate. No face exemplifies evil more than his." Even the politicians personalized the issue. Health Minister David Nantes stated, "In the past wherever Dr. Morgentaler goes he causes chaos, turmoil and a great deal of animosity between two sides. We would like him to stay in Toronto." Buchanan added more: "One of the problems with Dr. Morgentaler is that he raises a lot of emotional problems and emotional issues and the whole matter becomes an emotional matter when he arrives. We don't need that in Nova Scotia." A poll in February 1989 found that 63 per cent of Nova Scotians were opposed to abortion clinics in their province. It wasn't long before anti-abortionists were accusing Henry of being in the business for the money and were holding him personally responsible for any and all violence and street demonstrations in front of his clinic, then turning around and accusing him of being an "egoist" (Pat Tanner, president of Nova Scotians United For Life). Even the then provincial NDP leader, Alexa McDonough, wanted it known she was pro-choice but not pro- (private, for-profit) clinics.

The government acted fast, amending the Hospitals Act so abortions would not be covered by medicare and could only be performed in a government-approved hospital. When CARAL-Halifax challenged that, the government brought down a new bill in June 1989, known as the Medical Services Act, which prohibited abortions, as well as certain other procedures, from being done anywhere other than in a hospital. "The purpose of this legislation was obviously to prevent me from opening the clinic. The fine was increased from $500 to [up to] $50,000 per infraction...they did it in a hurry.... It's clearly fraudulent, dishonest camouflage. This Bill is aimed directly at me," Henry recounted for the record in his memoirs. The bill passed with "unseemly haste," as Bowes put it, in a matter of just a few days. CARAL was caught. The law they were challenging had been overtaken; now it was the Medical Services Act they had to fight, meaning they would have to push back their June court date a couple of months. Henry had promised he wouldn't open the clinic before their challenge was heard — according to CARAL-Halifax, he had "prevailed upon" them in the first place to challenge the law on his behalf — but he was paying a mortgage; he was paying staff; he had announced on May 24 the clinic was open, if only as a source of counselling and referral; and he was increasingly agitated and frustrated.

This provincial government was deeply committed to never having a Morgentaler or any other free-standing abortion clinic on their turf. "Thank you for your letter regarding abortion" read the form letter circulated in 1989 under Premier John Buchanan's signature, surely one of the most incautious letters ever sent by any politician anywhere. "You can be assured that the Government of Nova Scotia will fight and oppose any abortion clinics in Nova Scotia. We will use every Constitutional and legal means to defeat Dr. Morgentaler and have passed a law which will not permit abortion clinics. In addition, I can assure you that this Government will *not*, in any way, fund the abortion clinics for Dr. Morgentaler."

CARAL had hired Anne Derrick to win legal standing for them in court so the organization could challenge the Medical Services Act on the grounds that it violated the sections of the Charter of Rights and Freedoms protecting women's rights to freedom of conscience and security of person and equality. Derrick was a partner of Buchan, Derrick and Ring, Halifax's first feminist law firm, now located just off Halifax's boutique-strewn Spring Garden Road, but in the same no-nonsense fifties-style low-rise building as the Salvation Army headquarters. A striking woman, she wore her fair hair in a brushcut, and usually a single earring dangled to her right shoulder. In many ways her appearance belied her accessibility and enthusiasm, as well as her serious purpose. Since graduating in 1980 from Dalhousie's law school, she had defended the right of the now defunct feminist publication *Pandora* to not print a letter from any man. Derrick, together with Clayton Ruby, had also represented Donald Marshall Jr during the royal commission that investigated how Marshall had come to be wrongfully convicted of a murder for which he served eleven years. She was a brilliant, maverick lawyer with a commitment to social justice activism.

On October 17, 1989, CARAL lost their challenge when Mr. Justice Merlin Nunn ruled CARAL would get no legal standing because they had no more special interest in the issue than any other segment of society. Coffin immediately announced that CARAL would appeal, perhaps directly to the Supreme Court. Judge Nunn had made a point of saying that if CARAL wasn't affected by the law, Henry Morgentaler most certainly was. However, Henry was in no mood for more legalities. He had been sidelined and, for him, inactive too long. He hated being "somewhat fearful about running up a big bill with the government" should he open the clinic, but he wasn't happy paying out $2,000 monthly in salaries, plus another $3,000 in expenses (although he reduced that by laying off one staff member and cutting back Lanz's hours to eight over three mornings a week). Lately he'd been spending his own money — $100,000 to get an injunction for the Toronto clinic and another $45,000 towards the post-Supreme Court legal debt, even after Ed Ratcliffe's $30,000 cheque paid off what was owing for Winnipeg. There was no money left in the pro-choice defence fund. CARAL-Halifax had spent everything on their court challenge. Nevertheless, a month later a draft letter from Henry to CARAL spelled out the way things were going to be. Since their attempt at legal leadership had fizzled, he was back in the forefront, and here is what he wanted them to do:

> I believe I deserve your financial support and would like a commitment that the funds that you have collected for the Halifax battle will be available for me to pay legal expenses in a battle which may, and probably will, go all the way to the Supreme Court of Canada.
>
> Also, I wish to point out to you that, in retrospect, your rejection of my offer to challenge the Nova Scotia legislation in the name of CARAL and myself together was unjustified, proved to be bad judgement, and deprived us of valuable time to challenge the oppressive Nova Scotia [government] before the courts. As requested by you, I waited a few months before opening the clinic

at a considerable financial loss and finally did so after your request
for standing was denied.

I need not remind you that I was a founding member of CARAL,
that I supplied the first $5,000 for its beginning and have regularly
contributed financially when I was able to.[4] I gladly gave you my
name for appeals to the public for money. Twice my requests for
financial help in paying legal expenses have been denied by you.

Ultimately Henry launched his own fund-raising campaign with
ads modelled on the one designed by the Edelstones, and gave the
Halifax clinic as the mailing address. He received more than $60,000,
plus five hundred letters of encouragement. And CARAL gave Henry
an in-kind offering, which proved more valuable than cash. As other
abortion-related events began to outpace CARAL's sluggish appeal for
standing, and after the Supreme Court ruled in April 1990 that Henry
could better challenge the new provincial law than they could, they
donated all the legal research they had done to mount their challenge
for Henry to use in his own defence. "And it was a lot of work. Anne
and I and Nancy [Bowes] wrote out these documents until eleven or
twelve o'clock at night. That was a good year and a half of my life.
Nancy and I worked with Anne, getting stuff together, getting witnesses, doing research," Coffin said. Derrick was billing them on a preferred rate of $110 an hour, but Coffin said their challenge cost them
about $74,000, which the CARAL head office helped them to pay. Coffin
also telephoned Henry to recommend he use Derrick as his lawyer. This
would prove to be probably Henry's most effective legal partnership.
"[Henry] has enormous appreciation of the law," Derrick said. "He does
understand why he has lawyers. He has them for the legal advice....
And he listens and he says, 'Okay, I'm going to weigh that in.' Nobody
tells Henry what to do. He decides, but he will decide upon reflection."

Derrick was also the first of Henry's lawyers to be as profoundly pro-
choice and pro-child as he. Her three blond daughters were her "reality," her partner, law professor Archie Kaiser, her "sweetie." Derrick
often said she admired Henry's "guts and bloody-mindedness" but she
became as stigmatized as Henry was in Nova Scotia during the court

fight that was to ensue. She was intrigued that so many of her hate messages and mail assumed she was a lesbian. "It is interesting that is the
kind of labelling that occurs when you are a woman seen as going up
against powerful forces. You are a witch. It's a witch burning. You are
not doing what you are supposed to. That's what those messages mean.
You are stepping out of line." To Derrick they meant she was exactly
where she was supposed to be. She credits her schoolteacher father with
instilling in her "the view that the world's not fair and there's no good
reason for it not being fair."[5]

Derrick believed it was important to have a "woman lawyer and a
feminist lawyer at that. And whether the judges be put off or not, I
don't really care. I think I don't expect too much from the legal system
in Nova Scotia anyway." Convinced he'd hired absolutely the right person, Henry telephoned Sandra Lanz at the clinic on October 22, 1989,
and told her he would be coming back to town in four days and that he
would be performing abortions.

————

Were it not for the bullet-resistant thick plastic over the windows, the
deep red and slate-blue Morgentaler Clinic would look like the other
plain and proud houses on McCully Street. Outside in the back was a
substantial and gracious border garden, at which Lanz had worked
hard. The neighbours appreciated the greenery, as they did the fact that
she paid for the removal of all the trees in the shared back to make the
clinic parking lot. That's deliberate and that's important, "my good
neighbour philosophy," Lanz said.

Inside was her office and the waiting area, near the kitchen where
the *People* magazines were precision piled on a pine coffee table and the
radio always tuned to CBC-AM as receptionist-counsellor Janet Chernin
booked appointments for the Wednesday procedure day. The art on the
wall, some elegiac, some attention seeking, was created for the clinic by
women artists. Lanz made sure Henry was there for that art presentation and the wine-and-cheese celebration afterwards. She valued every
opportunity for a connection with the community outside when she
presented the clinic with a shy and earnest pride. A tour was thorough.

There was nothing to hide and much to point to — the recliner chairs upstairs were a shimmering teal and made of real leather, but the crocheted afghans slung over their backs were genuine homespun. Different visions, equal comfort. "People do say they feel comfortable here," stated Lanz, grateful, not boastful.

A midwife as well as a nurse, she had worked in Ghana for two years and had just returned from a year of world travel when she attended an 1988 potluck Christmas party at the home of CARAL member Jane Wright. One of the handful who knew there would be a clinic, Wright wondered if Lanz was interested in a job. After an interview with Arlene and Andrea Knight, who were in Halifax to furnish the clinic, Lanz was offered the job. She didn't know the clinic location, and she had never done an abortion or even an ultrasound. But on March 23, 1989, she flew to Toronto. She met Henry in the Toronto clinic operating room, where she learned about the instrumentation involved in doing the procedure. She made notes about everything, from what bolt cutters to buy to cut the chains of Operation Rescuers to the correct size of Post-it® notes to order. Even with the months of delays of the clinic opening, Lanz worried. "I was so stunned and serious," she said. "I felt I was never going to be ready."

But many women in Halifax were. CARAL had organized a meeting at Dalhousie's student union building at which the Pro-Choice Action Group (PCAG) was founded. PCAG's role was to be the Nova Scotia version of OCAC. At the meeting, Marie Paturel, then a law student newly committed to activism, remembered a woman from the International Socialists immediately criticizing CARAL for not doing anything. Henry paid for Carolyn Egan and Cherie MacDonald to come and train the Action Group as escorts and front-line workers, but as long as the clinic was open just for referrals, everything was theoretical. "There was no sense of urgency," Paturel said. She had dropped out of the group and was back on campus that fall when Lanz told her Henry Morgentaler was coming in the next day, October 26, and they needed women for a show of support. Lanz said the same thing to PCAG. Paturel responded; PCAG didn't.

Paturel gathered up friends from the campus and headed down to

McCully Street just as it was getting light, about 6:30 a.m. or 7 a.m. The street was quiet, the air was cold. At a few minutes after eight, Henry, Lanz and Sharon Broughton quietly slipped inside. The pro-lifers and the media wouldn't be there for another ninety minutes. The gate was locked. "I did not know that Morgentaler would be performing abortions — I was not told that. I'm semiglad Sandra didn't tell me, because when the police came by I could honestly say I didn't know what was going on," Paturel recalled. Seven women were having abortions that day. Lanz had asked them all to come at the same time. Paturel and friends met them at designated places within the neighbourhood and together everybody entered the clinic. "Everybody milled together so the protestors didn't know who was the client and who were pro-choice," Lanz said. When the police came to the clinic door, she wouldn't let them in. She phoned Derrick, who told her not to give them entry unless they had a warrant. They didn't.

Henry did the seven abortions "without a hitch." Two of the women were from Nova Scotia; one was a girl of twenty who had been date-raped. A woman from Newfoundland had only enough money for her $481 plane fare, Henry recalled, so they waived her fee. He didn't charge the last woman either, because the mother of two had been very frightened. She had come by car from Moncton with her husband. She was very anxious because she feared police might interrupt the procedure. Outside, nobody knew whether or not Henry was doing abortions. The media trampled on the next-door property in their attempts to peer through the clinic windows. Undercover police officers were trying to mingle with the pro-choice crowd, and finally settled for circling with the pro-life picketers. The first woman to leave walked out the back door and was chased down the street by the media. "It was heart wrenching," Paturel said. "We hadn't realize what we were up against. We made sure that never happened to anybody else." As far as she and Debbie Mathers were concerned, the media were the transgressors that day. "One guy kept swinging his camera in my face," said Paturel. "The cameramen were awful. The reporters had started to understand they had to co-operate to get a story." And that they would have to wait for the press conference scheduled that evening at the Sheraton Hotel.

Lanz had everybody back to her house for a low-key spaghetti dinner and Anne Derrick stopped by. She wanted to attend the press conference to experience as much of the issue as she could. Henry was impressed.

It was near bedlam in the hotel meeting room. The podium was covered in microphones. Cameramen elbowed one another for maximum position as reporters jammed the room. Even Henry was agog. "I've never seen such a big crush of reporters since my days in Winnipeg when I had opened my clinic there," he marvelled. "I was in good form. My statement said that basically, yes, I am happy to announce that we opened the Halifax Morgentaler Clinic to serve women from Atlantic Canada and that I personally had performed seven abortions today. I realized that it was a violation of the provincial statutes, but I said the statute was in violation of the Supreme Court of Canada ruling on the abortion issue and a violation of the Charter of Rights, and therefore let them take me to court." Lanz had arranged that some members of the media could have private interviews with Henry in his hotel room, but waiting there for him were two police officers. "We shook hands. They were very polite. I wasn't very surprised. I expected to be charged. I didn't expect to be charged that night," Henry recalled. He went ahead with the interviews, then took a group of supporters downstairs to the bar, where they danced till closing time. "We all felt elated. Things had gone off very well, just the way I had scheduled it to start off with a bang. [Performing] a few abortions...especially [for] women from outside the province and then the press conference." Nothing could mar his celebration, not even when Derrick pulled him aside to say the police had just told her someone was threatening to kill him and destroy the clinic, and did Henry want police protection? He shrugged, said he'd been through this many times before, but added "inside I was a bit worried. It was actually the kind of constant worry that really is quite a deterrent in the sense that I have to fight against the image of someone coming up behind me and pumping a few bullets in me."

The next day, October 27, two undercover agents were assigned to Henry as he gave interviews all morning. Lanz worried: Henry insisted on walking slowly from one destination to the next. "He was not going to change his life for them. The undercover guys — there was one man and one woman — had trouble following him around. He was not going to make it easy for them." She relaxed only when he was safely on board his flight back to Toronto that afternoon.

But exactly one week later Henry was back, to perform seven more abortions and hold another press conference. Facing seven charges under the province's Medical Services Act, Henry decided the media should see for themselves how essential the service was that he was providing. Partway through his workday, as one woman lay in recovery in the downstairs waiting room, and two others awaited the procedure upstairs, Henry asked the woman on the table before him if she would consent to being interviewed by media — anonymously, of course. The woman agreed. Lanz, who was doing instrumentation for Henry, was "stunned." She asked Henry how he intended to do these interviews. "He hadn't thought of that. It was a detail." Typically, Henry assumed Lanz could handle it, and she did. She put Paturel in charge of getting identification from every reporter and assigning an interview time. Television reporters would be allowed only one camera operator, she decided. They all had deadlines: television needed their interviews before 2 p.m., print before 4 p.m.; but as well, CBC wanted a live hookup at 5 p.m., which necessitated two hours of setup time.

Lanz flew around the clinic. One other woman agreed to be interviewed, although she was fearful she would be recognized. Lanz was afraid the women who had not consented to interviews would be seen or, worse, filmed or photographed. The phone rang; it was a woman needing an abortion. Henry readily agreed she should come down right away, as Lanz hastily ushered the women into her back office and closed the door. The members of the TV media came in through the side door, were instructed to leave all cell phones by the entrance ("We didn't want anybody calling a colleague outside, saying anything like 'There'll be a brunette coming out. Get her picture,'" Lanz explained) and were then led to the clinic's front room. Behind closed doors, they talked with Henry as staff brought from the recovery room the women who had had their abortions and escorted them into Lanz's back office. In the former living room, they met one of the women. Her back was to them; a shawl covered her head and shoulders and Lanz stood between the woman and the reporters to ensure anonymity. "The woman was great. She was from New Brunswick. They asked her questions like could she have got an abortion somewhere else," Lanz recalled.

Meanwhile, staff were hastily cleaning up the procedure room, where an abortion had just taken place. Then, when Henry took reporters on the clinic tour, Paturel and other escorts walked out and away with the woman. The print media were warned they would see something a little strange. The woman they were to interview, a twenty-one-year-old Newfoundlander in the media and otherwise recognizable, wore a huge cape and an orange balaclava with holes for eyes, nose and mouth. "They just cracked up," Lanz recalled. Some reporters were disdainful, "but the minute this woman started talking, she was so articulate, so calm, so concise the whole atmosphere in the room did a 180-degree turn from disbelief and craziness to one of great respect for this woman doing that. And they asked intelligent questions." Even so, one reporter recognized the woman and made them a deal: he wouldn't name her if Henry would give him a personal interview. "It was real base stuff, but we said sure, and Henry never minded, ever," said Lanz. It was well after three o'clock when the print and other television reporters left to file their stories, and the CBC camera crew for the national news was pressuring Lanz to get inside the clinic to set up. But there was still the last-minute abortion to perform. The woman had been taken upstairs by the escorts, where she was having her ultrasound, testing and counselling done while an oblivious CBC crew set up downstairs. Henry came downstairs to the office for their live interview straight from doing the procedure. He took off his white coat, checked to make sure there was no blood anywhere, then stepped in front of the cameras. "He was fabulous. I couldn't believe it," Lanz said.

That night at his press conference he announced he had performed another seven abortions. Earlier reports from the media stated he had performed six abortions, but that was before he had performed one for the woman who'd called for a last-minute appointment. Four days later, on November 6, the provincial attorney general's office got an injunction from the Nova Scotia Supreme Court to close down the clinic.

Henry was forced to cut the clinic's function back to referrals. "Henry hated obeying the injunction .... If left to his own devices he would have performed more abortions. I advised him to obey [it]." Derrick explained. "That was the main event. We needed to get into court to make the constitutional argument to cut the legs out from under the leg- islation. And that is ultimately what we did and we did it successfully."

Henry would concede only that it was a "temporary victory" for his foes, "petty, vainglorious men who are trying to deny women a legal and essential medical service."[6]

———

Nova Scotia's provincial courthouse is a grand and soothing rust-coloured building directly across Spring Garden Road from the Bud the Spud chip wagon, another Halifax landmark. Henry's case was being heard on the second floor in a room with elaborate ceiling cornices, velvet curtains and curved benches of old, gleaming wood. He was so confident he was bored. These were beautiful June days he was wasting. On the first day, as Derrick paraded a long lineup of expert witnesses, Henry kicked off his shoes, wiggled his feet under the long table and strolled over in his socks to deliver her a note. On the second day he briefly snoozed, the Halifax *Daily News* reported. His relaxed, insouciant behaviour was the flip side of how Henry had felt a few months earlier on February 12, 1990, when he had sat, "sizzling with contained rage and fury and anger," in court for the challenge he'd launched after the Nova Scotia government had won the right to close down his clinic. Although Anne Derrick had whispered this was as good as he was going to get, he wasn't at all happy with the threesome sitting in judgement, one of whom had previously quashed an earlier attempt to speed up the appeal process. The judges decided to reserve judgement.

This trial had started in March 1990, under Judge Ross Archibald, who insisted Henry be present; then the judge changed his mind and decided to postpone everything until June. Two weeks later Archibald suffered a heart attack and Joe Kennedy took over. Henry liked the man immediately when Kennedy announced that anyone could tell from his name that he was a Roman Catholic, but that if Kennedy thought his religion would affect his judgment he wouldn't be hearing the case. Henry approved of such forthrightness, as well as the fact that he was a Liberal appointee, and therefore, Henry reasoned, not in debt to the current government. Henry had decided to capitalize on his trial press coverage with another round of newspaper advertisements asking for money. Already he'd received more than $30,000, although some colleagues told Henry they thought it unseemly for him to run ads asking for money for himself, and felt that an organization should plead on his behalf. Henry viewed the matter differently:

> I agree it would have been better. Selma used to do that with The Issue Is Choice, and this time I just didn't have the patience to go round and ask somebody to do that for me and I decided to do it on my own. So too bad, some people might feel bad about it and I made them feel guilty.... But I think I am perfectly justified and I'm glad I've done it. It mobilizes some people into being able to participate in an important cause this way and that's perfectly all right. I think that for many people in Canada now I'm seen as a hero who is fighting for the rights of women and justice and decency, for their rights, and who is not afraid to do that. It's true I've arrived at a stage in my life where I'm not afraid to do it. I think I have a contribution to make. I like to make it. I get a lot of satisfaction from doing it and I get a lot of public acclaim for it as well and so I'm just doing the right thing. I feel good about myself and I feel really good about this trial.

On Friday, October 19, 1990, Judge Kennedy acquitted Henry of all fourteen counts of breaking Nova Scotia's Medical Services Act. "In its pith and substance it is a criminal law," Kennedy said, and therefore constitutionally a federal matter and "*ultra vires* and of no force and effect." Henry had always assumed Kennedy would "bend backwards to be objective because he was Roman Catholic"; he was so confident he would win his fifth Canadian acquittal of illegally performing abortions that he didn't need a sleeping pill the night before the verdict was handed down. Henry hailed the ruling as "courageous" for flying in the

face of the government in power, even though Buchanan, by now appointed to the Senate, had left amid an RCMP investigation into whether
charges of patronage and misuse of public funds should be laid against
him, and Nantes had resigned as health minister after being accused
of releasing confidential medical information. (The RCMP couldn't find
enough evidence to lay any charges against Buchanan; Nantes was
acquitted.) "[After the verdict] Anne Derrick had the presence of mind
to stand up immediately and to ask that the court decide the question of
costs," Henry recalled, but the judge later decided to postpone any decision until November 30, 1990, the last day on which the province could
appeal the decision.

At the press conference after the ruling came down, Henry announced the clinic was open as of that minute, and once again forgot to
publicly acknowledge his lawyer. "I told myself I was going to thank
Anne Derrick for her brilliance and perseverance and good work. I
actually forgot to do that" until answering a later question. He also said
the trial had cost about $200,000, which he later realized was "an exag-
geration. I think it's more like $150,000."

Driving to the airport to attend a conference in Montreal on laughter and play, Henry heard one radio reporter comment that Henry
was so self-assured he appeared arrogant. Better arrogant, he reassured
himself, than to seem shaky, hesitant, nervous or intimidated.

He had told Lanz he'd be back in Halifax Tuesday to do abortions,
and she spent the weekend trying to figure out how to hire nurses,
obtain supplies and find patients. That Sunday evening at about 11 p.m.
Henry called to say Lanz should phone a Janet Chernin, a former staff
member from his Toronto clinic now living in Halifax. Typically, that
was about all the information on Chernin he passed on. Again, typically,
if Henry liked someone, thought her bright and energetic, he wanted to
hire her. (His clinics' support staff are all female). But Lanz balked. "I
said no. I had never met Janet. I figured I should have at least the opportunity to meet someone I was going to work with. It was the only time
I absolutely refused to do something for Henry," she recalled. Blithely,
Henry himself phoned Chernin and told her to report for work. In
Toronto, Chernin had helped handle an Operation Rescue in which

some of the two hundred protestors had locked themselves with bicycle locks to oil drums of freshly poured cement. She was as sardonic as Lanz was serious, and equally as dedicated to the cause and the clinic. Eventually, the two became good friends as well as professional colleagues. Together they handled just about all of Henry's surprises.

After Henry's dramatic arrival — this was the day he was trapped in the centre of angry anti-abortionists and rescued by a pair of escorts — and midway through the day's schedule of twelve abortions, Henry invited a prominent anti-abortionist into the clinic. He knew Anne-Marie Tomlins from the trial; she had attended the court so regularly that she and Henry used to glance at each other and break into grins. They chatted inside the clinic for about half an hour, neither softening in his or her stance, but each courteous and respectful of the other. "The gesture was probably good in the sense that it diffused some of the implacable hostility among the two groups," Henry said. It was Tomlins who asked Henry to come outside and shake hands with her in front of the media cameras. Henry did, then went back inside the clinic and wrote a letter "on the spot" to the demonstrators. "Dear fellow human, anti-choice protestors," it began. "I appeal to you to stop picketing my clinic thereby causing additional distress to women wanting to receive medical abortions here. I understand your concerns although I do not share them. I believe you are misguided in your belief that every pregnancy, no matter how conceived, has to go to term." He suggested they direct their efforts to caring for abused children and helping single mothers "with the chores needed to take care of their children." He urged them to "be gentle to your own children (if you have any) and give them quality time — they will be much better off if you are able to give them love and caring rather than waste your time trying to victimize women (you will not succeed anyway)." The protestors did not appreciate receiving parenting advice from Henry Morgentaler.

That Friday, November 2, the health minister for Ontario's ruling New Democratic Party, Evelyn Gigantes, held a conference on how to improve abortion service within the province. Appearing with Henry were the owners of Toronto's other three abortion clinics — Colodny, Scott and Manole Buruiana, another former Morgentaler employee.

Henry was only ten minutes into his speech when Gigantes had to leave for another meeting, but he managed to slip in a suggestion the Independent Health Facilities Act be curtailed.[7] Henry had already written Gigantes, congratulating her on her new position and suggesting he was willing to be a consultant to help set up a province-wide system of free-standing clinics. "I am very hopeful this is going to happen," he said before flying off to Bavaro Beach, a resort in the Dominican Republic, for a holiday. He didn't expect what awaited him on his return around five o'clock on Sunday, November 11. Word of Henry's secret New-foundland clinic had leaked out in that province.[8] Henry immediately placed a call to clinic manager Peggy Misener. He would fly in Tuesday night, and Wednesday he would hold a press conference making the clinic's existence official. It would begin what became, he later said, "one of the most dramatic weeks of my life."

CHAPTER 19

"UNCLE HENRY'S SHOE STORE FRANCHISE"

FOR THREE SATURDAYS NOW, Sandra Lanz, Janet Chernin and Dr. Claude Paquin had quietly packed up equipment and supplies from the McCully Street clinic to take with them on their weekly flight to St. John's, Newfoundland. On this Saturday afternoon, October 27, 1990, they slipped into town, silently entering a white clapboard house in the subdued medical office district. There Dr. Paquin performed six abortions, bringing the total number of abortions that had been performed in the unofficial clinic to eighteen. This was the newest Morgentaler abortion clinic, codenamed "Uncle Henry's shoe store franchise." Only five CARAL members knew of its existence. Earlier that month, one of them, Noreen Golfman, a Memorial University professor and CBC commentator, had stood in front of more than a hundred supporters in a downtown park on a sunny afternoon and shouted that it was about time Henry Morgentaler came to town. "Everybody whooped it up enthusiastically — if not in ignorance," she later reported.

A Newfoundland clinic had been in the works since November 1989, when Henry borrowed the phone in Anne Derrick's Halifax office to put a call through to Toronto and to Elinor Ratcliffe.

"What would you say if I said I was ready for Newfoundland?" he asked her.

She'd been waiting so long to hear those words. Ratcliffe was one of Newfoundland's first pro-choice activists and had met Ed Ratcliffe, her future husband, when she'd attended the inaugural meeting of CARAL in Ottawa. Since then, CARAL had maintained a small but hardy presence in the intensely religious and isolated society of Newfoundland.

A September 1980 CARAL newsletter described many of the group's problems:

> There are some people in these areas supportive of our activities
> but each of these areas are one-industry company towns where it is
> difficult to "make waves." Within St. John's our membership num-
> bers 65, although members are fairly generous financially. Local
> people are very hesitant to get involved and most of our workers
> and members are people who have settled here from elsewhere.
> We can only speculate that local people are too intimidated by
> being in a small area.

In May 1980, Cornerbrook's hospital folded its therapeutic abortion committee, leaving the Health Sciences complex in St. John's to serve the entire province. They would only take women who were less than twelve weeks pregnant. "Right now we are in dire straits," CARAL representative Sally Grenville wrote in the newsletter:

> Pressure has been increasingly heavy by the Anti-Choice groups
> here. Every day during Lenten season, high school girls from our
> largest Catholic high school picket the hospital. On Good Friday
> they are joined by their parents, relatives, friends and clergy. Press
> coverage is extremely biased in their favour. The press, especially
> the CBC, wouldn't cover our public meeting... said it had no
> local interest! We have consistently and constantly lodged com-
> plaints.... In St. John's we have 2 daily papers. Letters to the
> Editor average 5-1 for anti-choice. We have been trying to keep a
> record of the Pro-Choice letters that have not been printed, but
> this is sometimes difficult to do.

By 1981, only one doctor in the province would perform abortions, and only on one morning a week. Women could easily find themselves on the waiting list for six to seven weeks. Pro-choice spirits were buoyed when Henry flew into St. John's in October of 1981 for an extensive round of interviews, followed by a public meeting, but by 1983 Liberal opposition leader Steve Neary was calling the St. John's Health Sciences Centre "a slaughterhouse." Optimistically (and inaccurately), a CARAL member announced that year that Newfoundland would have a clinic within twelve to eighteen months. But all that ensued within the time frame was Henry's March 1985 jab at then minister of justice (and Newfoundlander) John Crosbie — if he wasn't about to change Canada's abortion laws, then Henry would have to open a clinic in Newfoundland anyway.

Elinor Ratcliffe had often urged Henry to live up to his rhetoric, to say, as he was now, "You get me the clinic and I'll open." He didn't have the money to buy a place himself, he explained, and he knew no one there would rent to him. "Of course I bought the clinic," Ratcliffe stated, a clapboard building located on 202 LeMarchant Road, in a respectable part of town, close to two hospitals and accessible to patients. CARAL began the work to build a community support group stealthily and slowly. For once, Henry was in no hurry. He had assumed he would wrap up his legal affairs in Nova Scotia by 1990, the next summer, and would resume operating the Halifax clinic, before pushing the public relations button activating the St. John's operation.

Meanwhile, he appeared briefly in a Manitoba court, fighting the government about its refusal to pay health insurance money for women having abortions at his clinic. And he had agreed to participate in a public debate — "Christianity Versus Secular Humanism: Which Is a More Rational World View?" — at three universities in Southern Ontario. His opponent was Dr. William Craig, an American born-again Christian and a research scholar at Belgium's University of Louvain. The one at the University of Toronto, before an audience of academics, was particularly worrisome to Henry. According to the *Toronto Star*'s former religion editor Michael McAteer, Craig had "obvious debating skills" and the Campus Crusade for Christ's national director told McAteer that Craig had handily won the debate with Henry at the University of Western Ontario. Henry was transparently eager to speak about more than abortion; however, he was rarely asked his opinion on other subjects. He was Canada's foremost Humanist, the organization's only well-known advocate, and he was all too aware it had not become the home for stellar intellectuals and moral leaders he wished it to be. But its members were thoughtful and sincere, and many didn't want Henry to participate in the debates with Craig. Some thought Henry was being set up. Others believed Henry was out of his intellectual depth. Henry may have had his doubts, as well. After the debate at Western, he asked a Humanist colleague to draft his text and said he would pay $500. His colleague, well versed in Craig's arguments, worked up a paper providing Henry with a response to every one of Craig's points. But Henry fell back on his well-used arguments and was intellectually sideswiped during the University of Toronto debate. Henry's colleague cringed in the audience.

After the debate, Henry flew south to join Arlene, Benny, the child's nanny and, a day or two later, Yann, at Club Med in St. Lucia. He felt so good he would no longer take his Verapamil pills for hypertension. Arlene had been indirectly responsible for that. Under her tutelage, Henry was eating more vegetables and less red meat and drinking teas instead of his morning coffee. He had begun to exercise and swim regularly. On that holiday he cut out alcohol, started tai chi and did so much exercise his muscles ached. He attributed his hypertension to "stress and inner tension due to the fact the small arteries always constrict, so it's basically psychosomatic." He decided he would conquer that. Already the nature of his dreams had altered. He still awoke in sweat-soaked agitation, after having been surrounded and smothered by menacing Nazis, but such dreams were outnumbered now by other dreams in which he was safe, respected and powerful. In those he talked with Mikhail Gorbachev, a man whom Henry then believed had "single-handedly almost changed the course of the limits of the atomic armaments race," with France's famed General de Gaulle and with Claude Ryan, a respected if not revered former journalist and education minister of Quebec. In all dreams, the conversations were cordial, the discourse was between equals. Although he couldn't stop battling the system, Henry could at least now acknowledge that he had arrived.

Well, you could say, of course, that I am famous in my own right, but [I had these kinds of dreams] even before I was famous. I think that the possibility of [my] greatness or fame was always there. Some of these people obviously became household words and you can relate to them because of their image, and this is similar, probably, to the way people can relate to me now when they see me and they get all moved and flustered and excited and stimulated by the fact they met a famous person. So in my dreams I relate to these people on an equal basis where I evaluate things, ask them questions, offer them advice and become intimate with them.[1]

He and Arlene had moved into a fine, large home of their own, which was deliberately not located within one of Toronto's coveted neighbourhoods but was, again deliberately, on a quiet street not far from one of the city's green and private ravines and one of its finest public schools. Benny was thriving. He was small, with a wiry grace, and he brimmed with energy. He had his mother's dramatic pale skin tones and dark curling hair, but his face was the same elongated oval shape as that of his father, whom he called "Henry." Benny amused Henry, while Arlene controlled her husband, if only in this domestic sphere, by catering to his every need. Arlene had set out some rules for her and Henry's relationship the way she set out the shirt and tie each morning that he was to wear. Heading the list was monogamy, and Henry was faithful, at least for a while, before his exuberant, spontaneous, sensual — and needing — side re-asserted itself. He loved women. He respected them, appreciated them and genuinely enjoyed being in their company. Despite his status in the movement, and perhaps because of his physical stature, he has always appeared boyish and warm to many women he encountered. Lesbian women found him safe and lovable, but more than a few heterosexual women had experienced how Henry's appreciation of women included an open invitation. "Oh, yeah, I've seen that look in his eye," said one. "Every parting with Henry is an opportunity to go to another level with him. It's intense. He's looking. He's interested. But you have to be interested back, and a lot of women have been." There have also been miscues — a hand straying too far up a supporter's leg after a press conference in Winnipeg, a sexual overture at the home of a clinic employee — but they were not repeated after the first rebuff, and the original affectionate working relationships were restored. Henry's image was too tied in with the cause, and the cause of reproductive freedom was too important or at too-critical a juncture for women to be offended. And many understood how important sex was to Henry to feel connected and to feel intensely. When Arlene realized Henry wouldn't ever be monogamous, even though he had thought he could be at different times, but that his extracurricular relationships didn't lessen Henry's commitment to her and Benny, she said all right, had a bit of a celebration and declared neither of them had to be faithful. That did confound Henry temporarily, but he wanted his freedom enough and Arlene so much then that he reluctantly agreed to that equality clause.

In Arlene he had found a strong woman, which he knew he needed, and a generous woman, which he was now learning he also needed. She encouraged him to telephone Mike, who was still angry but never refused his calls. She worked hard to build a relationship with Yann, who was courteous, never close, with her but whom Benny worshipped. When Yann was with them, Henry was transported with happiness. With Yann's birth, Henry was finally much of the person he wished to be. And Yann was his witness. He had been at the press conferences; seen the attention, respect, gratitude his father culled. Yann was a natural and eager entertainer, and at all the Club Med holidays he would leap onto the stage with Henry, imitate Elvis, make the people laugh and jump up in standing ovations. On the hills at Quebec's famous Grey Rocks ski resort, they were in sync on the snow, a son at ease reflecting his celebrity father. He looked like his mother, but in his spirit Yann was a miniature Henry — and Henry was reliving himself through Yann. Charming but undisciplined when younger, the boy could command every fibre of his father's attention just by entering the room, and he knew it. "When Yann came everyone else might as well have disappeared," Jean Rankin noted.

Carmen and Yann had moved back to Montreal late in 1989. An enthusiastic consumer of yoga and New Age–style alternative therapies, she had become a therapist. Her shingle read Dr. Carmen Wernli because she had taken a course in New York State on alternative medicine. "It was a five-day course. Five days," sputtered Mike Morgentaler. "When I saw [Bamie's wife] Suzie, who has a Ph.D. from Harvard in psychology, I said, 'How many years did your Ph.D. take you? Why did you waste so much time? See what Carmen can do!'" Her therapy involved channelling, diet, massage and more; she told Henry she could cure diabetes and some cancers. Henry just laughed. "She said she was getting wonderful results. She even believed it." He wasn't going to argue, not when she had brought back his boy. She was eager to have Henry establish a $200,000 pension fund for Yann. "As if I would leave him out [of my will]. He is one of my heirs," Henry said. "But Carmen was suspicious and wanted to make sure, and in the bargaining, she said she would return to Montreal if I set up a fund for Yann." They proceeded to work out the divorce settlement. Henry agreed to pay her $2,600 a month, even during the six months a year Yann lived in Toronto. She agreed to stay in Montreal at least three years. As far as Henry was concerned, he had negotiated the optimum arrangement. He did not want Yann ever to be in the position of having to choose; the child knew he was all his mother had. This way Henry saw more of Yann without having to sacrifice time from the abortion crusade, which was about to experience a major setback as Bill C-43, the proposed new abortion bill, came to a vote in the House of Commons.

At a springtime rally in Ottawa led by the National Action Committee on the Status of Women's new president, Judy Rebick, and attended by seven hundred people, he declared "no self-respecting female MP could vote in good conscience for such a law."[2] Compared with past performances, his protest appeared somewhat perfunctory. It was women in CARAL and other pro-choice groups who were sounding the alarm about Bill C-43. Henry later admitted he never thought it stood a chance of passing. He considered the legislation so vague that it left the government only one option: to introduce a subsequent bill that put an upwards limit on the number of weeks of pregnancy at which an abortion would be permitted. "I was sure the government would have to abide by the Supreme Court decision," he said. Failing that, "Bill C-43 would have been easy to circumvent." He could live with Bill C-43, but he preferred not to. When he said as much, he was told by some CARAL members that the justice minister, Kim Campbell, was taking his word and bandying it about as an endorsement. "She was on live radio saying if Dr. Morgentaler can live with it, it should be satisfactory to the pro-choice forces, which obviously it wasn't," Henry recalled. "I was urged to rebut, but I never got around to it. Somehow it didn't seem important. If the law would force us to be hypocritical, we would be hypocritical." Mulroney himself had advised his cabinet to support the legislation. When the vote was taken in the House of Commons on May 29, 1990, only thirteen Tories voted against it, none of them women. Mulroney was absent. The bill passed by 140 to 131 votes. "They are sending us back to the coat hanger," Carolyn Egan despaired,[3] as many doctors across the country immediately announced they would stop performing the procedure. In Toronto Henry told four hundred protestors in front of the clinic that he had no intention of stopping. "We will, however, have to get the women to sign a paper to confirm that they feel the pregnancy is a health risk. The new law figures us all to become hypocrites," he said.[4] When a twenty-year-old Toronto woman bled to death after a self-induced abortion, pro-choice supporters blamed the government's new legislation now on its way to the Senate for the final vote. "We demand that the federal Tories let their bill die and let the women of Canada live," Cherie MacDonald said.[5]

On October 30, Henry was scheduled to make a presentation in his own name to the Senate about Bill C-43, but at the last minute decided to appear not on behalf of the pro-choice movement but as part of the Humanist Association of Canada. He asked psychiatrist Wendell Watters and longtime Humanist colleague Blodwen Piercy to appear with him. Henry remembered thinking of his appearance as a "historic occasion":

> Twenty-three years ago, on October 19, 1967, I presented a brief of the Humanist Fellowship of Montreal in which, backed by the Humanist Fellowships in Toronto and Victoria, we claimed that women should have a right to abortion at least in the first three months of pregnancy as a right and not as a privilege. This brief to me was a historic brief in that it changed my life . . . and here I was

again presenting another brief in the name of the Humanist Association of Canada, which I had created as a result of my initiative to present the original brief, and it was a nostalgic experience for me.

The Society of Obstetricians and Gynaecologists of Canada had announced that 59 per cent of their members had stated they would stop providing abortion services when the bill became law. The government of Ontario, CARAL and many other groups had already been before the Senate to insist that the bill be defeated. Henry said about his own appearance:

> I answered all the questions and I finished the presentation by asking the senators to abort this bill. I said it may sound facetious coming from me, but basically what we are asking you to do is abort this bill, to do an abortion on this bill. Surprisingly none of them laughed or smirked. I had a sideways view of some of the reporters — they were laughing, smirking. It was very good — I was very proud of myself. I was in front of the cameras in both English and French and I had done a good job of knocking that bill.

After the presentation Henry fielded questions — simultaneously pleased and embarrassed that they were all directed at him — including one from an Alberta Tory asking if he would ever defy the law again. "I said I might but that it wasn't really relevant, that I probably wouldn't need to because circumstances were different. I didn't go into details, but it was clear there was no need for me to defy this bill personally. The difficulty would be with the many doctors being afraid to perform abortions or even counsel a woman to have an abortion because of the probability of prosecution, and the possibility of going to jail for two years. This would be a deterrent for many, but it certainly would not be a deterrent for me."

These were the same old words he'd used in the marches and demonstrations of the seventies and the eighties, in the battle for abortion rights, which had been won two years before. He may never have looked back. And he didn't intend to start looking back, so he turned to New-foundland and the birth of his newest clinic for consoling proof that his battle had not been lost or even stalled. But he and everyone else in the know had to keep the clinic a secret for a few weeks longer for the sake of one of their own, Wendy Williams, who was running in (and won) a tight race for the Ward 1 seat on St. John's city council. A for-mer co-ordinator of Planned Parenthood and an outrageous and effec-tive feminist president of the provincial Advisory Council on the Status of Women, Williams had been at the heart of Newfoundland's CARAL chapter and had worn her pro-choice stance on her t-shirt sleeve for years, but she didn't want the clinic to become an election issue. The election was on Tuesday, November 13; Henry offered up a compro-mise. The clinic would open in October, as planned, but he agreed to wait until after the election before announcing its existence. He cut it close: the press conference took place at 8:30 the morning after the elec-tion, at the Battery Hotel. Henry had been forced to act fast as news of the clinic had broken in time for it to become an eleventh-hour cam-paign issue, for Premier Clyde Wells to grimly respond that there would be no legal challenge from his government and for Henry to be named newsmaker of the week of November 11 by the *Sunday Express* "for cre-ating such a hullabaloo and capturing headlines all week without so much as stepping foot on the tarmac at Torbay Airport." Anti-choicers had already held their first vigil outside the clinic, and as Henry spoke to about fifty supporters and members of the media, council members, under outgoing St. John's mayor John Murphy, were preparing to meet to revoke the clinic's zoning permit.

The press conference was packed; Henry had galvanized the island's journalistic community. Euphoric and oblivious to any adverse reaction, he eagerly invited everyone to come and tour the clinic. A clinic nurse drove him, Golfman and clinic manager Peggy Misener there in her van, but about four hundred people were outside waiting for them, a thick procession of stern and angry people with placards, led by Newfound-land's Archbishop Alphonsus Penney. The gathering was ominous and obviously organized. Golfman scanned the crowd; she knew none of the faces. Henry decided they would get out of the car, which would keep going and return to the clinic sometime later. Golfman was rattled, but Henry had been through this before, she thought; he knew what to do, because she certainly didn't. Out of the van they scrambled, Golfman, Peggy Misener, then Henry.

The crowd saw him and surged. Immediately two dozen or more men in nylon jackets and peaked hats pressed in, completely surrounding them; burly, big men, bearing down on them with rage-filled faces, hurling screams of "Nazi murderer." There was no one to intervene. The two plainclothes policemen were caught back in the crowd and helpless. The two other uniformed officers were at the door, fifteen metres from where Golfman, Misener and Henry were trapped inside this furious mob, which had rimmed their quarry and were closing in, pushed nearer by the hundreds behind them. Misener was a small woman, shorter than Henry, and Golfman, who was about five-foot-eight, tried to shield them both. But the seething crowd lunged towards Henry, knocking his glasses askew, smashing his shoulder. He was punched in the back of the head, thrown off balance. He lost his momentum and was being swallowed up by the crowd. They hated him. At that moment, they were totally mad with hate for him. One of them leaned on Misener's shoulder and pushed down on her as if she could be ground out of sight into the earth. She was on her knees, immobile, seconds from possibly being trampled by the untrammelled crowd, when Golfman reached down, grabbed her by the wrist and pulled her upright. "Noreen is so fast. It was all in one motion. She looked down, realized what was happening and pulled me up, saying, 'Good thing I lift weights, eh?'" Misener recalled. The cries of a man on a nearby balcony tore through the air. "Murderer, murderer, murderer."

They got inside and closed the door, pushing away the sound and the horror. "That was the only time I ever saw Henry scared," Golfman said. "And he was scared. There's no doubt about that. For about a minute, maybe two. I was scared for an hour." The media had followed them in. As the camera lights went on, Henry pulled himself together and began the comforting ritual of the interview. This would not deter him. More than four hundred women from Newfoundland came every year to his Montreal clinic; altogether, about twelve hundred left the province for abortions every year. Newfoundland women needed and deserved a clinic in St. John's. "It was hell. It was exactly like going through hell," Golfman said. "I know the reason I calmed down and the reason I didn't pass out or freak out or whatever it is you do when you are paralyzed by stress was…Henry. I looked at this guy who had to give a press introduction and say, 'Welcome to the clinic,' and I watched him collect himself. He adjusted his tie. Took his coat off. Fixed his glasses. We were all shaking and he was collecting himself."

Later Golfman found out many in the crowd had been bussed in from Glace Bay and places in Nova Scotia like North Sydney. It was no consolation. Nobody in the clinic wanted to repeat the experience. The police decided they should all leave by the front door. Police reinforcements halted all traffic on the street to allow their car to pull in, pick them up and deliver Henry to a number of radio stations for more interviews. That afternoon he left for Winnipeg, where he was to work the next day. A nervous Misener hurried him through the airport, asking the Air Canada clerk to take Henry Morgentaler immediately to the first-class lounge. Accompanied by the same pair of plainclothes officers, Henry headed, instead, for a small concession stand to buy Benny a present. And, Misener said, he never once mentioned what had happened that morning. "He just kept saying that I should get some people to infiltrate the Right to Life movement," Misener recalled.

He was due to return to St. John's on November 22, for the party celebrating the clinic opening. "I'm a bit queasy about going to St. John's again in view of what happened," he admitted in his memoirs the evening before he was to leave. "I had not anticipated so much hate [being] thrown at me. Again the realization came back to me that I was such a hated person in Canada. It's true I am also loved and admired, but there are so many people out there who hate my guts. Call it fanaticism. Call it rage by people who are ignorant, who are anti-Semitic, who are steeped in traditional religious thinking. Whatever it is, it was very disquieting. Up to now I'm still waking up in the morning with the image of all that mob trying to lynch me or killing me or to do things to me." But he did return for the celebration with staff and supporters. Before the party shifted into high gear as it always did with

Henry, running long into the evening and well into the morning, Golf-man took Henry aside to tell him she finally understood what he had told her in the clinic that morning about Auschwitz having taught him he could face fear and that he could and would recover from it. "Fear is fear. At some level it is absolute," she said. Now that she had experienced it, she understood his certainty that everything was possible.

Henry instinctively had chosen the only moment in Newfoundland's recent history when a clinic could have been opened. The people there were distracted and unsure, shaken by the televised testimony of the boys of Mount Cashel and their awful, graphic descriptions of the violence and sexual abuse done to them by the Christian Brothers who had run that orphanage. "All the poison had come to the surface after years and years of denial. There was no hiding," Golfman said. The church had lost its moral authority. It could no longer lead the people it had betrayed. This was a society that had been completely dominated by the Roman Catholic church. Golfman, who had lived in St. John's since 1984 and married into one of the island's most established and prestigious families when she wed Bill Romkey, had never believed she belonged. She was Jewish, and St. John's was not anti-Semitic as much as it was un-Semitic. Jews were rare enough to be exotic. Once when she, Henry, Selma Edelstone and Judy Rebick were walking along LeMarchant Road, Golfman exclaimed, "Do you realize there are four of us in St. John's?"

In the summer of 1989 when Golfman was doing commentary on a popular local morning radio show, she did one three-and-a-half minute spot about Chantal Daigle. She was astonished at how many women thanked her for speaking out. "It was my first indication of how repressed, underground, the whole issue had been here." One of the callers was Misener, who had been deliberately keeping a very low profile while preparing for the clinic. By that time, Golfman had learned more about what was beneath the surface of this community, "how the women here had been fighting for years against so much crap, how they would do anything, not for Henry — Henry was irrelevant — but for the cause. They had so much guts." She was an academic, living then in a beautiful high-ceilinged, restored wooden house in downtown St. John's and teaching women's studies. In the classroom, in her life, she talked the talk. She could have witnessed what she knew was about to happen from the safety of the sidelines; she could have said she was too busy to get involved, and she would have been telling the truth. But she couldn't. "No, it was absolutely raw, very demanding. There was no choice about it."

Golfman became active in the Women's Centre. Many women there were "absolutely not" her middle-class colleagues from CARAL. "We're talking fierce-looking women, archetypal tattooed, male-eating, boot-kicking, every stereotypical lesbian characteristic," said Golfman. They told her about their lives in the outports, why they were radical, why many were re-examining their sexuality. They had lived the issue, scrambled for money to go off-island for an abortion. "And these were the women I needed — to escort the women to the clinic, to keep the secret, to have telephone trees, emergency backups, the whole plan, the whole elaborate game plan, like a military strategy of some kind." The women wanted her as their spokesperson. "It was absolutely vital to hear them say to me it is important you are doing this because you are a woman who is educated, you are a woman who can talk, you are not afraid to do this," she said. "These were women who didn't feel they had that sort of power. I felt this was something they were allowing me to do and I respected that."

Henry recognized that, as well. He took fifteen of the women from the Women's Centre to dinner at the Radisson Hotel for the belated clinic opening party and demanded they all sing "We Shall Overcome." "We're talking linen tablecloths and people making Hibernia deals," said Golfman. Henry was the only man at a table of tattooed women, hugging, kissing everyone, toasting, ordering more wine. The waiters were becoming more stiffly formal as the celebratory volume increased; the hotel detective hovered. Henry made speeches, acknowledging everyone, predicting continued success and ever more victories.

Misener had worked hard to make appropriate links, quiet connections with the community. Henry had found two doctors willing to perform the procedures, even though it often took them six hours to drive in from Burin Peninsula, where they worked. The city council's attempt to revoke the permit ultimately failed. Even Clyde Wells's government would ease up a year or more later and soften its payment policy. Newfoundland's Medical Care Commission began paying physicians $85 per abortion in September 1992. That night at the hotel, Henry made it all seem inevitable, as it turned out to be. Down the hall at the Radisson, Premier Clyde Wells was addressing a conference of teachers, and one of Henry's party decided to crash the meeting to have a word with the anti-choice premier. She was ejected, but that only increased the evening's hilarity. Henry announced to the dining room at large that he was "the singing abortionist," then he inquired, loudly, "Is there a Papist anywhere?" It was absurd, triumphant, outrageous, and an acknowledgment of the anti-authority rage that motivated Henry and so many of these women who had never been able to be themselves in the communities where they had grown up.

Every year since then there has been an anniversary party at the St. John's clinic, marking not only the clinic, but a turning point for many of the women involved with it, including Golfman. "After walking through that line, I knew anything was possible," she said. "Henry didn't heroize the experience at all. He talked about its necessity. That was tempered, of course, by the other Henry, who likes to go through it, to go through hell and have everyone say he is a hero. To be heroic just reinforces the power he has to keep doing it." And when Henry was heroic, Golfman learned, it reinforced the power of women. "It made me much stronger than I ever thought I was to survive something like that. That's the thing he has given women. He has given them the sense of their own strength. It's an odd thing for a man to do, but he has done that."

CHAPTER 20

OF A BOMBING AND BELONGING

ON THE FINAL DAY OF JANUARY 1991, Senator Pat Carney flew from one end of the country to the other to vote against Bill C-43. She and six other Conservative-appointed senators — including Manitobans Mira Spivak and Janis Johnson — voted no, bringing matters to a stunning 43 to 43 tie vote and a dramatic halt. In the Senate a tie vote was a defeated vote; abortion would not be put back into the Criminal Code and, as Justice Minister Kim Campbell made immediately clear, the federal government was walking away from the issue. She tried to sound a solemn note: "I think you'll find action by the provinces and that will generate a fair amount of litigation and legal challenges," she said after the vote. "We will have to wait for issues to make their way to the Supreme Court of Canada to provide the kind of national certainty that people want."[1]

But nobody on the pro-choice side was listening. "Abortion is now legal in this country and I believe it will be legal for another generation," crowed NAC president Judy Rebick. In Halifax, where Henry's case would go all the way to the Supreme Court of Canada, CARAL's Kathy Coffin declared the anti-abortion movement "a spent force in this country," the issue of abortion decided once and forever. "What we need to look at now is access and prevention."[2]

And in Edmonton, Henry was so jubilant he threw away the notes for his speech. That night he strolled onto the stage of the Jubilee Auditorium, all bravura and glint, eager to jostle with the sold-out crowd of fifteen hundred, most of whom were there to support his opponent, the ubiquitous theologian William Craig. Another evening sponsored by the Campus Crusade for Christ, it turned out like no other. When Craig said, disparagingly, that the day's Senate vote was a miracle, Henry immediately demanded, "How many of you believe in miracles?" of the born-again crowd. "I was in a great mood that day. At the debates I had been getting bored with my set speech and I had decided to wing it," he said. During intermission his opponent expressed surprise at Henry's improvisational skills. Henry's speeches were often cobbled together a few days, or even hours, before he was due to give them, but he rarely spoke in these settings without a written text. That night he was re-laxed, witty and touching. He talked about his time in the concentration camps and why he was an atheist, and as hostile as those in the audience were to his ideas and beliefs, they listened. Some even laughed when he announced he had been hanging around lawyers too much, so he wanted proof of the validity of those stories of their Jesus. "Don't tell me they came the next day and the cave was empty. Maybe it was the wrong cave." Laughing loudest was a small group of pro-choice advocates not even numbering twenty. These were the lawyers and their families with whom Henry had been consorting. They were high-powered, respected legal minds, employed by some of the city's top law firms, and they had been quietly working on creating a local Morgentaler Clinic for about eight months, ever since one of them, Ellen Ticoll, had decided to call up Henry and ask him to come to Edmonton and start a clinic.

"We were so surprised when he said sure. He hardly asked any details," said Ticoll. "He just said that if we organized it, if we found the building, did all the work, he would come." They found a squat, one-storey office not far from the Royal Alexandra Hospital, just off Stony Plain Road, theirs for $125,000. Over the phone, Henry agreed to buy it sight unseen. They were taken aback and activated by his trust. "The clinic was our field of dreams. If we build it, he will come," said Marie Gordon, lawyer and pro-choice activist.

That evening, after his speech, Henry joined the women for a party at Ticoll's casual, comfortable home to celebrate his performance and the end of Bill C-43, the last legal obstacle. He hugged everyone as he crowed, "I knew we would win," and claimed his hard lobbying had turned the tide. (Henry had written every senator a letter, including a personal one to John Buchanan reminding him this was his chance to redeem himself. But it was CARAL that targeted Pat Carney. "They worked on her for months," said Marcia Gilbert, CARAL's current executive director.) He would open a clinic in Saskatchewan next, he said, then Fredericton. It was thrilling and entirely perfect, they all agreed over many glasses of white wine. "It was an outrageously good party," said Gordon, who had just been given the rusty old key to the building. At 1:30 that morning she decided Henry should see the place he had bought. They drove there from the party. "It was decrepit, incredibly ugly. The floor was filled with gunk, and really, it was pretty discouraging," she recalled. They preferred to view it as bricks-and-mortar proof they had evolved into "active feminists rather than just theoretical feminists. It ground us in experience. We weren't just talking or changing the law, but working for the real major changes we had all been hunkering for. It was why we became lawyers," said Gordon. And at least Henry seemed to be very enthusiastic about its location.

They didn't know he was worried about opening in Edmonton. He saw that he should; too many Edmonton women came to his Winnipeg clinic, some enduring sixteen-hour bus rides each way. But the Alberta he knew was "Bible belt and redneck" and intolerant of his presence. After Henry's jury acquittal in Ontario, when Edmonton lawyer Sheila Greckol predicted there would soon be a clinic in Alberta, a petition with the signatures of thirty thousand people against it landed in the legislature. Greckol represented Abortion By Choice (ABC), a small CARAL affiliate that had started with a meeting of mothers and toddlers in Ellen Ticoll's backyard. "I was tired of seeing the pro-life posters showing little babies' feet all over town," Ticoll explained. For the first few years, the group met in backyards and basements and their goal was to convince more doctors to perform the procedure. Ticoll also wanted to change the law, but in those days Edmonton was so resolutely anti-choice they had to work from the ground up. The first time the media took any notice of their point of view was on January 16, 1985, when they brought in Henry to speak at the university. He had been splattered with ketchup twenty-four hours earlier at the Calgary airport, and that day he was compared to mass murderer Clifford Olson by the same Baptist minister (Jake Johnson) who stated, "If one woman was put to death for murder-abortion it would have a great effect on other attitudes."[3] But Henry was effusive and confident, coy only about whether his clinic would be in Calgary or Edmonton. (Since the abortion unit at Foothills Hospital in Calgary opened in 1983, the number of women leaving Calgary to go to Montana for abortions had sharply declined, as had the number of those on the waiting list. Edmonton seemed the obvious, if unstated, choice.)

The authorities didn't want Henry Morgentaler anywhere in the province. Although only thirty-two of the province's 124 hospitals had therapeutic abortion committees, Henry shouldn't "intrude," Alberta's attorney general said. The provincial abortion rate of 6,500 was "alarming," said the health minister, and "girls who get pregnant are at fault" for it, according to the then registrar of the Alberta College of Physicians and Surgeons. As Judy Rebick, Henry's fellow speaker accompanying him on this tour, noted, it would take a lot more groundwork to change community attitudes before Alberta would be ready for a freestanding abortion clinic.

The women in ABC brought in more speakers, including Nikki Colodny in 1987, raised funds and invited themselves out to schools and meetings of other women's organizations. They were making small but significant progress and alliances. But on October 1, 1987, many doctors stopped doing abortions when Alberta moved to ban extra billing. Until then, abortions had cost $200; provincial medicare paid $85 and doctors had extra-billed the rest. The government had raised its medicare fees for other medical procedures, but not for abortion. To compensate, some doctors began charging $75 to write the letter to the therapeutic abortion committee, but the province declared that it, too, was extra billing. "It didn't say much for the medical profession that they should refuse women this type of service because they weren't paid enough," Henry said. Premier Don Getty's health minister of the time, Marvin Moore, announced that "many abortions are used as birth control," neatly summing up the source of the government's resistance.

The situation in Edmonton, where abortions were being done at only one hospital and only up to twelve weeks, was "desperate," according to another lawyer, Deborah Miller. By this time the Abortion By

Choice group was meeting weekly but unofficially at Ciao, a chic Italian restaurant, to talk about access and the six-week wait for abortions in Edmonton. When Henry said he'd come to town with a clinic, "we went into a year and a half high," said Miller. Gordon had been narrowly defeated as a New Democratic candidate in the 1988 election; they hired her campaign manager, Deb Bowers, then later Pat Paradis, to do the detailed organizational work. Plotting in each other's oak-panelled office board rooms, they took turns handling, pro bono, various aspects of the clinic's legal work. Gordon faced the College of Physician and Surgeons and convinced it to grant Henry a licence under special registration, after it had initially refused his application because he had not had the necessary minimum eight weeks of postgraduate training in pediatrics. The new health minister, Nancy Betkowski, refused Henry's standard offer to set up a clinic and train doctors, but Henry did get a licence in November 1990. Edmonton would have its clinic within six months, Gordon told media.

It took almost a year. "Every step of the way was a battle," said Henry. If he hadn't become friends with Greckol, Gordon and Ticoll, he would have dropped the project. Tradesmen willing to work on the clinic were scarce; those who were hired charged beyond-premium rates. A Calgary doctor whom Henry had trained and hired to work at the clinic blurted its existence to the media; immediately the Right to Life forces challenged the clinic's renovation permit, effectively stopping all work while council debated the issue. Petty vandalism dogged the clinic for months after it opened. One architect quit after being harassed by Right to Life protestors. Construction site gates were locked, a contractor's paint compressor flooded and slogans were smeared on the walls. Absurd pamphlets were distributed, including one that read: "Wednesday Henry Morgentaler offered the provincial government that they could take over the operation of the abortion clinic. The reason, Henry Morgentaler can no longer perform abortions. Reason, Henry Morgentaler has AIDS." Legal action set back the schedule by about six months; the necessary extra security added another $20,000 to the clinic costs.

In July, flammable liquid was ignited at the back wall of the clinic, causing about $1,000 damage. Police said it was a professional job. That same month in a special supplement to the *Interim*, a Roman Catholic newspaper, the pro-life organization outlined everything they had done to keep Henry Morgentaler out of the province. They had met with Health Minister Nancy Betkowski, and delivered a petition with ten thousand names to the College of Physicians and Surgeons; their president had had a private interview with the College and every sitting provincial politician and all board members of the College of Physicians and Surgeons had been sent a video and copy of their organization's policy. On April 3, they had appealed Edmonton council's decision to allow the clinic's renovation permit, and although they lost, the appeal stopped work almost another full month until the hearing. Daily pickets frustrated workers on the site, the group reported. They were also picketing any firm working on the clinic, from the electrician to the waste management conglomerate. One of their group had fasted for forty days and "there was a profusion of miraculous medals" or medallions of various saints known to have special powers to heal, on the property next door to the clinic on 150th Street.

Disheartened, Miller called Henry one day to discuss the bleak situation. The architect had quit, every inch of the building was either in disrepair or ruins (renovations would end up costing $250,000) and the anti-choice people were launching another appeal. Henry wasn't alarmed. "It's not that big a deal. We'll just keep going. We can't let those zealots run our lives," he told her.

He was accustomed to setbacks. The Saskatchewan cabinet had vetoed a College of Physicians and Surgeons' by-law that would have allowed doctors to perform abortions at clinics outside hospitals. Even after the Nova Scotia government lost its Supreme Court appeal division ruling against Henry, the Saskatchewan government was mulishly appealing to the Supreme Court of Canada for their own hearing. Alarmist headlines appeared about the number of abortions hitting record highs in 1989 (up 6.8 per cent to 70,779) when Statistics Canada released its report in April. Few caught the good news: the medical complication rate from abortions had dropped from 3.2 to 1.6 per cent of all operations in 1988.[4] The mortality rate from abortions had also decreased dramatically. From 1965 to 1969, sixty-one women were known to have died from abortions; because abortion was illegal and then dangerous, there were probably many more fatalities whose cause was never, or was inaccurately, recorded. Between 1985 and 1989, four women died, including one from an illegal abortion. Close to 90 per cent of abortions were performed during the first thirteen weeks. "The rate of self-induced or clandestine abortion is probably minimal, and thus the biggest danger to the life and health of young women has almost disappeared in Canada due to our efforts to make abortion safe and legal," Henry wrote to the CARAL membership in a letter read out at their annual general meeting on April 24, 1991. (He was at the National Abortion Federation meeting in Chicago at the time.) A major coup occurred in June of that year when Ontario's NDP government quietly began full funding for Toronto's four free-standing clinics.

And in Edmonton, the sixth Morgentaler Clinic was ready. They had dealt with eleventh-hour restrictions from the College of Physicians and Surgeons that prohibited rhesus blood testing and the use of ultrasound in the clinic ("stupid, senseless," Henry fumed, "and made me extremely angry and frustrated"), when Gordon arranged for the law society president to have a conciliatory and convincing talk with the College. The ultrasound machine shipped from Toronto refused to work, and the College staff insisted on conducting an on-the-site inspection the day before the clinic was to open. Word of the opening date, Tuesday, September 17, 1991, had leaked and plenty of protestors were expected. Henry hired a security advisor, who organized the opening like a military manoeuvre. John Begg met with Henry and some of the women the night before at the Ramada Inn, where Henry was staying, and laid it out. He had hired a darkened-windowed white limousine, which would drive past the clinic and around to the back, drawing the protestors after it. Marie Gordon was to immediately follow with Henry in her beaten-up old Mazda and drop him at the front door. The staff, including Calgary doctor Ted Busheikin, would be expecting his arrival. This was to occur precisely at 8:30 in the morning. "We synchronized watches," said Gordon.

That night Henry didn't sleep well:

Deep down I was scared someone might want to attack me and
kill me. I know how easily these hate-filled people can target me. I
didn't have much fear of being killed outright, although that
would have been so sad for a man with so much overflowing
energy and the ability and determination to accomplish much
more in his life. What worried me most was the idea of being crippled, like a victim of a bullet that severs the spinal cord and causes
paralysis below the neck, or else a head injury that would take
away my mental capacities. However, even in such a case I still
would have the option of suicide or assisted suicide. What bothered me most was that I might not be there to be a strong influence
and role model for Benny and Yann, not to see them grow up,
which I want to see very badly.

Everyone was on tenterhooks. Gordon, Miller, Ticoll and the other
women took the day off work to be at the clinic. They brought friends
and husbands — "we figured we needed men there," said Miller — and
worked staggered shifts, beginning at six in the morning through to
noon. One woman was assigned to take photographs of the protestors
and any of their actions for the injunction affidavit being prepared that
same day by Sheila Greckol. (Henry was impressed when they got their
injunction the next day. "Sheila Greckol had prepared the injunction
against the picketers. It was served on them yesterday, and bingo, it was
granted today," Henry recorded. "Hurrah for Sheila. I like her a lot.
She is beautiful, intelligent, simpatico — what a sweet woman.") About
a hundred protestors showed up, most lured to the back of the clinic by
the limo. A few stayed up front, trying to prevent patients from entering. Security staff managed to keep the protestors contained, although
they repeatedly carried off Lianne Laurence each time she scaled the
chain-link fence. Laurence was a former journalist in her early thirties
who believed she had to rescue the unborn by "non-violent, direct protective action"[5] inspired by the resistance movements of India's Ghandi
or black civil rights leader Martin Luther King Jr. A part-time cook at
a local retirement home for priests, she felt it was her duty to appear
daily at the clinic. Greckol's injunction specifically named her, as well

as two other pro-life leaders, and Laurence served prison sentences amounting to almost three months as a result of several convictions for disobeying the clinic injunction. Ticoll represented the clinic many times in the next few months because Laurence continued to disregard the injunction.

Laurence and fellow protestors Gerard Liston and Leo Coyle were served with documents that first morning as, inside the clinic, Henry performed six abortions with a nurse holding a flashlight over his shoulder. The ceiling operating-room light had not yet been installed. "Pandemonium. Disorder was reigning supreme," Henry remarked. "However, we accomplished our job. Security was tight, and supervised ably by John Begg. Sharon [Broughton, from the Toronto clinic] was there. Otherwise nothing would have got off the ground." The party that night was again at Ellen Ticoll's home, the press conference the following morning went well, and as Henry flew back to Toronto that afternoon he toasted himself with two Scotches. "A new Morgentaler Clinic was born. Mazel Tov. May you grow and last a long time and accomplish many good deeds. I am proud of my accomplishment, proud of being able to overcome my fears and anxieties. Arlene, Bamie, Yann, Benny, you can be proud of me."

————

Two months later, protestors came back to the clinic, twice as many as on opening day, with signs and plastic fetuses and pictures of babies. They were going to shut it down that day, November 13, 1991, on the occasion of Edmonton's first-ever Operation Rescue. Anti-abortion protestors hurled themselves in front of cars coming into the clinic parking lot and lay down under them. They sat, shivering and determined, in clusters on the steps at the back door, refusing to let anyone pass. One nurse huddled in her car for three hours with a patient as the crowd pressed baby pictures against the car window. For hours patients couldn't get in or out. Eleven security guards hauled off kicking, punching and screaming protestors, while the police stood by. Only one patient didn't make it in as the staff worked in the operating room until nine o'clock that evening, then helped the lawyers gather information for affidavits

they would file for a broader injunction that would include all protestors who harass women seeking abortions. That was granted the
following day, which was also the first day on the job for Susan Fox,
a lawyer and clinic escort who had been named the new clinic manager. She inherited a clinic in chaos, and not just because of the anti-
choice action.

"The clinic had been floundering for three months," Fox said. It
needed a new business system, new floor plan, new paint, new lighting
and another $20,000 — "which Henry gave to me on blind faith." She
had few allies — even Planned Parenthood was angry the clinic
charged money. (In 1995 its fees were $375 for pregnancies of six to
eleven weeks, $475 for pregnancies of twelve to thirteen weeks and $575
for pregnancies of fourteen to sixteen weeks. The Alberta government
pays the physician fee of $107.97. If the patient doesn't have a health
card the clinic charges her another $125.) But the Edmonton police were
"excellent," Fox said, putting one man in charge of clinic protection and
sending him to Fargo, North Dakota, to study protests and gather information. The police had not interfered in the beginning because they
were testing the injunction.

By February the injunction was permanent, and most of the protestors obeyed the ruling, staying across the street from the clinic. About
twenty-five to thirty procedures were being done during the clinic's two
procedural days, even when the low-slung building flooded and water
ran in the back door throughout the newly carpeted building. Security
camera wires were constantly cut, the posted injunction was ripped
down and bottles were smashed on the front sidewalk, although that
may have had more to do with the pool hall two doors away. On its second anniversary, the clinic had its water hose stuffed through an air
vent and the water turned on, causing more flooding. "The protestors
were bigger and louder when Henry was here," Fox said, but there were
no more Operation Rescues. Later, Laurence moved to Ontario. The
clinic won a permanent injunction with the consent of a pro-life leader.
Campaign Life Calgary president Mike O'Malley told reporters that
pro-life proponents don't believe they are bound by the permanent
injunction, but are bound by the earlier, temporary injunction barring

protests or harassing activities by unknown persons. "We are [in the process of] challenging this temporary injunction in court."[6] There were no more unruly protests, just two or three dutiful protestors silently keeping vigil across the street on procedure days. When Henry came into town, Fox made sure everything was orderly and in order, including having milk for his tea and the *Globe and Mail* newspaper on his desk. After he spent the morning doing procedures, she would drive him to interviews, buy the hostess gift if he was staying at the house of Gordon, Paradis or Greckol and perhaps arrange a speaking engagement for him. Once the clinic was open, Henry never held another press conference in Edmonton.

His fights were with provincial governments now, and they were no less crucial, but much less dramatic. They were all about funding. "The Governments of Newfoundland, New Brunswick and Prince Edward Island all refuse to pay the doctors' fees for therapeutic abortions performed in clinics. They also refuse to pay for the facility fee for clinic abortions. Not only do they show a callous disregard for women's health needs, they in fact profit from women's misery by saving money for abortions not being done in their own province. How despicable," Henry wrote to supporters in what he called a "victory letter" after the defeat of Bill C-43 in the Senate. "I intend to sue the Governments of Newfoundland, Prince Edward Island and Nova Scotia for the recovery of doctors' fees," he added. He took the Manitoba government of Progressive Conservative Gary Filmon to court to get it to pay for clinic abortions. "I'm still angry, but it is a good change from before," he said. "At least now instead of being hauled into court by the government, I am hauling the government into court, which is a nice change for me."[7] (Six months after the 1988 Supreme Court decision, the province had passed a law stating no doctor would be paid for performing an abortion outside a hospital. Women paid about $300 for an abortion at the Corydon Avenue clinic.). Henry won the June ruling, allowing clinic doctors to bill for $145, the same amount then paid to doctors who performed abortions in hospitals. Declaring women shouldn't have to pay a cent, Henry initiated more court action to force Manitoba to pay the whole bill.

But a CARAL survey had found inequities across the entire country. For example, in Saskatchewan abortions were funded only if performed in a hospital and deemed medically necessary by two doctors. In Quebec, abortions were free in hospitals and the community health centres but only partially covered in women's centres and free-standing abortion clinics. To fight on all these fronts meant hours in faraway courtrooms, battling entrenched, mundane and stubborn laws. It was not the stuff of headlines. Henry could couch the issue in terms of access, talk about putting out a thousand small fires before they become one raging destructive blaze, but the issue was also about money, and even for someone as skilled as Henry with the media, it would be hard to appear a hero when the bottom line of the cause was cash.

Few media outlets could be as generous as CARAL's *Pro-Choice News*, which gave over two full pages to a question-and-answer interview with Henry in its Spring 1992 issue. "Governments should pay for women having abortions in clinics just as much as they pay for women having abortions in hospitals," he said, laying out his logic, step by step:

> The distinction is one that should not exist anymore. Before the 1988 Supreme Court Morgentaler decision, clinic abortions were technically illegal, whereas hospital abortions were legal and consequently abortions in hospitals were paid for under medicare. Before the ruling, provincial governments claimed that abortions were not legal if they were performed in a clinic, so why should they pay for them. This distinction's now gone. All abortions are legal, and the only justification for the government not to pay is to say "Clinics are outside the hospital system and if women choose to go to clinics, they should pay themselves." The problem with that argument is that very often they choose to go to clinics because there's no access, or access is insufficient, or the waiting list is too long, or the procedure involves more visits to the doctor's office, or because some hospital abortions are still done under general anaesthesia, which involves greater risk for the women.
>
> Clinic abortions, the way we provide them, are much better and safer than hospital abortions, especially if hospitals use general

anaesthesia. But, it's also true that many women choose abortion clinics...for other reasons as well. Women are here by choice in an atmosphere of support, understanding and empathy, which you don't have in many hospitals.

But very often the basis is that women don't have access: they have to wait too long and we know that every week of delay increases the complication rate by twenty per cent. So it's very important that these procedures be done as expeditiously as possible.

Henry made it clear the women's movement should take up his cause. "I think that this should be one of the actions of the women's movement in Canada — to press the provincial governments to make all abortions a procedure paid for under medicare so women are not penalized when they go to a clinic. The arguments are very good; clinic abortions cost at least half as much as abortions in hospitals. Their quality is excellent and their complication rate is low," he said in the interview. Although some women within the movement actively opposed Henry's profit-oriented clinics, most were fervent supporters of his fight for universal access. But even CARAL, by then an efficient and established Toronto-based national lobby organization sharing office space with a prolific and independent educational component in the Childbirth by Choice Trust, wasn't as sharply or solely focused on the Henry Morgentaler–activated aspects of the abortion issue. They continued to support him and his fight for increased abortion access, but CARAL was also busy encouraging the testing and marketing of the abortion pill RU-486 in Canada. "We believe that RU-486 has proven to be safe, effective and potentially private and accessible; it should be released for testing as an abortifacient," CARAL president Kit Holmwood wrote in the same issue of *Pro-Choice News*. Henry also supported the use of RU-486 as "an additional method which should be available to women," but he warned it would benefit only a small percentage of them because the drug was good only for seven weeks after the last menstrual period, or about five to six weeks postconception. Nevertheless, it looked like this next stage of his battle would be a long and wearying legal struggle, which his supporters could only witness, not in which they could engage.

Then, at 3:23 on the morning of May 18, Victoria Day, 1992, a bomb destroyed the Harbord Street clinic. The double-bricked east wall buckled and broke; the front bulletproofed window was hurled across the four-lane road; the back wall blew apart. The explosion was heard a kilometre away, while the couple sleeping upstairs next door were blasted from their bed, glass and debris raining down on them. A thick, foul-smelling smoke filled the air; flames four and a half metres high leaped into the night from the clinic's back second- and third-storey windows.

The video cameras, two out back, two more in trees in front — part of an elaborate, newly installed $50,000 security system of glass-breakage detectors, shock sensors and motion detectors — had recorded a gloved hand pushing open the back gate at ten minutes after three. Because the pairs of cameras worked in sequence, one camera cut away, before coming on again in time to catch a man with two containers of gasoline, then later, the man coolly drilling a hole through the clinic's back door. The last frames showed the man retreating with the two gas cans. Forty seconds later the clinic exploded. Police said two people were involved, one of whom poured gasoline under the door, which spread over the basement floor, as the vapour from it crept throughout the building. A Roman candle was later found nearby; police believed it ignited the gas, setting off the bomb that destroyed the clinic but, miraculously, took no lives. "I was walking home from a friend's house at about 3:30 in the morning of Monday, May 18. I had just passed the clinic, and had just put my key in the door, when the bomb in the clinic went off. This was no more than thirty seconds after I walked by," a young woman later wrote Henry. Less than five hours after the blast, the president of Choose Life Canada (and the clinic's former neighbour), the Reverend Ken Campbell, issued a press release, in which he wondered whether the explosion was "an Act of God."

Grim-faced, Henry looked at his gaping, crumpled, teetering clinic and knew at once that it wasn't. Just a few months earlier, youths had set fire to a gasoline-soaked tire they had hauled onto the porch, which had gutted the clinic foyer. The same week, a woman who had booked an appointment planted a stink bomb in the clinic washroom. Those were annoyances, but this was cruel, deliberate violence, a swift and destructive strike from enemies bent on extermination. "This is a sign of the moral bankruptcy of the so-called pro-life movement. They cannot act by democratic means, so they resort to criminal acts — violence and arson," he said. He had handed over to police photographs taken by clinic security of a pair of men seen loitering about the clinic two week before the bombing. He believed, and still does, the firebombing was the work of American anti-abortion activists, although no arrests were ever made and he has no concrete proof of the perpetrators' identities, let alone their nationalities. According to the National Abortion Federation, there were thirty-four bombings, sixty-one arson and forty-four bombing attempts at American abortion clinics between 1977 and 1991. In a third of the cases, arrests had been made, but no one had been directly connected with an organized pro-life group. Nevertheless, Carolyn Egan and other activists noted that Operation Rescue had just finished trying to close down Buffalo's four clinics the previous month and had failed. "Yes, we're scared," Maria Corsillo, the Scott Clinic manager and Bob Scott's wife, told media. But that afternoon, Henry stood defiant on a plastic milk crate before a crowd of about a thousand. "What happened here is no doubt a setback," he said. "But if these people believe that they will deny women access to abortion — no, they made a big, big mistake."[8]

That morning he had appeared close to cowed as he wandered outside the brick-strewn rubble. The lines on his face cut deep; for once he looked all of his sixty-nine years. In the back of the building were mocking mementos: the metal sign stating the premises were protected and monitored remained unscathed, as did the Morgentaler Clinic sign. Damage was close to $600,000. He vowed to rebuild, but admitted the clinic had long before outgrown the building and he had been thinking of relocating.

Meanwhile, Henry began operating out of Bob Scott's Gerrard Street clinic on Wednesdays, evenings and weekends when Scott was not using it. The Morgentaler Clinic's clerical and nonnursing staff set up lawn chairs in the laneway behind the Harbord Street clinic for the first week, and were using cell phones to contact insurance firms and to try to find new premises even as firefighters combed the rubble for clues. "I don't remember being frightened of more violence happening. We were running on adrenaline," said Linsey Macphee, who was then Henry's executive assistant. They found an unused space behind a neighbouring hairdresser on Harbord Street for the administrative staff. Henry finally rented cramped temporary clinic premises in a three-bedroom Victorian row house on a raw and hopeless section of Gerrard Street a few doors away from Scott's clinic. Henry did his paperwork at home and his medical work at the Gerrard Street clinic, and stopped in on his administrative staff in the room behind the hairdresser only to drop off typing he needed done and to pick up messages. They saw little of him and were becoming demoralized, Macphee said. Henry organized a lunch and several dinners for all staff to revive the esprit de corps, but by the end of the summer "things started to go wrong and the excitement faded away," Macphee said. "I think it was a delayed reaction with everyone." Henry's friend Jean Rankin was working at the clinic then. Her income from psychotherapy had dropped and Henry had offered her a counselling job. "The place on Gerrard was awful," she recalled. "Outside it was disgusting. There was a lady next door who stunk to high heaven, who would come out and sweep the sidewalk every day. There were condoms all over the place — it was hooker heaven down there. But once you walked inside [the clinic] it was heaven. Henry knows how to be with people and how to get the best out of them."

The NDP provincial government pledged $420,000 over two years to monitor the harassment of abortion service clients and providers to determine what to do to improve security at Ontario's four abortion clinics. Backed by CARAL and OCAC, Henry asked the province to push for a public injunction to keep away protestors from all free-standing abortion clinics. But the attorney general's office suggested Henry dip into the $420,000 already pledged for monitoring to gather the information, which they could use to apply for an easier-to-obtain private injunction. This occurred as Henry lost his first court bid to move his three-year-old Harbord Street injunction to his temporary quarters at the Scott Clinic. "The problem is that violence follows Henry. It's not just because of the location," said his lawyer, Clayton Ruby,[9] before permission was finally granted for Henry to move his Harbord Street injunction to his new location. Meanwhile, Henry launched a cross-country fund-raising campaign of newspaper ads to rebuild the clinic, "bolster security at existing and future clinics" and pay off his legal bills.

Everyone was keeping a watch on the United States, where the Supreme Court went to the brink of replacing the landmark 1973 *Roe* v. *Wade* decision and overturning legal abortion. Justice Sandra Day O'Connor wrote that there had been no change in Roe's legal underpinnings that declared abortion to be a constitutional right for American women. But the vote had been close — 5 to 4 — and the Supreme Court had upheld a Pennsylvania law restricting access to abortion. Although it struck down a provision that a wife must notify her husband and reiterated that individual states must not apply "undue burden" on those seeking an abortion, it upheld some restrictions, including a mandatory twenty-four-hour waiting period and parental consent for anyone under eighteen. Henry viewed the American law as "hanging by a thread" and predicted more and more Americans would cross to Canada to have abortions. He was already advertising his Montreal clinic in northern New York State, he told an *Edmonton Journal* staff writer, and he would soon place ads for his Winnipeg clinic in North Dakota and Minnesota, where abortions were difficult to obtain. But he also had to deal with foes closer to home.

He had found a site for a new Toronto clinic — a sleek, grey office building, where he could rent most of the spacious second floor, have his own entrance and design the most advanced and beautiful clinic in the world. No more sandblasted, wickered and wallpapered renovations, with quilts and quirks and charming inconveniences. Abortion was legal and a medical procedure, and it deserved the respect of professional and top-notch surroundings. Feeling secure enough to rent, he triumphantly signed a ten-year lease in October, as six of the other eight building tenants met hurriedly to worry about what effect an abortion clinic might have on their businesses. Henry didn't care about what the neighbours thought. He was moving his clinic (and his injunction) uptown, away from the relaxed, Bohemian jumble of New Age bookstores and smart cafés spawned by Harbord Street's proximity to the

university, right onto the front steps of the middle-class burghers
of North Toronto and Leaside. The office building was on Bayview
Avenue, a respectable centre of neighbourhood hardware stores and
bakeries, as well as upscale lifestyle accessory shops. Officially the clinic
was around the corner on Hillsdale Avenue East, a residential street of
family homes with brass or porcelain number plates on renovated fronts
and minivans parked in mutual drives or on the road out front. Alerted
by a tenant worried about the clinic's effect on his business, the powerful and vocal area ratepayer groups protested vigorously, handing out
anti-choice literature that detailed the clinic's history of bomb threats
and predicting that property values would plummet. OCAC and CARAL
countered with their own information campaign. Clinic renovations
were temporarily halted on a technicality. An ad hoc group called Let's
Preserve South Bayview petitioned the City of Toronto's planning
department to re-assess the clinic's right to relocate in their neighbourhood. They had the support of at least one of the local councillors. The
flustered landlord offered Henry equivalent space in a building on
University Avenue across the street from the Toronto General Hospital,
but he refused. He was embarking on renovations, he wanted to be
right where he was and he was not leaving because an advertising
agency believed it was losing business.

He was determined to belong there.

CHAPTER 21

GRAND STARTS AND GETTING EVEN

Tᴴᴇ ᴍᴏʀɢᴇɴᴛᴀʟᴇʀ ᴄʟɪɴɪᴄ that opened at 727 Hillsdale Avenue East in February of 1993 had steel-clad security, a low-lit and spacious waiting room that didn't double as a recovery area, a staff lunchroom, a sound system sensitive to every nuance in the compact discs playing classical music whenever Henry was in the operating room and "the most up-to-date techniques and equipment," as he never tired of telling every visitor. It was also fully funded by the Ontario Ministry of Health.

Henry threw a large, festive opening party, heavily secured, but none of the other tenants in the building came. Nevertheless, Henry thought his new clinic was near perfect, except, he paused thoughtfully, "maybe for an elevator." Incoming patients never saw those leaving; the aspirators, which tended to be noisy, were behind a soundproof wall; the lighting was soothing, the security top of the line. "It is one of the best appointed clinics in the world," he boasted. With these 630 square metres, Henry had achieved the medical mainstream, and not by capitulating, but by staying his own course.

On the office wall opposite his desk, positioned so he could see it whenever he looked up from his paperwork, was the most important item he'd rescued from the bombing: his framed poster of Albert Einstein, bearing the words "Great minds have always encountered violent opposition." He asked a nurse, also a medical photographer, to take a picture of him standing by the poster. As she prepared for the shot, he began speaking, as if to Einstein, for it was momentous for him to have this clinic, which represented the culmination of everything he had

worked for for twenty-five years and everything he wanted. Even down
to the colours. There was nothing striped, nothing homespun; everything was the finest, the latest. The corner office was his, spacious
enough to easily accommodate his large, burnished rosewood desk,
matching recliner, credenza and wardrobe. On a pillar was a colour
photo of Arlene proudly holding a newborn Benny, and on the wide
ledge of the low-slung window overlooking Hillsdale Avenue sat a
framed photo of Bamie, a photo of and artwork by Benny and a portrait
of Yann. Three smiling handsome sons, but nowhere did Henry have
a likeness of his daughter.

Goldie Morgentaler had not spoken to him for three years. Nor has
she ever publicly spoken about him. "It's an accident my being related
to him," she told this writer. She had moved back into the house on
Barton Street to live with her mother, with whom she was very close
and who also remained estranged from Henry and angry with him.
Goldie was preparing her doctoral dissertation on Dickens and working as a translator, as well as writing an occasional column on language
for Montreal's English-speaking newspaper, the *Gazette*. In *Morgentaler: L'Obstiné*, Sylvie Halpern's biography, published in French in 1991
just after the defeat of Bill C-43, Henry was quoted as saying some
things that angered Goldie intensely, including referring to her as a per-
petual student. But she had been estranged from her father for years
before that. There was tension when Henry had stayed at her place in
New York for his primal therapy sessions, because Goldie had stopped
and started several graduate study courses as she searched for her academic niche. Bamie acted as emissary between the two, aiming for reconciliation, and asked his sister on behalf of his father why she was so
angry. He reported back that Goldie said Henry was excessively critical
of her while she was growing up, demanding excellence in maths and
sciences, and wasn't good at hiding his exasperation when she didn't
achieve high enough marks in those subjects, which came so readily
to him.

"Is that all?" Henry exclaimed when he heard. But he knew it wasn't.
He had written her, sent her money and cried because of her hatred for
him. It was so much easier to approve of Bamie's life path, swift and

straight into the familiar, familial field of medicine, to applaud that he was practising and doing research in Boston, and teaching at Harvard Medical School; that he was married and had fathered two daughters, the younger born on Henry's birthday. The families often vacationed together — Arlene and Susan were not too far apart in age and Henry and Bamie competed on ski hills and at the Ping-Pong table. Bamie Morgentaler's medical specialty was male impotence; together father and son would joke about opening up shops across the street from each other. "I don't think it's a coincidence I ended up in the United States," Bamie acknowledged. "I didn't like being known as Henry Morgentaler's kid. I wanted to be known for me, rather than my father, and within my field people do know me and that's important to me." He credited Henry for "one of my most affecting memories," handed down when he was about five, he said. He had been at loggerheads with some friends, and had definitely held the minority opinion. "My father told me it was possible for everyone in the world to have a different opinion from you and you to be right. He has lived that way. That was a gift — to know that public opinion may not be the truth and that having a sense of justice is okay." His father always had internal confidence that "what he wants to do is worth doing and that he was right," said Bamie Morgentaler. "Some might call it stubbornness, depending on the outcome." He didn't know what had caused the rift between his father and sister, but a book Henry gave him when he was twelve might have an explanation. It was about astronomy, stars and constellations called red giants and white dwarfs and "some stars which burn so incredibly bright there are casualties."

Henry wondered if Goldie's feelings originated in her childhood, not when his marriage to Eva ended or even when he began to stray from the marital bed, but sometime earlier. Goldie had had scoliosis of the spine, for which Henry had found expert, innovative treatment — but it was painful treatment, especially for a child to endure. He knew she had to have the treatment and had used his parental authority to have her undergo an operation against her wishes when she was twelve years old. Now, years later, he cautiously had begun to write her occasional letters, commenting carefully on the content of her newspaper columns, which Gertie Katz regularly clipped and sent to him. His only daughter had turned her back on him more than a decade ago, but her absence in his life was even more marked now that he had lost another son.

Yann and Carmen had moved back to Chile. Henry had thought they were going there only for a four-week vacation over the 1992 Christmas holiday. He didn't know Carmen had packed up the Montreal apartment and shipped everything on to Santiago. Yann had been living a part of the year with each parent. Adept at shifting from one world to the other, he had been enrolled in two schools and had a computer in his bedroom in each home. After attending Hillcrest Public School in Toronto, then passing the entrance examination for Upper Canada College, the prestigious private school for boys that Henry so wanted him to attend, Yann decided, instead, to stay enrolled in Montreal's Collège Marie-de-France. He was living with his mother as she packed everything up to leave Montreal forever, not for a holiday. But Yann said nothing about it to Henry until he phoned him in mid-January from Santiago. It was a tough call for both of them. He liked it in Santiago, Yann said to his dad haltingly; he wanted to stay in South America, and he had already enrolled in a school where he was happy. Henry was stricken — and powerless. If he hired lawyers to enforce the joint-custody agreement, Carmen might disappear with Yann again. And his son was almost a teenager, old and courageous enough to tell his father what he wanted for himself. Henry wouldn't be fighting Carmen for Yann; he would be fighting Yann, which he could never do. Carmen had no man, nobody but Yann, while he had a partner and another child, Henry told himself. Yann had chosen Carmen over him because of his sense of loyalty. This was not the time "for protracted legal wrangling," Henry said as, for the first time in his life, he gave in. Yann would fly up to be with him for a week once or twice during the summer, and for six weeks the following winter. It would have to do.

Henry was busy, anyway. He was soon to sign another deal with the Ontario government to train medical students in the clinic, a labour of love signifying one more small but important personal victory. The clinic had evolved from symbol of a grass-roots political movement to a state-of-the-art medical facility, *his* state-of-the-art medical facility, although the government of Ontario paid the bills and its Independent Health Facilities Act governed the clinic's very existence. Still, Henry wanted letters available in the clinic asking patients to contribute to the Morgentaler Defence Fund, and he got them, even though some staff thought it was inappropriate. Scattered among the back issues of *Vanity Fair* magazines in the waiting area were yellow sheets. "Dear Friends," they read:

> As you know I have fought for the last twenty-five years for the right of Canadian women to have access to safe legal abortion. After four trials and a prison term, I have succeeded in overturning the abortion law and making abortion legal and safe. In Ontario now you don't have to pay for it — it is under medicare. However, women in other provinces still don't have what has been achieved for you. I am still fighting for the rights of women to reproductive freedom in provinces like Nova Scotia, where the Government has appealed my acquittal to the Supreme Court of Canada. I have recently won a case in Manitoba where I was suing the Manitoba Government for non-payment of doctors' fees for abortions performed in my clinic. I intend to open additional clinics in provinces where access is difficult or non-existent. I intend to pursue other provincial governments for non-payment of clinic abortions.
>
> It is for these reasons that I ask you to make a donation to the Morgentaler Defence Fund to help me defray legal costs of litigation so that women across the country may share the same rights and privileges that Ontario women now enjoy. Such a donation is entirely voluntary. If you feel you are unable to contribute anything you will be treated with the same care and compassion as anyone else. However, if you want to show solidarity with women and help me continue the struggle for safe medical abortion under medicare across the country and to help me be able to provide abortions for these women unable to pay the facility fee please give your donation to the receptionist or the counsellor.... Unfortunately we are unable to provide receipts for income tax purposes.

Childbirth by Choice Trust researched and printed a province-by-province breakdown of the situation later that fall. It began well enough. In British Columbia the Everywoman's Clinic, the province's first free-standing abortion clinic, opened on November 4, 1988, followed by the Elizabeth Bagshaw Clinic in Vancouver in 1990. On March 19, 1992, the NDP government designated thirty-three public hospitals as abortion providers to ensure access in all regions. It also announced full funding for abortions done in the two private clinics. The Alberta government paid for abortions done in hospitals but paid less than one-quarter of the actual cost of an abortion done in a clinic. Access there was still a problem. In Grande Prairie, abortion was available only to women in the area. With two hospitals and one private clinic providing abortion service, Calgary offered the best service used by women from all over the southern part of the province, western Saskatchewan, eastern British Columbia and the Northwest Territories. In Edmonton, only Henry's clinic and one hospital provided abortion service. In Saskatchewan, the new NDP government of Roy Romanow got legal advice that it couldn't de-insure abortions even though the results of previous premier Grant Devine's election plebiscite showed the majority of people wanted the funding of hospital abortions stopped. But it was only after Henry threatened to open a clinic there that the Regina General Hospital unveiled a Women's Health Centre, the first facility in Regina to offer access to abortions, on July 20, 1992. In Manitoba after Henry won an appeal court decision upholding the illegality of the province's refusal to pay for clinic abortions, the government passed the Health Services Amendment Act, which excluded payment for nonhospital abortions, to counteract the decision. Henry would later challenge that legislation, as well. In Ontario, despite a supportive NDP government, anti-choice groups had forced doctors to quit performing abortions in places such as Cambridge and Kitchener-Waterloo. The Quebec government paid for hospital abortions and for those still performed in its CLSCs, the provincial community health centres, some of which no longer offered abortions because they were being run by anti-choice proponents. But it paid only a small portion of the cost of abortions performed in three women's health centres and the four free-standing abortion clinics. Since 1985, Henry had talked of opening a clinic in New Brunswick. Only three hospitals (all in the south) provided access, but Fredericton did not have enough operating-room time to service everyone; Moncton provided the service only to area women; and in Saint John there was only one doctor, who was available only to his own patients. Although 24 per cent of the women using the Halifax Morgentaler Clinic were from New Brunswick, the government refused to pay for any out-of-province abortions. Any woman from Prince Edward Island needing an abortion had to leave the Island to get one, and the province refused to pay for the procedure unless it was first approved by a five-person committee, who had to be informed of the reason the woman wanted an abortion. Nor would the government pay for any procedure done in a clinic, although only one hospital in Atlantic Canada accepted women from the Island.

On March 17, Henry announced he was taking the P.E.I. government to court for not paying for abortions for Island women that were performed in his Halifax clinic. Anne Derrick would represent him. Even when the media discovered Newfoundland was paying up to $4,000 to send women for an out-of-province abortion rather than use Henry's clinic in St. John's, the government still refused to fund clinic abortions until late in 1992, when it agreed to cover the $85 physician's fee. It continued to pay hospitals more than $500 for each abortion performed. The Northwest Territories were rocked in March 1992, when it became known that women in one hospital were routinely and deliberately not given anesthetic during the procedure. That news launched a committee of inquiry, which eventually made thirty-two recommendations, including that access be extended by having three other hospitals provide the service. The government covered the cost of all travel. In Nova Scotia, the government paid Henry physician fees for abortions performed in his clinics even as its appeal of his 1990 court victory was heard in February at the Supreme Court of Canada. Anne Derrick argued that only Parliament could legislate abortion access through its enactment of criminal law and that the Province of Nova Scotia was illegally trying to recriminalize abortions by banning private clinics. Derrick's position was supported by lawyers representing CARAL and the federal government. In separate legal actions, Henry launched suits against Nova Scotia to recover more than $100,000 in legal fees and to force the government to pay the entire cost of a clinic abortion. It was Henry's third appearance in the country's top court, and although he was absolutely confident the Supreme Court wouldn't uphold what he called "a dishonest, fraudulent law," he didn't underestimate the importance of this case. "At stake is how far any provincial government can act legislatively to restrict abortion," he said. "That is the basic question."[1]

Then, on March 10, 1993, a doctor was shot dead outside the Pensacola Women's Medical Services clinic in Florida. Dr. David Gunn was an abortionist who had ignored protestors at the clinics where he worked in the southern United States for seven years. But on the twentieth anniversary of the *Roe* v. *Wade* decision that past January 22, an event marked by President Bill Clinton in his lifting of several abortion restrictions, Gunn had held his own celebration outside a Montgomery, Alabama, clinic. Dancing and singing along into a megaphone to Tom Petty's "I Won't Back Down," he'd told the anti-abortion protestors, "I'm going to sing 'Happy Birthday' to you."[2] Gunn, forty-seven, commuted one thousand miles every week to clinics in Alabama, Georgia and Florida to perform abortions. According to the *New York Times*, he kept three guns in his car — one in the glove compartment, one under the seat and one in the trunk — but rarely took them out of his vehicle. He had thought any trouble he would encounter would be on the road, between clinics. He had been the subject of an anti-abortionist wanted poster and the object of hate mail and death threats. The man who shot him three times with a .38 calibre revolver was a local fundamentalist Christian, Michael Griffin, a loner and a newcomer to an extreme anti-abortion group led by a former Ku Klux Klan member.

The first-ever murder of an abortionist sent out a wave of shock and fear that spread quickly north. "Doctors are terrified," said Scott clinic manager Maria Corsillo. "You worry not only about staff and patients but about your family." Dr. Manole Buruiana, the head of Toronto's Cabbagetown Women's Clinic, admitted he had been forced off the road in his car once and been verbally accosted many times. The home of London, Ontario, gynecologist Fraser Fellows had been picketed daily for fifteen months. In Winnipeg, Dr. Robbie Mahood said his home had been picketed by people shouting, "God knows what's going on, and Hell's hot." One screamed, "Why did you decide to keep her?" when he saw Mahood's six-year-old. Ontario abortion workers went public about their fears at a press conference because they wanted more legislated protection. CARAL demanded a "multisite injunction" to protect people who work in abortion clinics. "If the 'responsible' anti-choicers are willing to picket our houses, what would people with more militant anti-choice positions be willing to do?" asked Mahood.[3] As American abortion rights groups and two congressmen called for an FBI probe of the anti-abortion movement, Canadian pro-choice activists said they were afraid someone could be murdered here. Only Henry declared he was neither afraid nor worried for himself; he was just concerned that other doctors would now be too afraid to perform abortions. His clinics would stay open "no matter what." "There's Henry again undermining the movement," said one longtime activist. "He marches to his own drum. He's off to one side, saying, 'I'm not afraid. There's no problem,' when there is a problem and when other doctors are afraid."

At his private seventieth birthday dinner at Toronto's Splendido restaurant, he congratulated his staff because none of them had quit after the Harbord Street clinic was bombed. "That's because you get one bombing free," quipped executive assistant Linsey Macphee. But, she noticed, her boss didn't laugh. "I hope you don't think I'm responsible for the bombing," Henry replied, referring perhaps to a recent visit to CARAL offices by police propagating the theory that a pro-choice person had bombed Henry's clinic to discredit the pro-life forces. Some six weeks after Gunn was murdered, the Ontario government applied for a court order to ban anti-abortionist protest activities outside abortion clinics, doctors' homes and hospitals.

———

She couldn't have picked a better or worse time to leave. Less than a week before she was to fly into Toronto for the gala birthday tribute to Henry organized by Selma Edelstone, Peggy Misener wrote to say she needed time away from her job. She said she needed to heal; from what

she didn't say — only that she had to leave Newfoundland and go to her
mother in Vancouver. Henry, Sharon Broughton and others at the
Toronto clinic, Henry's head office, first thought the worst. Worried,
they tried unsuccessfully to make contact with her. On May 14, Misener
wrote again, assuring them she was not critically ill, but burnt out and
tired. She complained she had received little support or understanding
from Henry and Sharon about the unique nature of the problems running an isolated clinic. She said she needed the next few weeks to recuperate and would take longer if necessary. That meant the clinic would
be without a manager for an unspecified period of time.

But Broughton was too busy the day of the tribute to tend to the
Newfoundland situation. With the exception of Peggy Misener, all clinic
managers had shown up and were meeting and having dinner together
before the event. Late in the afternoon of the next day, Broughton, general manager for all the clinics, signed on Henry's behalf a letter faxed
to Misener indicating her letter had been accepted as a resignation.
Henry then got on the phone to offer Misener's job to Peggy Keats, the
clinic assistant manager he had given Misener permission to fire six
months earlier. When Misener had told Henry the working relationship between Misener and Keats was untenable and that one of them
had to leave the clinic, Henry had sent Broughton to assess the situation.
A friend of Misener's, Broughton reported back that Misener was well
respected by many, so Henry decided Keats was expendable. "Peggy
Keats was pissed off, since she had spent the last six months unemployed," Henry admitted, "but she did accept the job."

Henry also met with Edmonton manager Susan Fox that same day.
Alberta was in the throes of an election, and although Liberal leader
Laurence Decore was pro-choice, he nevertheless had promised to outlaw abortion clinics if elected. "I just think there's something repugnant
about [clinics]," he had said. In response, Henry had drafted one of his
favourite kinds of missives — lambasting, lofty and addressed to a political leader.

"Tone it down," Fox told him. A political insider, she knew her
territory. Westerners could take offence, she warned; the letter could
backfire.

"I can be offensive if I want," Henry bristled.

"Then don't ask me for my advice," Fox countered, rising to her full height and slapping her hand for emphasis on Henry's gleaming desk. At five-foot-one, Fox was one of the few Morgentaler Clinic staff shorter than Henry, but Henry had huge respect for her. He often boasted that his Edmonton clinic manager was a lawyer. He did tone down the letter, although the news report in the *Edmonton Sun* that Friday led with the sentence "Dr. Henry Morgentaler jumped into the middle of Alberta's campaign yesterday." Decore never commented on the letter, which chastised him ("You have raised a non-issue as if you were living in a time warp") and analyzed him ("I interpret [your comments] as meaning that abortion is repugnant to you and your promise to shut down the clinics is obviously an attempt to impose your own idea of morality on the province by diminishing access to abortion, thereby causing enormous suffering to women"). After Decore lost the election to Ralph Klein, he resigned the Liberal leadership.

It was a small but satisfying skirmish, a welcome diversion from Edelstone's tribute, which had been worshipful and full of laughter. But "thank you" to a man turned seventy included a farewell, and tacit permission to withdraw from public life. He had helped lead the broad political left and the feminist movement to their biggest victory. For that he was sacrosanct and they would always be grateful. No one would question — in fact, most would respect and all would understand — if he turned inwards now, back to his young family, "who needed him," in the phrase of all retiring — or defeated — politicians, or devoted himself to his chain of six medical clinics. There was a danger in any man lingering past his prime and his time. The longer Henry stayed on the public stage the more he invited assessments not as flattering as those taken immediately after the warm glow of victory. Already some had noted his habit of walking into a room late, allowing things to stop as he was acknowledged. Others had begun to question why he still wanted and courted media attention, even after the grand victory for the cause had been won, and wondered why he still needed to win — whether it was at Ping-Pong or in a provincial courtroom — every single scuffle.

But Henry had no intention of stopping, or even of slowing down. He was going to Moscow and to Riga in Latvia, where he thought he might open clinics in partnership with a local entrepreneur. In 1992 he'd met Alexander Dubcek, hero of the Prague Spring, as that country's brief freedom from Soviet troops and tanks in 1968 came to be known, at an international Humanist conference in Amsterdam. There he had also spoken with some women from Poland. He had agreed to meet with them in Warsaw that summer, when he would be visiting Moscow and Riga. Henry refused to attach any significance to his decision — "I was there — it was almost like a moral obligation. It would have been unthinkable that I should have been there and not gone" — but unlike Mike, he had never returned to his birthplace. The day Henry was shoved onto the crowded, dark railway car with his mother and brother and transported to Auschwitz was his last in Poland. "If I lived with the memories of that, I couldn't live in the here and now. My way was to get away from all of that, to try to forget it. Enough. I wanted to live in the here and now. I don't want to live forever as a victim of the Nazi concentration camp," he said. His past had marked him; it belonged to him. But it had been assimilated by him, and it would not interfere with his daily life. He had seen it "poison" other survivors; when Italian author-survivor Primo Levi committed suicide, Henry knew it could kill, no matter the number of years that had passed. It would always haunt, lurking at the edges of memory; unless, he said, "you have something in your life on which you can concentrate, it will come to a point where it is too much."

When Henry and Arlene took Benny and Yann to Australia for a month during the winter of 1991–92, he looked up old Bundist colleagues he had not seen since Belgium. They were still close-knit, a circle of old friends and fellow travellers living by reliving their shared past. Henry loved their singing and the music, but he was uncomfortable and somewhat awkward, because he knew, even if they didn't, that he was no longer one of them. He'd lived by avoiding films and books about the war, or tried to. But what he disparagingly termed his "morbid fascination" propelled him to buy the books and read them, hardbound volumes as heavy as tomes and as indisputable, including one account by a doctor in Auschwitz whose job was to treat the officers; that robbed Henry of sleep for a week. He said he wouldn't, but he went to see Steven Spielberg's film *Schindler's List*, and the victimizing nightmares returned. He was in Washington attending another National Abortion Federation annual conference when the $6-million American memorial museum to the Holocaust opened. He was too busy to see it, but others were going, so he accompanied his Toronto office manager, Sharon Broughton. After five minutes, he turned on his heel, white-faced, and left. There had been photographs of Lodz; he had seen faces he knew. Back at the hotel he had a brandy, then another.

But he believed he could visit Poland. "I know I have the ability to do it and not fall apart." He was a hero now, no longer the pale youth huddled in the middle of other frightened Jews under a malevolent government's hateful Nazi watch. He was returning with a cause allowing him to challenge and taunt the Polish rule. This time he would win for the sake of his mother, sister, father, on behalf of that newly formed group of Polish Humanists he'd met. Many of them were women worried about the situation in their country, where abortion — which had been free and legal for thirty-four years — was outlawed the summer of 1992. Now any doctor performing an abortion could receive up to two years in jail. The cost of illegal abortions had skyrocketed to as much as $1,100, but women were so desperate they paid. The group asked Henry if he would meet with famed Polish freedom fighter Marek Edelman when he was scheduled to visit Montreal that fall. Henry was honoured; Edelman was a national hero who had written *The Ghetto Is Dying*, a book about the Warsaw ghetto uprising he had helped lead. He'd survived by scrambling through the sewers of Warsaw as soldiers surrounded the burning city. He had known Henry's sister; he'd fought beside her martyred fiancé. Now he was a cardiologist working in Lodz. They talked about how Henry could help Polish women, perhaps by speaking up on Canadian television about the situation. Henry never did, but when he knew he was going to Latvia and Moscow, he telephoned some of the Humanists he knew in Poland and asked them to organize a meeting to discuss the possibility of opening a clinic in Russia just a few kilometres from the Polish border. He told them he would come to Warsaw and stay for two days. He was flattered when they asked permission to translate his book, *Abortion and Contraception*, into Polish, and moved when Edelman made the two-hour train ride from Lodz to come to Warsaw.

They met for lunch, after which Henry asked Edelman to accompany him to the monument commemorating the Warsaw uprising. Their taxi driver recognized Edelman. Although only about five thousand Jews still live in Poland, a country where the anti-Semitism was subtle but omnipresent, he had become a national hero again. It was Saturday afternoon, and the cobblestone city square was almost deserted. A few last-minute shoppers hurried by; otherwise they were alone in the quiet of the former ghetto. This was where the Jews, including Henry's sister, had been rounded up and sent by train to Treblinka for extermination. A few days before in Riga, a guide had shown Henry a synagogue torched by Russians after they had herded all the Jews into it, and offered to point out the forest where they used to hang Jews. Henry refused: "You get so full of terrible things that happened there. The forest near Lithuania and Poland where Jews were brought to be shot — they're so full of blood, and they were all over the place. It brought back a lot of things which I had kept under wraps, the pain and longing." Seeing the monuments to Jews who had refused to be victims and who had committed collective suicide instead of passively going to their death would assuage the fear bubbling back to his mind's surface, cut off the inevitable recurrence of those dreams. But he couldn't go alone. Edelman was a hero when Henry was a stripling; he was still a hero. "He was the right person," Henry said. Henry asked a passerby to take a picture of the two of them in front of a stone memorial. But he could not bring himself to visit Auschwitz or Lodz, although he could, and did, go back to Canada and visit Mike.

It was one of their few real talks. Since the breakup, Henry had phoned Mike several times for brief and superficially cordial chats, and in 1990, he flew to Montreal specifically to see his brother face to face to sort through things. That's when Mike said Henry never gave him any credit. "You have reflected glory," Henry protested. But Mike wanted to be acknowledged, publicly and often, with saving his brother's life in the concentration camps. In his speech at the birthday tribute, Henry had, but it was not enough. Sick and more and more confined to his apartment, Mike lashed out at his frenetic, globe-trotting brother. Henry had betrayed Mike in the camps. Would Henry acknowledge that? Henry's anger burned. "He is nerves. I don't need nerves." But he didn't understand Mike's anger. Henry would phone. "I forgive, let's forget and go on from here," he would say to Mike, then to his daughter and even to his first wife. Eva Rosenfarb told him she preferred their current standoff to whatever friendship might be forged. When he telephoned Goldie from Riga on her birthday, he was thrilled she actually took the call. Even though Goldie seemed to want only to tell her fat her why she was upset with him, he hoped the reconciliation had begun. "We had a nice chat," he reported to sceptical friends, who were accustomed to Henry's habit of putting a positive spin on most things.

His optimism was not as unfounded on the business front. That 1993 summer the Ontario government announced it was taking bids on proposals to establish a new nonprofit abortion clinic in Ottawa. In July 1991, Henry had submitted an unsolicited proposal for a clinic to the Ottawa District Health Council. Although three Ottawa hospitals provided abortion services, 242 women from Ottawa had been to his Toronto clinic in an eighteen-month period, and 507 women from Ontario, probably Eastern Ontario, he added, had travelled to his Montreal facilities. At a Saturday afternoon pro-choice march organized by the Pro-Choice Network in October 1992, Henry complained that his proposal was "lost somewhere in the bureaucracy." CARAL's Ottawa chapter continued to lobby and write letters and hold "polite private meetings," as member Anne Burnett put it. The following month the government commissioned a needs-assessment report by the ubiquitous Dr. Marion Powell, and in December of that year an Ontario task group on abortion service highlighted Ottawa and Eastern Ontario (as well as the Kitchener-Waterloo area and Northern Ontario) as being most in need of new abortion facilities. Powell recommended a comprehensive multiservice, community-based clinic for women in her February 1993 report, which the Ottawa District Health Council readily adopted because it believed a women's health centre wouldn't attract as much

anti-abortion activity as an abortion clinic, although a centre would cost
more. Henry argued that that style of clinic would never get off the
ground because it would be duplicating services already available. The
same day Health Minister Ruth Grier announced the NDP government
was funding and licensing the province's first abortion clinic outside
Toronto, Henry announced his bid. Everyone assumed it was his, anyway; except Peggy Misener, the former Newfoundland clinic manager.

She decided to mount a rival bid. At an information meeting organized by the government she met some area women, including Planned
Parenthood board member Sue McGarvie, who had been dreaming of
a women-centred clinic with lots of counselling, big bowls of free condoms and sponges and plenty of follow-up care ever since Marion
Powell had first come to talk to the board. "Not to take away from
Henry, but I felt it was time to have a different kind of clinic, which
would be run by women of Ottawa-Carleton with a full board of directors," McGarvie explained. "I thought it was time for a new model.
Misener gave interviews stating much the same thing. Henry was in his
seventies and he hadn't designated his successor." At least one columnist
supported the alternative bid; Henry recalled the *Ottawa Citizen*'s Susan
Riley writing that he liked things his own way, after she'd interviewed
him. She supported the broader-based model. "Everybody knew there
was an anybody-but-Henry campaign going on," said CARAL's Burnett.
She and other CARAL members wanted "a clinic that works," not one
that might flounder, as the clinic in Newfoundland so recently had.
They lobbied hard to ensure that Henry would promise to build in a
community board comprised of people truly involved in reproductive
issues. "We nagged and nagged him. We knew it was a strategy we
should really push," Burnett said. Henry's bid was unquestioningly supported by the Pro-Choice Network, with whom Henry had marched
two years earlier.

Nevertheless, McGarvie sold her vision to key women in the area,
high-profile feminists and professionals, including former politician
Marion Dewar and Glenda Simms, who was then president of the Canadian Council on the Status of Women. Also on board was the head of
the nursing department at the University of Ottawa. "This was going to

be the model for the rest of the country. This was going to be it."
McGarvie put aside her doctoral studies and encouraged some friends
to work full time on their bid. "Peggy [Misener] told us what to get and
we got it," she recalled. Misener was living in Picton, Ontario, and seemed
determined, if not driven, to win the clinic bid. She had McGarvie call
medical supply companies for quotes on the cost of everything from
oxygen to gauze pads. She was at the core of their bid. "You had to have
run a clinic to do the proposal," said McGarvie. Even Henry, an old
hand at the business, complained about the paperwork required for the
application. "We sent in about sixty pages of paper listing all kinds of
things, staff, salaries, the kinds of medicines. It was terrible."

Just before the October 1993 deadline for the proposal, word came
down from the Supreme Court of Canada on Henry's Nova Scotia
court case. By a unanimous 9 to 0 decision, they had ruled that Nova
Scotia's Medical Services Act was invalid. "Only the federal government, through the Criminal Code, can legislate access to abortion,"
wrote Mr. Justice John Sopinka. "The decision was a big surprise to
me," Anne Derrick recalled. But not to Henry. This was the third time
the Supreme Court of Canada had ruled in his favour. And, in fact,
Henry told media, he was not surprised. But when Derrick heard that
the appeal was dismissed, it took her a few moments to comprehend.
"What about dissents?" she asked. "There weren't any," she was told. A
partner went out and bought a bottle of Mumm's, "expensive champagne — I'd never before had it," even though she knew hers was not
the most significant case in the annals of the Supreme Court because it
was not a charter case. "It's too bad the [Nova Scotia] government
couldn't have said that the Supreme Court case of 1988 is absolutely
clear that provincial clinics can operate legally. The case doesn't explic-
itly say that, so legally the 1993 case is a necessary piece of the law
around how abortion is delivered," she said. It also, she added, shut the
door on New Brunswick, or any other province that might have wanted
to enact legislation prohibiting free-standing abortion clinics.

At the same time, McGarvie learned that Misener was inexplicably
dropping out of their clinic bid. "She said she had fallen in love and
wanted to get married. She left us at the altar. She had all the information,

everything, because she had been formulating it," McGarvie said. She had to beg Misener to send her the proposal information — by courier, collect. "When she shuts down, she shuts down." McGarvie spent the next four nights nailing down the clinic lease for their proposed Glebe area location and co-ordinating the clinic blueprints and equipment lists. Her proposal was 550 pages long, including an index, and it cost $500 to make the six copies required by the government. McGarvie dared to hope, even though she suspected Henry and everyone in the government knew from the beginning that he was going to win the application. His successful bid was announced at a press conference on February 17, 1994. McGarvie said she was not informed of the decision or of the press conference. She found out through a friend involved in the Pro-Choice Network. Shaking with anger, she telephoned the office of Evelyn Gigantes, her MP for Ottawa Centre and at that time the NDP's housing minister. She said she had been calling weekly; they knew she represented the alternative model, yet they had said nothing to her. "How dare you treat us this badly?" Now a sex therapist who also hosts a television show, she is still angry. "This was something I did for my community, but I will never get involved again. I was sickened. Had not Pro-Choice Network called me, I would have read about it in the paper." Henry had flown in to Ottawa for the afternoon announcement, where he said later that he was told, in confidence, his proposal was the superior in fifteen categories.

CHAPTER 22

HAPPY AT LAST?

H E WAS DINING WITH A FRIEND in Toronto when it happened. March 9, 1994. A frisson sped up his left side, then there was nothing except the clatter of cutlery and plates slipping away. Arlene was also out with a friend. She arrived home to a flashing red signal on the message machine: Henry was in hospital, recovering from a mild stroke; a brain hemorrhage had affected his left arm and leg. The next morning as Bamie Morgentaler was readying himself for an 8 a.m. live appearance on a Washington, D.C., television program to promote his first book, *The Male Body*, he got a call saying his father was in the emergency ward. By the time he arrived in Toronto later that day, Henry was able to tell him he intended to still go on with the vacation the two families had planned for the following week. "We'll get a wheelchair."

Henry did his exercises, everything he was supposed to, and he could feel the strength returning. He didn't go on the vacation, but that March 19, his seventy-first birthday, he celebrated at home with friends and family. Bamie had told Mike of Henry's stroke. "Okay," Mike said. "I'll come down." He stayed with his cousin Sara Schwartz, and she and her husband accompanied him to Henry's birthday dinner. It was the first time Mike had been in Henry and Arlene's home, which was crowded and noisy, filled with well-wishers. "Too many people," Mike said. He never got to talk to his brother. "From then on I made it a point never to be in his home." Mike's health quickly deteriorated to the point where he could no longer leave his apartment. He began to need constant care from his companion, Emilia, a Polish-born doctor. Over the

telephone Mike still sounded vital and combative — his voice, so like
Henry's, was always more animated — but many nights he couldn't
sleep, and he remained angry, as Henry knew all too well. A year later
Henry was in Montreal frequently while moving the clinic to move into
glorious new renovated space on the seventh floor of a medical building
on St. Joseph Boulevard East in downtown Montreal. But he didn't visit
Mike. "He hasn't resolved his resentments, so what's the point?"

But when Mike left Henry's house for what would be the last time
the night of the seventy-first birthday party, Henry was determined to
show that everything was fine, that *he* was fine. If there was an edge, a
slight manic tinge to his hosting ministrations that evening as he circulated, laughed often, would not be tired, it was because this was the way
he had always quelled the doubting, defeatist voices inside. But the
stroke had frightened Henry and he did slide into a depression. Morbid
and lethargic, he mourned his lost vigour. He was so very tired all the
time, and would not forget that a month before he would have swum
forty lengths of the YMCA pool, skied the Laurentians, then laughed and
drunk red wine into the night. Now he believed himself old, sick and
frightened. The doctor told him his recovery, although rapid in the first
forty-eight hours, would take time. For most of the numbness to retreat
he had to be patient, quiet, to rest, not brood — an impossible assignment for someone like Henry. Instead he withdrew, kneading thoughts
of being struck down again, of becoming useless, a burden to Arlene,
vital and thirty years younger, who had fallen in love with a dynamic,
restless man of action and would not be able to love, or even live with,
someone used up and weakened. He was an automaton, wedded to this
worst-case scenario, and he ran it over and over in his mind so it blocked
out anything Arlene tried to say to him. She began playing tennis two
hours a day, working out, swimming; to be physically exhausted was the
way she coped. They went for couple counselling and gradually Henry
understood that Arlene wanted him to take it easy and look after himself because she wanted him to be around for many years, not because
she thought he was weak and old.

But the depression lingered like a still and heavy summer's day
before a storm. Henry just wanted to sit and read; occasionally, very

occasionally, he would go out for a walk, always by himself. Some days he would spend upstairs, in his silent study or in bed, as Arlene painted downstairs. Never had they spent so many twenty-four-hour days together; never had their life been so quiet. Arlene phoned Jean Rankin and asked her to visit. Henry could talk only of his unhappiness and fear to his friend. He didn't comprehend that his depression could be a residual of the stroke or of the medication he was taking for his high blood pressure. He believed he was depressed because he was old and tired and his hearing was going, and not that he felt old and tired and increasingly hard of hearing because he was depressed. Selma Edelstone called to try to coax him out for lunch. Eventually he did go, and then a few weeks later he went out again. "Then we had dinner at the Four Seasons, an expensive dinner. It helped," she said. He was getting better, feeling well and courageous enough to meet with people and travel. In early May he went to New York to visit a friend, a primal therapist. When he returned the smile was back on his face, and Arlene said she knew "that was the beginning to beginning again."

Somehow on June 28 of 1994 he opened his clinic in Fredericton. The local newspapers reported Henry "marched into his new clinic in downtown Fredericton" and performed five abortions. That was not how Halifax clinic manager Sandra Lanz remembered it. She and Janet Chernin were there to help clinic manager Alison Brewer with the opening. A worried Lanz knew Henry was battling depression and still recovering from his stroke, and she knew he would be facing the habitual crowd of press and protestors. "It was a hot day. We had to take him out back and make him sit to cool down. His blood pressure was up — he was turning red in the face," she said. When he was in the operating room, she watched him closely, at one point dragging him away again to drink some spring water. "All the women around Henry tend to protect him, act as his bodyguards," she explained. At the ensuing news conference he performed as expected: he was feisty and combative. "Here in New Brunswick, it's as if we're in the Middle Ages again. Where have all these people been? Haven't they noticed what's been going on in the rest of Canada? Here, they're threatening me with closing the clinic, not paying for this and doing this and that — I mean,

what's going on? Is this a different country?" he said, adding Premier
Frank McKenna had promised him "the fight of his life" if he ventured
into New Brunswick. Pro-choice sources in Fredericton close to the
premier had told Henry that McKenna was not posturing, that he was
genuinely and deeply and unequivocally opposed to abortion and would
invoke the province's 1985 law banning abortions outside a hospital.

But Henry needed to do battle. Newspaper photos taken at the
opening show Henry assuming the jaunty posture of prideful ownership, yet vulnerability and entreaty shadow his features. On the late-
night news, the cameras picked up a tired man, sitting and speaking
slowly in a weary voice about his newest crusade, his depression infus-
ing the resignation and disgust. He recalled later: "[The situation]
reminded me of previous defeats. After the Nova Scotia [Supreme
Court] decision, there was nothing they could have done. Premier Clyde
Wells didn't do anything — he knew the challenge wouldn't work.
McKenna knew, too, but he had to do it. It had become a personal vendetta. Who was going to win? Crazy. Not caring for a moment he was
harming two hundred, maybe three hundred, women who still had to
go to Halifax to get an abortion. That didn't count. He had to show
Morgentaler he was the boss."

For years Henry had been taunting McKenna. In 1989, Henry sent
lawyers to court seeking payment under the province's medical insurance plan for three Montreal clinic patients from the province, known
as X, Y and Z. He won. It was back in August 1991 that Henry had first
announced he would open a Fredericton clinic and that he expected
the province to pay for all procedures. About two months before the
Supreme Court ruled on the Nova Scotia case, Henry purchased the
house Carl Katz had found for him at 88 Ferry Street. It backed onto
a stream that flowed into the Saint John River but looked out across
the parking lot of a busy mall, onto a bustling McDonald's outlet and a
movie house. The following February he wrote McKenna about his
intentions, reminding him of the Nova Scotia decision and informing
him his cadre of lawyers were of the opinion that both the New Brunswick Medical Act and the New Brunswick Medical Services Payment
Act were "unconstitutional":

I understand that your opposition to free-standing clinics has to do with your Catholic upbringing and your religious outlook.... I wish to convey to you my opinion, and I hope you will agree with me, that as a Premier of a province your secretarian religious views should not influence public policy.... It strikes me as that you represent yourself as a defender of women's rights and do not see the contradiction in opposing a medical facility which would alleviate the pain, the stress and the suffering to which so many women in New Brunswick are exposed to [sic] due to the policies of your Government.

If you do not see this contradiction, or you have a good explanation for it, I would like to hear from you....

He did. McKenna's answering volley was not the usual bland political fare. "....Stripped of the offensive allegations relating to my Catholic upbringing, that I have misogynistic inclinations and that I desire to inflict unnecessary suffering on hundreds of New Brunswick women, the purpose of your letter appears to be an attempt to persuade me to invite you to establish your clinic or clinics in New Brunswick. I must say I personally find advocacy based on insult, threat and abuse quite unpersuasive," he wrote. Saying McKenna "completely misunderstood what I had written. I didn't want his blessing," Henry turned over their correspondence — all marked "Personal and Confidential" — to the *Telegraph-Journal* newspaper, where it was published under the headline "Personal and confrontational." Given that history, Henry wasn't surprised when, a few hours after the Fredericton clinic opening, McKenna's health minister read to reporters a prepared statement that the province was asking the College of Physicians and Surgeons to restrict Henry's licence. Dr. Russell King also called for an inquiry into Henry's conduct. A week later the College complied, restricting Henry's licence. "Physicians are afraid of governments — governments have too much power. So I guess they just gave in to the government. I blame the government for this absolutely useless fight and waste of taxpayers' money," Henry retorted, announcing his appeal. He'd invested $450,000 in an operation he knew would adversely affect his financially struggling Halifax clinic and would never make money. The Toronto clinic would be supporting it for years to come, maybe forever. McKenna's "rear-guard action was an insult to me personally," but he never expected him to close down the clinic. And Henry was furious when that action was dressed up and delivered as a legitimate conciliatory offer of granting a medical licence to practice everything but abortions — therefore making it appear Henry chose to close down his own clinic when he refused their offer.

He appealed the College decision and lost, but he was expecting to win in August, when the larger and more crucial court case concerning the banning of clinic abortions was to be heard. The day before the New Brunswick clinic opened, Anne Derrick also launched Henry's court challenge to the Prince Edward Island government for its refusal to pay for abortions at private clinics. Henry expected to win that fight, too — and in February 1995 when David Jenkins, the P.E.I. justice minister, set down his ruling, he did.

He won in New Brunswick, as well: in September 1994 Judge Ron Stevenson agreed with Henry that the 1985 law had been enacted to prohibit abortions outside a hospital environment, not to control or ensure health quality. As the province appealed, Henry re-opened the clinic, flying in doctors from his Montreal and Toronto clinics a week later to do the procedures when no local physicians volunteered their services, a practice he continues. New Brunswick ultimately lost its appeal, as well as its bid to be heard in the Supreme Court of Canada. As the headline in the May 23, 1995, issue of the *Medical Post* said: "Morgentaler 4, Provinces 0." (British Columbia lost in February and March 1988 and Manitoba lost a 1992 ruling and a 1993 appeal to opt out of funding clinic abortions.)

New Brunswick conceded defeat — "There is no other forum to appeal to. The clinic can certainly exist in its present form," said Health Minister Russell King. But the province has yet to pay Henry a nickel. Manitoba paid briefly while it changed the law to clearly stipulate the province would not pay. Henry was amused by these machinations: "Now I have to attack their new law. Crazy." He resigned himself to similar stubbornness on other provincial fronts. In P.E.I., another fiscal holdout, Henry called for Health Minister Walter McEwen to be fired or resign. "It's all a last-ditch effort on the part of governments. They're going to lose anyway. I'm absolutely positive they are going to lose," he reasoned. In a letter to Premier Catherine Callbeck, he added, "Until your Government comes to its senses I can only say: Shame on you." Within two weeks Callbeck had replied: "I have no intention of asking for [McEwen's] resignation."

———

"All right, on October 13, 1994, we declare victory," Henry announced with a flourish, as he opened Canada's sixteenth free-standing abortion clinic in Ottawa. It cost $450,000, it was going to cost about $600,000 a year to operate and it was all being paid for by an NDP provincial government led by Bob Rae, the man who had refused to support Henry's Toronto clinic when it opened in 1983 because it was illegal. The elevator doors of the building just off the Spark Street Mall opened onto a triumphant and huge sign: Welcome to the Morgentaler Clinic. The health ministry had wanted the clinic to move into available space in a building Henry deemed "rundown." Henry held out for "first-class space," 360 square metres right where he wanted it — which just happened to be in the neighbourhood of the Supreme Court of Canada and the Parliament Buildings. "In the heart of the nation," he said, unashamed of such raw and obvious symbolism. "It tickled my imagination." He hadn't realized — but was even more pleased when he learned — that the neighbouring office housed the Reform Party of Canada.

A dozen police officers were at the opening, as were a respectable number of journalists, given that the Canadian-born Hollywood film star Dan Aykroyd was also in town, but the only trouble emanated from clinic supporters. Trained and eager to defend the clinic, a large crowd of Pro-Choice Network members gathered outside the building on opening day, brandishing placards and shouting supportive slogans. Henry asked them to leave. " . . . the women who come here should come in to an atmosphere of calmness and serenity, and a big crowd, whether it is pro-choice or anti-choice, will scare them off." Many didn't like

what he said. They were as angry as OCAC had been when he'd applied
for the injunction for the Harbord Street clinic in Toronto, and for the
same reasons. But in Ottawa, six years after the Supreme Court decision, the time for street theatre had passed. Sure, a couple of provinces
remained stubborn holdouts, but Henry was certain they, too, would be
tamed in time and in higher courts. Canada's Health Act stated that if
abortion (or any other insurable procedure) was covered under a provincial health plan, the province must pay either all or none of the cost
— no matter where that procedure was done. Canada's health minister
of the time, Diane Marleau, had said that meant any province paying
the doctors' fees for abortions (or any other insurable procedure) must
also pay the full facility fee. Only British Columbia and Ontario were
complying. In Alberta, there were further complications when Ralph
Klein's government supported establishing private health care facilities
catering to people able to, and in favour of, purchasing their own health
care, which would have included the province's two abortion clinics.
Edmonton clinic manager Susan Fox reminded people and politicians
the clinics filled needs not being met by public hospitals. She then pitched
regional health authorities with the idea that the Morgentaler Clinic do
all the abortions in the northern part of the province (and Calgary's
Kensington clinic could look after the south). Fox once told a reporter
her hobby was "overthrowing governments." She loves political brink-
manship; later that summer she would show her skill at it when Klein's
Conservatives voted to limit abortion services by de-insuring "unnecessary" abortions. By October 10, 1995, they had backed down because
the province's doctors refused to be responsible for defining which abortions were necessary and which were not, and because CARAL's national
and regional groups went to work, creating a coalition that organized
a huge letter-writing campaign and lobbied all members of the legislature. Fox has always been confident of their success, just as she has
always been sure that, ultimately, the Alberta government would, one
day, fully fund clinic abortions. "We're going to win this one," she said
in June of 1995.[1]

Meanwhile, in Ontario the government won an interim injunction against pro-life picketers in eighteen locations, including abortion

clinics, doctors' homes and their offices. Henry was ecstatic. Where there were no injunctions, picketers waxed and waned, sometimes aggressively engaging in sidewalk counselling, occasionally gluing shut a lock or chaining themselves in front of clinic entrances, many times simply standing in silent rebuke as women walked by. All clinics had been the subject of death threats and hate mail, which was troubling and at times frightening, but in Canada there did seem to be an unconscious but clearly demarcated limit to abusive behaviour. Nevertheless, abortion workers worried about the Americanization of the anti-abortion movement. Their Canadian foes had embraced the tactics of Operation Rescue. Would they be as enthusiastic about the publication of the hit list of a "deadly dozen" abortion doctors, the manuals for attacking abortion clinics allegedly published by an American underground group known as the Army of God and the monthly magazine *Life Advocate* for militant abortionists, which made a point of listing the name and address of every known doctor performing abortions?

Canadian militants were still bearing polite placards requesting women to *please* not kill their babies, but American extremists had moved into a war mode. Five months after Gunn's death, an Oregon housewife wounded Dr. George Tiller outside a Kansas clinic. She was arrested as she obediently returned her rental car. Less than a year after that, Gunn's successor was murdered. Paul Hill, a former Presbyterian minister, walked up to a station wagon and emptied the contents of a 12-gauge shotgun, shooting dead Dr. John Britton, sixty-nine, and his volunteer driver, retired air force officer James Barrett, and wounding Barrett's wife, June. Hill had been on television shows such as "Donahue" and "Nightline," talking approvingly of taking any necessary action to stop abortions, but had always said he personally would never gun down anyone. Among his admirers was C. Roy McMillan, self-styled "abortion abolitionist" and subject of a cover story October 30, 1994, in the *New York Times Magazine*. In it he spoke admiringly about Hill being the first person in Jackson, Mississippi, to actually go to an abortion clinic to try to stop procedures. Several months after Gunn was killed, Hill circulated a petition stating that what Michael Griffin did was justifiable. That convinced McMillan it was "not a sin to go out and shoot an abortionist." When Hill killed Britton, another petition was circulated, supporting Hill's actions. McMillan signed that one, too, although, he told the *New York Times*, he did not understand "why would a person do it publicly when maybe he could have done it clandestinely with a high-powered rifle."

On November 2, 1994, Hill was convicted of two counts of first degree murder, the first person brought to trial under the Freedom of Access to Clinic Entrances Act, which President Bill Clinton signed after the American Supreme Court ruled anti-abortion groups fell under the purview of federal racketeering laws and that creating a buffer zone around clinics didn't violate the First Amendment. Early on November 8, McMillan's words became cruelly prophetic when a Vancouver doctor was shot by a sniper as he sat in a bathrobe, eating breakfast in his kitchen. Dr. Garson Romalis was an obstetrician-gynecologist whose practice included abortion. He endured an eight-hour operation to repair a burst femoral artery and the other damage from the AK-47 bullet that had pierced his upper left thigh bone. Previously Romalis had been harassed at Vancouver General Hospital and had put up with demonstrators leaving roofing nails on his driveway at home. More than a tragedy, this shooting brought the long-simmering abortion dispute into some alien, terribly un-Canadian place. No gunman was ever arrested, (pro-choice activists remain sure the shooting was the act of an American or Americans), but the event set off fast and loose talk, and suddenly, local pro-life activists were sounding eerily like their American counterparts. "I do condone violence," said Gordon Watson of Vancouver, who had been convicted two weeks earlier of criminal contempt of court because he refused to adhere to an injunction banning him from picketing the Everywoman's Health Clinic. He had also asked the B.C. health ministry for the names and addresses of all doctors in the province who do abortions.[2] "This man [Dr. Romalis] is a mass murderer," said Christine Hendrix, another activist.[3] "We responded with some indignation people would think [the gunman] was us," said Campaign Life's Jim Hughes, adding, "you can't consider [abortion] a non-violent act."[4]

Henry had never met Romalis, but he did know the women who

worked at Vancouver's two abortion clinics. He sent them a reassuring telegram. In response they told him they had seen him interviewed on television saying he was not frightened and that he would not be giving up. He was told one of the women who worked in the Everywoman's Health Clinic said, "If Henry Morgentaler, after everything he's been through, is not giving up, why should we?" and was pleased to have made that strong an impression. He wanted to be the role model of courage, and he would ignore those fear-riddled dreams that had come back to him after Dr. Gunn was murdered — which was a far more adult response to dreams, he told himself, and a good and gratifying sign of his freedom from fear. But many other Canadian abortionists freely admitted they were frightened. "I may be next," said Buruiana. Scott had already released the contents of a letter in which he was called a "murderer of innocent newborn babies" but which also named his wife and stated "the same fate will be hers . . . her death will occur before yours." Henry made sure he did not express fear — the media had never been told of his stroke or depression — and that he presented himself as a man who had withstood years of anti-abortion-generated stress and would not crumple now. He was the victor, never again the victim. He saw this as an opportunity to blame the religious leaders and their "vile, lying propaganda." He preferred to comment on the violence as a sociological phenomenon — "These people in Vancouver are fanatics, you know" — not as an act that infringed on his life or affected his psyche. His depression had finally subsided, but Henry feared a recurrence — because it was the marker that he had not withstood the stress after all, that he was not as strong as he needed to be and that he had really been frightened these many years. Anti-abortionists were desperate, he reasoned; they had failed trying to convince "one hundred thousand women not to have abortions," so they're now trying to stop the doctors who provide them. "Basically terror tactics designed to reduce health and welfare and empowerment of women, and it should be seen as such." He would continue his shoulders-back, head-up evening walks in the neighbourhood ravines. "I don't believe in absolute security. I don't think it's possible."

Not so Arlene, who had panicked when she heard of the shooting, he said. She was frantic for Benny's safety, as were his teachers. Henry appeared to shrug the shooting off. "There's not much you can do. I hope they don't go after the children." Their home had an elaborate alarm system, but the back wall was a floor-to-ceiling window that was "not even shatterproof," Henry noted. Appointments were made with tradespeople to rectify that. Many in his clinic were frightened, as well. The Saturday following Romalis's shooting, one of the clinic staff asked the building security guard for permission to use the Bayview Avenue entrance, accessed by employees of the other businesses in the building, instead of the clinic's private entrance off Hillsdale Avenue. Building management refused and followed up with a letter stating the request was evidence the Morgentaler Clinic was a dangerous tenant. Henry was asked to leave by May 31, 1995. He was disgusted, and not just because he had a ten-year lease and this meant another useless court fracas he would inevitably win. He was impatient with his employees. They had survived bomb threats, including one recently when they'd had to evacuate the building for half an hour. This was just more of the same; he couldn't comprehend why they were so fearful. He had expected better, more, of them. They should understand it by now: becoming frightened was letting the other side win; show weakness and the other side would attack. "It takes one person to be scared and infect all the others."

But when an unemployed hairdresser killed employees in two Massachusetts abortion clinics and wounded five others in a December 30, 1994, rampage, Henry acted quickly to increase the clinic security. No longer would the receptionist have a sliding-glass window; it would be replaced with an immovable, impenetrable bulletproof pane of inch-thick glass. Two security guards were posted at the entrance. The clinic would have ten emergency intercoms, eight panic buttons and a lock-cut feature that could disable all clinic entry cards. Staff attended a seminar on how to recognize a letter bomb. None of them quit.

The man charged with killing Shannon Lowney, twenty-five, the receptionist at a Brookline, Massachusetts, clinic, and Leanne Nichols, thirty-eight, the receptionist at Preterm Health Services, was arrested the next day as he fired shots at a clinic in Norfolk, Virginia. Police stated John Salvi appeared to be the prototypical single gunman — he was a loner and a misfit — but some anti-abortionist protestors held prayer vigils supporting Salvi. The National Abortion Federation faxed all their members an update on January 4, 1995: "This latest act of terror has struck at all our hearts. At a time like this, we all need to huddle a little closer together for warmth. In the next few days and weeks, you will want to set time aside for staff to get together to talk, to vent and to discuss your security systems. Take care of yourselves and one another. ... "

Henry appeared at a Toronto press conference with other members of the pro-choice movement, re-united and presenting one voice in their outrage at the other side. "At this point in our history we have to view every aggressive picketer in front of a clinic as a potential murderer," he said. He added the Canadian Conference of Catholic Bishops was "morally irresponsible" for not calling for an end to protests and violent anti-choice rhetoric. Two days later Campaign Life Coalition announced they were posting a $10,000 reward for any information leading to a conviction in the Morgentaler Clinic bombing. "We are sick and tired of allegations that pro-lifers are violent. We have always condemned violence and believe the only way to change the hearts and minds of Canadians about abortion is to work within the law," Jim Hughes said on January 18. Henry had no choice. This was "a cheap publicity stunt" and "a bit late," but he said he'd match their $10,000. As a diversionary tactic, it was short-lived. Halifax police had obtained a letter on January 24 addressed to all abortion clinic workers. Written entirely in capital letters, the letter read:

THE SHOOTINGS OF DOCTORS; [sic] WORKERS AND PATIENTS IN USA CLINICS ARE MADE OUT TO BE HORRIBLE ACTS OF VIOLENCE. WHAT OF YOUR HORRIBLE VIOLENT ACTS AGAINST UNBORN, INNO-CENT BABIES? ARE THEY TO GO UNANSWERED? NO, NO, NO!! PLEASE TAKE THIS MESSAGE SERIOUSLY ....

I HAVE IMPORTED THE FINEST HANDGUNS AND ONE SILENCER. ALSO INCLUDED IS A MARKSMAN'S RIFLE AND SCOPE. AFTER JANUARY 30TH/95, I SOLEMLY [sic] PROMISE TO TAKE ACTION

AGAINST ANY AND ALL PERSONS INVOLVED IN THE OPERATION OF
ABORTION MILLS, CLINICS OR GOVERNMENT RUN AND PUBLICLY
FUNDED HOSPITAL; ABORTION CLINICS. TAKE HEED DR. ▇▇▇▇▇▇▇
OF DARTMOUTH. HE KNOWS JUST WHO I MEAN. I HAVE A LIST OF
NAMES AND ADDRESSES OF PERSONS THAT HAVE AND STILL WORK
IN THESE DISCUSTING [sic] JOBS. TAKE WARNING!!! I AM NOT
INSANE BUT I AM AGAINST THE TAKING OF INNOCENT LIVES.
I DO NOT CONSIDER CONSENTING ADULT ABORTIONISTS TO
BE INNOCENT.

Lanz was not told of the letter until January 31, and when the four doctors who performed abortions at the Victoria General Hospital were notified, two of them quit. "I think it just gave them the out they wanted," Lanz said, although she did admit that the local pro-life movement was now heavily influenced by American tactics. Henry told everyone it was an "empty threat," but as the hospital scrambled to find replacements, it began to refer patients to the clinic. Henry just as quickly demanded full funding, and sent out a fund-raising letter. His postscript said, "Please write me, even if it is a short note. I need your encouragement."

Yet guest books from his clinics offered up page after page of people pouring out their relief: "Thank you on behalf of a concerned mother. Your procedures in explaining the process to my daughter and the compassion shown was [sic] greatly appreciated"; "The non-judgmental and HELPFUL attitudes of the staff members are something I will always remember. I was treated as a woman first — with dignity, respect and compassion. All of you helped make a difficult experience as positive as possible"; "I'd like to thank you all for saving me from a desperate situation.... I have followed Dr. Morgentaler in the news and read his books and I never imagined that I would meet him, let alone under these circumstances"; "I have noticed that all your grateful recipients have naturally been female of course. Well, I would like to express thanks on behalf of the male.... It is not that easy either for the male counterpart to watch the person they love have to suffer the consequence of foolish mistakes. Thank you."

Sheepishly, Henry explained his request for fan mail: "I couldn't resist. It's important to have a response from the public. When you don't hear anything, it's nice to hear that some people appreciate what I'm doing. It's not good for me to be in a cocoon surrounded by my legend." He needed to know he was still central and integral to the movement. But with the five murders of abortion providers in the United States and the attempted murder of Dr. Romalis on the West Coast, the abortion issue had slid into a shadowy realm, where Henry would never belong and where he long ago had decided he would never go. He was comfortable fighting for it in the courts, where the issue stayed clear and contained, rational and able to be legislated; where he made his speeches and plotted strategies as he would his game of chess, deliberately and boldly. And in the media, where he could see proof of his day's progress on the night's newscasts.

But now it was different. Many hailed the Supreme Court decision as the women's movement's greatest victory and then moved on to other causes represented by other spokespeople, other heroes. CARAL struggled, their ability to fund-raise curtailed by the win. Henry lent his name to one of their appeals, then asked for $10,000 of the money they'd collected to sustain their weakened organization for his legal bills. Everyone in the pro-choice movement in Canada was in strange limbo — protected by no law but by innate Canadian civility, they still had no security, no sense of completion, and because, mercifully, they had no martyrs, they had no momentum.

The talk that year at the National Abortion Federation annual conference was all about guns and the killings. "How many of you are packing heat?" the doctors and abortion providers were asked. Many of them said they were armed as they went to their work. They had taught their children where the weapons were kept in the house and their wives had signed on for shooting lessons. On the final day at the special breakfast meeting for Canadian abortion providers, Henry was the featured speaker. He tried to wipe away the content of the previous day's conference with an upbeat update on Canada's new clinics, the injunction, the court victories — reassuringly familiar topics to all those longtime front-line workers, most of whom were his employees. He told them not to be afraid because there was nothing to be afraid of. He told them he wasn't afraid; he was confident they would win every remaining battle if they simply stayed the course. They were on the right road. The women of Canada were behind them, supporting every new clinic and every new court appearance.

Or were they? Did they recognize his new fights were as integral as his former triumphs? He had to know. Hundreds of women had already spoken out and told their abortions stories — at CARAL's tribunals, in chapter eight of the *Report of the Committee on the Operation of the Abortion Law* (Badgley Report, 1977) and for CARAL-Halifax's Nancy Bowes when she researched *Telling Our Secrets: Abortion Stories from Nova Scotia*. When CARAL's headquarters sent out a questionnaire asking donors why they chose to contribute to CARAL and did they have anything to tell CARAL, they received hundreds of responses. "I come out of the old days, nearly lost my life twice trying to terminate an unwanted pregnancy and lived in fear the rest of the time"; "I had an illegal abortion and became very ill. My own doctor would not speak to me on the telephone"; "Thirty-four years ago as a school girl I became pregnant. A kitchen-table butcher-type abortion failed. My forced marriage to an alcoholic lasted four weeks. But it took six years to obtain a divorce. I am a single parent to a mentally handicapped child. No financial support, no family support, no support from society, i.e. daycare. Your endeavours are too late to help me, but I support your efforts to free young women of burdens that can destroy their lives"; "I have always believed in freedom of choice in principle. Two and a half years ago I was faced with an unexpected pregnancy and decided against having an abortion. However, I was happy to have the choice."

For years people — women — have written Henry himself to tell him their truth. He'd received awkward misspelled thanks written on notepaper decorated with frolicking kittens; stilted letters in the rounded handwriting of young teens: "Thank you very much for helping me," using the format they'd been taught for thank-you notes. Some told him their stories because he wasn't there for them: "I am seventy-five years old, never had any children, but remember well my mother's dilemma, who out of eight pregnancies had four abortions.

Probably during her twenties and early thirties. It was probably because of botched attempts to abort herself or with the help of wives' tales that she injured herself and died at the age of fifty." Some women wrote him because they did not have an abortion — "Just a small something ($2.00 cash) to help all women who want control over their own bodies even, like me, those that make their own choice and go the opposite direction and have a baby (in my case twins, yet I cannot find out what has happened to them in the past twenty-two years)." Or because they did not get pregnant:

> I was widowed thirty years ago, left penniless with two children.... I worked eight to ten hours a day outside...holidays were kept to fall back on when the children were sick. Many times I left them alone.... At one time I worked for a VIP. He was happily married.... Twice I accepted his dinner invitation — at his apartment. Twice we had sex. I still shudder in a cold sweat at what might have happened. It was truly God's hand, his blessing that I did not become pregnant. What would I have done? I was very well known in the community. My family, my later husband's family as well. I had no money. Everybody knew that I had no friends — worked throughout weekends, even though my boss was not there! I could not have contemplated suicide because my children needed me so. They were ten and eleven.... You deserve all the support you may receive, morally and financially. I can only send you one dollar — but I feel at least I am contributing to what I consider a worthwhile cause.

And this time when Henry asked them to write, they said: "For a brave man — not forgetting the brave people who work with him"; "In my forty years this is the first fan letter I've ever written. I just want you to know how special you are"; "Please thank Dr. Morgentaler for his magnificent courage"; "I just want to say that I very much admire your fortitude and determination"; "I once again feel it is an honour and a privilege to help you so that you can continue to help me and my 'sisters' throughout Canada."

His days were filled with accidental testimonials — from the Ottawa agent processing his airline ticket who told him she had been a patient and now had three beautiful daughters to an unsolicited donation of $25,000 from a prospering businessman. He appreciated the cheques, but he still needed those letters; they were his applause and his cause, reminders of why he wouldn't stop, or step down, or aside. Technically Henry was still fighting because there was still ground to be covered and won. He still does abortions four mornings a week in his Toronto clinic because he is skilled and compassionate, and a good doctor: he personally has done more than sixty thousand procedures without a fatality.

There have been close calls — an Edmonton woman sued him for malpractice for an abortion performed at the Harbord Street clinic in September 1988. She had had an incomplete miscarriage and Henry had evacuated her uterus. Because she was an unusual case, Henry called her doctor to follow up and was told everything seemed fine. But three weeks after that, she experienced pains, and further tests found that she had had a tubal pregnancy, as well. They settled out of court. In Montreal one woman stopped breathing during her procedure. As Henry frantically tried to resuscitate her, his nurse yelled "*Respirez*" ("Breathe") into her ear. The woman did. Then, just after Labour Day in 1995, a mother of two inexplicably experienced massive bleeding after what appeared to be a routine and successful operation. She was rushed to a nearby hospital, where she was given a hysterectomy and her life saved. He could have lost a patient. This was hard for him to admit. Telling himself it was his quick thinking in getting her to the hospital that saved her didn't help. Years of work, his entire record, would have been wiped away. He believed in the method he had developed; he believed in his own talent and experience; now he believed he was riding "a false sense of security." What had he done or not done? Was the never-receding stress seeping into his work? In all his years, there had been — maybe — twenty cases of complications, including a few perforations, but none in the last three or four years. But that could be just luck, he told himself. However, the following morning the abortion he performed went so well, so smoothly, he felt a long-forgotten pinprick of professional pride. It had been years since he had so enjoyed doing his job well. Abortion had long ago become his issue more than his craft. It was a medical procedure that had enabled him to act out his humanistic moral and ethical world view, fight the state and the church, get even and get ahead, and become the person he wanted to be. Yet there were many friends and colleagues who wanted him to stop doing the procedures, stop doing the crusading, stop battling for bucks, because it would mean he would be at peace with himself.

Henry's response was to work harder, run faster. That fall he did his annual East Coast celebratory trek, this time starting in Ottawa to mark that clinic's first anniversary. "This clinic in particular is very symbolic. It means a lot to me, Ottawa being the seat of power and where I first presented my [Humanist] brief." His good mood was buoyed by the following-day opening of the first official office of the Humanist Association of Canada. It was modestly situated in a small shopping centre on the outskirts of town. Henry, who cut the ribbon, nevertheless regarded it as the beginnings of a national presence for humanism. He wanted Humanists to become respected, sought-after advocates and spokespeople, quoted by media as often as the members of the Roman Catholic church hierarchy, if not more often. But when he returned that afternoon to the Ottawa clinic, a message from Arlene awaited him. Janek Laskier had called. A friend from Lodz who had managed to stay close to both Morgentaler brothers had news about Mike. He was back in hospital; his kidneys were failing; it was serious, possibly the end.

Henry caught the next flight. He approached his brother's bedside cautiously. "He wasn't antagonistic," Henry ventured, always the optimist, but admitted the words Mike said to him fell like physical blows: "I could have killed for you. I loved you with a passion and I hated you with a passion." Mike was heavily medicated with morphine for his pain, but Henry couldn't comprehend how his own brother could harbour that kind of hatred. He didn't think he deserved it, not just for ending their business arrangements in a businesslike manner and bringing in lawyers. Henry looked at his younger brother, always physically the stronger, now hooked into dialysis and intravenous tubing, lying on a hospital bed from which there was no guarantee he would ever get up, and decided he was grateful that Mike was at least speaking to him and allowing him to be affectionate with him. When a nurse entered with more medication for Mike, Henry slipped outside into the corridor to collect himself. He was there when Goldie and Bamie walked up. Stunned, grieving and alone, he opened up his arms to Goldie. She came into them. Henry laid his head on his daughter's shoulder and wept.

But this was not to be the reconciliation he craved. Collecting himself, Henry forced out small talk — "pleasantries," he called it. He asked Goldie about the status of her doctoral dissertation, complimented her on a recent newspaper article she'd written criticizing the language of the Parti Québécois separatist manifesto that spelled out the conditions of the referendum question. He told Goldie that when she received her Ph.D. she would become "the third Dr. Morgentaler," and they laughed together.

Henry stayed outside when she went into the hospital room to visit her uncle, with whom she had always been close. As she was leaving the hospital, he said to her, "Goldie, I love you." He hoped she was pleased by his words; but he admitted she was noncommittal. "I'm trying to be gentle and not push things too far too fast."

Two weeks later, Henry was in Newfoundland, celebrating the fifth anniversary of the date they'd first operated, albeit secretly, in that province. If he has a clinic that's his sentimental favourite, it is the one in St. John's. Henry loves the exuberance and humour of Newfoundlanders; this time he appreciated what he saw even more. He realized how warm and inviting his clinics were, that they really were the highly professional and compassionate places he had boasted of in so many speeches and interviews. It was as if he fully felt, for the first time, the unshakable truth of his words. "I really did make a difference here," he said to himself as he looked around the St. John's clinic; then, a few days later, he experienced the calm warmth of his Halifax clinic.

When he returned home and flew again to Montreal to see Mike, this time with Arlene, he was less diffident, and strode eagerly up to Mike's bedside. With Mike's permission, he had phoned Mike's daughters, who lived in the United States, and offered to pay their airfare so they could visit with their father. Mike's adopted son, Joe, had previously told them of their father's hospitalization, but the seriousness of Mike's illness had somehow not been communicated. Cindy and Linda came at once. It was a good visit and Henry was pleased, especially since he'd also convinced Mike to draw up a proper will and get it witnessed. The young articling student with whom Henry had lived so many years before in Montreal did the will. Like so many of the people in Henry's life, Joyce Yedid had remained friends with Mike after his brother had moved on.

Believing he had enabled Mike to attain "the peace of mind to survive better," Henry took Arlene and Emilia, Mike's companion, out to lunch. He hadn't realized Emilia was seething. She accused Henry of taking over his brother's life — again — then promptly went to Mike and spoke her mind. When Henry and Arlene came to Mike's bedside to say goodbye before returning to Toronto, Mike erupted, blasting Henry one more time for hiring lawyers to terminate their business arrangement. Henry tried to placate him. "Mike, I'm leaving now. Can't we talk of pleasant things?"

"I've got a right to talk about whatever I want," Mike snapped.

"Of course you have the right, and I will listen to you," Henry conceded.

"Maybe I'd better not," Mike replied.

All during the flight home and into the next morning, Henry brooded. Over breakfast, Arlene said, "Mike spoiled your homecoming. He won over you. You like things to have a nice, happy ending." She asked if Henry would call Mike again.

Henry wasn't sure. He didn't want another session dealing with Mike's long-held anger and resentment.

"You can rise above it," Arlene told him.

Henry called Mike then and there. Their conversation was cheerful and warm. The next day, Mike called Henry.

"Maybe I've been a little rough on you," Mike said.

There it was, the apology Henry so needed from his brother, the signal that Mike acknowledged Henry may not have been to blame for everything between them. When Henry hung up the phone, he cried from relief, because he had been waiting so many years for those words and because he was saddened it had taken Mike so long to acknowledge Henry's pain. A frightened Benny ran to get Arlene. The little boy thought Mike had died.

"Look, Benny," Henry told his son, "if I cry it means I am sad. It doesn't mean I am weak. It takes strength to be able to cry."

When Henry next talked with Mike, he learned Mike had rallied and was being discharged. When Mike was first admitted, the doctor had given him anywhere from two days to a maximum of three more weeks to live. They should think of every minute he remained alive as a minor miracle. He hadn't reckoned with the Morgentaler stubbornness. Mike would be going home that weekend, but Henry had already scheduled a visit with Bamie and his family in Boston. Mike seemed disappointed Henry wouldn't be able to make his homecoming. The following day Henry rescheduled his flight to accommodate an overnight visit in Montreal. "Bring a bottle of Veuve Clicquot and we'll celebrate," Mike said when he learned of Henry's change of plans. Emilia cooked a dinner, holding it for ninety minutes when Henry's flight was delayed so the three could together toast the joy of living. "It was the first time we had relaxed together. It was absolutely great," Henry said.

In Boston, Henry and Bamie went out to dinner. They needed to talk about Mike, with whom Bamie also was very close, and Henry wanted to explain himself to his eldest son. Perhaps because his brother's time appeared to be nearing its end, Henry was convinced he was experiencing a nascent sense of inner peace and contentment. "You're looking at a happy man," he said to Bamie, and later to many others. Bamie has long since come to terms with Henry's restless, driven nature and for years has offered up his father unconditional love and approval as well as respect. He has always managed to witness his father's triumphs, re-arranging his own crowded schedule to fly in to Toronto for a few hours to be part of Henry's combined tribute and birthday celebration, for instance. Bamie knows he is his father's confidant, even, ironically, Henry's father confessor. Without taking sides, Bamie understood his father's struggle with his uncle was "an open wound" for Henry, agony for him, because it had been the one battle Henry Morgentaler could not win. As often as Henry had tried to reconcile with Mike, he had been forced to retreat. Granted, Henry's idea of rapprochement was telling Mike he had forgiven him, but he could never comprehend why Mike retaliated with blasts of anger, which, as hard as he tried, Henry could never rationalize away as he did the hate-filled ravings (as he saw it) of those on the other side of the abortion issue.

So when Henry confessed to Bamie his euphoria-tinged relief that the struggle with Mike appeared over, Bamie understood everything Henry meant. Mike was very ill and this was probably as reconciled as the brothers would ever be. Henry was beginning to accept that it was the rage that had kept Mike alive the past few years. The energy he got from hating Henry may have prolonged Mike's life, just as by loving Henry, Mike had saved Henry's life in the camps. For Mike, it had always been about Henry. Henry's colleagues had become his friends (Eleanor Wright Pelrine, the women in Winnipeg, Maria Corsillo and Bob Scott, Norma Scarborough all adored Mike); one of Henry's employees was Mike's longtime lover; Henry's two eldest children were as close, maybe closer, to him than his own offspring. Mike was hurt when his successful, famous and driven elder brother wouldn't give him as much of the credit as Mike believed he deserved, because he alone understood that Henry's fearless fight for abortion rights was keeping the convenant and honouring their martyred parents.

An elated Henry flew home to Toronto — and Arlene. That Sunday night in late November Henry proposed marriage. Arlene replied, "Henry, of course I'll marry you." Then the pair laughed because it was ridiculous that after nearly eleven years of partnership, the prospect of marriage felt so sublime.

CHAPTER 23

WEDDING INTERRUPTUS

THE WEDDING WAS SET FOR MAY 3, 1996. Arlene wanted Judy Rebick, the woman who'd introduced them, to stand up with her; Henry wanted the ceremony to be secular and at Toronto's city hall. They both hoped the reception at an estate within the city would be a joyful, wonderful party, where their friends could sing, say a short speech if they wished and celebrate. Of course Yann would be there — performing two songs. Declaring Arlene the best woman Henry had ever been with, Mike also promised to attend. The enthusiastic reaction of delighted friends and family to the news surprised Henry. Only Benny wasn't too happy with the announcement. When Henry asked him why, the small boy said he didn't want them to be married because then they could divorce, like many of his friends' parents.

Henry assured him that wasn't their intention. His youngest son's droll, original mind had always amused him; this was no exception. But how could he communicate to a child how much he had felt he had been altered, when he was struggling with the explanation himself? Unlike his life story, his stock of anecdotes, his reasoned defence of his actions, he had not said this many times before. With friends, he seemed suddenly vulnerable, not the usual polished, practised Henry Morgentaler. "I feel as if there's been a tremendous change inside me. It's as if I've grown into the role I designed for myself," he admitted. He spoke of having been transformed, using the term in its most profound sense. He felt he had been altered at the very core of his being; he said he was content, a word he had never before used or wanted to. His whole visage was softer; he appeared to have finally dropped his guard.

He was proud he had booked an appointment to be fitted with a hearing aid, after procrastinating for more than a year and impatiently denying what he considered an infirmity and a sign of the onslaught of old age.

In Montreal twenty years earlier when he was on trial and his future in real jeopardy, he had walked his dog, Beebee, and Goldie's collie, Pasha, every day on the Mountain. "I'm a free man," he had told himself over and over. He was saying the same thing now, but with more fervour and meaning. He wasn't a sick man; he wasn't in a hospital bed. Unlike another abortionist, watching television in the den of his luxurious home in suburban Ancaster outside Hamilton, Ontario, he hadn't been shot. A sniper's bullet had pierced the picture window and permanently maimed Hugh Short's elbow on November 10, 1995, one year and two days after Vancouver physician Gary Romalis was shot. Henry learned about it the next day, as he was about to meet Arlene and the Edelstones for their annual joint birthday dinner. "We still went out and had a good time," Henry reported. He had decided the Vancouver sniper and the Ancaster sniper were the same person who was making a statement by deliberately choosing the same time of year for his attacks. Henry also reasoned he was in no danger because the sniper was not targeting a nationally known figure like him, but low-profile doctors like gynecologist Hugh Short who perform few abortions, to scare off more abortion providers. But Henry agreed with Arlene to have another $25,000 worth of bulletproofing and safety features installed in their home. She was not as certain as Henry that he was not a target. Her parents, who often house-sat when they travelled, had been unnerved one recent night. Arlene's mother had inexplicably woken up at 3 a.m., looked out the window and seen two men in a parked car outside, one of them pointing to the house as if to say, "That's the place." Henry agreed to move his office to the basement, to a bigger but also safer and less exposed space.

Then, at the Toronto clinic's annual Christmas party, he announced his happiness. "I'm a happy man, a lucky man that I've been able to create these centres of excellence. I have so much joy in my heart I want to share it with you. I want to spread it around." He made changes, beginning with attaining some resolution to the escalating strife and factiousness among his staff. A year earlier he had called in a professional mediator to calm the work environment, but the animosities had not receded. Henry, whose habit was to duck or delegate confrontations, had been content to put the conflict down to personality clashes. But when one of his nurses came to him in tears, saying the nurses were insulting one another in front of the patients, that she had not slept the night before and would have to quit, he finally acted. Duties were rotated, a clinic staff manager appointed, both factions appeased. Sharon Broughton instigated weekly staff meetings after Henry told her, "You're the manager. I'm getting older. I want to ensure an orderly succession, and that means I'm delegating a lot of the power and responsibility to you."

Many had reason to doubt that Henry could delegate, but he believed he could — and must. He had other, bigger, things to do. He'd decided to revive his proposal for a Moscow clinic, dormant since his stroke and since his erstwhile on-site partner had stopped taking his calls and hastily departed the capital city for unknown business ventures elsewhere in the former Soviet Union. Now that a pro-choice government had been elected in Poland, Henry had dropped his idea of a Latvian clinic. As for righting his loss of the scholastic medal he'd been denied by his Polish schoolmaster, he was convinced he was now past that need.

But he was restless; he wanted action — what Henry called his contentment had not calmed but enervated him. He decided the Toronto clinic needed brightening. The waiting room, a dim, calming, dull mustard colour, must be repainted, and he wanted art, lots of it, on the walls. He asked staff to bring from home any paintings or posters they might not be using. Along with the photo of him with Gloria Steinem, he banished the framed poster of Albert Einstein, which had hung in the place of honour directly opposite his desk in his office in the bombed-out Harbord Street clinic as well as at Hillsdale. Both now hung off-centre in the staff lunchroom. He replaced them with prints of famous art — the golden-toned *Before the Bath*, *After the Bath* and the voluptuous *Birth of Venus*. He decided there should be more emphasis on counselling, that the women should be counselled in the clinic before and after the procedure. He had clinic councillor Sheri Krieger draw up a short list of four applicants for a new counselling position — then to her surprise hired every one of them for part-time work. Suddenly she was the head of a department, with work schedules to draw up. He was determined his clinics, particularly the one in Toronto, really would become the best in the world. In mid-December he called a press conference in Toronto to announce he had written the pope, chastising him for his stance on abortion and for not calling for an end to the violence against abortion providers. By the time Henry left in mid-December for a month-long African safari holiday with Arlene, Benny and Yann, his personal assistant, Catherine Colombo, had lost ten pounds trying to keep up with her employer's new, inflamed pace.

When he returned in January 1996, he hung in the clinic waiting room an enlargement of a charming, candid holiday photo taken by Arlene of a grinning, tanned Henry lifting up a small, laughing African boy. And on the bulletin board there was a money collection box and a very large poster asking patients for donations to fund Henry's ongoing court battles in other provinces.

And there was a new task waiting for him. Maria Corsillo and others in the pro-choice establishment told Henry they wanted him to publicly articulate their stance against the new American feminist ideology categorizing abortion as a tragedy, albeit a necessary tragedy.

Only semifacetiously was it being called "the awfulization of abortion," and it was right up there on the agenda at both the 1996 international abortion conference and the National Abortion Federation meeting that year in San Francisco. Feminist writer Naomi Wolf launched the first volley in the October 16, 1995, edition of the *New Republic*: she is pro-choice, but she accused pro-choice rhetoric of dehumanizing the fetus. "Sometimes the mother must be able to decide [that] the fetus, in its full humanity, must die," she wrote. "But it is never right or necessary to minimize the value of the lives involved or the sacrifice incurred in letting them go. Only if we uphold abortion rights within the matrix of individual consciousness, atonement and responsibility can we both correct the logical and ethical absurdity in our position — and consolidate the support of the center." Wolf believes abortion rights are safest "when we are willing to submit them to a morality just beyond our bodies and ourselves" and stop characterizing the decision as "an intensely personal decision," because, she says, it is more than that. "One's struggle with a life-and-death issue must be understood as a matter of personal conscience. There is a world of difference between the two, and it's the difference a moral frame makes." Keeping the abortion decision outside the moral frame means losing millions of potential supporters for a woman's right to have an abortion who won't and can't deny that the "death of a fetus is a real death" and entails much pain, grief and suffering. Wolf wanted a "radical shift in the pro-choice movement's rhetoric and consciousness about abortion," and that is precisely what she got. Maria Corsillo had been at caregiver meetings lately where Americans had referred to having an abortion as a bad thing having to be improved upon because it is a necessary thing. "That's why we really value Henry. He has never had this attitude that what he does every day is somehow tragic," she said:

> All this stuff coming out of the States now — that to appease the Right to Life we have to agree abortion is an evil act — leaves out why a physician would think it is actually fine to use his or her hands to do something intrinsically evil. Henry has never felt that about the act he has done every day. I think that is what he has given that is most wonderful. He has always felt that abortion is a creative act, that if you have thought about why and are clear about why and you feel good, then you are doing something positive. That's very different from the United States, where they are always apologizing for what they do.

When Corsillo's husband, Dr. Robert Scott, opened his elegant clinic, located on one of downtown Toronto's meaner streets in 1985, she told him she would work there for one year. More than ten years later she's still there, and just finished organizing the first extended meeting of local hospital abortion providers, social workers and nurses to make sure the Canadian scene never disintegrates to the state of the American situation, where abortions are done only in free-standing clinics and consequently the procedure and those who perform it are marginalized from mainstream medicine and easily scapegoated. "People like Henry have always said, 'No, there is no guilt. This isn't something someone has to bear guilt for. This is a good thing and it can lead to good things if it's the right decision,'" she said.

Henry said he was "disgusted" by Wolf's article:

Terrible — the religious overtones, sin, that we left the high moral ground to the other people. So crazy. To me it's a liberating thing for a woman to be able to make a decision and to follow through. It's like taking power for herself to decide what to do with her body, and she should offer no apologies. I tell my women [patients] who feel guilty, "Take it from me. Instead of feeling guilty and knocking yourself, which doesn't help anybody, feel proud you were able to make a decision which is in the best interests of yourself, your children you have and the children you are going to have. Feel proud. A long time ago you might not have been able to do it or to have [an abortion] under these conditions. You have the power now and the ability and the legal right to do that, and the moral right to do it." They usually brighten up and say, "Yeah, maybe I should think that way."

Partly as a reaction to this latest idealogical assault, Henry has started periodically popping into his waiting room to assure the slumped boyfriends, the clusters of whispering friends and families there that the women are getting the best possible treatment available, it is a safe procedure and he personally guarantees it. He also has begun striding into the clinic's other, smaller, waiting room, where usually a half-dozen women in paper gowns and socks are readying for their preprocedure ultrasounds. "People," he announces, raising high an arm, "I don't want you to worry about a thing. This is a perfectly safe procedure which will not affect your fertility." Always there are some more entranced by seeing the famous Dr. Morgentaler himself than by his words. Henry enjoys that, almost as much as he does the surprise on some patients' faces when they recognize the man at the end of their bed. "Wow, it's you," gasped one. Henry laughed, after all these years still delighting in the adulation.

His annual celebration of the January 28, 1988, Supreme Court decision outlawing the abortion law as unconstitutional is a lavish party he pays for in a large private room downstairs in a restaurant across the street from where the Harbord clinic used to stand. This year — 1996 — the event, always on a Sunday evening, fell on January 28, and Henry was so buoyant his speech included anecdotes about each person in the room and lasted past the midnight hour. Before everyone hurried away, Arlene managed to tell Norma Scarborough to expect to receive her invitation to the wedding, since she would be sending it out soon. The next day most of the celebrants were together again, at CARAL's first-ever fund-raising dinner marking the anniversary of the Supreme Court decision and honouring the work of *Toronto Star* columnist Michele Landsberg and CARAL's former president, Norma Scarborough. Henry purchased a table and invited some staff to join Arlene and him, as well as his friend and fellow abortionist Warren Hearn, from Boulder, Colorado, and Dr. Garson Romalis and his wife, Sheila, from Vancouver. It was Romalis's first public appearance since he was shot in the leg. He kept his remarks short: "It's a pleasure to be able to stand here before you on both legs," he said, electrifying the room.

More than 640 people attended; CARAL took home $24,000, $22,000 of which went to pay off their looming bank debt. More important, CARAL was revitalized and the women reminded why continued access to legal abortion was so crucial to their independence and well-being. Women such as Ruth Miller, author Anne Collins, Dr. Linda Rapson and June Callwood, who had all worked for the cause for years but had moved on to other issues, were there. So were representatives from some key government and social agencies. The NDP's new national leader, Alexa McDonough, flew in from Halifax. The first reunion in years for many, it was a noisy, joyful night that revived forgotten fealty to CARAL and again made women realize how powerful they could feel in the company of other like-minded women.

Nor was Henry ignored, even though the evening was rightfully dedicated to Landsberg's and Scarborough's work. Author Pierre Berton took the microphone to announce to loud cheers that Henry had once again been nominated for an Order of Canada. "If he doesn't get it this time, then why have the medal at all?" he asked.

————

Three weeks later, Henry dropped his head into his arms at his desk and broke down into sobs. Huge, wracking sobs, the kind a teenaged boy makes the last time he cries. He had just told a visitor he and Arlene had broken up. He tried to stem the tears, but he couldn't. "I told my son not to be ashamed to cry," he managed to say as the sobs become heartbreaking howls. He had moved into a two-bedroom suite in a luxurious downtown hotel, Arlene and Benny were still in the house. He was unable to say any more without tearing up again.

Yet he was the one who ended the relationship, called off the wedding. So many rumours had been sweeping through the clinic that he was advised to call together his worried and confused staff, who were already reeling from the frantic pace he had been setting, to tell them his news himself. Several of the staff were close to Arlene before they came to work at the clinic, including Sheri Krieger. "It is hard," Krieger admitted, "but Arlene is taking [the breakup] well — she's strong — and she understands."

And Henry was off and running, deciding he himself would replace three part-time doctors at the Montreal clinic who he thought were becoming too territorial, finding a penthouse condominium near the all-night heart of downtown Toronto, and leaping at any and all media invitations. He appeared without glasses or hearing aid on Pamela Wallin's Newsworld program in early March, eager to talk about himself as well as the abortion issue. "When I look back at what I've accomplished, I'm awestruck," he said, not once but three times during the hour-long interview. On another interview show, this one called "Up Close and Personal," he happily discussed his "new maturity." He seemed eager to get personal, mentioning again that novelization about his life he may yet write.

But some topics were still off-limits, such as his stroke in 1994. Nor would Henry speak of the second but very mild stroke he had suffered recently. He was frantic to maintain the euphoria of the previous fall that still engulfed and buoyed him. Gertie Katz gently tried to ease her friend into accepting that they were aging, they were slowing down. Life's highs weren't as majestic, but neither were its lows as stinging, she reminded him. Nevertheless, he continued to create his own dramas, crises and pagentries. He was impatient — even ruthless — with those trying to slow him down, even though they were motivated by concern for his well-being, and that included Arlene. "I am the man I always wanted to be" he told her.

Instead of riding this giddy wave of happiness with him, Arlene had remained worried and rooted firmly outside its influence. She was fairly certain that this round of Henry's rash and compulsive spontaneity would play itself out and that he would crash. And she had witnessed first-hand how low he could sink when in a depression. She had also been wary of his marriage proposal. It had arrived out of the proverbial left field and it wasn't something she had wanted, especially as it was not accompanied with a pledge of fidelity. Because Arlene loved Henry, she agreed to marry him, but she wasn't sufficiently joyful or festive. It was clear she wasn't swept away. Henry thought she was trying to ground him, which would be like standing still, dropping out of sight, or just not being. The idea of this so frightened him that he broke off their relationship.

Then, on May 13, a numbing phone call came from his old nurse and friend, Joanne Cornax. Mike was dead; his heart had finally given out. Henry had last seen Mike in Montreal two weeks before when he and Mike and some of his family had gone out to Troika, Mike's favourite restaurant, for a wonderful evening of Russian food and strolling musicians. But now it was over; the last taut thread with the past broken. With Henry's grief came a sense of release. He was now free to live in the present and for the future. In his eulogy, Henry said Mike would be in his heart until the day he died. After the funeral the mourners gathered for champagne at Mike's apartment with Emilia, just as Mike had requested. Afterwards, Eva Morgentaler asked Henry over to the house. It was the first time in twenty-four years he had crossed the threshold of their former home on Barton Street. It was the first time in twenty-four years that the entire family — Henry, Eva, Bamie and Goldie — had been there together.

———

Henry returned to Toronto and his work. He decided to find new doctors to work in the Montreal clinic. On August 23, the anniversary of the day Henry and Mike arrived in Auschwitz, Emilia followed Mike's dying wish and scattered his ashes on the site of the abandoned concentration camp, "to join the ashes of our mother," Henry said. Henry did not go with Emilia. And he rarely speaks of his younger brother's death.

He decided to open a new clinic in the Caribbean, but, perhaps showing the first signs of caution, on an island where abortion was already legal and there were no "unjust" laws to overturn. He saw it differently: this was the first step to beginning his work in the Third World, he announced. When he'd terminated the relationship with Arlene, Henry had telephoned the executive director of CARAL to say he'd have more time to devote to the fight for abortion rights, even though the organization, working full time but quietly to maintain the ground he and they had won for the pro-choice forces in Canada, was not seeking any fresh challenges.

But Henry was. Possibly for the first time, he needed the cause more than it needed him. It had enabled him to be a man in motion; to fight, to rail, make noise and reap attention in the name of justice, and he needed to do all that to feel alive. It was that simple and that basic. And that binding. Henry would never be able to let the battle go or let others take it from him. Nor will he ever have to. He will always be ready for the next fight, no matter when and where — and whatever — it will be.

ACKNOWLEDGEMENTS

Now that it's finally over — this living I did inside another person's life (because that is ultimately what a biographer has to do) — I need to first thank my own family for being so understanding and accepting during these last three years. Then I need to acknowledge my agent, Helen Heller, for handholding and hanging tough at the halfway mark and Doug Pepper and Sarah Davies of Random House Canada for their rock-hard and so-necessary support during the final months of work on this manuscript. Does that last sentence intimate that writing this book was no easy task? So be it. I wonder — now — if writing any biography isn't ignominious work. Why should I or any other incipient fact-gatherer collect, peer at and label pieces of another's life? Especially when it's still being lived, as it is with Henry Morgentaler. Yes, he's changed Canadian law and lives and is blatantly proud of it but he isn't very comfortable with the reality of a lengthy biography about him, not even now, after hours and hours of interviews. He wasn't the only one: there were people who refused to make any comment, good or bad, on or off the record, about the man behind the headlines.

What did sustain me were all the others who did talk to me, who trusted me with their memories, opened their files and told me the truth. They were Henry's friends, lovers, lawyers, as well as newspaper reporters and activists, feminists, humanists, members of CARAL, Childbirth by Choice, OCAC, unions, the indomitable women in Winnipeg, Edmonton, Toronto, Nova Scotia and Newfoundland and the staff in each one of the Morgentaler clinics. Put simply, this book could not have been written without them — and not just because they were of such help to me, but because they were there on the front lines in the first place.

Catherine Dunphy
Toronto
August, 1996

Chapter 1

1. Michele Landsberg, *Toronto Star*, May 7, 1993.

Chapter 2

1. Alan Adelson and Robert Lapides, editors and compilers, *The Lodz Ghetto: Inside a Community Under Siege*. New York: Viking Penguin, 1989.

    Much of the information in this chapter was derived from this collection of writing. I am grateful to Henry Morgentaler for lending me his personal copy.

2. Nechama Tec, "A Historical Perspective: Tracing the History of the Hidden-Child Experience," an afterword in *The Hidden Children: The Secret Survivors of the Holocaust* by Jane Marks. New York: Fawcett Columbine, 1993, p. 279.

3. Ibid.

4. Adelson and Lapides, *The Lodz Ghetto*, p. xvii.

5. Ibid., pp. 55–56.

6. Before he died unexpectedly in Toronto in June 1995, Lodz survivor Louis Lenkinski recounted to me his memories of the Bund, the Lodz ghetto and the importance of the work of Josef and Golda Morgentaler did there. "Henry Morgentaler," he said then, "is a visible example of those who keep the socialist ideal." So was Lenkinski, an Ontario Human Rights Commission officer, active unionist and Bundist until the day he died. As a young Bundist ghetto leader, he worked to keep spirits alive, even as his own parents starved to death. "We cannot believe after all this we still survived it. It is too gruesome to remember...but my memory is good and I am not trying to suppress it."

7. Adelson and Lapides, *The Lodz Ghetto*, p. 146.

Chapter 3

1. Mike Morgentaler would not agree to an extensive interview. However, he willingly spoke to me about his recollections and his version of the past during several telephone interviews which took place throughout 1995.

2. Chava Rosenfarb refused several requests to be interviewed. Any biographical information comes from Henry Morgentaler and from biographical data from *The Tree of Life*, an award-winning novel she wrote about the Lodz ghetto, originally published in Yiddish as three volumes, and in Hebrew in 1980, 1981, 1982.

An English-language trilogy was published in Australia in 1985 as a single volume by Scribe Publishing. Rosenfarb has also published four books of poetry and five other works of fiction. She is regarded as an expert in Yiddish literature and lectures extensively.

On Saturday, May 7, 1995, the *Montreal Gazette* printed an excerpt from *Letters to Abrasha*, her new novel, in which she finally tackles her 1944 experiences in Auschwitz, then Sasel and Bergen-Belsen concentration camps, before she was liberated by the British in April 1945. In *The Tree of Life*, Rosenfarb couldn't face the subject; instead ten blank pages appear in the book. In an introduction to the *Gazette* excerpt, journalist Elaine Kalman Naves noted that *The Tree of Life* has been compared with *War and Peace*. "[Rosenfarb] has lived since 1950 in Montreal; had she abandoned Yiddish for English, she would indubitably be known as one of Canada's most compelling writers," Kalman Naves stated in her introduction to the excerpt.

Chapter 4

1. I am indebted to Dr. Vivian Rakoff, former chief of psychiatry at the Clarke Institute of Psychiatry, Toronto, for his discussion with me of the variety of ways in which the simple but profound fact of just living through the madness of the Holocaust has affected many Jewish survivors. As he stated during our interview in 1994, "I could argue this ten different ways."

2. In an interview on June 2, 1996, award-winning author Irving Abella, also a professor of history at Toronto's York University and former president of the Canadian Jewish Congress, said Jewish students wanting admittance to McGill's art faculty needed 750 points out of 900 (a tally reached by designating 100 points for each required subject). Non-Jewish students only required 600 points. The same discrepancies existed in the professional faculties such as law and medicine. "Not until late in the 1950s and into the early 1960s were these inequitable standards lifted," Abella said. "It's provable because no one denied it." In his book *A Coat of Many Colours: Two Centuries of Jewish Life in Canada*, Abella writes: "Universities...had quotas against Jewish students. Most notorious of these was McGill's. For years it was an open secret that standards of admission were far higher for Jewish applicants than for anyone else. An examination of the correspondence of university officials from the president down makes it clear that they were determined to limit ruthlessly Jewish enrolment at McGill. They were worried that by accepting too many Jews McGill would become, in the words of one official 'the Yeshiva University of the North'...it was not until well after the Second World War that the quotas were dropped." (Toronto: Lester & Orpen Dennys, 1990, p. 220).

3. On June 12, 1996, Quebec's education minister Pauline Marois stated the province intended to replace the Protestant and Roman Catholic school systems with

French and English language school boards by mid-1998. *The Globe and Mail*, June 13, 1996.

4. Excerpts were taken from the official transcript of the Health and Welfare standing committee meeting, 26952–1.

Chapter 5

1. From the magazine article "Abortion Rights: A Chronology," assembled by Judith Doyle, *Impulse*, 1985, and "Abortion in Law and History: The Pro-Choice Perspective," a booklet published by Childbirth by Choice Trust, Toronto, revised edition 1992.

2. Angus McLaren and Arlene Tiger McLaren, *The Bedroom and the State*. Toronto: McClelland & Stewart, 1990, p. 34.

3. Ibid., pp. 34–35.

4. Ibid., pp. 52–53.

5. Doyle, "Abortion Rights: A Chronology," 1985.

Chapter 6

1. Robert McCallum was not the only Canadian doctor to be convicted of performing an illegal abortion. In her 1971 book *Abortion in Canada*, Eleanor Wright Pelrine quoted experts estimating that eight to ten abortionists from Ontario alone were convicted during the sixties.

Chapter 7

1. Eleanor Wright Pelrine, *Morgentaler: The Doctor Who Wouldn't Turn Away*. Agincourt, Ont: Gage Education Publishing Co. Ltd., 1975, p. 75.

2. From statements reprinted in the anthology *Women Unite!* Toronto: Canadian Women's Educational Press, 1972, p. 121; also statements made in *The Struggle for Choice*, Nancy Nichol's 1986 documentary.

3. *The Struggle for Choice*, documentary by Nancy Nichol, 1986.

4. "The Women are Coming," *Kinesis*, Oct. 1993, p. 14.

5. *The Struggle for Choice*, Nancy Nichol, 1986.

6. "The Women are Coming," *Kinesis*, Oct. 1993, p. 15.

7. Krista Maeots, *Canadian Forum*, p. 157.

8. Janine Brodie, Shelley A. M. Gavigan, Jane Jenson, *The Politics of Abortion*. Toronto: Oxford University Press, 1992, p. 47.

9. Bobbie Spark, *Socialist Worker*, 162 (Dec. 1990–Jan. 1991) p. 5.

10. Wright Pelrine, *Morgentaler*, p. 83.

Chapter 8

1. *Toronto Star*, Sept. 24, 1973.

2. Wright Pelrine, *Morgentaler*, p. 147.

3. *Toronto Star*, Nov. 14, 1973.
4. Ibid., p. 146.
5. *Morgentaler*, a film by Dan Garson, 1977.
6. Wright Pelrine, *Morgentaler*, p. 140.
7. Ibid., p. 146.
8. *Calgary Herald*, Nov. 9, 1974.
9. Wright Pelrine, *Morgentaler*, p. 148.

Chapter 9

1. *Kitchener-Waterloo Record*, Mar. 27, 1975.
2. Dan Garson's film *Morgentaler*, 1977.
3. *Ottawa Citizen*, Apr. 23, 1975.
4. *Toronto Star*, May 23, 1975.
5. Wright Pelrine, *Morgentaler*, p. 189.
6. Ibid., p. 192.
7. Ibid.
8. *Toronto Star*, June 14, 1975.
9. *Toronto Star*, June 18, 1975.
10. *The Globe and Mail*, June 19, 1975.
11. *Toronto Star*, June 20, 1975.
12. *The Globe and Mail*, Feb. 16, 1976.
13. Ibid.

Chapter 10

1. *Toronto Star*, Jan. 26, 1976.
2. Larry Collins, "The Politics of Abortion: Trends in Canadian Fertility Policy." *Atlantis*, Vol. 7, No. 2, Spring 1982.
3. Wright Pelrine, *Morgentaler*, p. 214.
4. *Toronto Star*, Feb. 18, 1976.
5. *The Globe and Mail*, Feb. 3, 1976.
6. F. L. Morton, *Morgentaler v. Borowski: Abortion, the Charter and the Courts*. Toronto: McClelland & Stewart, 1992, p. 125.
7. *The Globe and Mail*, Dec. 14, 1986.
8. Comments from the Professional Corporation of the Physicians of Quebec have been translated from the French.
9. *Toronto Star*, Dec. 16, 1976.
10. 271 out of 559, according to *Morgentaler v. Borowski*, p. 244.
11. Judith Doyle, "Abortion Rights: A Chronology."
12. *Toronto Star*, Dec. 3, 1977.
13. Ibid., Feb. 28, 1978.
14. Nichol, *The Struggle For Choice, Part III*, 1986.

Chapter 11

1. *Toronto Star*, Nov. 4, 1982.
2. Ibid., Dec. 15, 1987.
3. Ibid., Sept. 30, 1993.
4. *Morgentaler v. Borowski*, p. 129.
5. In January 1991, NARAL announced they had revised their name to National Abortion and Reproduction Rights Action League, which enabled the acronym to stay the same. The organization's broadened mandate included sexuality education, improved contraception, increased access to pre- and post-natal care, as well as safe, legal abortions. Childbirth By Choice executive director Robin Rowe commented that NARAL was not only combining aspects of the work of Canada's Planned Parenthood organization with their baby care, but also placing abortion rights in the centre of the entire reproductive rights issue. It is notable, however, that the Americans never mentioned a need for free abortion services.
6. *Morgentaler v. Borowski*, p. 116.
7. Joe Borowski died in September 1996 of cancer at age 62 in Winnipeg.
8. *Winnipeg Sun*, Dec. 1, 1982.
9. *The Globe and Mail*, Dec. 1, 1982.
10. Ibid.
11. *Montreal Gazette*, Dec. 1, 1982.

Chapter 12

1. *Saturday Night*, Sept., 1983.
2. *Winnipeg Free Press*, June 28, 1983.
3. *Toronto Star*, July 5, 1983.

Chapter 13

1. *Winnipeg Free Press*, Sept. 13, 1983.
2. *Winnipeg Sun*, Sept. 14, 1983.
3. Ibid., Oct. 7, 1983.
4. Ibid., Oct. 6, 1983.
5. *Toronto Star*, Feb. 21, 1988.
6. Ibid., Nov. 22, 1983.
7. Canadian Press dispatch in *Toronto Star*, Jan. 6, 1984.
8. Anne Collins, *The Big Evasion: Abortion, the Issue That Won't Go Away*. Toronto: Lester, Orpen & Dennys, 1985, p. 151.
9. Gordon Edelstone died in the late summer of 1996.

Chapter 14

1. *The Globe and Mail*, Nov. 28, 1984.
2. *London Free Press*, Jan. 8, 1985.

3. *The Globe and Mail*, Jan. 18, 1985.

4. *Vancouver Sun*, Jan. 16, 1985.

5. *Winnipeg Free Press*, May 26, 1983.

6. *The Globe and Mail*, Mar. 28, 1985.

7. *Victoria Times Colonist*, Mar. 27, 1985.

8. *Winnipeg Sun*, Apr. 19, 1985.

9. *Winnipeg Free Press*, Aug. 2, 1985.

10. *The Globe and Mail*, Oct. 23, 1985.

11. Ibid., Nov. 20, 1985.

12. *Winnipeg Free Press*, April 26, 1985.

Chapter 15

1. *Toronto Star*, Aug. 15, 1985.

2. Ibid., Oct. 4, 1986.

Chapter 16

1. *Toronto Star*, Mar. 18, 1987.

2. Ibid.

3. Ibid., Mar. 22, 1987.

4. Ibid., Jan. 29, 1988.

5. Ibid.

Chapter 17

1. *The Globe and Mail*, April, 20, 1988.

2. *Toronto Star*, Oct. 11, 1986.

3. Ibid., July 4, 1989.

4. *Fireweed*, Issue 33, Summer 1991, p. 68.

5. Ibid., p. 71.

6. *Toronto Star*, July 29, 1988.

7. Ibid., Jan. 28, 1989.

8. *Time* magazine, May 1, 1989.

9. *Interim*, Oct. 1988.

10. *Toronto Star*, Oct. 30, 1988.

11. 'Unbending Faith' aired on "Sunday Morning", CBC Radio, Sept. 20, 1993.

12. *Time* magazine, May 1, 1989.

13. Ibid.

14. *Interim*, supplement, July 1989.

Chapter 18

1. *The Globe and Mail*, Aug. 7, 1985.

2. Henry has always been somewhat discomfited by Kathy Coffin, a CARAL powerhouse

in St. John's, Newfoundland, before she helped start things going in Halifax. Coffin was chosen to be honoured at CARAL's tribute in Halifax on January 29, 1996, the eighth anniversary of the Supreme Court decision. Her loyalty to the cause has never been questioned, unlike her loyalty to and appreciation of Henry. During successive interviews in Halifax in the summer of 1994, then 1995, Coffin said she credits Henry Morgentaler for the pro-choice Canadian victory and for the continued existence of a Halifax clinic. But she has a wicked sense of humour and at parties has kidded Henry that he should have a vasectomy. "Don't you think you're getting too old for these?" she once asked Henry, pointing to the infant Benny. Nor did she let the sight of Arlene fetching food from the buffet table for a recumbent Henry pass without comment. "Did you break your legs?" she inquired. There was a significant pause before Henry laughed, she said.

3. *Toronto Star*, Jan. 18, 1989.

4. Henry claims it was his $5,000 contribution that started CARAL. Ed Ratcliffe says he funded the creation of CARAL, renting Toronto office space for them, paying the salaries of employees Eleanor Wright Pelrine and his daughter, and covering the cost of the airfares of all the women who flew into Ottawa for CARAL's inaugural meeting and lobby in the fall of 1974.

5. *Dalhousie Magazine*, Winter 1992

6. *Toronto Star*, Nov. 7, 1989

7. In fact the Independent Health Act was never defeated. On March 2, 1989, the Ontario Liberals passed it as Bill 187 at the end of the second longest sitting of the provincial legislature — the honorable members sat for 157 straight day. Then Health Minister Elinor Caplan introduced some government control amendments to the Bill which were passed 54 to 21 on November 22, 1989. With the subsequent election of Bob Rae's pro-choice New Democratic Party government, many Tory backbenchers complained that Caplan's amendments had made it easier to create new private clinics. But the new Progressive Conservative majority elected in June 1995, under Mike Harris swiftly brought forth Bill 26. Bill 26 was so pervasive and all-consuming in its recommendation of sweeping changes to and less funding of Ontario's health, education and social services systems, it became known as the Omnibus Bill. Critics, who were plentiful, accused the Harris government of Americanizing the province's health system. After a public outcry because Harris planned to put the Omnibus Bill to a vote without any public participation, the Tories relented and set aside two weeks for public depositions. That accomplished, the Tory majority passed the bill on January 29, 1996. Among its many items was one permitting for-profit, foreign ownership of clinics, laboratories and health care centres. At the time of publication, the two Ontario-based Morgentaler clinics had not been directly affected by any edicts in the Bill.

8. During the June 1990 Nova Scotia proceeding in which Henry was on trial for performing fourteen abortions at his McCully Street clinic contrary to the province's

Medical Services Act, the Crown asked him outright if he intended to open another clinic. Henry had already begun work on opening a clinic in Newfoundland, but he skirted the question by saying — truthfully — he would first like to settle his affairs in Nova Scotia. When the St. John's clinic was ready before the Nova Scotia verdict was handed down, Anne Derrick was adamant: it would not be a good idea to open another clinic before Judge Kennedy's ruling; even though Henry hadn't said he wouldn't build another clinic, the judge could well take umbrage.

Chapter 19

1. From Henry Morgentaler's private memoirs, transcribed from a tape he made on a January 1990 holiday in St. Lucia.
2. *Toronto Star*, May 13, 1990.
3. Ibid., May 30, 1990.
4. Ibid.
5. Ibid., June 14, 1990.

Chapter 20

1. *The Globe and Mail*, Feb. 1, 1991.
2. *Halifax Daily News*, Feb. 1, 1991.
3. *Edmonton Journal*, Jan. 19, 1985.
4. *The Globe and Mail*, Feb. 20, 1991.
5. *Alberta Report*, Nov. 25, 1991.
6. *Edmonton Journal*, Feb. 21, 1992.
7. *Winnipeg Free Press*, Apr. 22, 1992.
8. *Edmonton Sun*, May 20, 1992.
9. *Toronto Star*, May 26, 1992.

Chapter 21

1. *Toronto Star*, Feb. 4, 1993.
2. *USA Today*, Mar. 12, 1993.
3. *The Globe and Mail*, Mar. 12, 1993.

Chapter 22

1. Almost a year to the day later, and about nine months after the federal government began docking the Alberta government $422,000 monthly in federal funding, the province caved in and announced it would pay facility fees at the forty semi-private clinics in Alberta, including the Edmonton Morgentaler Clinic. Fox told *The Globe and Mail* the clinic had been getting a $107 physician fee per procedure from medicare but had been charging patients facility fees of between $375 to $675. "What it means is that [now] women will be fully insured for a medically necessary service. Women will no longer be penalized."

2. The government refused his request, but that was not enough for the worried
   pro-choice activists in and around Vancouver. The B.C. Coalition for Abortion
   Clinics (BCCAC) subsequently helped spearhead a campaign for legislation protecting providers and women seeking abortions from anti-choice harrassment. In
   September 1995, they got it — an Access to Abortion Services Act which included
   a 50-metre "bubble zone" outside abortion clinics, a 160-metre zone around private
   houses, and a 10-metre zone around doctors' homes in which pro-life protesting
   and sidewalk counselling and hassling were prohibited. But on January 23, 1996,
   as reported in the Spring 1996 edition of *Pro-Choice News*, Judge E.J. Cronin ruled
   that the ban was unconstitutional. His decision is currently being appealed.

3. *The Globe and Mail*, Nov. 10, 1994.

4. *Toronto Star*, Nov. 10, 1994.

INDEX

Abella, Irving, 453

abortion: cause of death, 69, 78, 79–80, 87, 321, 386–87, 434; legal penalties, 83, 84; medical complications, 108, 386–87, 434; methods, 5-8, 69, 79–80, 82–83, 98, 108, 184–85; pill, 393; rhetoric, 444–46; self-induced, 69, 79–80, 98, 387; statistics, 157, 183, 347, 386–87; stories, 432–33; on television, 107; unequal access, 74–75, 94, 173, 299

abortion clinics: counselling, 5–6, 331–32, 444; daily caseload, 262, 288, 327, 331–32; fundraising at, 402, 444; patient escorts, 202, 225, 256; patient interview with media, 357–58; women's control over, 195–96, 223–24, 227–29, 329–31, 329–32, 414

abortion fees, 70, 183, 322–23, 327; government funding, 311, 379, 384, 391, 404–6, 459; at Morgentaler Clinics, 83, 86, 89–90, 163, 390, 391

abortion legislation, 67–71. after 1988 Supreme Court ruling, 332; Bill C-43, 340, 346, 371–73, 381, 382, 391; constitutional validity, 235, 238, 241, 460; and fetal age, 371; Health Act (Canada), 424. *See also* Criminal Code; individual provinces; Supreme Court.

abortion providers, 69, 70, 79, 80; abuse of women, 185; gynaecologists, 184, 320; international conference, 319–20; professional organization, 320, 431, 445; training, 101, 163, 175, 320, 402. *See also* doctors.

abortion: referral services, 94–95, 95, 113, 174, 185, 202; Morgentaler Clinics, 221, 271, 350, 358

Abortion: The Big Evasion (Collins), 71, 231

Abortion and Contraception (Morgentaler), 176, 180–81, 412

Abortion by Choice (Alberta), 382, 384–85

Abortion Caravan, 94–99, 100

Abortion in Canada (Eleanor Wright Pelrine), 454

Abortion Information and Referral Service (Nova Scotia), 347

Abortion Stories (film), 301

Abortion Tribunal to Defend Dr. Morgentaler, 118

ACALA, 151

Advisory Council on the Status of Women, 138, 140, 374

Alberta, 311, 384, 390, 404, 408–9, 424, 459

Allard, Madame, 43

Allen, Helen, 70

Alliance for Life, 101, 112, 125, 156, 198

Allmand, Warren, 63, 106

Alter, Victor, 43

Amnesty for Morgentaler, 140, 148

anaesthetic, 7, 78, 332, 405

Andrews, Joan, 333

anti-abortion. *See* pro-life

anti-choice. *See* pro-life

anti-Semitism, 9, 14, 15, 46–47, 51, 349, 412, 453

Arabella, Rosalie, 125

Arbeiter Ring (Workmen's Circle), 48

ARCAL (Association for the Repeal of the Canadian Abortion Law), 82, 100, 123

Archer, David, 140

Archibald, Ross, 359

Aristotle, 67